THE HEBREW BIBLE
IN ITS SOCIAL WORLD
AND IN OURS

THE SOCIETY OF BIBLICAL LITERATURE
SEMEIA STUDIES
Edward L. Greenstein, Editor

THE HEBREW BIBLE
IN ITS SOCIAL WORLD
AND IN OURS

by
Norman K. Gottwald

Scholars Press
Atlanta, Georgia

THE HEBREW BIBLE
IN ITS SOCIAL WORLD
AND IN OURS

Library of Congress Cataloging in Publication Data
Gottwald, Norman K. (Norman Karol), 1926–
    The Hebrew Bible in its social world and in ours/ by Norman K.
Gottwald.
        p. cm. — (Semeia studies)
    Includes bibliographical references and index.
    ISBN 1–55540–856–7. — ISBN 1–55540–857–5 (pbk.)
    1. Bible. O.T.—Criticism, interpretation, etc. 2. Sociology,
Biblical. 3. Bible. O.T.—Influence.   I. Title.   II. Series.
BS1192.G675   1993
221.6'7—dc20
                                                    93–7356
                                                    CIP

Printed in the United States of America
on acid-free paper

For Laura Lagerquist-Gottwald

Contents

INTRODUCTION   XI

PROLEGOMENON:
How My Mind Has Changed or Remained the Same   XV
    [address, SBL annual meeting, November 1991]

PART I: THE HEBREW BIBLE IN ITS SOCIAL WORLD

A. SOCIAL CRITICAL METHOD AND THE ORIGINS OF ISRAEL

CHAPTER 1.   Domain Assumptions and Societal Models
in the Study of Pre-monarchic Israel   5
[*Supplements to Vetus Testamentum* 28 (1974): 89–100]

CHAPTER 2.   John Bright's New Revision of *A History of Israel*   17
[*Biblical Archaeology Review* 8/4 (1982): 56–61]

CHAPTER 3.   A Response to John W. Rogerson on "The Use of
Sociology in Old Testament Studies"   27
[panel response, Eleventh Congress of the International
Organization for the Study of the Old Testament,
Salamanca, Spain, August 1983]

CHAPTER 4.   Two Models for the Origins of Ancient Israel:
Social Revolution or Frontier Development   37
[*The Quest for the Kingdom of God: Studies in Honor of
George E. Mendenhall*, ed. H. B. Huffmon et al., Winona Lake:
Eisenbrauns, 1983, pp. 5–24]

CHAPTER 5.   Historical Material Models of the Origins of
Israel in the Light of Recent Palestinian Archaeology   57
[ASOR-SBL symposium on "New Perspectives on the
Emergence of Israel in Canaan," annual meeting, 1987]

CHAPTER 6. Religious Conversion and the Societal Origins
of Israel—A Reply to Jacob Milgrom 71
[*Perspectives in Religious Studies* 15/4 (1988): 49–65]

CHAPTER 7. Israel's Emergence in Canaan—an Interview
with Norman Gottwald 89
[*Bible Review* 5/5 (1989): 26–34]

B. PROPHECY, MONARCHY AND EXILE

CHAPTER 8. Were the "Radical" Prophets also "Cultic" Prophets? 111
[lecture, the Graduate Theological Union, Berkeley,
CA, spring semester, 1972]

CHAPTER 9. The Plot Structure of Marvel or Problem Resolution Stories
in the Elijah-Elisha Narratives and Some Musings on *Sitz
im Leben* 119
[lecture, the Graduate Theological Union, Berkeley,
CA, spring semester, 1975]

CHAPTER 10. The Rise of the Israelite Monarchy—
A Sociological Perspective 131
[panel presentation, Consultation on Sociology of the
Monarchy, ASOR-SBL annual meeting, November 1980]

CHAPTER 11. A Hypothesis about Social Class in Monarchic Israel
in the Light of Contemporary Studies of Social Class
and Social Stratification 139
[paper presented to the Sociology of the Monarchy Group,
ASOR-SBL annual meeting, November 1985]

CHAPTER 12. The Book of Lamentations Reconsidered 165
[lecture, Yonsei University, Seoul, Korea, May 1989]

C. CANON, THEOLOGY AND TEACHING HEBREW BIBLE

CHAPTER 13. Social Matrix and Canonical Shape 177
[*Theology Today* 42 (1985): 307–21]

CHAPTER 14. Max Weber and Yehezkel Kaufmann on Israelite Monotheism
—a Review of Irving M. Zeitlin, *Ancient Judaism: Biblical
Criticism from Max Weber to the Present* 193
[*Religion* 16 (1986): 383–87]

CHAPTER 15. On Integrating Multiple Truths in Biblical Texts—A Review
of Walter Brueggemann, *David's Truth in Israel's Imagination
and Memory* 201

[*Biblica* 68 (1987): 408–11]

CHAPTER 16. Literary Criticism of the Hebrew Bible:
Retrospect and Prospect 207

[*Mappings of the Biblical Terrain: The Bible as Text* = Bucknell
Review 37/2, ed. V. L. Tollers and J. Maier, Lewisburg, PA:
Bucknell University Press, 1990, pp. 27–44]

CHAPTER 17. Teaching the Hebrew Bible: A Socio-Literary Approach 225

[*Approaches to Teaching the Hebrew Bible as Literature in
Translation*, ed. B. N. Olshen and Y. S. Feldman, New York:
Modern Language Association, 1990, pp. 59–64]

PART II: THE HEBREW BIBLE IN OUR SOCIAL WORLD

A. SOCIAL CRITICAL THEOLOGY

CHAPTER 18. The Theological Task after *The Tribes of Yahweh* 237

[*The Bible and Liberation*, ed. N. K. Gottwald, Maryknoll:
Orbis Books, 1983, pp. 190–200]

CHAPTER 19. Human Sacrifice and Religious Scapegoating—A Review of
Hyam Maccoby, *The Sacred Executioner: Human Sacrifice and
the Legacy of Guilt* 249

[*The New York Times Book Review*, December 18, 1983]

CHAPTER 20. The Politics of Armageddon—Apocalyptic Fantasies,
Ancient and Modern 255

[lecture, eleventh annual Social History and Theory Seminar,
University of California, Irvine, April 1988]

CHAPTER 21. The Exodus as Event and Process: A Test Case in the
Biblical Grounding of Liberation Theology 267

[*The Future of Liberation Theology: Essays in Honor of Gustavo
Gutiérrez*, ed. M. H. Ellis and O. Maduro, Maryknoll: Orbis
Books, 1989, pp. 250–60]

CHAPTER 22. God, Community, Household, Table—A Review of M.
Douglas Meeks, *God the Economist: The Doctrine of God
and Political Economy* 281

[*Christianity and Crisis* 50/7 (May 14, 1990): 150–54]

B. SOCIAL AND POLITICAL ETHICS

CHAPTER 23.   Prophetic Faith and Contemporary
International Relations.   291
[*Biblical Realism Confronts the Nation,* ed. P. Peachey, Nyack:
Fellowship Publications, 1963, pp. 68–87]

CHAPTER 24.   Are Biblical and U.S. Societies Comparable? Theopolitical
Analogies Toward the Next American Revolution   307
[Bicentennial paper, Pacific Coast Theological Society, May
1976, and published in *Radical Religion* 3/1 (1976): 17–24]

CHAPTER 25.   Sociological Method in Biblical Research and
Contemporary Peace Studies   325
[SBL special lecture discussion, annual meeting,
December 1982, and published in *American Baptist
Quarterly* 2/2 (1983): 142–56]

CHAPTER 26.   How Does Social Scientific Criticism Shape Our Understanding of the Bible as a Resource for Economic Ethics?   341
[lecture, Union Day Conference on "Ethics and Economics,"
Union Theological Seminary, New York, April 1988]

CHAPTER 27.   The Biblical Prophetic Critique of Political Economy:
Its Ground and Import   349
[*God and Capitalism: A Prophetic Critique of Market Economy,*
ed. J. M. Thomas and V. Visick, Madison, WI: A-R Editions,
Inc., 1991, pp. 11–29]

CHAPTER 28.   Biblical Views on "Church-State" Relations and Their
Influence on Existing Political Ideologies   365
[*Christian Community in a Changing Society: Studies from the
World Alliance of Reformed Churches,* ed. H. S. Wilson, Geneva,
Switzerland, 1991, pp. 1–18]

LIST OF WORKS CONSULTED   385

ABBREVIATIONS   411

AUTHOR INDEX   413

SUBJECT INDEX   417

Introduction

*T*he present volume is a collection of pieces originally prepared for various audiences in the period from 1963 to 1991. They articulate the emergence and progress of my interest in the social critical study of the Hebrew Bible. Taken as a whole, they supply context for—and offer modifications and elaborations of—my two major works written during this same period: *The Tribes of Yahweh* (1979) and *The Hebrew Bible: A Socio-Literary Introduction* (1985). At the same time, they contain the fruit of my thought about the implications of Israel's social reality for our social world.

The works gathered here are of diverse provenance: classroom and public lectures, working papers for professional societies and conferences, periodical articles, contributions to anthologies, and book reviews. One-third of them are previously unpublished, and the pieces I have chosen to reprint are drawn largely from periodicals and other sources not widely or normally read by scholars in the biblical field. Accordingly, I exclude all articles that have appeared in publications of the Society of Biblical Literature on the assumption that they are already known or readily accessible to most readers of *Semeia Studies.* By the same token, several SBL working papers and oral presentations previously unpublished are included in this collection. In particular, I have been guided in my selections by requests from colleagues to make available certain of my oral presentations that they remember hearing at the time, or subsequently learned about, particularly when they treat topics or aspects of method not developed in my published oeuvre.

The thematic unity of this collection is the social world of ancient Israel, visible in its history and literature, and impinging on our social world through the Hebrew Bible as the scripture of Judaism and Christianity. The volume is organized around a bipolar structure that is both historical and hermeneutical. Part I is composed of a series of studies on ancient Israelite society arranged in historical sequence, with considerable attention to how social scientific criticism relates to other forms of biblical interpretation such as literary and canonical criticism. Part II consists of attempts to appropriate Israel's social history for contemporary theology and social ethics.

Within the subdivisions of Part I and II, the entries are grouped chronologically according to their dates of composition. This will permit the reader to see how my ways of treating the same or similar subjects have developed over the years. I have made no attempt to revise the text or to update the notes and bibliography, since that would have required substantial re-writing, although occasionally I refer to the subsequent publication of works originally cited in less complete or less accessible formats. More ominously, such revision would have been to "second guess" what I might or should have written one or two decades ago in the light of what I now know. Instead, I have supplied brief abstracts for each entry, in which I sometimes comment on instances where later developments in my thought, or in biblical studies at large, would require modification or amplification of my views were I to write on the subject at present. Similarly, I have allowed the entries from earlier years to retain their non-inclusive language as testimony to my social conditioning as a scholar. To facilitate ease of access, all titles referred to in the essays are arranged alphabetically by author at the end of the volume under Works Consulted. An asterisk (*) prefixed to entries under my name in the Works Consulted section indicates that these titles are included in the present collection.

Lastly, I have placed the most recent of these pieces at the head of the collection and entitled it "Prolegomenon." It is my address at the 1991 annual meeting of the SBL on the topic, "How My Mind Has Changed or Remained the Same." That address is admirably suited as an orientation to this volume as a whole, presenting as it does the way I view the course of my professional career and contribution in biblical studies. A close reading of this Prolegomenon, with its outline and assessment of the major trajectories of method, hypothesis and hermeneutical framing that have characterized my work over time, will give context to all the entries that follow in this collection.

I wish to thank Edward L. Greenstein, editor of this series, who first proposed the idea of bringing together a collection of my shorter writings, and who has been unfailingly helpful in his counsel about the content and structure of the volume. Special credit is due Kathleen Tice who has used her skill in word processing to reduce the clashing formats of the originals to one coherent format. Above all, I must express my unbounded appreciation to students, colleagues in biblical studies and other fields, clergy and lay audiences, who in person and in writing have struggled with me to understand the social shape and meaning of ancient Israel.

New York, NY
July 1992

Prolegomenon:
How My Mind Has Changed or Remained the Same

*T*he honor of the invitation to address this forum, although admittedly tempered by the daunting character of the assignment, presents me with the challenge of assessing my work to date and charting directions for the future. In my reflections I strive to transcend a narrowly self-focused approach, mindful of the observation of the poet Thomas McGrath that "all of us live twice at the same time—once uniquely and once representatively. I am interested in those moments when my unique personal life intersects with something bigger...." (Des Pres:164). Accordingly, I shall be considering the development of "my mind" in the company of "other minds"—including many minds in this audience—and within the context of what we loosely call "the mind of our age."

I have decided to organize my remarks in two parts. The first section will be an overview of what I understand to be the core of my work as a biblical scholar and how I conceive my scholarly function in academy, church, and society. The second section will recount the trajectory of my scholarly work as it has developed over forty years, with specific focus on my understanding and practice of social critical methodology and the direction in which my work has moved since the publication of *The Tribes of Yahweh* twelve years ago.

The Content and Context of My Work

As for the content of my work, the first thing to be said is that I have always understood myself to be primarily a historian of ancient Israel. This needs underscoring no doubt because of my wide range of intellectual interests. In every one of my forays into other scholarly territories, whether within or beyond biblical studies, I am constantly asking myself what they offer or imply for historical understanding. My interest in texts has been as a historian, and my orientation to Israel's religion has been to grasp the development of the religion over the course of its history. Fine points about texts and religious institutions and practices are of course the indispensable ingredients of good historical judgments, but without the larger interpretive historical framework the details swiftly lose their weight and significance.

Because of this abiding historical orientation, in adopting a social scientific approach from the late sixties on, I was not turning my back on history but taking an absolutely necessary step to complete the historical project. This move into social scientific methodology signified to me the enlargement, enrichment, and consequent recontextualization of biblical religious history and biblical political history by embedding them in a wider process of social history. Furthermore, during the decade I was working on *Tribes*, I came ever more firmly to the conclusion that social history necessitates a method far more analytic and radical than social description. To see history socially is to see it as the interplay and conflict of humans busy about what we all must be occupied with, namely, securing our physical survival and well-being, gaining a measure of power over the conditions that affect us, and achieving a sense of meaning as persons in community.

Thus, precisely as historian, I have had to become social analyst and political economist, and to do that I have had to consult theorists and analysts who have taken a similar large view of what human historical existence consists of, in particular how its various sectors are linked to one another and how change occurs in social formations. With the aid of large-scale social theory and comparative studies in sociology and anthropology, I have sought to offer a reading of ancient Israel of a sort familiar enough in many other fields. Apart, however, from Max Weber and a handful of lesser known scholars, a controlled systemic social outlook has been foreign to biblical studies until the last two decades. Fortunately, in part due to my work and the fruitful labor of a good number of like-minded scholars, the social critical study of the Bible now has a solid, if not wholly secure, place within biblical studies.

At this juncture, I want to say a word about my explicit use of Marxist social theory. My encounter with Marx as a serious social theoretician began in 1966, after I had for some time explored the strengths and limits of Durkheim and Weber. It was almost immediately apparent to me that, without canceling out the merits of Durkheim and Weber, the Marxist social analytic apparatus provided the comprehensive and dynamic grasp of the social subject matter that I had been groping for in my earlier work. I do not hesitate to say that my encounters with the biblical prophets, Jesus included, and with Marx are the two most formative intellectual, ethical, cultural and religious encounters of my life. Both the prophetic heritage and the Marxist heritage continue to engross me in the form and content of my biblical research, writing and teaching, as well as in my efforts to understand, renew, and commit myself as a human being and as a Christian in church and society.

The frequency with which my work has been dismissed, not because of disagreement over particulars, but because of its Marxist methodology has taught me at first hand how deeply anti-communist ideology has penetrated intellectual traditions in this country. I can only liken the ignorance of this dismissal to the way we would regard the wholesale dismissal of psychological work that used a Freudian framework or work in the natural sciences that used a Darwinian perspective. Some have made Marx a god, and others have made him a devil. My contention is that Marx is a first-rate guide in matters of human social life whose misjudgments, omissions, and imbalances are more easily corrected than those of any other guides I have met.

The social axis of my work as a historian reveals itself not only in the object and manner of my study, namely, ancient Israel as a social formation, but refers at the same time reflexively to the social context in which all of us do our work. For one thing, this means that I understand my personal contribution to be part of a larger effort, with all its achievements and failures more widely shared than is the usual mind-set of professional scholars. It is to see how specialized and bounded our work as biblical critical scholars is, how our capacity to understand our objects of study and the capacity of others to see what we see is profoundly conditioned by both the social history of our discipline and the way it is inserted into late twentieth-century capitalist societies.

This notion of the social ground and limit of biblical scholarship is, of course, intimately related to hermeneutical understandings of the close dialectical relation between the interpreter and the interpreted, probably beginning theologically with Schleiermacher and vigorously propounded in biblical studies by Bultmann. Most of this European-derived hermeneutics stressed the intellectual and cultural pre-understandings we bring to texts, but, as Dorothee Soelle has astutely noted, it did so in a markedly attenuated, so-called existentialist manner that largely ignored the social and political dimensions of interpretation.

It has remained for liberation theologies in their many forms to extend the map of hermeneutical pre-understandings into the realm of social systems and conflicts. The long-dominant interpretive paradigm of Enlightenment-aimed-at-overcoming-ignorance has been contested in our time by the interpretive paradigm of Liberation-aimed-at overcoming-oppression. The struggle over social pre-understanding of our work may be put in this simplified form for hermeneutical purposes: does the paradigm of Enlightenment subsume Liberation, or does the paradigm of Liberation subsume Enlightenment? Will people be liberated chiefly by the steady spread of more and more knowledge and education, as it is being generated within the several scholarly specialties, including biblical studies? Or will those who seek liberation have to take responsibility for reworking and applying this scholarly knowledge to their own oppressive conditions, since the generation of knowledge does not automatically serve any particular social ends?

My own judgment is that, although Liberation necessarily requires Enlightenment as a step in its realization, Enlightenment is decisively subsumed by Liberation in a means-ends relationship. Consequently, it is incumbent on me to identify those spheres of oppression in which reworked biblical scholarship may be potentially liberating. Among those that stand out today are feminist and ethnic communities of discourse and action, as well as sectors within third world countries where determined resistance and struggle against imperialism and local colonialism is taking place. The social reality, however, is that I am not immediately a part of these most articulate oppressed communities. My most immediate community is that of left or radical liberalism, which is fractured and nearly voiceless in the wider society. The radical critical impulse behind early nineteenth century biblical criticism is by now long lost in a conservative academic establishment that rewards individual technical brilliance and ignores the social meanings and uses of our scholarly output. As a socialist who employs Marxist social theory, I should be most at home among Marxist theorists, but, in a mirror image of religious scholars, they for the most part have as little interest in religion, much less ancient Israel, as most biblical interpreters have in Marxism. Moreover, merely to seek my community among other intellectuals is not to touch the most urgent oppressions of our society, since by and large biblical scholars, left liberals, and Marxist thinkers alike are not at present significantly serving the needs of oppressed peoples.

As a partial resolution of this dilemma, I have come to accept a vocation in an ecumenical metropolitan New York City seminary that fully reflects the ethnic and gender diversities of the city's churches and, to a considerable extent, its class divisions as well. New York Theological Seminary provides education for academic slow starters who are often where they are because the realities of oppression in our society have handicapped them along the way. In that context, my understanding of Israel's social history as a class conflict concretizes the biblical themes of exodus and social justice in a manner that urban blacks, Hispanics, Asians, and whites can appreciate more readily than most seminarians who have come, so to speak, by way of the more conventional "middle class" route. I have also found my work widely responded to in the third world. Recent visits to Brazil, Chile, Colombia, Korea, and China, together with correspondence with many other parts of the world, confirm my confidence that what I have been able to articulate about ancient Israel as a society is deeply relevant to the churches and societies of those lands. Feedback from these domestic and foreign connections has enabled me to see why it is so easy for us in the academic establishment to deny or depreciate social conflict in the Bible: simply enough put, we are living inside the equivalent of biblical Assyria or Babylon or, if you will, inside the royal court at Jerusalem. Only a consciousness awakened through alternative experience is likely to shake our intellectual and sociocultural serenity.

This has been a long introduction which serves, I think, not only to highlight the major considerations in my scholarly work but also to clarify why my work has met with heated responses, both pro and con. Something is at stake here beyond the usual scholarly debate over the details of textual readings and historical judgments, of which there has been an abundance with respect to my work, and appropriately so. Concerning this debate over alternative interpretive scenarios and their various details, I would insist that it is only through such lively dispute that I am able to separate the wheat from the chaff in all historical work, my own included. Because I have been explicit in my presuppositions about social history and about the social construals and applications of biblical scholarship, and because I have tried to work these out with methodological consistency, my position has a sharp profile that, if it is to be understood at all, demands an engagement with my presuppositions about social history and the social context of our scholarship.

My explicit deliberation about the presuppositions of my social historical work has elicited a range of responses. For some it is liberating to recover the long-elided social dimensions of Israel and of academic scholarship, even when they go on to do rather different things with those insights from what I have done. For others it is inadmissible that the field should be disturbed in its traditional contours, even when they happen to agree with particular observations I make on texts or issues. Still others see little value to social approaches but grant a "live and let live" stance of the sort they would ask in return for their prized interests. Yet others are conflicted and struggling with social pre-understandings of the text, attracted to some of my presuppositions and put off by others.

Very much as with responses evoked by newer forms of literary criticism, social critical biblical studies of the sort I engage in throw into question the conceptualization of biblical studies as a discipline and as a force in society. For this reason I do not become overly elated at praise or greatly disappointed at criticism. If I have gotten my presuppositions across as I intend, then precisely such a conflictual response is what should be expected for theory and method that read social conflict as the driving force of history.

The Trajectory of My Work and Where I Stand Now

Professionally, my work in biblical studies has developed along a clearly traceable path from an almost exclusive commitment to old-style literary and historical criticism toward an emergent social scientific criticism that supplements and enriches former methods and increasingly recognizes that an adequate social theory must comprehend textuality, aesthetics and psychology—precisely as aspects of ideology. This course of development has had both an inner-biblical logic and a sociopolitical/ecclesial contextual logic. In terms of the biblical subject matter, I have moved in a reverse chronological order from the Exile to the preexilic prophets and eventually to the premonarchic origins of Israel. In terms of the theories and methods employed, I have progressed from an undisciplined sociopolitical interest to an application to Scripture of more exact and self-conscious social scientific methods and theories with Marxist social theory as my most inclusive frame of analysis. Recently, as I have struggled to write a social history of preexilic Israel, I find myself concentrating on political anthropology and ethnographic reflection on the effects and implications of writing up what you think you know about a society in one form or another. In terms of social and ecclesial contexts, I have moved from vague awareness of biblical hermeneutics as the practice of "applying" to my own world certain principles or analogies drawn from the Bible to a recognition of the full hermeneutical circle in which my social structural stance and consciousness correlates with biblical readings.

The major steps in my professional engagement with biblical studies may be summed up as follows:

1. My doctoral dissertation was on the historical setting, literary form, and theology of the Old Testament Book of Lamentations. Although a considerable body of graduate study in theology, philosophy, ethics, and history of religion served as backdrop to my dissertation, it scarcely entered into the formulation and execution of the project

in any deliberative way. Ironically, the one extrabiblical resource that was later to press its significance on me, namely, the social sciences, was virtually a closed book at this stage.

2. Early in my teaching career, I became engrossed with the prophets as political actors and thinkers, particularly with reference to their knowledge of and attitudes toward foreign nations. This interest was greatly affected by my efforts to think through the ethical dimensions of conflicting political systems in the context of nuclear weaponry. In order to carry out this project I had to immerse myself in political theory and in the literature on international relations. This was my first exposure to the social sciences in any depth.

3. My study of the prophets pushed me increasingly into the question: what after all was the social experiential ground for the prophetic judgments and actions? In short, what gave the prophets the insight and power to offer such sustained and comprehensive critiques of their societies? I was altogether unwilling to settle for the "revelation alone" answers given by the biblical theology movement. I was driven to investigate the social structure of ancient Israel and how its various biblical spokespersons were grounded in that structure. By this point, my experience in conflictual politics and my reading in sociology and Marxism were pressing me to more exactitude in characterizing the nature of Israelite society as a developmental phenomenon. This carried me increasingly into that murky origin period of Israel before the rise of the monarchy. Looking at biblical scholarship from the point of view of the social sciences, I was astonished to realize that, isolated as it was from developments in the social sciences, it was not capable of conceptualizing the social grounding of Israelite beginnings. Instead, it offered up a confused array of quasi-sociological notions about pastoral nomadism and amphictyony, depending largely on outmoded anthropology and sociology, and heavily seasoned with assumptions of religion as an autonomous self-generating force rooted in "revelation."

4. Slowly the outlines of a theoretical and methodological program of research took shape in my mind. As I saw it, this program would have to bring *all* elements of Israel's life under rigorous social scientific examination, including its religion, its traditional leader Moses, and the deity Yahweh. Simultaneously, this program would have to keep in mind its own location in modernity, the intellectual ideas that informed it, and the social realities in which I the researcher was embedded. I was not simply about a piece of "objective historical research," although I had to respect the extent to which Israel's past was something I could not freely invent or manipulate. As liberation theologies became ever more articulate through the early seventies, I was able to grasp more

clearly the reality of the complex reciprocal exchanges and flows of energy and meaning that pass between an ancient "canonical" subject matter—even when it is studied "historically"—and the interpreter's stance in church and world. *The Tribes of Yahweh* ends with theological reflection because it had in fact begun that way and was shaped in part by a theological matrix.

As I proceeded deeper into the project both on the biblical and the social scientific fronts, I read voraciously in macrosociological literature, precisely because I had decided that Israelite origins could only be grasped by means of large-scale social modeling. I gained much insight and many analytic tools from Durkheim's articulations of religious beliefs as social facts and of the division of labor in society. I was broadly informed by Weber's fascination with the interplay between economics and religion and his analysis of traditional, charismatic, and bureaucratic forms of authority, and vastly stimulated by his shrewd but erratic analysis in *Ancient Judaism*. It was, however, Marx who provided the superior heuristic framework for gathering and categorizing the data, on the one hand, and for keeping the categories or interlocking planes of social relations dynamically interactive, on the other hand. Specifically, the expropriation of surplus or uncompensated labor proved to be a crucial entrée into the structure of Canaanite and early Israelite societies, even though the precise conceptualization of pre-capitalist forms of expropriated labor is still a matter of great debate and little detailed agreement, even among Marxists. At this stage, my attention was drawn to anthropology as a field exemplifying various forms of social theory and offering valuable comparative material for an understanding of early Israel.

The culmination of this theoretical and methodological research program, extending from the late sixties through the seventies, was the publication of *The Tribes of Yahweh: A Sociology of the Religion of Liberated Israel, 1250–1050 B.C.E* (Maryknoll: Orbis Books, 1979; corrected second printing, 1981). In this forum, I have neither time nor inclination to summarize the argument of *Tribes*. Instead, I will hazard a brief evaluation of its place in the field, what it accomplished, and what it left undone or misconstrued. This will lead me on to reformulations of my perspective on early Israel and to a brief prospect of directions that need to be taken in our ongoing social critical studies. In retrospect, it seems to me that the fundamental achievement of *Tribes* has been twofold: (1) it has helped to make social scientific criticism respectable and attractive as a valid method in biblical studies, and (2) it has shown that a social critical study of Scripture is integral to contemporary ecclesial practice, social ethics, and theology. Of course, not all readers draw these conclusions, but those who value *Tribes* seem to do so for one or both of these reasons.

Closely connected with these accomplishments is my particular way of construing the origins of Israel as a composite of largely inner-Canaanite peoples who advanced from an inchoate movement to an organized stateless society with the help of their religion but not as the sole creation of that religion. We are still too early into a social study of early Israel to be confident of how much of my portrait of Israel's emergence will stand up over time. Over the last decade we have seen a significant array of proposals about early Israel's formation. No two of them agree with one another or with me on all issues, but it can be said that my perspective has had impact and considerable concurrence at a number of points.

Allow me to state what I construe as significant elements of consensus in the current debate over Israelite origins, elements that resonate with and extend the main line of argument of *Tribes in* an open-ended way. Pastoral nomadism was only one, and not the sole or even major, means of subsistence in earliest Israel. The origins of Israel as a society must be looked for within Canaan, even if some elements within Israel came from abroad in recent memory. The character of the initial Israelite society was broadly analogous to stateless societies known elsewhere in the world, and is therefore open to comparative elucidation from many sources other than the once-popular Greek amphictyony. Israel's agrarian society must be examined in its adaptation to the highland environment where it took root, and in relation to the state societies with which it interacted. Archaeological evidence is absolutely essential to understanding early Israel, but so far its data are sufficiently opaque and ambiguous that they do not confirm any single detailed social historical reconstruction. The emergent Israelite society had an extensive social matrix that cannot be circumvented or bypassed by positing Israel as a singular religious product. The religion of early Israel requires examination as an emergent novelty from Canaanite religion and as a distinctive force within the Israelite movement-becoming-society.

In a sense this presumed legacy of *Tribes* may be seen as so generally formulated that it would fit several scholars who have given very different accounts of early Israel. What this means is that *Tribes* was a provocative and suggestive work but not a definitive one, if only because it tackled many more issues than it could fully pursue and it broached others that could not have been grappled with given the state of our knowledge at the time. Moreover, my study included a considerable number of explicitly labeled heuristic probes or speculations, such as exploring the pejorative sense of *yôšēb* (literally, "one who sits") as a term for "ruler," and the proposal that holy war is viewable as a social mechanism for confiscating and giving communal ranking to expropriated goods. Amid our disappointment that we are still "in the dark" about many aspects of early Israel, I think we should take heart that we now have an ongoing scholarly tradition, with recognized theoretical and methodological tools, and a community of discourse in which the issues can be debated with confidence that researchers will understand one another's concepts and can offer one another intelligent fair-minded criticism, even as they disagree on many things.

I would be foolish to think that the existing community of discourse on Israel's origins is solely the creation of my book. Rather, the truth is that my book participates in and gives expression to a wider current of inquiry. In the first place, many papers and conversations with colleagues in a San Francisco Bay Area study group on sociology of the Bible and in the SBL Consultation and Working Group on the Social World of Ancient Israel contributed to *Tribes*. Subsequently the work of the ASOR-SBL Seminar on Sociology of the Monarchy and the recent SBL Consultation on Ideological Criticism of Texts, as well as other units in the Society dealing with form criticism, semiotics and exegesis, newer literary criticism, and sociology of the Second Temple period, have stimulated me to write a series of papers and articles that elaborate and modify *Tribes*, and to extend my work into areas not touched in that volume. The encouragement of colleagues in teaching and publishing has supported me in extending my social critical approach to the whole of Israel's history in my 1985 textbook. As indicated earlier, feedback from church workers and laity the world over has shown me that what I have had to say "taps into" prior understandings and insights they have reached by other means. Finally, in my perpetual "rethinking" of *Tribes*, I owe an incalculable debt to a stream of trenchant studies by such scholars as Ahlström, Bal, Bird, Chaney, Coote, Crüsemann, Finkelstein, Flanagan, Frick, de Geus, Halpern, Hopkins, Jobling, Lemche, Malamat, Mayes, McNutt, Meyers, Rogerson, Stiebing, Thompson, Whitelam, and Wilson. Their inquiries over much of the same ground that I surveyed have confirmed, corrected, and motivated me in what has come to feel like a collective project. The continuing reality of this community of discourse, even as we joust and wrangle among ourselves, is promising for future breakthroughs in our efforts to recover Israel's beginnings, as well as its later social history.

Twelve years after the publication of *Tribes*, I make an emphatic separation between the social theory and methods I employ and the particulars of my historical reconstructions arrived at through use of a social critical apparatus. Indeed, I discover that proper use of the fundamental theory and methodology continuously corrects and revises all historical reconstructions including my own.

My current reading of the origins of Israel and its premonarchic life can be succinctly put. First, I strongly dissent from the view that the relative paucity of our sources for the period is incapacitating for social historical reconstruction. Two realities stand out at this point. One is the profound continuity in social developments from Canaan in the Amarna Age, through Canaan two centuries later as Israel emerged, and on into the Israelite monarchic era. The other is the inexplicability of the extensive anti-statist traditions about the communitarian nature of early Israel when they are dismissed or played down as fabrications from the monarchic period. This means that I continue in the methodology of Albrecht Alt by progressing from the better known to the less well-known, working forward from the Amarna period and backward from monarchic times to try to grasp what happened in the "dark tunnel" of the tribal period. My project is analogous to what New Testament scholars do in attempting to establish "criteria of authenticity" for the words and deeds of Jesus when they compare Jesus with Judaism as his given matrix and with the subsequent early church.

Reconstruction of the social history of Israel precisely as political economy depends on an analysis of modes of production. In *Tribes* I had not yet developed a consistent mode of production analysis that extended to the whole ancient Near East and to all periods of Israel's history. I also did not give sufficient cognizance to the reality that within any dominant mode of production other modes of production may co-exist as survivals or forerunners.

My present understanding can be crystallized around certain changes in terminology which reflect conceptual reformulations. In *Tribes* I spoke of Israelite beginnings as a *peasant revolt* against a *feudal society* that produced an *egalitarian society*. These terms have come under severe criticism, some enlightened and some unenlightened. As a result of merited criticism and further developments in my thought, I now speak of Israelite beginnings as a *social revolution* against a *tributary mode of production* that produced a *communitarian mode of production*. I will now characterize the nature and significance of my reformulations, starting with the mode of production analysis.

Tributary and Communitarian Modes of Production

In *Tribes*, although uncomfortable with the category, I chose to describe Canaanite city-state society and the later Israelite monarchy as a form of feudalism. This usage soon frayed and I grappled with the intensive inquiry into what Marx had called the Asiatic Mode of Production and others labeled Oriental Despotism. In recent years I have come to the conclusion that feudalism is one variant of a larger mode of production which, following Samir Amin, I call the Tributary Mode of Production (1980: chap. 3). In the ancient Near East this took the form of a strong bureaucratic state that taxed the vast majority of peasants and nurtured merchant and landholding clients who indebted and expropriated land from these same peasants. Technology and social organization at the grassroots level of the populace, however, were only modestly changed by these tributary impositions. The local infrastructures could be severely damaged, but the tributary state had nothing to replace them with.

By all accounts, Israel first emerges at odds with this tributary system both in its ideology and in its social practice. Because there was such a great gulf between the rulers and their clients, on the one hand, and the agrarian populace, on the other hand, I believe it correct to posit that the populace of these ancient Near Eastern states constituted virtual sub-cultures that depended in no essential way on the authority, power, and ideology of the state that governed them. In early Israel we see a coalition of such people gaining autonomy and carrying on their life so as to do for themselves what states claimed to do for them: to guarantee their livelihood, to defend them against enemies, and to keep them in good graces with the gods. Israel found other ways to deal with all these needs. For this alternative mode of production, in which there was no place for taxes, rents, or interest-laden loans, I have coined the term Communitarian Mode of Production.

The concept of Communitarian Mode of Production eliminates, or at least minimizes, a recurrent misunderstanding generated by my calling early Israel an egalitarian society. Even though I have reiterated the anthropological sense in which I use the term egalitarian for approximately equal access of all the primary social units to basic resources, egalitarian is a term so freighted with specific political meanings since the French Revolution that I have decided to abandon it as a primary designation for early Israel. Egalitarian carries too many individualistic connotations of equal merit, personal property rights, and civil rights and liberties to do justice to the fundamental communalism of early Israel which it shared with all the ancient Near eastern peoples. What set Israel apart from these other peoples was that it enjoyed two centuries of independent life without the tributary overlay that it later acquired with the introduction of the monarchic state. It is in this context of communitarian equality, concerning which anthropological studies have much more to teach us than political theory since the French Revolution, that we may best explore the participation of women and servants/slaves.

There are a good many implications of adopting a mode of production analysis that distinguishes both the independence and interdependence of Tributary and Communitarian modes of production. For one thing, it allows us to carry through an analysis of the whole trajectory of social history in Canaan from pre-Israelite through late biblical times. It enables us to see that tributary domination in the ancient Near East was always an overlay on a communally-oriented populace. It helps to clarify the autonomous communitarianism of early Israel as a recognizable outcropping of a communal populace and not some arbitrary product of a religious reformer. It further illuminates why religion as the ideology of such a people would be of great social significance in the face of the religious legitimation of tributary rule. Finally, as a contribution to what has proven to be one of the most valuable gains of the last decade of debate on Israelite history, it helps us to see how tributary tendencies would be latent even in the most robust communitarian movement and, at the same time, how even the strongest tributary state could not stifle communitarianism among its people. It could not undertake the social transformation that modern nation-states have come nearer to achieving, since it had neither the technology to transform production and replace traditional social relations nor the cultural media to successfully indoctrinate and reshape the subjectivity of the agrarian populace. Once again the critical role of religion as an instrument of communitarian resistance to the state emerges as critical, since the very circumstances of Yahwism's communitarian origins prevented the Israelite state from coopting and domesticating Israelite religion with entire success.

Social Revolution

Peasant revolt was of course the term that Mendenhall first employed but abandoned in his later writing. It was an appropriate term insofar as it highlighted that the majority populace of Israel was agrarian and that it was in conflict with city-states in its environment and managed to gain autonomy over against them. The peasant revolt analogy, however, depended heavily on sporadic peasant uprisings in Europe in late medieval and early modern times. Eric Wolf's study of peasant wars in the twentieth century drew attention to how peasant militancy related to the unrest of other socioeconomic sectors and to the protracted rather than sporadic nature of a number of these peasant involvements in struggles to gain national independence and to change the social order.

Social revolution seems the correct term for a change in the mode of production effected over a considerable territory for a span of two centuries. In earliest Israel, a communitarian mode of production replaced a tributary mode of production. The primary means of production in both the tributary and communitarian modes were agrarian. What changed was not the means of producing but the mode of appropriating what was produced and the related changes in social structure flowing from the rejection of tribute in the form of taxes, rent, and interest on debts. Although the great majority of Israelites were former peasants who became free agrarians, their revolution clearly involved others, including pastoral producers and various servants of or renegades from nearby tributary state systems, such as soldiers of fortune, brigands, priests, artisans, and the like.

Does this untidy tattered assembly of peoples in the highlands of Canaan in the twelfth and eleventh centuries deserve to be called a social revolution? My judgment is that it does, but how one reasons for or against that conclusion is closely entwined with the disputed issue of "social intentionality" in early Israel. What were these people up to? Our view of these first Israelites hinges, I believe, on our conception of how their communitarian mode of production emerged. There are three explanations. Some believe that tribal Israel's communitarian mode of production was a carry-over from its earlier life as pastoral nomads, and was thus a wholly predictable cultural inheritance which Israel outgrew as it settled down. Others believe that communitarianism developed in Canaan because of a breakdown of the city-states so massive that rural communities were thrown on their own resources and learned to cooperate to survive, and thus reluctantly adopted a lesser-of-evils strategy for coping with an undesired happenstance. Still others, myself among them, believe that this communitarianism—however much aided by city-state decline—was an insurgent movement recruited among a coalition of peasants, pastoralists, mercenaries, bandits, and disaffected state and temple functionaries, who simultaneously worked to oppose city-state control over them and to develop a counter-society, and was therefore in considerable measure "intended" by them. This is not to say that they all agreed on precisely what to do, or that they all adhered to the agreements and institutions they worked out, or that they were able to foresee the consequences of what they were doing. It means that by and large they wanted to be free of state sovereignty and they wanted to develop loosely coordinated self-rule in spite of all the problems decentralization created for them.

It is customary nowadays to dismiss the social militancy and intentionality in the Joshua-Judges traditions as the fabricated nostalgia of monarchic traditionists and thus of a piece with the Deuteronomistic schema of a monolithic national entity composed of twelve parts. My considered view is that these testimonies to tribal Israel's will to build a counter-society are rooted in pre-Deuteronomistic materials that derive in their essentials from tribal times and are clearly detachable from later notions of a harmonious twelve-tribe social order soon to be logically crowned with statehood. I believe that much of my social analysis of these pre-Deuteronomistic materials in *Tribes*, tentative and incomplete as it was, is likely to stand the test of time, although it is obvious to me that we have far more social exegetical work ahead of us than we have behind us. In this task of discerning social reality enshrined in texts, the notable contributions of the Marxist literary critics Terry Eagleton and Frederic Jameson are just beginning to be felt in our biblical work.

I am optimistic that along the lines indicated it will be possible to proceed ever more deeply and concretely into a reconstruction of Israelite social history and that, despite all continuing and constructive differences among us, we will be able to achieve a working consensus. In any event, what we have so far accomplished, and may yet accomplish, is of tremendous consequence for our assessment of the place of Israel and the Bible in our churches and synagogues and in our societies the world around.

PART I

THE HEBREW BIBLE IN ITS SOCIAL WORLD

A

*Social Critical Method and
the Origins of Israel*

CHAPTER 1

Domain Assumptions
and Societal Models in the Study
of Pre-Monarchic Israel

ABSTRACT

Generations of biblical scholars have uncritically assumed that the social changes in ancient Canaan which produced early Israel were the result of population displacement as desert nomads settled down to an agrarian life and proceeded to shape a new society by the mandate of their unique religious ideas. A more sophisticated grasp of social theory and history, requiring a very different set of assumptions about social change, greatly alters our perspective on early Israel as "a new society." It is now widely recognized that social change is frequently—even normally—precipitated through inner-societal pressure and conflict, that pastoral nomadism is a limited source of population and culture under conditions such as obtained in ancient Canaan, and that a complex of cultural factors is at work in all social change, among which the role of religion must be demonstrated rather than posited in advance. Taking these updated "domain assumptions" into account, we are in a position to develop societal models of early Israel that do justice to its indigenous rootage in a village-based agrarian society, including the practice of a religion congruent with, rather than simply predetermining, its social formation.

The American sociologist Alvin Gouldner speaks of "domain assumptions," by which he means the key or master conceptual frames of reference that affect the kinds of models and hypotheses that are imaginable—and therefore possible—in an epoch or circle of scholarship. The commanding domain assumptions are characteristically unexpressed or half-expressed and unargued. Shifts in models and hypotheses occur when new domain assumptions arise under the pressure of accumulating evidence and, more especially, under the impact of new extra-scholarly intellectual and cultural climates.

Precisely such a shift in domain assumptions is under way in the study of Israelite beginnings. In a volume shortly to be published [*The*

Tribes of Yahweh], I attempt to articulate the old and the new domain assumptions and to offer a societal model for pre-monarchic Israel consonant with the new domain assumptions. I shall here summarize the main outlines of my argument, with particular attention to the links between the domain assumptions in ancient Near Eastern and biblical studies, on the one hand, and the models of Israelite society, on the other. By way of more detailed application, I shall have a few comments about the historical peculiarity of Israelite tribalism or "retribalization."

The history of the study of Israelite beginnings is a history of very slowly emerging self-consciousness about domain assumptions and societal models, chiefly I think because anthropology and sociology never have had the impact on biblical studies that the humanities have had. The traditional conquest/invasion model of Israelite origins scarcely raised a single sociological question because it contained an implicit unexamined, albeit rudimentary, sociology of Israel. It assumed a twelve-tribe system composed of clans and families as sub-sets of tribes operating as an unquestioned counterpart to the miraculously formed religious community of Israel. The immigration model, especially in the form it assumed under Noth's amphictyonic analogue (1930, 1960:85–138), pushed sociological considerations a bit farther into the foreground, but not so far after all—and perhaps for three main reasons:

1. Noth's welcome systemic approach to Israel was really mainly focused on one societal segment, the cultic institutions, rather than on the entire social system.

2. Noth's approach took for granted the semi-nomadic origins of Israel without argument.

3. Noth failed to compare the structural locus of the amphictyony in Greece with the structural locus of the "amphictyony" in Israel. Had he done so, it would have been clear that the amphictyony in Greece was a secondary or tertiary formation within the wider society, whereas the presumed "amphictyony" in Israel was the encompassing framework of the entire society.

Within the last decade the revolt model of Israelite origins has exposed the social structural and developmental questions about early Israel in an emphatic and insistent manner. The fact that Mendenhall prefaced and framed his model of "peasant revolt" or "withdrawal" with a discussion of pastoral nomadism and tribalism in relation to urban and rural modes of ancient Near Eastern life thrusts the problem of the modes of Israel's occupation of the land into a larger context, namely, the problem of the social organizational modes of the Israelite occupiers (1962, 1973).

Until very recent years the inquiry into Israel's early history was massively under the sway of at least three master ideas which I shall characterize as:

1. The Domain Assumption of Social Change by Population Displacement.

2. The Domain Assumption of the Creativity of the Desert in Initiating Social Change in Sedentary Regions.

3. The Domain Assumption of Arbitrary Social Change Produced by Idiosyncratic or Prominent Cultural Elements.

These domain assumptions may be briefly stated as follows:

1. It is assumed that a major sociopolitical shift or hiatus is most likely to have been the result of one demographic or ethnic group displacing another, either wholesale or as a ruling elite, whether by immigration or by military conquest.

2. It is assumed that the breeding ground and source of many such population displacements in the ancient Near East was the desert and that these displacements entailed an influx of military and cultural élan typical of the desert group, followed by an eventual transition of the immigrants or invaders from nomadic to sedentary life with resulting socio-political acculturation.

3. It is assumed that the most idiosyncratic, prominent or distinctive element of a new sociopolitical phase, especially as viewed in retrospect, must have been the nuclear factor which initiated other sorts of changes and constellated them into a new social system or culture. Since the religio-symbolic and cultic dimensions of Israelite society appear to be the most idiosyncratic elements, particularly as viewed from the perspective of later Judaism and Christianity, Yahwism is to be regarded as the isolate source and agent of change in the emergence of Israel.

The pressures and forces which have eroded these long-standing domain assumptions are numerous and I shall cite only a few of them in catalogue form: (a) evidence from pre-history and ethnography that pastoral nomadism is a secondary outgrowth of plant and animal domestication in the sown land; (b) indications from the study of zones of social organization and from cultural anthropology that seemingly sudden cultural and social change is as often the consequence of slow growth and sharpening social conflict within a population continuum as it is the result of fresh incursions of peoples, that conflict occurs as regularly within societies under single political regimes as between opposing states, and that technology and social organization shape ideas more profoundly by far than humanities-oriented scholars have understood; (c) demonstrations from sociology of religion that the social functions of religion are intrinsic to the form religion takes even in its most distinctive higher features; (d) signs from historical data on the ancient Near East and early Israel of the subsidiary role of pastoral nomadism within the village-based economy, of the desert as a zone of political resistance and asylum rather than the locus of alien political and military initiatives, and of Israel's fundamental cultural continuity with Canaan over a very wide repertory, including language and religious formations, simultaneously combined with Israel's sharp divergence from Canaan in the development both of tribalism in opposition to the state and of a distinctively elaborated religious system. Probably not the least as a general encompassing factor in the deterioration of the old domain assumptions is the direct experience of social upheaval in the modern world which more often follows from technological change and from tension and conflict within populations over control of resources and their distribution than from actual population displacements.

New domain assumptions are implicit in sociological work on Israelite beginnings now going on in the United States, so far most fully published by George Mendenhall, soon to be enlarged by this lecturer's publication, and shared in by a growing number of younger scholars. Among others, students of Mendenhall at the University of Michigan and of Frank Cross and Ernest Wright at Harvard University have contributed measurably to this development, generally in the form of unpublished dissertations and brief articles. Similar trends toward the application of social scientific methods to ancient Israel are beginning to surface in Israel, in western Europe, and in the third world. A parallel phenomenon is visible among students of the ancient Near East.

The emerging master concepts, in each case challenging and replacing its outmoded predecessor, may be characterized as:

1. The Domain Assumption of the Normalcy of Social Change by Inner Societal Pressure and Conflict.

2. The Domain Assumption of the Subordinate Role of the Desert in Precipitating Social Change.

3. The Domain Assumption of Lawful Social Change Produced by the Interaction of Cultural Elements at Many Levels.

The substance of these new domain assumptions may be briefly stated as follows:

1. It is assumed that major sociopolitical shifts or hiatuses are to be expected within societies as the result of new technological forces, social conflicts and contending ideas in volatile interaction and that social change due to population displacement or political conquest is to be posited only when specific evidence warrants.

2. It is assumed that semi-nomadism in the ancient Near East was economically and politically subordinate to and broadly integrated

within the dominant agricultural zone and was never the source of massive population displacement or political conquest as commonly attributed to it (Gottwald, 1974).

3. It is assumed that the initially or ultimately prominent or distinctive features of a society or culture must be viewed in the total matrix of generative elements and not over-weighted in advance as the all-powerful sources of inspiration or as the selective survival factors in the societal development. Thus, a critical generative role may well have been played by cultural elements which have been lost to view and must be recovered by careful research. In particular, ideational factors must be looked at not as disembodied prime movers but as the ideas of human beings in determinate technological and social settings in which the total mix of culture will tend to exhibit lawful or patterned configurations (Harris).

Congruent with these domain assumptions, I propose a societal model for early Israel along the following lines: Early Israel was a slowly converging and constellating cluster of rebellious and dissenting Canaanite peoples distinguished by an anti-statist form of social organization with de-centralized leadership. This Israelite "devolution" or "winding down" from the city-state form of social organization took the shape of a "re-tribalization" movement among agriculturalists and pastoralists organized in economically self-sufficient extended families with egalitarian access to basic resources. Israel's religion, which had intellectual and cultic foundations in ancient Near Eastern-Canaanite religion, was idiosyncratic or mutational in a manner that its society was idiosyncratic and mutational, i.e., one integrated divine being existed for one integrating and egalitarianly structured people. Israel became that segment of Canaan which wrested sovereignty from another segment of Canaan in the interests of village-based tribally-oriented "low politics" over against city-state hierarchic "high politics."

So far it can be seen that I am in broad agreement with Mendenhall's basic design of Israelite origins. One of the points where we diverge, however, is the point at which he denies the sphere of politics to early Israel. Mendenhall reads Israel's rejection of state power as tantamount to the rejection of sociopolitical power per se: "The starting point of politics is the concern for power, but the whole theme of early biblical history...is the rejection of power" (1973:195). It is obvious, however, that without a central concern for marshalling and employing power Israel could never have come into existence. Prompted by his fascination with the suzerain-vassal treaty as the supposed model for Israel's early covenant, Mendenhall has bracketed out the divine monopoly of power from sociopolitical analysis. Clearly, we face two interlocking sociological phenomena to be accounted for in their peculiar combination: (1) Israel challenged one form of power by means of another form of power, and (2) Israel consciously exercised power even as it consciously attributed the source of all power to its deity. In failing to deal with the Israelite power formation sociologically, it appears to me that Mendenhall has not adequately assimilated the new domain assumption concerning lawful social change.

At this juncture I propose to follow up and extend somewhat the tribal model of early Israel, first in synchronic terms and then in diachronic terms.

A considerable body of social organizational work on the tribe suggests the following broad formal features or traits of tribal organization (Sahlins; Helm):

1. The tribe represents a sharp increase in demographic size over the hunting and gathering or primitive agricultural band, normally a leap from fewer than one hundred people to several hundreds or thousands.

2. The population increase is closely connected with a more secure control over an enlarged food surplus.

3. The enlarged food surplus is secured not only by technological improvements but by more intricate social bonding by means of many cross-cutting associations or sodalities which interconnect the residential units, notable among these associations being the exogamous clan.

4. The sub-divisions of the tribe are typically segmented, i.e., they are structurally and functionally equivalent and politically equal, so that in principle any one of them could be destroyed and the tribe would survive.

5. The tribe carries out its political functions by diffused or temporary role assignments in such a way that there is no political leadership network distinguishable from the network of social leadership, although the rudiments of specialized political leadership appear with the tribal chiefdom.

Viewed in the broad design of social forms, pre-monarchic Israel was clearly tribal in character. Israel's economy was a form of intensive rain agriculture with animal husbandry, an economy which capitalized on the recent introduction into the highlands of Canaan of iron implements for clearing and working the land, of slaked lime plaster for constructing water-tight cisterns to hold reserve water through the annual dry season, and of the art of rock terracing to retain and control the erratic rainfall. The members of Israelite society were arranged not only in large extended residence groups which were relatively self-contained socioeconomic units and political equals but also in cross-cutting sodalities or sodality equivalents. Among these cross-cutting groupings were the protective associations of extended families (the *mišpāḥōt*, which were *not* exogamous clans in my view), the citizen army, the ritual congregation, the Levites (landless and distributed among the tribes), and probably also the Rechabites (understood as itinerant specialists in metal [Frick, 1971]).

On the other hand, Israel was not yet a state, which it became only fully under David. Tendencies toward the chiefdom and monarchy are clearly evidenced in Saul and even earlier in some of the diverse functionaries called obscurely "judges," notably Gideon and Abimelech, and perhaps also some of the so-called "minor judges" such as Ibzan. At its founding Israel had no specialized political offices rooted in a superordinate sovereignty, and it resisted such institutions and offices strenuously even after reluctantly resorting to them in the face of the mounting Philistine military threat, which was itself a powerful and effective regrouping of sociopolitical formations from the preceding era of Egyptian imperialism and Canaanite quasi-feudalism.

The defining feature of politics in old Israel was that political functions were diffused throughout the social structure or focused in temporary ad hoc role assignments. While the details of Israel's social structure (and especially of its "offices") are as yet unrecoverable in many respects, so that we do not possess the fully rounded cross-section we desire, all available information supports consistently the view that early Israel was tribal with fiercely resisted tendencies toward the chiefdom. And we are also able to establish beyond any shadow of doubt that this political feature of Israelite tribalism was not derived from pastoral nomadism but was securely rooted in a form of agricultural tribalism for which there are ample parallels in ethnography.

Of course the gross typological-evolutionary scale of band, tribe, and state does not provide a finely calibrated historical understanding of specific societies. The historical locus of early Israel is thus of decisive importance for understanding the precise mix of factors and tendencies at work in its social organizational development.

The insights of Morton Fried concerning tribal formations as "secondary phenomena" are pertinent for understanding Israel's peculiar tribalism (154–74), granting that Fried's position is adjudged extreme by most anthropologists when applied to all tribal societies (Helm). Fried points out that many tribes are known to us in colonial situations, where the external pressure of more highly organized and dominant civilizations leads to administrative synthesis and consolidation of the threatened society internally, so that it comes to present the form of a tribe to those who dominate the society. He cites the Makah of

Washington State, the Tonga of northern Rhodesia, and the Chiga of Uganda.

> Most tribes seem to be secondary phenomena in a very specific sense: They may well be the product of processes stimulated by the appearance of rela-tively highly organized societies amidst other societies which are organized much more simply. If this can be demonstrated, tribalism can be viewed as a reaction to the formation of complex political structure rather than a necessary preliminary stage in its evolution (170).

Fried notes that this is hardly a development peculiar to European colonialism since "the Roman, the Chinese, and other expanding state societies had grasped the essentials of divide and rule" (173).

If we modify his "most tribes" to "some tribes" or "many tribes," Fried's insight may be taken seriously as an indication of the way a centralized state may intrude on simpler societies and harden them into certain social formations. But surely Fried does not mean to imply that these simpler societies were entirely indisposed to the tribal direction in which the more organized societies pushed them. It would be stretching his argument ridiculously far to claim that segmentation and the exog-amous clan were imposed by colonial powers. These integral elements of tribalism must be closely connected with economic production. Fried himself admits the pertinence of Elman Service's contention that the tribal organization extends the peace group and enhances military effec-tiveness in a world of competing bands and tribes, quite apart from and prior to the entrance of state societies on the tribal scene (164–65).

Under the circumstances, Fried's model must be altered consider-ably to apply to Israel. This can be done fruitfully if we allow not only that colonial centralized states can shape tribalism within a subject people, solidifying and skewing elements already present, but if we also posit that elements of the population within or adjacent to a centralized state may withdraw from it or rebel against it and develop less central-ized social forms both as defensive mechanisms against the state and as constructive alternatives to the state. What these two versions of the social organizational effect of opposed centralized and uncentralized societies have in common is the abrasive or openly conflicting juxtapo-sition of societies at different organizational levels and the critical selec-tive organizational impact of the "stronger" and more complex party upon the "weaker" and less complex party.

In my assessment we should view Israelite tribalism as a form chosen by people who consciously rejected Canaanite centralization of power and deliberately aimed to defend their own uncentralized system against the effort of Canaanite society to crush their movement. Israel's tribalism was an autonomous project which tried to roll back the zone of political centralization in Canaan, to claim territories and peoples for an egalitarian mode of agricultural and pastoral life. Unquestionably there were significant antecedent forms of struggle and modes of organization which fed into Israelite tribalism, but in terms of demographic size, organizational novelty, and political effectiveness there was a far greater qualitative leap from pre-Israelite to Israelite tribalism than there was from pre-colonial to post-colonial tribalism among the Makahs, Tongas or Chigas. The sum of these qualitative differences suggests that we should speak of Israel's adaptive tribalism as a "re-tribalization" movement.

All the evidence for early Israel points to its tribalism as a self-constructed instrument of resistance and of decentralized self-rule rather than tribalism as an administrative structure imposed by Canaanite rulers in order to govern their proto-Israelite or Israelite subjects. Seen from the perspective of Canaanite society, Israel was not a resistant colonial underling to be subdued but a foreign growth in its own body to be cut out. Seen from Israel's perspective, its tribalism was not a continuous ancient development to be preserved but a freshly constructed instrument for "cracking open" the centralized and stratified appropriation of natural and human resources of which the people forming Israel were an essential part prior to their act of revolt. Israel's tribalism was politically conscious social revolution and, more loosely, a civil war in that it divided and counterposed peoples who had previously been organized within Canaanite city states.

At this point, however, I would introduce another factor into the sociopolitical dynamics of Israelite origins, for it is the omission of this factor from Mendenhall's model which contributes to the air of unreality which many critics have detected in his hypothesis. I refer to the fact that in virtually all such revolutions and civil wars the polarization of the populace is far from complete. There is evidence that a sizable part of the Canaanite populace was "caught in the middle," staying neutral as long as possible and only reluctantly moving toward one side or the other, thus constituting a sociopolitical segment whose loyalty or passive cooperation was actively sought by the contending parties.

The implications of this concrete historical understanding of Israel's leap to tribalism are enormous. It means that our image of Israel's formation cannot be that of a continuous line of cultural evolution upwards from the band society to tribal forms of segmentation and sodality formation, nor can our image be that of a spill-over or eruption of pastoral nomadism from the desert into the settled land. Our image of Israel's formation must be that of a profound discontinuity in the hierarchic feudal social fabric of Canaan, a rupture from within centralized society. This rupture was accomplished by an alliance of peoples who withdrew directly from the Canaanite system with other peoples who, beyond the centralized system's immediate reach in the hinterland of Canaan, refused the customary path of being drawn into that system and accommodating themselves to it.

In terms of Fried's typology, Canaan did not make an "appearance" in a long-developed or latent tribal society called Israel. To the contrary, Israel, with a mutant sophisticated tribal mode of organization, made an "appearance" within the social system and territorial domain of Canaan. The people who came to be Israelites countered what they experienced as the systematic aggression of centralized society by a concrete coordinated symbolically unified social revolutionary action of aggressive self-defense against that society. Appropriating the land and economic means of production, this body of people organized its production, distribution, and consumption along essentially egalitarian lines. The specific historic rise of old Israel was thus a conscious improvisational reversion to egalitarian social organization which displaced hierarchic social organization over a large area which had been either directly or indirectly dominated by Canaanite centralization and stratification for centuries.

The above model of Israelite re-tribalization as an inner Canaanite phenomenon raises whole chains of additional questions for further research and theoretical reflection. Is anything to be learned about the re-tribalizing confederacy of Israel from the history and typology of other inter-tribal confederacies such as the Iroquois Five Nations? Is there an analogy between post-Minoan and post-Mycenean Greek society and early Israel, as Mendenhall has briefly suggested? Is anything further to be learned about the earliest Greek amphictyony of pre-Delphic times, which centered at Pylae and which might after all be more cogently analogous with early Israel than the relatively late, perhaps already much decomposed, form of the amphictyony which Noth treated? With what relevant social systems are we to compare early Israel? Certainly the Canaanite city-state and the Egyptian empire are prime units for comparison. But what of the ʿapiru, who appear in part as a special deviant form of passive resistance to Canaanite society and in part as a forerunner and contributory component of early Israel? How can our view of the previously over-inflated and misconstrued pastoral nomadic society be phrased so as to include it as a special ecological nuancing either of the city-state system or of the village-based agricultural system in conflict with the city-state? What allowance must be made for Mendenhall's recent contention that there was a considerable movement of Luwians, Hittites, Hurrians and other northerly peoples into Palestine attendant on the incursion of the Sea Peoples? (1973:142–73). Were these people carriers of a major new social system or, more likely, did they join the ranks of both sides of the inner-Canaanite struggle between low and high politics, or opt for uneasy neutrality? What are we to make of the Ammonites, Moabites, and Edomites of whose beginnings we still know so appallingly little? Will the present slight improvement in our archaeological data on these trans-Jordanian peoples allow us to form any clearer picture of their social structure? This glaring blank in our knowledge of Israel's neighbors becomes all the more tantalizing in the light of the model advanced above for early Israel's social origins. Why were those Ammonites, Moabites, and Edomites, whose origins are presumed to have been rather similar to Israel's origins, *not* a part of Israel? Why did the social revolutionary movement of early Israel extend only so far in the trans-Jordanian highlands and no farther? Were social elements among the Ammonites, Moabites, and Edomites part of the general social uprising which failed to develop to a breakthrough point as it did with Israel? Finally, can a re-oriented Palestinian archaeology be of increasing assistance in checking social and cultural hypotheses, comparable for example with the function of "the new archaeology" in checking out hypotheses in new world ethnography?

These are but a few of the proliferating questions which sharply pose the need for new research strategies and new forms of collaboration among specialists in order to seek additional evidence and to reassess old evidence within the framework of rapidly maturing sociological analyses of old Israel.

John Bright's New Revision
of A History of Israel

ABSTRACT

As was true in the previous edition, this third edition of Bright's *A History of Israel* (1981) accepts Mendenhall's hypothesis of a peasant revolt as a major contributing factor to the formation of Israel but fails to integrate this social construct with the other historical and religious data which he continues to treat in a highly traditional manner. The result is a schizoid portrait of Israel as a historically obscure and undistinguished people who nonetheless possessed a creative new theology that held them together in a religious league. Bright's confusion, typical of most biblical historians, is revealed in his imprecise use of the terms "Hebrews," "Israelites," and "Yahwists." I propose that a thoroughgoing integration of all the socioreligious data concerning the emergence of Israel requires us to distinguish among the socially restive/revolutionary elements in Canaan: (1) Proto-Israelites, including both those who later became Israelites and those who did not; (2) Israelites joined in El worship; and (3) Israelites joined in Yahweh worship.

Since its publication in 1959, John Bright's *A History of Israel* has been the standard English-language work on the subject, especially provocative for its treatment of the obscure premonarchic period. The changes in the new third revised edition, largely confined to the premonarchic history, underscore the current maelstrom of conflicting interpretations of biblical Israel's origins. Describing this controversy, the author remarks that "almost everything seems again to have been thrown into question. At many points...one now finds a veritable chaos of conflicting opinion" (15).

Bright quite correctly recognizes that his subject consists of an interlocking series of historical problems extending from the patriarchal migrations through the descent into Egypt, bondage, exodus, wilderness wandering, conquest, and the formation of the intertribal Israelite league. Not content merely to examine isolated historical topics, Bright struggles for a coherent method and theory that will get to the bottom of the entire sequence of events as reported in Israel's traditions. If he is frustrated in this quest, the difficulty is not in his talents so much as in the fragmented and stalemated interpretations that biblical scholarship has bequeathed him. In this third edition, Bright has not altered his position on any major issue set forth in the second revised edition (1972). However, this appears to be less the result of firmness of opinion than of frustration over scant and conflicting biblical and archaeological data and over scholarly theories that hang in the air as they cancel one another out. Striving to unravel it all, he resorts to theological solutions that bring an *appearance* of definitive explanation but do not have convincing historical *substance*.

The central problem Bright faces as a historian is this: There are substantial literary traditions in the Bible concerning the patriarchs, Moses, Joshua, and the judges. In what sense do these *literary* works tell a *history* directly, or at least provide information that helps us to reconstruct a history? His primary answer is that the narratives, poems, lists, and laws of early biblical tradition are by and large not the kinds of writings that tell history directly. However, they do provide indirect indicators of a history occasionally sketched in outline, hinted at in some details, or presupposed as the sorts of happenings broadly necessary to produce the biblical literature. Archaeology and the political and cultural history of surrounding nations can assist in filling in parts of the outline and in testing the plausibility of alternative reconstructions of early Israelite history.

As for the patriarchal period, Bright argues that no history of the patriarchs can be written because the biblical traditions about them are not contemporaneous records but instead come from a later period. Not a single person in Genesis is attested outside that book. Moreover, there are no archaeological materials connected with the patriarchs that can compensate for this deficiency. There is no reliable patriarchal chronology, nor any coherent geographical itinerary for patriarchal movements because many migrations of many clans are compressed into the artificial unity of the stories. Finally, no patriarchal biographies can be written because the patriarchs are so heavily, although not exclusively, symbols for groups.

Where does this leave the historian? The only recourse is to place the patriarchal traditions in their broad cultural horizon, which Bright takes to be, in the main, the Middle Bronze Age (c. 2000–1500 B.C.E.) with some elements fitting better into the Late Bronze Age (c. 1500–1200 B.C.E.). This cultural match is made by analyzing the kinds of names, the customs and laws, and the migration patterns contained in the patriarchal narratives. Bright's most confident conclusion is that the patriarchal groups originated in Upper Mesopotamia as part of Middle Bronze Amorite and Late Bronze Aramean migrations. For centuries, they entered Canaan as semi-nomads who then settled down at varying places. During this period they had no overarching social framework nor any consciousness of unity.

Among these patriarchal groups were three clans led by the chieftains Abraham, Isaac, and Jacob, who worshipped personal gods of a type that covenanted with their worshippers and promised land and progeny to the clans. These gods slowly coalesced with the Canaanite high god El who was eventually conceived as a manifestation of Yahweh revealed to Moses. Segments of these patriarchal clans entered Egypt; some came forth in the exodus.

In connection with this reserved reading of patriarchal realities, Bright repeatedly speaks of the traditions as "firmly anchored in history," marked by an "authentic flavor," and even exhibiting "historical facts." There is a definite stretching of language in his way of speaking that invites methodological confusion. Most of the time Bright makes it theoretically clear that the patriarchal traditions are not historiography. Again and again, however, he converts the cultural "lifelikeness" of the traditions into historical assertions. This permits him, for instance, to assert confidently that the three Genesis patriarchs were actual historical individuals, even though the substance of their traditions is not at all directly historical.

Similarly, Bright acknowledges that our principal interest in the patriarchs stems from their place in the history of religion; he then uses the frail bridge of Albrecht Alt's theory about personal clan gods (1966b) to assert that these patriarchal cults contributed major covenantal and promissory elements to later Yahwism (98–103). This move from general cultural authenticity to specific historical connections is made in defiance of his announced working methodology.

Much of the difficulty lies with Bright's insufficient attention to a consideration he, in fact, urges: "All literature is to be interpreted in the light of the type to which it belongs" (75). If the literary genre of the patriarchal narratives is barely "historical" enough to permit connecting their sociocultural contents with various groups spread over as much as 800 years, what purpose is served by using historical categories to evaluate these narratives? Doesn't this lead to disappointment? Are we not reduced to forcing this "poor history" into a mold of specificity and exactness that must inevitably be unsatisfying?

Bright suggests that the patriarchal narratives may once have been "heroic poems" worked eventually into prose "epics." Other scholars have characterized them as legends or sagas. Like most scholars oriented to archaeology and history, what Bright does not do is to inquire systematically into what sorts of external references to culture, society, and historical events we are likely to find in this kind of non-historiographic literature that has been cast into family sagas.

Fortunately, we know a good deal about folklore and sagas among peoples the world over. In some cases, as with the Icelandic sagas, we have external historical controls for assessing the way historical and social realities get filtered and refracted in this type of literature. It is high time to focus cross-culturally informed attention on the way the form and content of the patriarchal stories are structured; then we can perhaps determine more exactly the extent to which this structure reflects the external environment in which the literature was created. Bright readily concedes that the patriarchal narratives, as well as the conquest narratives, have probably combined or "telescoped" once separate persons, groups and events (83, 85, 133, 138, 140). That being the case, it seems futile and arbitrary to search, as he does, for a kind of "redeeming historical value" in the sagas, without first inquiring carefully into the precise ways the sagas have undergone "a process of selection, refraction, and normalization" (73).

On the use of the Ebla texts, Bright is commendably circumspect. He remarks that when these texts are published, they may throw light on the patriarchs. Mindful of the sweeping claims of some scholars and the flat denials and cautious reservations of others, he refrains from embracing premature correlations of Ebla and the Bible, like those that clouded past major textual discoveries at Mari, Ugarit, and Qumran. In this, Bright shows himself a careful historian—he knows that his thirst for new information is not a license to invent it or to grasp untested interpretations of texts convenient to his purposes. Accordingly, Bright tells us of reports that the Ebla texts contain patriarchal personal names such as Abram, Eber, Ishmael, and Esau; patriarchal place names such as Peleg, Serug, Terah, Nahor, and Haran (78); Sodom and Gomorrah and other Cities of the Plain (84); a second Ur in the vicinity of Haran (90, n. 48); and the short form (ya) of the divine name Yahweh (126, n. 43). In each case he notes that these identifications have been flatly disputed and that no historical conclusions can be based upon them without further study.

Bright's treatment of the Mosaic period reflects the growing awareness of the Midianites' importance. In the late 13th and 12th centuries, the Midianites constituted a large confederacy of tribes that attempted to control trade in Sinai and Transjordan (124). Bright accepts the view that a Late Bronze Egyptian temple to Hathor at the Timna mines in the

Arabah was modified about 1150 B.C.E. into a Midianite tent shrine that contained a recently recovered bronze serpent. This archaeological evidence, he believes, strengthens the likelihood that Midianites (Kenites) as well as early Israelites were Yahweh worshippers (127, 168, n. 57).

Bright notes that the literary traditions about Moses are in many respects no more historiographic than the patriarchal sagas; he nonetheless claims that "the events of exodus and Sinai require a great personality behind them....To deny that role to Moses would force us to posit another person of the same name!" This type of argument is a frequent ploy among biblical historians when direct evidence is thin, but it does little except obscure historical analysis. Bright is certainly correct that single founders are prominent in the history of religion, but it is also well known that legends have tended to embellish their careers. Moses might have filled a singular role, but the traditions about him may also have been singularly distorted. We should not overlook the biblical traditions of Moses sharing leadership and of the repeated challenges to his authority. Thus, when Bright invokes the "necessity" of Moses as depicted in the Bible as an explanation for Yahwism, this is either a literary truism that simply restates the traditions, or it is Bright's longing for historicity. In neither case is it a historical judgment.

Indeed, at key points where Bright deals with "great men" and "great ideas" in the historical process, he leaps into unpremised historicity. With regard to Moses, for example, he asserts:

> It is, to be sure, difficult and frequently impossible to isolate the distinctive contribution of Moses and beliefs of the desert days from features that developed on the soil of Palestine. But there is no reason whatsoever to assume that Israel's faith changed in any essential way with its appearance in the settled land (147).

I should have thought, however, that the historian's way of proceeding from the first sentence would be to say something like this:

> Consequently, there is no reason whatsoever to assume that we know in advance, or can precisely or confidently determine in the end, how much continuity there was between the religion of Moses and the religion of the intertribal Israelites in Canaan.

To claim or to deny change "in any essential way" requires that we specify the changed and the unchanged elements, structures, and settings. Instead, Bright gives the impression of a Mosaic faith that was not subject to historical change, the very thing he elsewhere warns against when he says, "It is human events that he [the historian] must record. These he must seek as best he can behind documents that interpret them theologically" (75). Bright occasionally lets those theological interpretations in the documents substitute for historical assessment.

Even by the second edition, Bright had abandoned the theory of the Israelite takeover of Canaan as a massive military conquest. This well-known version of events had been advanced by W. F. Albright and G. E. Wright. In the second edition, Bright favored the hypothesis of a peasant revolt within Canaan ("an inside job") that coincided with an influx of Moses' group of Israelites from the desert, as proposed by G. E. Mendenhall (1962, 1973). Bright completed the third edition in August 1979; consequently he did not have at his disposal the amended and refined version of this social revolutionary model systematically developed in my book, *The Tribes of Yahweh* (1979).

Although Bright was once a strong advocate of the Albright/Wright method of correlating archaeology and biblical history, in this third edition he introduces severe cautions about the difficulty of correlating external archaeological evidence with any particular reconstruction of Israelite origins. He notes that the archaeological data from Gibeon, Hebron, Arad, Hormah, and Khirbet Rabūd are either contrary or inconclusive for the conquest hypothesis as reported in the book of Joshua (129, 132–33). He is also inclined to agree with those who now shift the date of Israel's takeover of the Canaanite highlands from the last quarter of the 13th century to the first quarter or so of the 12th century (133, 174).

Bright notes some of the far-reaching implications of using a social revolutionary model to interpret archaeological data. He observes, for instance, that the absence of archaeological evidence of destruction may mean that a city was taken by internal uprising and preserved by its inhabitants as part of the Israelite movement (132).

But he must be careful, because archaeological evidence presents a range of possible interpretations. Destruction of a city or the absence of destruction at the time of the Israelite takeover could be interpreted consistently with a military conquest or a peasant revolt model. Bright, as we have seen, observes that non-destruction may mean that a city was taken by internal uprising. While I might welcome that conclusion, the truth is that non-destruction could also mean that the city surrendered to a military conqueror to avoid destruction. Similarly, a city might be destroyed because a local ruler took refuge in his fortified palace at the center of the city, making large-scale or total destruction necessary to topple him from power. Another possible explanation for the destruction of an administrative center is that in the tribal society of Israel there would have been no place for fortified administrative centers and at least some of these centers might have been destroyed to prevent their re-use or to make a strong symbolic statement against hierarchic government.

The language Bright uses to describe the Israelite takeover of Canaan is evidence that the peasant revolt hypothesis has taken root in Bright's thinking. In the second edition, he habitually called the process "conquest" or "settlement." Now he typically refers to Israel's "control over," "mastery of," or "hold upon" the land. This shift in terminology makes the need to replace the old terminology clear. Henceforth we should speak of *Israel's Rise to Power in Canaan,* or the like, in place of "Conquest" or "Settlement." Likewise, it would be best to speak of *Israel's Village-Based Confederate Tribal Social Organization,* or the like, rather than of "Amphictyony,"[1] "Religious League," or "Pastoral Nomadic Tribalism." Unfortunately, Bright continues to be enthralled by the explanatory power of an "Israelite religious league," though he is unhappy with the amphictyonic form Martin Noth advanced fifty years ago (1930).

Bright's various usages of "Hebrews," "Israelites," and "Yahwists" point up the problem of putting all the parts of the puzzle about Israelite origins together smoothly. For him "Hebrews" refers to some of the Canaanite ʿapiru, social misfits who became Israelites. Sometimes these "Hebrews" are conceived as social revolutionaries and at other times as a vaguely ethnic "stock." "Israelites" for him seems to refer to those who gathered in an earlier El-worshipping confederacy called Israel, as well as to those who joined in the Yahweh-worshipping confederacy of the same name after the Moses group entered Canaan. Sometimes the Moses group is called "Israelite" because it eventually came to be a part of the Yahwist confederacy; sometimes it is called "Israelite" because of the possibility that its ancestors had been part of the older El-worshipping confederacy before their bondage in Egypt.

While Bright has certainly been more careful in his terminology than many biblical historians, an awkwardness and inconsistency of terms remains. We need a new set of categories to describe the component members and stages of early Israelite development. Operating with a social revolutionary model, we might distinguish these categories:

1. *Social Revolutionary Elohist Israelites,* who formed an El-worshipping confederacy before the arrival of the Moses group of Yahwists in Canaan and who used the name Israel ("Israel, Stage One").

---

[1] An amphictyony is a sacral-religious league organized around a central sanctuary. The term is used to describe Israelite tribal structure by analogy drawn from the Greek institution of this name.

2. *Social Revolutionary Yahwist Israelites,* who formed a Yahweh-worship-ping confederacy after the arrival in Canaan of the Moses group of Yahwists. This confederacy included old Elohist Israelites, the Moses group, and additional Canaanite affiliates. It retained the name Israel ("Israel, Stage Two").
3. *Social Revolutionary Proto-Israelites,* a term applied to social revolutionary groups in the process of becoming (or of not becoming) Israelites. It is applicable to at least three subgroups:
   3a. Canaanites who formed the ranks of the emerging Israelite move-ment, entering either the El confederacy or the Yahweh confederacy.
   3b. Canaanites who, while rebellious against their overlords, did not or could not enter either Israelite confederacy.
   3c. Newcomers or returnees to Canaan, such as the Moses group, who joined in either the El or the Yahweh confederacy of Israel.

Some such clarification of terms is presupposed in my book, *The Tribes of Yahweh,* and now seems urgently required in order both to carry out coherent and testable research and to theorize on the complicated question of Israel's rise to power in Canaan.

Bright regards the religion of Yahwism as having come from the Moses group. The fundamental form of that religion was the covenant between Yahweh and his people. Bright believes this covenant was structured as an analogue to an international suzerainty treaty between an imperial overlord (Yahweh) and a vassal (Israel). This religious form created "a covenant society" providing a framework that additional groups of socially rebellious peoples in Transjordan and Canaan could enter. Bright has dropped the term "amphictyony" in favor of the more neutral term, "tribal league." But he continues to defend the basic con-tours of an amphictyonic interpretation because he does not entertain the possibility of any other inter-tribal mechanism for early Israel.

Bright is unable to bring the *religious* drive of Yahwism into concep-tual congruity with the *social revolutionary drive* of the proto-Israelite peasants, herders, artisans, mercenaries and bandits. Yahwism remains for Bright a mysterious force whose primordial—and essentially inexpli-cable—desert character created Israel. The process by which Yahwism spread and developed in Canaan as the ideology of a social movement is not greatly enlightened, however, simply by reciting how unusual that religion was. In fact, as I observe in *The Tribes of Yahweh,* Bright argues that Yahwism was a self-generative *novel faith* which alone distinguished Israel; in all other regards, he contends, Israel was an *ordinary people.* Such a conclusion flies in the face of the social revolutionary origins of Yahwism that Bright has just described. To the contrary: Israel was *extraordinary* in being the one socially revolutionary people in the ancient Near East to produce a literature and to survive as a distinctive cultural and religious entity (Gottwald, 1979:592–99).

A serious failure in Bright's analysis is the absence of middle terms by which the social symbols and organizational forms of Yahwism worked their way into and worked their way out of the social organization and the interpreting minds of the Israelites as they fought their revolution. Instead Bright pictures the Yahwistic tribal league as being formed only *after* the revolution. It is far more consistent with our knowledge of how strong ideologies take form in social movements to assume that the confederacy grew incrementally and that its religious practice and understanding developed simultaneously as the revolution went forward.[2]

Yahweh as the divine warrior enlisted cosmic power in the cause of rebels who fought against the state political organization. Yahweh promised the blessings of the earth to the dispossessed of the earth. Yahweh "acted" in the sociohistoric process to break the grip of hierarchy over the bounties of nature and to return those bounties unplundered to the people who did the actual productive labor.[3]

In the end Bright misses the organic unity of society and religion in the creation of a socially revolutionary people. This is because he is wedded to an "unchanging essence" of biblical faith that initiated everything worthwhile in Israel's history. His conclusions are certainly legit-

---

[2] Ironically Bright stands on one side of a frustrating split among scholars who have managed to move beyond earlier models that ignored the social foundation and framework of the early Israelite movement, or simplistically equated it with pastoral nomadism. Recent theories have been one-sided and incomplete, lacking comprehension of the specific social and religious mix of factors that ignited Israel. One scholarly trend, typified by C. H. J. de Geus (1976) and W. R. Wifall, Jr., grasps the sociocultural unity of Israel as an ethnicity formed of many strands such as intermarriage and grass roots communal discussion and decision-making. The other trend, voiced by Bright and Mendenhall, has laid hold of the hitherto missing key of social revolution as the catalyst for forging Israel.

Regrettably, those who see the organic sociocultural and religious unity at Israel's birth miss the revolutionary matrix of that unity, while Bright and Mendenhall have not been able to formulate and elaborate the dynamic unity of the social and religious facets as a single process within the revolutionary matrix. Far from opposing one another, these hypotheses separately possess the partial insights that complement and fructify one another in the theory of a combined revolution— at once social, political, cultural and religious—with roots and forerunners that reached a decisive detonation point in the late 13th–early 12th centuries B.C.E.

[3] See Gottwald (1979:903-913) for the implications of the study of Lynn Clapham on "divine warrior" theology for Israel's way of relating nature and culture to covenant, and for a critical reflection on Walter Brueggemann's way of relating Israelite society and Yahweh's sexuality (1977).

imate for a theologian or philosopher. However, the steps he takes to reach these conclusions are not those the historian uses to trace an unfolding phenomenon in its own rich and complex terms. This is especially strange because Bright as historian has already recognized how intimately Israel's religion was linked to and shaped by the peculiarities of its social revolutionary context.

Bright has the key to early Israel's faith in hand, but he does not turn the lock. The key lies in the restive movement of free peasants that was renewing and extending an older tribal structure in the face of city-state opposition; one that was struggling to develop rainfall agriculture, with modest irrigation possibilities, under precarious conditions in the terraced hill country of Canaan (Gottwald, 1979:650–63).

John Bright's history of Israel remains the best overall account written in English, but it will only become the full-bodied synthesis he aims for when he discovers that the social revolutionary "key" turns the covenantal religion "lock."

A Response to J. W. Rogerson on "The Use of Sociology in Old Testament Studies"

ABSTRACT

Rogerson's address, subsequently published in *VTSup* 36 (1985) 245–56, is well informed about developments in anthropology and sociology, as it is judicious in its survey and assessment of recent influential applications of social scientific method and theory to the study of ancient Israel. He points out some of the grievous errors that arbitrary and random use of sociology has led to in biblical studies, and he argues for pluralist social theories that are disciplined in distinguishing the series of methodological steps that all good sociological work must recognize and honor. Rogerson articulates these steps in the form advanced by W. G. Runciman, and contends that, in *Tribes of Yahweh*, I have collapsed the separate steps of "explanation" and "description" by reducing theology to socioeconomic terms.

In response, I judge Runciman's cautions well-taken in that they mark "breaking points" in any cumulative sociological argument that the researcher must constantly keep in mind, but I go on to take issue with an overly "neat" separation of the steps which fails to recognize that they constitute "moments" in one connected discourse that is multi-directional and strongly informed by the observer's own pre-understandings of social existence. Over against the rather "flat" model of Runciman, inclining toward an uneasy mixture of positivist and idealist notions, I prefer the Marxist historical material model of inquiry, as articulated by the sociologist of religion, Otto Maduro, because it is more holistic in its grasp of the interacting dimensions of society and because it involves a rigorous self-involving and self-questioning stance. This difference is illustrated by the way theology is conceived in *Tribes*, i.e., as an authentic but integral aspect of Israel's social life—neither "materially" reducible to nor "spiritually" isolable from socioeconomics—steadily and dependably exhibiting the wider social reality in its own distinctive discourse.

The timely presentation of Professor Rogerson calls attention to work being done in Great Britain and the United States, and to a lesser extent elsewhere, in biblical sociological research and publication. Rogerson highlights the paradox that, although applications of sociology to the Hebrew Bible have been practiced by one or another scholar for more than one hundred years, the recent burst of interest in social critical biblical studies shows little agreement as to what this subdiscipline includes and the methods it mandates.

It is perhaps a sign of how isolated and uncoordinated these various undertakings are that our panel has no representatives from continental Europe or from the third world. The far-flung responses I have received to my own work in this area of study lead me to believe that we urgently need to hear from all geographical, ecclesial, and sociopolitical quarters to get an adequate overview of what is happening in this rapidly exploding subdiscipline. Accordingly, it is highly appropriate that, instead of trying "to survey" the field as though it has a well-defined scope and content, Rogerson focuses upon types of sociological theories that have been influential in biblical work to date and on and the most productive methodological format for employing sociology in biblical studies.

In my remarks I wish to respond to Rogerson's paper, making clear my basic agreement with and appreciation of his critical assessment of what we are about when we do "biblical sociology." In the course of doing so, I will indicate reservations and points of difference, concluding with a brief articulation of the theoretical placement of my work in *The Tribes of Yahweh*.

That Rogerson reports and advocates a plurality of methods is a fair-minded and accurate way to open up what is taking place in the field. My reading of his intention is that he would not wish this advocacy of pluralism to breach or violate his equal concern for rigor of method. Rogerson is rightly insistent that every sociological model, together with the reconstructions it fosters, must be tested against competing models in the light of all available data. Such testing of models or hypotheses is only possible if the integrity of the models and methods is respected. If a kind of eclecticism develops from case to case, which Rogerson favors over a foreclosure on any single approach, it must be made clear how the various elements or methodological moves have been selected and how they connect with one another in the larger body of sociological conclusions. Rogerson has elsewhere warned us of the pitfalls of undirected eclecticism in the way anthropology has been used and misused in biblical studies (1978). Probably more than any other factor, failure to explain the basis for "picking and choosing" theories and methods, and sometimes combining them in diverse ways, has served to discredit and delay the application of sociology to biblical studies.

Given this erratic history of the fortunes of sociology in biblical studies, Rogerson has good reason not to rush too quickly into a definition of sociology. Nonetheless, I am sure that any actual application of sociological method to biblical subjects will entail, from the start, some conceptual sketch of what is being looked for and within what frame of reference, and Rogerson's own work demonstrates that he shares this view.

Broadly, it seems to me that there are two things about our social explanatory models that need to be underscored: first, in studying society we are also studying ourselves, i.e., we are social "fish" in the larger social "sea" we are trying to comprehend; and, second, in seeking to understand society, we seek to explain social phenomena socially and not reductively through biological, psychological, personal, moral or religious categories—even though all these are dimensions within the society and may play varying roles in our social explanation. Both of these insights will often work against "common sense" social observations such as Rogerson has warned us about.

Otto Maduro, a Venezuelan lay philosopher and sociologist of religion, has given apt expression to the "unnatural" rigor that authentic sociological inquiry demands of us:

> ...the spontaneous consciousness we have of our life in society—our spontaneous consciousness of its causes, for example, or of its mechanisms, or of its consequences—does not afford a scientifically acceptable explanation of life in society. It is almost the other way around: it is this spontaneous consciousness that needs to be explained sociologically. The genesis, development, and social functioning of these superficial explanations demand a sociological explanation themselves.

> In other words, we find ourselves confronted with the fact that *the underlying motives of our conduct in society—like its results and consequences—are not spontaneously or directly knowable*....So here is yet another reason for engaging in a critical, cautious, and perspicacious study of our society....But at the same time it is a reason for us sociologists to oblige ourselves to be suspicious of our own explanations—however spontaneous, attractive, "evident," and acceptable to our audience they may be.

Maduro goes on to characterize sociology as the disciplined study of social relationships that have a definite structured shape but are nonetheless malleable human constraints:

> Sociology, then, is a science of society that seeks to understand and describe social processes (including individual conduct within society) in order to analyze and explain them on the basis of the *relationships* that individuals and groups establish among themselves (generally in an unconscious, unintentional, involuntary manner) within their society. This is the object of sociology: *social relationships*.

What happens is that sociology makes an effort not to renounce the insight that gave it birth—the insight that all the relationships that we human beings set up among ourselves are our own work, a human deed, resulting from other relationships with which we ourselves have knotted together various individuals or groups; the insight that the opacity and nonconsciousness of our own social relationships are in large part our work as well, a human deed; the insight that we ourselves, precisely because our social relationships are our own doing, are ultimately capable of undoing, redoing, or transforming our social organization; the insight that the very obstacles we encounter at every step in our attempts to undo, redo, or transform our social relationships are themselves social relationships, which we have manufactured without knowing it, or have forgotten about or blocked out of our consciousness.

Finally, Maduro sums up the sociological enterprise as a humanistic study with a collective reference point.

In this sense, the profoundly humanistic nature of sociology comes to light. It refuses to explain social processes or individual conduct in society by recourse to causes that escape human knowledge and control. It insists upon finding a *social* explanation for social processes. Nor does it yield to the temptation to explain the social by the individual. Far from it. Sociology takes its point of departure in some manner from the supposition—likewise humanistic—that our life is our *collective* doing, and that therefore our destiny (whether we know it or not, and whether we like it or not) will be our collective doing as well (12-14).

I have quoted Maduro at some length because I want to relate his self-involving and self-questioning view of sociology to the program for developing social theory put forward by W. G. Runciman (1983) and advocated by Rogerson as a guideline for biblical sociological inquiry. Rogerson summarizes Runciman as proposing four clearly separate steps in sociological understanding:

1. *Reportage*: description of the events, phenomena or attitudes to be investigated in language which is as far as possible value-free.

2. *Explanation:* discovery of the causes of what has been reported.

3. *Description*: exposition of what it is like for a person or group to be in a particular society or social situation.

4. *Evaluation*: decision about whether social phenomena or their effects are good or bad in the light of an observer's criteria for making such judgments.

I should say at the start that Runciman's proposal is known to me only through Rogerson's presentation of it, with the result that my remarks are necessarily probative and provisional. It seems to me that the thrust of Runciman's proposal is to remind us that, since we are likely to be doing a number of things when we do sociology—characterizing certain social relationships, attempting to explain how they have come into existence and what purposes they serve, grasping what it was like to be an actor in those relationships, and evaluating their merits according to criteria from outside the system of relationships—it is essential for us to be as self-conscious as possible about each aspect of our work, so that we do not jumble the tasks or the procedures proper to each of them.

The applications which Rogerson makes of Runciman's directives to Hebrew Bible studies are largely congruent with my own thought, since they are directed at identifying notoriously common errors of judgment, e.g., assuming that we know in advance what a term like "tribe" means when it appears in the Bible, thinking that a hypothesis is proven merely by stating it, failing to compare a preferred hypothesis with others covering the same phenomena, retrojecting a later social phenomenon such as postexilic Judaism into an earlier state of social development, ignoring the role of ideas held by actors in social systems, etc. The cautions expressed are entirely appropriate, but when Runciman's scheme is assessed for its overall conception of what sociology is about and how it is done, I have two major problems with it.

(1) There are indeed distinctions between reporting, explaining, describing, and evaluating, as Runciman uses the terms, but they are aspects or "moments" of one inquiry, even in cases where either or both of the last two elements are hardly visible in the sociologist's conclusions. In actual sociological work, these "steps" are involved virtually simultaneously, even as one or another is the focus of the moment. The sociological observer moves back and forth among these stances, in a movement that is less linear than it is spiral or oscillatory. I believe Runciman is absolutely correct that we need "breaking points" in our method where we can clarify and evaluate the state of our work in fulfilling the distinct demands of each "step," but the inquiry succeeds, comes to a satisfying interpretation, only as a totality in which the aspects legitimately influence one another, as when we find that a certain explanation influences what we think worth reporting, or when otherwise baffling reportage is given meaning by description emerging from within the society, or when evaluating alerts us to insights in any of the other steps.

In short, I am suggesting that the complex interactive social relationships we are investigating have their rhythmic counterpart in a complex interactive web of procedural operations enacted by the social observer. This is why in approaching the study of societies, and in concurrence with Maduro quoted above, I do so with a broadly Marxist understanding within which many methods may be used eclectically to carry through all of Runciman's steps. The Marxist method, which is to look for the critical linkages in the elements of social totality that inhibit or press for social change, is both comprehensive in aim and coverage and flexible in seeking the particulars of societies by means of all tools available from whatever theoretical or methodological source. The other major streams of social theory, Durkheimian and Weberian, both of which I have used extensively in *The Tribes of Yahweh*, share with Marxism—though I think not to the same degree—a comprehensiveness and flexibility which have made them such enduringly fertile traditions in sociological inquiry.

In working through the contest of models and methods in a healthy climate of pluralist debate, we need what Maduro calls "epistemological vigilance" and "autocritical partiality" (24-29), a deliberate ongoing self-critique about our models and methods (foreground of our inquiry) and about the place of our own scholarship in ecclesial and secular communities (background of our inquiry). Dogmatically unenlightening instances of allegedly Durkheimian, Weberian, or Marxist social theory invariably derive from this lack of self-criticism which can only lead to disregard or distortion of the particular societies supposedly under study, while the actual object of the enterprise is to prove or illustrate some larger principle or theory. Mushy eclecticism, on the other hand, which may pride itself on not adhering dogmatically to any school, ignores the coherence of the society under study and the self-critical responsibility of the investigator, leaving us all too often with collections of information accompanied by unsatisfyingly vague impressions as to their meaning.

(2) Moreover, on a first hearing, I suspect that Runciman may have delineated the formal steps of sociological inquiry in a way that is likely to create unnecessary confusion. His steps of reportage and explanation seem clear enough, although Rogerson wisely implies that a sharp separation of the two may be more difficult than Runciman recognizes. It does appear, however, that there are problems with Runciman's categories of description and evaluation. By description Runciman is referring to what many anthropologists call an "emic" approach,[1] i.e., getting the insider's view of a society. Indeed, the "emic" strategy is distinguishable from explanatory or "etic" theorizing[2] that offers

---

[1] From the term "phon*emics*," which is the study of the smallest speech units that mark distinctions between words and thus accord meaning to a stream of spoken sounds.

[2] From the term "phon*etics*," which is the study of the sounds of speech that in themselves possess no meaning, the latter being provided by cultural consensus and communicated in speech by the phonemes.

outsiders' interpretations of a society that its members may not recognize and may even deny. But to set off description from reportage so sharply is questionable, since it may be said that description so defined is a form of "internal reportage," i.e., the way social phenomena "feel" or "have meaning" to the participants. I shall return to this point below with respect to Israelite theology.

Finally, evaluation, in the sense of whether social phenomena are good or bad according to the social observer, is a clear enough category, and I think all careful social observers want to be aware when that is what they are doing. However, evaluation enters sociological inquiry in other ways. What is thought to be worth reporting about a society is affected by criteria which, even when not strictly moral, carry judgments of importance and relevance about why it is worth the effort to report on a certain society. Also, previous experience with social explanations in other contexts, which as a result are perceived to be more or less "valuable," will affect the social analyst in developing explanations in the immediate case. So it is not enough to hold a tight rein on blatant moral judgments about social phenomena; it is necessary also to be autocritical about a whole range of evaluations that affect our work and that can never be entirely excluded from it, only acknowledged and controlled. These evaluations, once we acknowledge them, may in fact propel us to greater understanding than we would have had if we came to the task lacking all judgments about the subject matter.

In sum, my initial impression of Runciman's schema is that it has undoubted cautionary value in insisting that we keep clear about the various kinds of observing and interpreting that we are engaged in when we do sociology. But beyond its cautionary utility, I have serious reservations as to whether it grasps the interactive subtleties of the steps as they are woven together in the practice of sociologists who are good at what they do.

Finally, I want to concretize this methodological response with a rejoinder to Rogerson's comments on Part II of *The Tribes of Yahweh*, in which he suggests that I appear to have collapsed "explanation" and "description" of what it was like to be an Israelite when I demythologize ancient Israelite theology into socioeconomic terms. I do not believe that I have done so, since I quite agree with Rogerson that biblical theology and biblical sociology are not mutually exclusive. Biblical theology without its social ground and social referents is in my view unexplainable, and biblical society without its religious practices and symbols is equally unintelligible.

Israel, like other peoples, certainly made symbolic claims that consisted of concepts or ideas. I would call them the conceptual, symbolic, or ideational aspect of their society. When, however, Rogerson speaks of these as "idealist," he uses the word in a way foreign to Part II of *Tribes*. To categorize and sum up the symbols of Israel is an aspect of adequate reportage, including the "internal reportage" of the biblical text which renders the voices of social actors at the time, and thus would be called "description" by Runciman. Such a treatment of concepts or ideas in Israel is, in my outlook, only *idealist* in the pejorative sense I employ the term if the Israelite religious system is forced to stand complete and isolated from its material and social base in a kind of "barren or false universalism."

This forced "idealization" occurs in two ways: both when the religious symbols (or "revelation") are posited to have created the material or social totality, and when it is assumed that the symbols can be adequately understood and appropriated by us apart from the Israelite material and social environment and in disregard of the material and social environment from which we observers look at Israel. That is the sense in which I understand John Bright's, George Mendenhall's, and G. Fohrer's views of Israel's religion as "idealist," taking those three scholars as typical of very many others (1979:591–607). It turns out, then, that I do not for a moment dismiss or minimize the theology of the Hebrew Bible, only that I reject it as the generator pure and simple of Israelite society. Sociologically, Israel's religion and theology are significant elements in Israel's society. The category of explanation operates in two directions: Israel's religion explains some things about the shape and function of Israelite society, but equally Israelite society explains much about the shape and function of Israelite religion. Moreover, we must grasp that the religion-society nexus was not a static "fit" but a shifting frontier of adjustments and conflictual encounters. I am at the same time aware that precisely what we mean when we say a theory "explains" social phenomena needs far more clarification than it normally receives.

An excerpt from my lecture on "The Theological Task after *The Tribes of Yahweh*" puts my point about religion enmeshed in society in another way:

> The socioreligious system of early Israel may be analyzed from as many angles as there were elements that composed it and as there are means for tracing the interactions among the combining and interacting elements. We may, for example, focus on the crops and agricultural technology that formed the base for the solidifying of the movement in the hill country, and go on to clarify the economic impact on residential patterns, forms of governance, and religious cults and symbols. We can also focus on the peculiar "retribalized" social structure of the Israelite movement and its adaptive relationship to the economic, military, and cultural priorities of the movement. Or we can just as legitimately begin with religious symbol and cult

and trace how the specific material environment and the forms of social organization came to expression in the religion. What we can no longer do in good conscience is to isolate the religious factors from the total social setting as though, once the historical and social "accidents" are noted as "background," we are free to move on to the self-contained religious essentials. For theology, this is of utmost consequence, not only because of the socially embedded nature of the subject matter in biblical texts, but because of our position as socially situated and conditioned believers and theologians (1983d: 191–92).

It appears then that the sociological task necessitates a more complex and subtle movement between the parts and the whole of society than Rogerson's appeal to Runciman indicates. The valid methodological moments of reportage, explanation, description, and evaluation are intricately related, and the "dance" of these approaches produces multiple data constructs and theoretical possibilities which do not simply pile up incrementally but emerge in configural patterns that provide shifting perspectives on "social facts." The configurations of social understanding that emerge in the course of our study of a society push us to reexamine and often to revise the initial understandings we entertained in any or all of Runciman's four categories. In this way, sociological study is a determined reading of society from parts to whole, and vice versa, proceeding through a series of methodological "fixes" on the subject. The whole task constitutes a movement whose "conclusions" are no more than the provisional results of a process which is necessarily without end. Clarifying the epistemological route we have followed in arriving at our understanding of biblical societies is obligatory for full-bodied interpretation. And it is equally obligatory for charting new lines of interpretation that may result from slight revisions or from major shifts in our way of orchestrating the multiple facets of the inquiry.

Two Models for the Origins of Ancient Israel: Social Revolution or Frontier Development

ABSTRACT

In a generally favorable review of *Tribes of Yahweh* by the sociologist Gerhard Lenski, published in *RelSRev* 6 (1980) 275–78, the proposal is advanced that early Israel may be better understood in some of its aspects as a frontier society rather than as a social revolutionary society. Lenski finds that the highland agrarian origins of Israel, beyond the reach of centralized political control, together with its eventual reversion to hierarchic politics are best explained as a frontier phenomenon. In reply, I concede the pertinence and utility of the frontier analogy for nuancing the specific conditions of Israel's emergence, but maintain that—unlike cited analogies in U.S., Australian, and South African history where even the "frontiers" were always under centralized political control—for early Israel the frontier paradigm must be subsumed under the larger paradigm of social revolution. Two further caveats of Lenski are addressed. The objection that I seem to have overstated the presence of social equality in early Israel is assessed as containing a measure of truth, since I was not sufficiently clear in *Tribes* in qualifying my use of the term. In substance, however, I argue that the social system of the first Israelites was deliberately structured and ideologically motivated to level preexisting social inequalities and to preclude the rise of new social inequalities. The further objection that I have passed simplistic moral judgments on Canaan and Israel is countered by a nuanced clarification of how I understand ethical judgment to be operative in historical hindsight.

With the publication of my recent book, *The Tribes of Yahweh* (1979), there is now available a substantial body of argument for the hypothesis that ancient Israel originated in a social revolutionary movement composed largely of peasants. Building on the pioneer work of George E. Mendenhall (1962, 1973), I have developed the major contours of a social revolutionary model in running dialogue with what have been to date the dominant models of Israelite origins: nomadic, conquest, and amphictyonic models.

The Social Revolutionary Model of Early Israel

My contention is that each of the prevailing models contains an element of truth but, standing alone and without the organizing perspective of social unrest and revolt, none is capable of doing justice to the emergence of premonarchic Israel. The *nomadic model* correctly refers to a component of pastoral nomads in early Israel and to a social organizational difference between Israel and its neighbors, but it vastly overstates the number of Israelite nomads, misconstrues the complex nature of ancient Near Eastern nomadism, and naively equates Israel's tribal social organization with a pastoral nomadic stage of development (Gottwald, 1979:293–301, 435–63; de Geus, 1976:124–87). The *conquest model* correctly identifies a major military dimension in Israel's rise to power, but mistakenly posits that the attacks were launched in a more or less unified way by outsiders invading from the desert (Gottwald, 1979:191–205, 207–11, 217–18, 220–23). In terms of their views of Israelites as "outsiders" to Canaan, the nomadic and conquest models tend to conjoin in support of one another. The *amphictyonic model* correctly observes that the several tribes of Israel were joined in a confederation, but it overlooks the sociopolitical matrix of the league arrangements and in its comparison between Israel and Greek sacral leagues misses the decisive social structural differences between Greek amphictyonic associations and the intertribal confederation of Israel (Gottwald, 1979:345–86).

One of the features that nomadic, conquest, and amphictyonic models share in common is an exaggerated concentration on the religious "uniqueness" of Israel, an almost exclusive focus on religious factors to the neglect of the sociopolitical matrix and constitution of Israel.[1] In advancing a social revolutionary model of early Israel we are

---

[1] De Geus, 1976: 1–68, beginning with B. Stade in 1887, traces a majority scholarly attraction to the virtually total autonomy of Israel's religion in the line of interpretation that culminated in Noth's amphictyonic hypothesis. Gottwald, 1979: 597–607, shows that reflections on the social context of early Israel's religion— surprisingly even among advocates of the social revolutionary hypothesis—have characteristically been marred by assumptions about the autonomy of religion, with the result that religion is separated from Israel's society (as with J. Bright), or the society is viewed as a spontaneous creation of the religion (as with G. E.

not only attending to the inadequacies in the other models but we are introducing a "demythologizing" or "secularizing" element that aims not to eliminate the religion, nor to reduce its importance, but to set the religion of ancient Israel in its necessary ancient social and cultural matrix, to give that religion a greater measure of social plausibility or credibility.[2]

The essence of the social revolutionary model is to see the emergence of ancient Israel as a combined sociopolitical and religious movement with its major base in the peasantry of Canaan. The movement aimed at creating an alternative society of independent farmers, pastoral nomads, artisans, and priestly "intellectuals" who were free from the political domination and interference of the hierarchic city-states that held the upper hand in Canaan. This movement was an intertribal alliance or confederation, based not on pastoral nomadic cultural life but on the revitalization and extension of rural agricultural institutions with real and fictitious kinship ties, neighborhood and regional residence, and communal mutual assistance (Gottwald, 1979:293–341, 474–97, 584–87). This counter-society had to provide for political self-rule, economic self-help, military self-defense, and cultural self-definition, which gave to its religion (so-called Yahwism) a very prominent role as an alternative ideology for understanding the legitimacy and efficacy of its revolution (Gottwald, 1979:65–66, 489–92, 594–97, 630–33, 636–37, 642–49, 692–709).

The historical reality underlying the two polarized equations of "Canaanite = bad" vs. "Israelite = good" was not in the first instance an ethnic or religious polarization but a social structural polarization around the divisions between those who upheld the reigning hierarchic social order and those who struggled to bring a more egalitarian free peasant society into existence. Nevertheless, one ought not to oversimplify or standardize the reactions of people in Canaan to this growing social struggle, for these varied greatly according to the spatial framework and the temporal trajectory of the revolution. I have attempted an initial rough plotting of these cross-cutting and confused loyalties under the categories of Canaanites as enemies of Israel, Canaanites as converts to Israel, Canaanites as neutrals toward Israel, and Canaanites as allies

---

Mendenhall), or the social influences on religion are confined to "non-essentials" (as with G. Fohrer).

[2] The significance of G. E. Mendenhall's formulation of the peasant revolt model of Israelite origins lies precisely in the forcefulness with which it opened the way to a recovery of early Israel as a socially understandable historical agent (cf. Gottwald, 1979: 220–27).

of Israel (Gottwald, 1979:498–583), a schematization that certainly calls for further nuancing and refinement.

The evidence for the social revolutionary model is drawn from biblical texts, extrabiblical texts, the material culture (especially the examination of rural agricultural complexes, Spencer and Hale; Ron; Golomb and Kedar; de Geus, 1975; Stager, 1976; Edelstein and Kislev), and comparative anthropological and sociological studies (ancient bureaucratic empires; retribalization and revitalization movements; peasant movements in unrest, rebellion, and revolution; social banditry).[3]

The initial responses to my articulation of the model have been a mixture of denial, skepticism, caution, fascination, curiosity, and varying measures of agreement. The agreements range from concurrence on limited points, through the recognition that the model is a respectable option—even if not clearly superior to the others—to the assertion that social revolution gives the most intelligible explanation of early Israel's origins and overall premonarchic form.[4] To show that the kind of modeling involved here is not a simple matter of "right/wrong," "yes/no" or "all/none," I want to share one particular response that stands in basic agreement with my notion that early Israel was a peasant movement in conflict with the surrounding society but suggests another way of looking at the same phenomena.

Early Israel as a Frontier Society

The sociologist Gerhard Lenski of the University of North Carolina prepared a critical review as a respondent to *The Tribes of Yahweh* at the 1979 Annual Meeting of AAR/SBL (1980). Lenski is a sociologist who stresses techno-environmental factors in human societies, has a broad understanding of peasant societies, and is also a neo-evolutionist in the sense that he believes archaeology, history, and sociology demonstrate that social change worldwide is natural, directional, immanent, continuous, cumulative, necessary, and proceeds from uniform causes—

---

3 Pertinent social scientific literature is extensively cited in the notes to *Tribes*, access to which is best gained through the Index of Subjects (N.B. the explanatory note on use of the Index, p. 842), and a brief list of social scientific titles for biblical studies appears in Gottwald, 1976c:467–468. [Additional titles will be found in Gottwald, 1992:88-89.]

4 Cf. the following reviews of *The Tribes of Yahweh:* Anderson; Brueggemann, (1980); Buss; Chaney, (1981); Christensen; Klein; Malina, (1981b); McCarthy; C. L. Meyers, (1981); A. C. Myers; and Woo, who compares the religious factor in the ancient Israelite and modern Chinese peasant revolutions.

although not evenly through time and space, as expressed by the important distinction between general and specific evolution (1976; cf. 1966;
Lenski and Lenski).

After summing up the gist of *The Tribes of Yahweh* sociologically,
Lenski proposes

> to inquire as to the degree to which Gottwald's analysis squares with what
> social scientists have discovered to date about social and cultural dynamics
> during the agrarian era (i.e., from the invention of the plow to the begin-
> nings of the Industrial Revolution)[1980:275].

In terms of the data on peasant societies vis-à-vis social and political
authorities, Lenski finds that my model of peasant unrest and revolt has
ample precedent.

> Studies of agrarian societies of the past in both Europe and Asia have made
> it clear that large numbers of peasants in these societies were unhappy with
> their situation and blamed the upper classes and their agents. Moreover,
> this unhappiness often led to violence, ranging from isolated actions by
> individuals to widespread uprisings as in England in the fourteenth
> century or Germany in the sixteenth (275).

Picking up on my observation that we do not have articulate
firsthand evidence about other such social revolutionary breaks in the
ancient Near East, Lenski goes on to focus on the *marginal territorial
element* in ancient Israel which seems to show a continuity with many
other societies where peasants have developed their own oppositional
forms of life in *frontier conditions* that are sufficiently removed from the
urban centers of power to allow a margin of freedom for independent
maneuver. Sometimes technological conditions (I would add political
conditions as well—NKG) transform such marginal territories into
expanding frontiers that give birth to new societies. Of these he notes
the United States, Australia, and Boer society in South Africa as examples. He then formulates the notion of a frontier model which, in his
view, needs to be joined to the peasant revolt model in order to account
for the peculiarities of Israelite beginnings.

> The interesting thing about these frontier societies is that they all share
> many of the social and cultural patterns Gottwald attributes to early Israel.
> All of them exhibit an antagonism toward the traditional centers of power
> and toward the institutional arrangements that supported those centers.
> Populist and democratic ideologies developed and often acquired a quasi-
> religious status. Small farms tended to be the rule, especially in the early
> stages of frontier expansion. And, perhaps to complete the story, frontier
> societies have had a relatively short half-life. In other words, as they grew
> and prospered, they tended to revert to the more traditional ways of life,
> although never entirely.

This is not to suggest that any of these societies has duplicated the experience of early Israel. That would obviously be impossible. I believe, however, that we may be able to get a better understanding of the dynamics of Israel's early development if we conceptualize the process in frontier-society terms as well as in the peasant-revolt-model terms Gottwald advocates. In other words, a combined frontier-society peasant-revolt model may explain more than a pure revolt model (276).

The "more" that the frontier model explains better than the peasant revolt model is, for Lenski, composed of three facets:

1. For one thing, he believes that a frontier model better accounts for Israel's origin in the thirteenth century rather than centuries earlier or later. He appears to mean by this that into the centuries-long hostility and friction between rulers and subject peasants in Canaan, the thirteenth century introduced new technological factors (such as iron for agricultural tools, intensive terracing, improved water supply) that opened up the Canaanite highlands as a viable frontier for Israelite occupation.

2. Lenski further suggests that the frontier model has a slight edge in accounting for the dramatic new character of Yahwism as a religion set off sharply from the Baal cult inasmuch as an Israelite movement based in the heart of the old Canaanite plains society would not so easily have broken with the ancient fertility cults as an Israelite society spawned in the hilly frontier region.

3. Lastly, Lenski contends that the frontier factor better explains the eventual reversion of Israel to the statist system and its abandonment of the tribal system. Frontier situations, being transitory phenomena, tend to fade back into greater likeness to the dominant society once material conditions improve and the circumstances of life are not so different between heartland and frontier. Even so, the distinctive history of the frontier lives on with sufficient force to make a cultural difference between the two regions.

By introducing the frontier model into a discussion of Israelite origins, Lenski taps a significant vein of historiographic and social scientific theory devoted to the explanation of major sociohistoric change since the beginning of the Age of Discovery about 1500 C.E. A major problem in evaluating Lenski's proposal is that, although he articulates "a *combined* frontier-society peasant-revolt model" (italics mine), he does not specify *how* they are combined. In my view, the way in which "frontier" and "social revolution" are articulated—whether the one subsumes the other or both are subsumed under some third schema—is critical for determining the precise relevance of the frontier analogy to early Israel. After reflecting on his observations and doing some modest study in the voluminous literature on the frontier hypothesis, especially in American historical studies, my basic conclusion is that in the case of early Israel a frontier conception helpfully *nuances* a social revolutionary model but is *subsumed* under it as a description of the special circumstances in which the social revolution was generated and in which it prospered.

To begin with, I would want to give a lot of thought to the extent to which particular frontier societies represented major social change or actual social revolution. The United States may be viewed as exhibiting an internal frontier that moved westward from the original Atlantic seaboard settlements. Or the United States may be viewed in its entirety as a frontier extension of its British, and more widely European, home base (Webb; C. J. H. Hayes). It seems to me that on either way of viewing matters, frontier America did not produce a major structural social revolution. As against England, there were certainly social changes. The aristocratic feudal institutions in the strict sense did not transplant successfully from England to the United States. It may be argued that in some respects the internal American frontier contributed toward more populist political measures and toward vigorous voluntarism in social forms, acknowledged as a "frontier process" by many who do not accept major aspects of the total frontier thesis. Nonetheless, the basic system of property relations did transplant and in fact the capitalist beginnings in England were developed more freely and exquisitely in this country than in the homeland. It is also patent that the U.S. frontier was an imperial frontier that shattered the native Indian cultures. It brought the outright conquest and plunder of one people by another people who held the advantage in military technology and political organization.

In 1893, the American historian Frederick Jackson Turner launched the frontier thesis with the programmatic statement: "The existence of an area of free land, its continuous recession, and the advance of American settlement westward, explain American development" (1921:1). Turner and others elaborated the frontier thesis at length in an effort to explain such diverse phenomena as American individualism, practicality, regionalism, nationalism, isolationism, and democratic institutions and values. The frontier thesis has been subjected to extensive criticism, as much for what it ignored as for what it claimed, and it is probable that some aspects of the thesis are far more cogent than others (Gressley; G. R. Taylor). Among the criticisms has been the contention that the frontier thesis neglects the high importance of urban industrial development and especially the role of conflict between labor and capital (Almack; Schlesinger, Jr.). It has been argued that the main population movements were from farm to farm and from farm to city, and not from city to farm, thus muting the claim that the frontier served as a "safety-valve" for urban social unrest (Goodrich and Davison; Kane; Shannon). It has been observed that the thesis misses the rapidity with which the frontier was monopolized and controlled by capitalist interests, as displayed in the activities of land speculators and railroads (Hacker; Abernethy; Hofstadter, 1949). The frontier thesis is said consistently to overlook the salient feature of rapid development of agriculture on the frontier in order to accumulate exports for the fueling of major industrial capital development (W. A. Williams).5 All in all, it appears that the notion of upward social mobility has been vastly overstated as a factor in American history—and with it the role of the frontier as the spatial symbol of that presumed mobility.

In summary, the U.S. frontier was very much a frontier of capitalist and imperialist expansion and domination. The value of the frontier hypothesis when the detailed patterns of settlement and development are studied is chiefly to show how American economic and political world power was amassed by drawing on vast continental resources in the context of intensive capital accumulation. If the frontier attenuated or delayed social conflict, it did nothing to change the fundamental structure of American property relations and the abiding political clout of capitalist wealth. Thus, the pertinence of the U.S. frontier at least for understanding the ancient Israelite "frontier" is limited. If Lenski's qual-ification of the social revolutionary model is to have more weight it will be necessary to uncover analogies from frontiers that actually produced social revolutions.6 Early Israel was not a frontier in which expanding Canaanite city-state organization populated and mastered the high-lands. On the contrary, it was a frontier in which elements of the indige-nous population organized a sovereign society that broke with city-state organization in favor of re-tribalization. In brief, the frontier context in Canaan produced a sharper social break in the case of Israel than did the frontier context in North America. I suspect that the same would be true

---

5 W.A. Williams traces the links between farmer pressure for expanded foreign markets and the growth of American imperialism abroad after 1898. In particular, he shows that Turner gave scholarly crystallization to a wide feeling in the American agricultural hinterland and that Turner's expansionist frontier notion was carefully studied by imperialist statesmen such as Theodore Roosevelt and Woodrow Wilson (see esp. pp. xii–xviii).

6 The drastically limited appropriateness of the ancient Israelite religion-society nexus as an analogy for the United States is critically evaluated from the viewpoints of American history and theological concepts in Gottwald, 1976a, 1981. On the application of the Turner thesis to world frontiers, see Wyman and Kroeber. Wolf (1969:293) remarks on frontier areas, peripheral to state control, that enhance the tactical mobility of dissident and rebellious peasants, as in China and Mexico.

of the two other examples cited by Lenski: Australian and South African Boer societies.

With this preliminary evaluation of the frontier thesis in mind, I wish to comment on Lenski's application of the frontier-society model to the above mentioned three aspects of early Israelite experience.

1. I have difficulty seeing that the thirteenth century origin of Israel can be satisfactorily accounted for by stressing either frontier or peasant revolt factors as separable or "pure" models. In fact, we seem to be in theoretical trouble when we divorce social movements from their material basis, including the topography and material conditions which frame the forces of production. As I understand Lenski, I judge that he would agree with me on this point. If we begin with a model of social revolution, we already have an interwoven skein of factors forming a combined technological, economic, social, political, cultural, and religious revolution. Within the combined revolution, we can readily identify a cluster of topographical, ecological, technological, communication, and control factors which organize nicely around the model of the frontier or marginal territory, more exactly elucidated by Lenski as a *technologically expanded frontier.* Indeed, more than fifty years ago, Albrecht Alt contributed much to our understanding of how the Canaanite highlands formed just such a special, somewhat privileged zone, for the entrenchment of early Israel (1966d).[7]

Unless we are careful, however, there is some danger of converting this insight into bare "technologism," so that the frontier becomes an independent spontaneous source of social restiveness. The frontier must be coupled with the broad-based grievances and restiveness in the direction of an alternative political economy and society that had deep roots in the Canaanite heartland, reflected inchoately in the Amarna age but at that time lacking organizational and ideological coordination. What is important about the frontier in the highlands is that it provided a suitable zone for giving expression to the discontent as well as opportunity for the embodiment of an alternative society. Frontier conditions, freshly expanding, facilitated the socioeconomic and political impulses fanning out from the broader Canaanite political economy and provided a

---

7 See Gottwald (1979:650–63) for comments on Alt's contribution. E. R. Wolf (1969:293) observes that "The tactical effectiveness of such [peripheral] areas is strengthened still further if they contain defensible mountainous redoubts," as was the case in Mexico, Algeria, and Cuba. M. L. Chaney (1983:61–67) welds the historico-territorial conditions of the Canaanite highlands pioneered by Alt with the factors conducive to peasant revolutions elucidated by Wolf.

milieu in which they could be realized in large measure.[8] As I expressed it in *The Tribes of Yahweh*:

> We can readily project a high rate of failure in efforts to erect a bronze-based agricultural tribal society in the highlands. In order to succeed, the renegades needed to gather enough people, well enough fed and housed, skilled enough in the new methods required by upland agriculture (including the construction of terraces and water systems), to be able to extend mutual aid to one another, to absorb and encourage newcomers, and finally to defend themselves collectively against the constant efforts of the politically declining Canaanite city-states to reassert their control over the upstarts and over that portion of the means of production which the rebels had "stolen" from them. It was a long, "uphill" struggle, and Elohistic Israel, which preceded Yahwistic Israel in the central highlands, represented the most successful effort prior to the breakthrough of biblical Israel (Gottwald, 1979:661–62).

2. Lenski raises the intriguing question as to how correspondent Yahwism was to specifically frontier conditions as against conditions prevailing in the coastal plains. It is difficult to know how to assemble evidence to test his argument. We do know that the established El and Baal cults were not restricted to the plains but appeared also in the hill country, and also that El theology and imagery were taken over by Yahwism. We also know that Yahweh's imagery and imputed acts were flavored frequently with "hill country" symbolism and addressed to the vital interests of marginal agriculture. At this point we must observe a pronounced caution in drawing a sharp line between the supposed overwhelming concern of Israelite religion with "history" and of Canaanite religion with "nature." As the incidence of divine warrior theology in Canaan and Israel clarifies, Canaanite religion was definitely committed to legitimating the "history" of hierarchic city-states, on the one hand, while on the other Israel fully appropriated "nature" as the proper domain of free peasants awarded by their fully accredited and empowered new deity (Gottwald, 1979:903–13).

It seems to me that here, too, social revolt and frontier conditions cannot properly be split apart. The cults of the high gods centered in the plains regularly appear to have penetrated the marginal hilly areas, possibly in diluted or mixed forms. And of course we must bear in mind

---

[8] A rather similar point is made about the initiating role of religious dissenting traditions in shaping frontier life in the U.S.: "Dissenting democracy, equalitarianism, system of calling, and organization did not spring from the wilderness. Instead, they moved in the opposite direction: Pioneer Dissenters carried these qualities into the forests and propagated them among their neighbors.... The frontier provided the physical setting and the limits but did not determine the pioneer social organization and culture" (Miyakawa:239).

that we know amazingly little about the popular forms in which Canaanite religion was entertained and practiced, say by peasants around Megiddo or Gezer in the plains or by peasants around Shechem or Hebron in the highlands.

All in all, however, it is evident that the specific thrust and intensity of Yahwism required more than frontier distance to come into play, since the new religion presupposes a powerful social impulse and effective organizational mechanisms. At this point the role of the Levites, as Yahwistic intellectuals, is probably of great importance, constituting one of the undeveloped aspects of my hypothesis that invites enlargement. My guess is that the Levites were not frontier provincials for the most part, or at least their key leaders were not. The tradition of their coming out of Egypt and their habit of moving about Israel and being distributed throughout the tribes suggest cosmopolitanism and a critical pan-tribal function. I am inclined to view them in the category of "'rootless' intellectuals of the new order" who, in many documented situations, have made common cause with peasant uprisings.[9] If this be so, then the religious counterculture of Israel had an impetus and a frame of reference from beyond the frontier, while its particulars and modes of expression satisfied and were shaped by the interests peculiar to the highland frontier peoples. The result was that the Yahwistic intellectuals merged their social and political fortunes with the Israelite peasants which in turn fertilized and energized the distinctive Israelite political economy and subculture within Canaan.

3. With respect to Lenski's point about the reversion of early Israel to monarchy and social stratification, here too the relevant conceptualization is not the frontier as an alternative to social revolution but the frontier as an area of lapsed social revolution, reinvaded by hierarchic institutions from within Israelite society. The structural changes constitutive of early Israel were eroded once the domain of political Israel was extended far beyond the hills to include the plains conquered by David and to absorb the venerable structures of sociopolitical domination which were then extensively reimposed on the hill country by Solomon. In this regard, I would point not only to the importation of hierarchic

---

9 Wolf (1969:287–88) describes these intellectually and culturally advanced petty officials, professionals, and teachers as "purveyors of skills...based on literacy." For the Levites, the competency may not have been so much literacy per se as their command of an articulate tradition that framed oppression and the possibilities of deliverance as code symbols of the society. Also worth close scrutiny is Wolf's specification of factors that make peasants hesitant to fuse with intellectuals and that are overcome only by sharply favorable objective circumstances (289–90, drawing on Hindley, 1965 and Adams, 1966).

political institutions into Israel but also to the incorporation of a large Canaanite population into the territorial state of Israel and the attendant introduction of non-Israelite personnel into the state apparatus and the military forces (Alt, 1966a:221–25). When I speak of "Canaanite" in this context I do not refer to ethnic foreigners in the customary ill-defined sense but rather to people who did not have the social revolutionary history that the highland Israelites experienced, people who were not in a position to comprehend the meaning of joining the social body of Israel as an intertribal movement toward social equality.[10] They were people who would require "re-education" to become Israelites in the full sociocultural sense, and it is by no means clear that David and his monarchic successors were interested in acculturating these newcomers to old Israelite consciousness since their main agenda was to strengthen the centralized power of the new Israelite state.

Social Equality in Early Israel

While for the most part Lenski absolves *The Tribes of Yahweh* of the charge of imposing modern categories to the distortion of Israelite social reality, he does suspect that I have overstated the degree of social equality among early Israelites. I concede that some statements in the book, particularly if taken in isolation from the total argument, may appear overdrawn or idealistic.[11] Since completing the book, I have also come to put more stress on the resistance to social equality within Israel itself that resulted from the mixtures of peoples from many different sociohistorical experiences who joined in the Israelite movement and from the tendencies toward social privilege within powerful families and affluent regions.[12] It is well known that within peasant societies there are frequent divisions among the more impoverished and the more affluent

---

[10] On the incorporation of Canaanites into David's kingdom, cf. Gottwald (1979:159, 175, 182, 204, 364, 368–69, 418–19, 576–77) and on various shifting biblical meanings of "Canaan/Canaanites" (55–56, 498–503, 586).

[11] In retrospect I now see that, given the range of meanings attachable to the term "egalitarian," it was unfortunate that my most exact clarification of Israelite "social equality" (the organizational principle of equal access to basic resources for all adult members of the society) was reserved for a note near the end of the study (1979:697, 798–99 n. 635) where M. Fried's conceptualization of the principle is cited.

[12] A considerable number of references concerning the incomplete social revolution of ancient Israel appear in the text, but none is developed at length (cf. Gottwald, 1979:43, 59, 318, 323, 325–26, 389, 409, 416–17, 429–33, 462–63, 485, 489–92, 495, 617, 641–49).

peasants (Wolf, 1969:290–92). The battle for social equality was not simply between Israel and its neighbors; it was a battle internal to Israelite society, which should occasion no great surprise, for just such internal struggle has characterized every social revolution that we know anything about.

It remains clear, however, that the catalytic social factor which precipitated the formation of large-scale Israel as an association of tribes was an intentional "opening toward equality" that deliberately set up institutional structures and pressures toward equality, understood as approximately equal access through extended families to the basic resources or means of production, and that was concomitantly expressed in the shaping of community decisions. An axial shift toward social equality shows up across an extensive field of institutional arrangements, socioeconomic practices, and literary and cultural features: in land tenure, in prohibition of interest on loans, in *gōʾēl* mutual aid customs, in limitations on the priestly establishment, in attitudes toward sex and death, in historiographic content and style, in ethical norms and legal motivations, in poetic imagery, in genealogical constructs, and probably also in so-called "holy war" practices, to name only some of the more striking instances.

At one point in the text I state that "Israel *thought* it was different because it *was* different; it constituted an egalitarian society in the midst of stratified societies" (1979:693). Lenski observes that he would feel more comfortable had I written that "Israel constituted a much less stratified society than its neighbors" (1980:276). Now it is certainly true that I could have written the sentence that Lenski prefers because I agree with it as far as it goes. Had I done so, however, I would find such a statement far too weak and much too incomplete to do justice to the decisive intentional break between Canaan and Israel, particularly in the context of tracing the internal relations between social organization and theological assertions such as Yahweh's exclusivity and abnormal jealousy and the special election of Israel by Yahweh.

What I might more exactly have said is something like this: "Israel *thought* it was different because it *was* different: it constituted an *intentional* egalitarian society in the midst of *traditional* stratified societies." The term "intentional" as I use it means more than strong subjective motives, preferences, or orientations of will (so-called "good intentions" in spite of predominantly contradictory behavior); it means objective action to make deliberate structural alterations in society which created sustained pressures and mechanisms to level unequal access to resources even though not all inequalities were removed or prevented from arising. In short, Israel was egalitarian in its conscious deployment of societal power.

Ethical Judgment and Historical Hindsight

In some ways the most challenging aspect of Lenski's critique of *The Tribes of Yahweh* is his uneasiness with what he detects as an inappropriately simplistic moral judgment of Canaan and Israel. It is best to hear his precise words:

> In reading *The Tribes of Yahweh*, especially the second half of the book, I could not escape the feeling that there was, beyond the scholarly analysis, an unfortunate judgmental element which cast Israel in the role of hero and the Canaanites in the role of villain. There is, of course, historical precedent for this. Virtually all biblical scholars, fundamentalist and radical alike, have done the same.
>
> One wonders, however, whether a somewhat stronger case cannot be made for the Canaanite social system. No less a scholar and moralist than Karl Marx was able to call the bourgeoisie a progressive force in human history when viewed in proper historical context. This does not mean that the same was necessarily true of the princes of the city-states of Canaan, but it should, at least, cause us to consider the issue.
>
> When we do this, we cannot fail to note that Israel herself quickly came to adopt much of the Canaanite social system once she won control over the cities of the plain. Was this merely a failure of will or a lack of proper leadership, or was this a reflection of an altered social situation which made the old tribal system unworkable? Or, to put the matter another way, how much latitude did the Canaanite elite really have? (1980:276)

Lenski's demurrers and questions definitely deserve response since they go to the heart of what present day discoverers of the social revolutionary origins of ancient Israel are to make of this strikingly novel reinterpretation of biblical origins. Lenski's difficulties are in fact related to my own objections to Mendenhall's tendencies to "moralize" and "idealize" Israel's social revolution (Gottwald, 1978:39–40, 43, 45; 1979:222, 226, 232–33, 591, 599–602, 608).

At one level in my study I am reporting on the ethical evaluations made by the early Israelites. Most of the time I am not so much making a case for or against Israel or Canaan as I am trying to see the case Israel presented for itself and what relation that argument bore to Israel's social organization in process. At one point I remark on the spectrum of ethical evaluations that Canaanites were likely to have made concerning Israel (1979:595–96). A close reading of those remarks will show that I understand just how strong a case Canaanites could make for their hierarchic social order and how really plausible and commanding it was, mustering as it did centuries of political and cultural hegemony brilliantly justified by its official interpreters. To be an Israelite was indeed a risky business in every way imaginable, including struggle with the ethical stigmas of folly and perverse evil.

I am also appreciative of Lenski's reminder that Marx regarded capitalist social relations as a progressive force vis-à-vis feudalism. I am still striving to assess how progressive the economic formation of the ancient bureaucratic state was when viewed at various points in its history. Much of the difficulty has to do with how the ancient Near Eastern political economic formations should be conceptualized, whether loosely as feudalism, or a combination of patrimonial, preben-dal, and mercantile domains, or an Asiatic mode of production involv-ing a strong centralized state imposed on traditional villages through the nexus of a "tax/rent couple."[13] If we adopt the argument that the strongly centralized state was necessary to develop large-scale irrigation agriculture, we can opt for a progressive thrust within it. Since, how-ever, there is still so much uncertainty and debate over this "hydraulic hypothesis" of the origin of the state in the ancient Near East, I am hesi-tant in drawing conclusions. In any case, Marx saw capitalist social relations as progressive only up to a certain point, namely, the point where the improvement of the forces of production was fettered by the relations of production so that the boons of the new productivity in goods, services, and ideas were restricted arbitrarily to a minority and denied or rationed to a majority, precisely when the means for their wider appropriation were technically available. If the earliest Near East-ern states had once been progressive, at some point they may have reached the limits of the "goods" (goods both as things and as social and cultural possibilities) that they could deliver and thus ceased to advance the over-all good or general welfare of society.

In such terms, Israel's attempted break with the ancient Near Eastern state structure could be evaluated as a progressive undertaking, although perhaps totally premature and in any case ultimately unsuc-cessful for any number of reasons. At any rate, Israel's social revolution

---

[13] On the evidence for Canaanite and ancient Near Eastern societies as broadly feudal in character, see Gottwald (1979:391–94, 737–38 n. 149; 755–58 nn. 293, 295, 303; 767–68 nn. 407–08, 410). Concerning patrimonial, prebendal, and mercantile domains, see Wolf (1966, esp. 50–59, 73–77). Concerning the Asiatic mode of production, see B. S. Turner (1978), and, for the formulation of "tax/rent couple," see B. Hindess and P. Q. Hirst (1975:esp. 192; 1977). For a discussion of these theories of the mode of production in relation to Canaan and Israel, together with bibliographic citations, see Gottwald (1983b; 1985b; 1992). [I now prefer the term tributary mode of production proposed by Amin (46–70) NKG.]

flowered objectively for a period of two centuries and left strong imprints on later Israel and on the whole history of the West. Just what we are to make of that early revolutionary upthrust and of its surviving imprints is a very large question. I find it possible and even necessary to respond positively to this Israelite undertaking without denying the social integrity and good faith of Canaanites and without prejudging how possible it actually was for such a retribalizing break with the ancient Near Eastern state to endure and spread. As far as I can see, the social revolution of Israel would have had to spread much farther than it did in order to have created a "balance of power" favorable to the continued success of its form of retribalized social organization. For instance, had Israel's social revolution spread to the Philistines, the immediate external threat that prompted the rise of monarchy in Israel would have been avoided. But as long as any strong centralized state existed in the ancient Near East or vicinity there would have been the threat of foreign conquest of the retribalized societies. Furthermore, social revolutions often lead to further internal conflict and sometimes to the recrudescence of hierarchy by means of counterrevolution.

As for the ethical judgments that interpreters will make of ancient Canaanite and Israelite social organization, they will depend greatly on the social location, assumptions, and commitments of the interpreter. Perhaps the example of a failed nonbiblical social revolution will help to illustrate my point. The Paris Commune of 1871 was a brief island in the capitalist seas of western Europe, and it was engulfed within months of its onset (Marx, 1871; Jellinek). Nonetheless, something was learned from the Commune to the benefit of later revolutions. I personally look with positive appreciation on the brief accomplishments of the Paris Commune, at the same time I see why it was incumbent on the wider French society to crush it. If I attempt to render my ethical assessment in terms of how I think I might have responded as a participant in the social movements of late nineteenth century France—or of thirteenth century B.C.E. Canaan—I am reasonably sure that my response would have depended critically on my social locus, recognizing of course that some of the advantaged classes do characteristically opt for revolution and some of the disadvantaged classes fail to be aroused. In any case, it is an illusion that any of us can make uncontestable "neutral" class-transcending judgments about past or present historical conflicts.

Lenski is correct that the Canaanite elite did not have much latitude in its choices as long as it faithfully adhered to its role within the hierarchic system, but other Canaanites at the bottom of that society and in its middle ranges found their latitude for choice much wider. As for Israel's reversion to hierarchy, national defense within the international system of militarized states was unquestionably a major factor. Precisely here we can grasp the enmeshment of ethical assessment in the limits of social systems. As long as "Canaanite"-type social organization predominated in the ancient Near East, the ethical argument for it would appear superior to the ethical argument for "Israelite"-type retribalization. Many of the prophets, it seems, favored Israel taking great risks with national security. If I judge rightly what underlies their argument sociopolitically, they were implying something like this: if we decentralize, either by total retribalization or by sharply limiting the monarchic institutions, we will not have the imperial ambitions and the piles of surplus wealth that invite conquest and plunder. I am not at all convinced that Assyria would have desisted from attacking a retribalized Israel but the attacks might have been less severe and hardly more catastrophic than what transpired.[14] Of course, all this is part of the unenviable position of a social venture that did not spread in a revolutionary way to other parts of the ancient Near East and so was isolated, contained, and destroyed, or at least thrown onto another plane in later Israelite-Jewish history.

Lenski properly highlights the ethical ambiguity of our historical hindsight and thereby he touches on the general problem of the relation of fact to value. It is evident that facts and values cannot be so neatly separated as disinterested scientific method proposes in its laudable endeavor to forestall premature conclusions based on tradition and "common sense." In *The Tribes of Yahweh*, I refer, for example, to "the critical intersection between lawful social process and human freedom," an intersection that continually recurs "amid the supersession of social forms through time" (1979:708). It seems to me that ethical judgments about history are estimations of how exercisable freedom has been used within the available factual options at the time. Thus the facts entail value judgments, are always valued in certain ways, but never incontestably because the facts are multitudinous and are always clusters or patterns of interconnected facts variously joined and weighted.[15]

The Israelites could give excellent moral reasons for their choices, and so could the Canaanites. The Israelites had "facts," openings for

---

[14] On the internationally-focused "political realism" and "theopolitics" of the prophets, see Gottwald (1964: esp. 350–87) concerning theories about the prophetic political orientation and a sketch of various prophetic models for international relations.

[15] For a perceptive discussion of the relation between facts and values in a historical material "ethical" outlook, interpreted according to a philosophy of the internal relations connecting and conditioning all social phenomena, see Ollman (chap. 4, esp. 45–47).

exercisable freedom, to sustain them, and so did the Canaanites. Different values were opposed in different arrays of social forces operating in the same broad field of facts. An ethical justification could be given for both and definitely was given. In the course of working through the data, I find myself valuing the Israelite break with Canaan positively as a needful thing and, at the same time, valuing the Canaanites for their resistance as the complementary needful resistance in order to clarify that this was not an abstract contest of ideas but a social struggle with high stakes and without any absolute arbiter, other than Baal and Yahweh, whose credentials were clearly acceptable only to those already committed to pursuing their vital interests as they saw them. Of course, this is not the whole of our interest in the Canaanite-Israelite social conflict. Israel's social revolutionary origins happen to lie at the base of the entire biblical tradition and thus at the foundation of Judaism and Christianity. Consequently there is an immediate religious interest and stake in Israel's social revolution that the Paris Commune, for example, does not possess. What we are to make of those revolutionary origins of our religious traditions constitutes a central issue in contemporary theology, an issue that cannot possibly be separated from the social stance of contemporary religious bodies and theologians any more than Israel's social revolution and religious faith were divisible.

The Internal Relations of the Social Revolutionary Process

It is apparent that this initial encounter between frontier and social revolutionary models calls for much more careful inquiry, not only into early Israel but also into the range of comparative sociological data relevant to the application of the models to Israel. It is worth stressing in conclusion that both models appear to share a common apprehension of the interconnectedness of material and non-material factors as facets of a social whole in process. Both models try to take into account the material factors more fully and integrally than the previous nomadic, conquest, and amphictyonic models. Consequently, it appears that we are involved here not merely with one or another model comparable to all the others in what it covers, but we are considering a new order of modeling: one that does not simply put material and non-material factors side by side in order to draw external connections between them, stressing now one or the other factor and one or another external connection between factors, but a model in which the vital internal relations among all the factors are sought after and brought to expression as an interacting totality.

It may be that my dissatisfactions with Mendenhall and with Lenski have to do with my perception that each in his own way is in danger of magnifying one element as an independent variable in the social revolution in such a fashion that the intertwined factors, once dissected, are not easily recoverable as an operative whole. In my judgment, Mendenhall's independent variable of Yahwism as the Kingdom of God leads toward a too-narrow "religious idealism," while Lenski's independent variable of the expanding frontier leads toward a too-narrow "technologism." I reaffirm my previous formulation of the internal relations of Israel's social revolutionary process in gaining a foothold in the Canaanite highlands and in defining its social structure and cultural style, together with my estimate of the theoretical explanatory yield of such a cultural material hypothesis (1979:662–63).

In a sense crucial to methodology, everything about ancient Israel proves to be both material and religious. Thus, clarifications of the circumstances and processes of Israel's early formation, such as Lenski has sought to sharpen by means of frontier categories, are not esoteric technicalities but simultaneous and integral clarifications of the full range of Israel's life and thought.

> In short, the basic tenet for future research and theory is clear and commanding: only as the full materiality of ancient Israel is more securely grasped will we be able to make proper sense of its spirituality (Gottwald, 1979:xxv).

CHAPTER 5

Historical Material Models of the Origins of Israel in the Light of Recent Palestinian Archaeology

ABSTRACT

After a brief exposition of the historical material method for analyzing social history, in which common caricatures are rebutted, it is shown that historical material models are "naturals" for integrating archaeological data with literary, historical, and conceptual artifacts. The prism of Palestinian archaeology is employed to look at several crucial issues in theorizing about the origins of Israel: (1) reliability of the literary sources for social-historical reconstruction; (2) indigenous vs. immigrant construals of the first Israelites; (3) agrarian vs. pastoral perceptions of Israelite means of production; (4) Canaanite decline vs. Israelite insurgency as the occasion of Israel's tribal polity; (5) ethnicity vs. social standing as Israelite identity markers; (6) society or culture vs. religion as the locus of Israelite distinctiveness.

It is argued that most discussions of these issues have mistakenly treated the paired terms as necessarily exclusive of one another. To be sure, the balance of evidence tilts toward the reliability of the sources for social history, the majority of the first Israelites as indigenous agrarians, Israelite insurgency as the critical catalyst in the birth of the tribes, social standing as the seedbed for ethnic consciousness, and society-cum-religion rather than religion alone as the realm of Israelite distinctives. Nonetheless, these nuanced conclusions can only be derived after carefully considering the measure of truth in the "opposed" terms that recognize the sources to be limited and even ineffectual for some purposes, the presence of immigrants and pastoralists within Israel, Canaanite decline coinciding with and abetting Israelite insurgency, an early bonding of Israelites that gave them a keen sense of "peoplehood" over against others who were of similar social standing, and the forceful way in which religion came to symbolize and cement the identity and polity of Israelites. Archaeology provides indispensable material content for assessing these issues without as yet being able to deliver indisputable judgments on any of them.

Introduction to Historical Material Models

Historical material theories are not well understood in North American intellectual circles, and particularly so among those who study religion, where it is so often assumed from the start that Marxist theories dismiss the human and religious subject matter out of hand. In fact, historical material theories serve to bring the human and religious subject matter into the context of the full range and scope of life conditions in all their concrete particularity.

Historical material theories claim that we best understand people as the makers of history, culture, and religion when we simultaneously grasp *both* their interaction with the material objects necessary to their livelihood *and* their interaction with one another in the course of producing and reproducing the life conditions that sustain them. This material interaction with things and people changes over time and is, therefore, of necessity *deeply historical.* This historical material interaction process involves who decides what is produced and who benefits from production and is, therefore, both *economic* and *political* in so intertwined a manner that it is proper to speak of *political economy.* At the same time, this historical material process also involves what people think, believe, feel, and plan and is thus ideational, imaginative and willful, even religious—in short, *ideological.*[1]

The totality of these historical material conditions in process constitutes the sphere of determinate freedom within which people at any given time can think and do some things, but not just any or all things. Consequently, historical material theories posit human subjects who can

---

[1] A lucid exposition of the Marxist historical material model for researching and writing history is given by the historical anthropologist Eric R. Wolf (1982:3–23). Wolf goes on to apply the model brilliantly as he establishes the integral and necessary connections between the accumulation of wealth by capitalists of Europe and North America and the industrial impoverishment of their own populations, on the one hand, and the colonial impoverishment of the rest of the world's peoples, on the other hand. Wolf's opening sentence is a methodological gem: "The central assertion of this book is that the world of humankind constitutes a manifold, a totality of interconnected processes, and inquiries that disassemble this totality into bits and then fail to reassemble it falsify reality" (p. 3). Other than in my own work, no biblical social historian has employed a full-fledged historical material paradigm. Flanagan perhaps comes closest when he proposes to model the interplay of diverse approaches to early Israel by means of the hologram as a commanding paradigm. His concept shows affinities with neo-Marxist efforts to free the historical material model of mechanistic economism, but in the absence of a clear focus on political economy, the hologram model of Flanagan seems to lack a cohering "center" (1988).

and do make socially constricted but effectual choices that have determinable consequences in history.

Historical Material Models of Early Israel

A historical material understanding of emergent Israel aims to grasp the precise conjunction of technological, environmental, social, political, cultural, and religious forces that came to embodiment and expression in this ancient Palestinian people through the choices they made. It aims to keep these Israelites in steady view as human subjects, as firmly conditioned but not rigidly determined historical agents. It refuses to split these historical agents into compartments suited to our disciplinary specialties or render them into programmed robots obeying externally imposed laws of history. Particularly in the light of one-sided "sacred" or "secular" conceptions of Israel, historical materialism resists the temptation to account for this people *either* by vapid religious idealizations *or* by narrow technological or economist explanations.[2]

In *The Tribes of Yahweh* and subsequent studies, I have argued by means of a historical material approach that early Israel was a social revolutionary movement, a coalition mainly of agrarians joined by assorted allies in varied socioeconomic niches (Gottwald, 1979, 1983b, 1985a, 1985b, 1988b). The exigencies shaping this Israelite free agrarian movement were the requirements for self-sustaining highland agriculture and the measures for getting and staying free of domination by city-state rule. These harsh pressures on the Israelite communities forged a collective identity within a loose pre-state (better still, sub-state) form of polity which, over time, issued in a distinctive culture and religion. I continue to regard this broad model as the most coherent and fecund perspective on early Israel.

Nonetheless, it is clear that other historical material readings of early Israel are possible, for it is neither in the intent nor the power of historical material strategies to conjure up social revolutions where they do not exist. Furthermore, social revolutions take numerous forms, and thus it

---

[2] In Gottwald (1992, vol. 6:79-99) I attempt to present a brief history of the political economy of biblical societies from the beginning to New Testament times, showing how such an account provides a comprehensive, intelligible framework for understanding the development of Israel's religion. A less technical reading of political economy and religion down to 63 B.C.E. appears in Gottwald (1985a; corrected printing 1990). I have also offered an historical material account of why Israelite free agrarians came to support the introduction of monarchy to Israel and with what aims and reservations they did so (1986b).

is imperative to specify and nuance the mode of Israel's social revolution, including its roots and its ongoing effects.

My option for a social revolutionary account of early Israel is based on a reading of the biblical and extrabiblical texts within the framework of political economy clarified by means of archaeology. In the twelfth and eleventh centuries B.C.E., cultivators and pastoralists over large parts of the Canaanite highlands passed over from a tributary mode of production to a communitarian mode of production, thereby gaining full use of their productive surpluses which they had formerly surrendered to their political overlords. In my judgment, this shift in mode of production involved sociopolitical, military, and ritual-symbolic initiative and intentionality on the part of those cultivators and pastoralists. Their exercise of determinate freedom within sharply limiting conditions produced the historic effect known as Israel. Had they chosen otherwise, we should have either seen no Israel at all or a very different Israel than eventuated. Neither transcendent religious ideals and revelations nor unrelenting laws of history preordained this Israel.

Obviously I reach my conclusions about the shape of Israel's social revolution on the basis of confidence in the witness of biblical texts. When ample allowance is made for the Yahwistic and Deuteronomistic biases of redaction, I firmly conclude that the early poetry of Israel, its laws in Exodus and Deuteronomy, and many features of its sagas in Joshua and Judges carry us into the world of premonarchic Israelite political economy and religion. I shall have more to say later on this much disputed issue of the sociohistorical reliability of the biblical sources.

Archaeology and Israel's Social Revolution

Recent Palestinian archaeology has made significant strides in bringing the Israelite makers of social history into clearer focus through minute attention to the rural settlements of highland Canaan (Stager, 1985; Finkelstein, 1988). A fair number of archaeologists are asking critical questions with historical material bite and substance: What were the concrete components of production and what were the social relations within and among these agrarian-pastoral communities? Along what trajectories did these communities move to self-conscious and collective identity as a people, adopting a loose confederation and then moving toward statehood? Has the way these communities thought about and practiced religion left any recognizable archaeological traces? It is absolutely certain that no historical material strategy for analyzing early Israel is remotely tenable without archaeology, and it can be said that historical material readings to date have been severely hampered by insufficient and atomistically rendered archaeological data (Finkelstein, 1988; Dever, 1990, 1992).

In the following remarks, I want to focus on what recent archaeological findings, and preliminary reflections on them, contribute to historical material reconstruction, both by crediting or discrediting elements in the reconstruction and by marking off aspects of the reconstruction to which the archaeological data so far do not appear to speak at all, or at least not in any decisive way.

I have chosen to organize my observations around certain vexed topics that recur in the study of Israelite origins: (1) the reliability of the literary sources for social historical reconstruction; (2) indigenous vs. immigrant origins of Israel; (3) agrarian vs. pastoral construals of Israel; (4) Canaanite decline vs. Israelite insurgency; (5) ethnicity vs. social standing as Israelite identity markers; (6) society or culture vs. religion as the locus of Israelite distinctiveness.

Reliability of the Literary Sources
for Social Historical Reconstruction

Redaction criticism has made so telling a case for late monarchic and exilic composition of the Pentateuch and Deuteronomistic History that grave doubt is now cast on the historical reliability of their contents (Lemche, 1985, 1988; Thompson, 1987; Coote, 1990). Moreover, some scholars claim that features of tribal or pre-state Israel survived, or first emerged, in the lower levels of social organization during the monarchy and exile. This suspicion leads Lemche for one to contend that the biblical accounts of allegedly premonarchic times contain little more than scraps of these late tribal survivals or inventions which in fact lack all verification of premonarchic origins (1985:294–99).

My starting point is that Israel did have a premonarchic self-awareness and identity; these were not created by Saul or David. From Genesis through Samuel, preserved within the redaction and standing in tension with the redactor's controlling conceptions, we find numerous "remains" of a way of life that obtained in Israel in pre-Saulide times. Among such "remains," I would designate the poems of Gen 49:2–27; Exod 15:1–18; Deut 33:2–29 and Judg 5:2–31a, along with elements in the sagas such as those about Judah and Tamar (Genesis 38), Rahab and her company (Josh 2; 6:17b, 22–25), the Gibeonite treaty (Joshua 9), the man of Bethel and his followers (Judg 1:22–26), and Abimelech and the men of Shechem (Judges 9). Various of the military encounters and sociopolitical annotations related in the sagas or mentioned in annals, though often distorted in context, do not seem to me intelligible as fabrications in later monarchic times. In addition, numerous provisions of the Covenant Code (Exod 20:22–23:19) are not reducible pure and simple to reform efforts under the monarchy, when they were no doubt compiled in their present form, but show signs of formulation under free agrarian socioeconomic conditions, which the monarchic institutions and policies either actively opposed or indirectly eroded.

To be sure, the textual "anchoring" of Israel's premonarchic social history needs to be extended and deepened, and toward that end it seems to me that a considerable number of close studies of specimens within each of the literary genres mentioned, joined with synthetic reflections of varying scope on groups of texts or on social institutions, have materially advanced our knowledge (illustrative are Glock; Mendenhall, 1976b; Freedman, 1979; Gottwald, 1979; Chaney, 1982, 1983; Halpern, 1983; Spina; Kennedy; Sperling, 1987; Boling; Hendel; C. L. Meyers, 1988).

In short, the common current claim that we can write no premonarchic history from the biblical texts, especially no social history, is in my considered judgment a gross and unwarranted over-reaction to the earlier naive uses of those texts as virtually straightforward history. As we draw more fully on the study of folk literatures, i.e., how they retain certain kinds of valid memories, even as they refract events, and how they articulate social organization (Vansina; McNutt) I think we shall begin to see good anthropological grounds for respecting the admittedly filtered testimonies that come to us from pre-state Israel.

Nevertheless, with all that said, the "pipe dream" of doing premonarchic history with the biblical texts alone or in undisputed first position, is surely gone forever. Since the biblical texts by and large have lost their original space-time anchor points within the pre-state period, they are far sharper on social ethos and process than on the sequence and synchronism of events. For this reason, it will be increasingly incumbent on all of us attempting premonarchic social history to specify the precise grounds for using particular texts in order to illuminate that period. In all this there is positive gain in pushing us to look at history from various angles. As "folkish" literature, the very historiographic resistance of these early biblical texts is a kind of testimony yet to be capitalized on for a social understanding of those who fashioned them, as also of those who in later contexts appropriated and reshaped them. By way of example, I have elsewhere tried to show how an ancient Israelite "exodus" tradition passed through three sociohistoric horizons in the course of its pentateuchal development, its core features shaped in each case by the respective modes of social organization prevailing in tribal, monarchic, and colonial Israel. Although the oldest level of the tradition does not conclusively anchor in an Egyptian locale, its genesis was among heterogeneous armed Israelite tribes actively opposed to Egyptian and Canaanite hegemony over them (Gottwald, 1989a).

In frequently surprising ways the "historical" biblical texts do provide vignettes which, when viewed sociologically, supply grist for our premonarchic sociohistorical mills. One of the most dramatic instances is Chaney's superb philological and sociohistorical demonstration that the caravans of Judg 5:6–7 were Canaanite, not Israelite, and that the peasantry of Israel did not "cease" or "languish" (*ḥādal*-I) but "grew fat" or "prospered" (*ḥādal*-II) on booty (cf. 1 Sam 2:5) when Deborah arose (Chaney, 1976, summarized and elaborated in Gottwald 1979:504–7). This well-supported sense of the passage is followed in the New Revised Standard Version of Judg 5:7:

> The peasantry prospered in Israel,
> they grew fat on plunder,
> because you arose, Deborah,
> arose as a mother in Israel.

Yet another cameo of tribal times, highly relevant to the circumstances of Israel's consolidation in Manasseh, is the overlooked poetic reference in Ps 68:11–14 to an Israelite defeat of royal forces near Mt. Zalmon in the vicinity of Shechem (cf. Judg 9:48). This incident is connected with the saying about Jacob's forcible seizure of Shechem in Gen 48:22 and probably also with the allusion to Joseph's victory over archers in Gen 49:23–24 (Gottwald, 1979:550–52). Taken together, these texts invalidate the frequent assertion that Israelites fought no battles of "conquest" in the region of West Manasseh but relied solely on alliances with related peoples living there.

Our goal as social historians is to establish more precisely the merits and limits of these types of literary genres and quasi-historical allusions for our historical material project. After all, we seek the full materiality of ancient Israel, and it is just such a comprehensive space-time grid for the material culture of premonarchic Israel that archaeology is constructing. To achieve the desirable depth and breadth in the retrieval of the material culture, with all its associated social implications, we must trust archaeologists to pursue the procedures and conclusions intrinsic to their inquiry, just as they must trust us as literary analysts to follow our "best lights." We do not serve our common interests well if, as nervous biblical scholars, we keep urging the archaeologists to locate this or that textual tidbit piecemeal on their space-time grid. The diachronic and synchronic dimensions of textual studies and archaeology, while complementary in the service of social history, are far from identical. The social history they yield is not a simple addition of two sets of inter-changeable conclusions but a very subtle intercalation of information drawn from different registers of knowledge (Brandfon, 1987a, 1987b). Flanagan intriguingly proposes a hologram as the appropriate metaphor for this process of synthesizing bodies of knowledge which never quite reach "closure" (1988:77–116).

Indigenous vs. Immigrant Origins of Israel

So far virtually all recent archaeological evidence appears to speak overwhelmingly for the indigenous origins of the Israelite highlanders, although the grounds for judgment are complex and problematic—and exactly what we mean by indigenous require much more specification. Some archaeologists argue that features of the highland settlements, such as the pillared house and the high incidence of animal husbandry, argue for immigrant origins, but their claims grow less and less com-pelling (Coote, 1990). Finkelstein advances the novel hypothesis that the Israelites had originally been sedentary in Canaan during the Middle Bronze period. Subsequently they withdrew into a pastoral semi-nomadic way of life for three centuries or so, only to "resedentarize" in the hill country (1988:315–56). Quite apart from the merits of this hypothesis, which certainly calls for further evaluation, Finkelstein's focusing of the rich detail of area surveys and excavations on an attempted paradigm of "settlement" is done with care and commend-able tentativeness, in effect presenting what one highly-informed archaeologist can say on the subject without pretending to command proficiency in biblical textual studies or analysis of political economy. It is now abundantly clear that this is the pathway we must follow, whether as archaeologists or as biblical scholars. Since W. F. Albright, who could still make a plausible claim to be at home in biblical textual studies and in archaeology, the burgeoning of both fields has made such a synthesis in any one scholar virtually impossible. What we each can do, as Finkelstein has done, is to offer a summation of our special knowledge as it bears on the overarching questions about the emergence of Israel.

More and more, the pronounced cultural continuity, with important variations, from "Canaanite" to "Israelite" is being impressively docu-mented. The aspect of my 1979 hypothesis about Israelite origins as a break-off from within Canaanite culture and society seems to be broadly corroborated by the archaeological witness.

Nevertheless, the immigrant traditions in the Bible demand to be reckoned with. The corroboration of Israelite "at-homeness" in Canaan does not exclude immigrants, even recent immigrants, from the early Israelite movement, nor does it speak to the issue of migration internal to Canaan, such as movement from the lowlands to the highlands or within the highlands proper. The case for the indigenousness of Israel does, however, throw into sharp relief the contrary biblical reports about Israel's origin in Mesopotamia and its subsequent stay in Egypt. It is distinctly possible that these claims speak less about geographical locales than they do about Israel's self-perception of cultural and political ties to those lands. It is noteworthy, however, that Israel's link with Egypt is a pronounced, richly developed feature of the traditions, and I will hazard the guess that the insertion of militant Levitical cadres from Egypt into the Israelite movement would not be inconsistent with the archaeological testimony to Israel's fundamentally Canaanite character.

Interestingly, the Egypt tradition also gives us Moses as a prototypical bicultural leader, what Eric Wolf calls "an intellectual of the new order," probably of the sort prominent among the Israelite leadership in Canaan (Wolf, 1969:287–89, 294–96; see also Chaney, 1983:65–66). Consequently, the Egypt tradition may be of considerable social historical value even if its strict geographical locale and historical placement is problematic and erroneous. Meanwhile, archaeological returns from Transjordan do not appear to support the notion of large-scale penetration of Palestine from the east, but this in itself has little bearing on the possible migration of a few hundred Levites through that area (Sauer; Boling). This situation further illustrates that we appear to get the solidest archaeological readings when we consider settlement patterns and approximate population size, whereas evidence on particular migrations and military campaigns is more difficult to discern.

Agrarian vs. Pastoral Perceptions of Israel

This topic was already touched upon in our consideration of the indigenous vs. immigrant character of early Israel, although it is important to caution that *indigenous* does not necessarily entail agrarian life, and *immigrant* encompasses the possibility of movement by displaced sedentary folk as well as by nomads. That the issues have sometimes been collapsed simplistically into indigenous = agrarian/immigrant = pastoral nomadic polarities is a measure of the relative theoretical "crudity" with which Israelite origins have too often been pursued.

Archaeological finds show that in the hill country the predominant agrarian mode of life was liberally mixed with pastoral pursuits, in part because some areas were suited only for pastoralism but, more importantly, because a judicious mix of crops and animals was vital for economic risk-spreading (Hopkins, 1985; Borowski). While this does not in itself argue for increasing our estimate of the numbers of pastoral nomads in early Israel, we do need to reassess the part that pastoral nomads played in Israel's social formation. Coote and Whitelam argue, for example, that the pastoral nomadic minority in early Israel played crucial roles from time to time in trade, in providing political asylum and in giving leadership as "judges" or "sheiks" over regions of the highlands (1987:117–39; in his forthcoming book on early Israel, Coote appears to make much less of this pastoral nomadic element).

I welcome the reassessment of pastoral nomadism in early Israel. What impressed me when I wrote in 1979, and still does, is the massive biblical witness to earliest Israel as a primarily settled agrarian people, the "wandering" of Israel being presented as an unhappy disruption of life, in sociological terms a migration in contrast to nomadism as a customary mode of subsistence (Gottwald, 1979:435–63, 584–87). It has, however, never been my intention to dismiss pastoral nomadism categorically from early Israel (Gottwald, 1979:889–94). It is altogether imaginable within my overall theory that pastoral nomads may have contributed roles and strategies that were vital for the successes of the larger agrarian populace. If so, it would not be the only instance where diversification of partnership in a social revolution has been decisive for victory (Wolf, 1969). What has radically changed is that, instead of assuming pastoral nomadism as Israel's sole and sufficient starting point, we must now try to specify it as a particular niche in the political economy, linked to the pastoral component in the wider agrarian society and perhaps politically significant because of the mobility it afforded vis-à-vis central authorities.

Canaanite Decline vs. Israelite Insurgency

This is an issue that has only slowly surfaced in its full dimensions. It appears most often in terms of the apparent cultural and political decline of Canaanite city-states in the Late Bronze Age, thereby "paving the way" for Israelite ascendancy. The immigration theorists Alt and Noth argued for a slow recession in Canaanite control of the highlands which allowed the Israelite nomads to fill the vacuum in a mostly peaceful manner. Mendenhall, who at first proposed an emphatic model of Israelite peasant revolt (1962), eventually backed away from that position by claiming that the Canaanite polity collapsed and Israel took over the spoils with almost no contest at all (1976a). Coote and Whitelam give a more sophisticated account of Canaanite decline or "transformation," which they attribute heavily to the interruption of international trade (27–80). The conclusion they draw is that agriculture in the hills became a necessary strategy for the survival of those who had formerly depended more on trade. The net effect of their reconstruction seems to come close to Mendenhall's revised position. Coote and Whitelam do not seem to envisage any sizable political or military tension/conflict between the city-states and the highland cultivators.

My own view is that these forms of reasoning about Canaanite decline are accurate in one sense but very one-sided and finally inadequate to explain Israelite identity and polity. Three points need to be made concerning this issue.

First, let it be said that this is not a question of either/or: either Canaanite decline or Israelite insurgency explains Israel's dominance in the highlands. Preceding successful social revolutions, it is customary that the regnant powers display weaknesses which the insurgents test and exploit as best they can. Therefore, to affirm Canaanite decline says nothing whatsoever about corresponding Israelite passivity or insurgency. The mutual interlock of establishment decline and anti-establishment insurgency does mean that the better we understand the specifics of Canaanite decline, the better we will be able to discern the actual shape of Israelite insurgency.

Secondly, my reading of the premonarchic witnesses is that the militancy in the texts cannot be wholly expunged as the retrojection of Josianic nationalist militarism (contra Nelson). Of course, the all-Israelite conquest framework of Joshua overstates the military action, but the contents of the enclosed traditions show a mixture of insurgent measures that definitely include force of arms. Early Israel fought many military engagements with Canaanites who, while weaker than in previous centuries, had not reached the point where they were helpless to contest Israelite gains, and most certainly they had not "collapsed."

Thirdly, the matter of Israelite insurgency is not simply a military issue; it is equally, even more importantly, an issue of movement-building. Mendenhall saw this with uncanny insight (1976b), but unfortunately attributed Israel's counter-society almost entirely to a religious-moral revolution introduced into Canaan from beyond history in the form of a religious revelation (1976a). Coote and Whitelam go in the opposite direction in excluding Israel's religion from their inquiry, but, sharing with Mendenhall the exclusion of political and military threat from the Canaanites, they describe a congeries of Israelite agrarians and pastoralists who hardly constitute a "movement" at all, much less a proto-Israelite or Israelite movement being "built" toward any particular societal ends beyond rather narrow economist goals. It is my view that the segmentary social structure, the juridical apparatus, and the ritual-symbolic forms of early Israel were directed not only toward meeting the stubborn requirements of marginal agriculture but quite as much toward developing a life-fulfilling society and culture that was worth defending against the still-dangerous Canaanite city-states, not to mention the raiders and nascent states from Transjordan and eventually the Philistines.

Ethnicity vs. Social Standing as Israelite Identity Markers

I spoke to this issue in my address to the International Congress on Biblical Archaeology (1985c), and developed the topic somewhat further in my treatment of religious conversion in early Israel (1988b). I take very seriously the warnings of Coote and Whitelam (1987:11–26, 167–77), already adumbrated by de Geus and Lemche, when they advise us not to use later Jewish ethnicity as a criterion for the identity of the Israelite highland villagers in the twelfth and eleventh centuries. They are surely completely on target in this admonition.

Historians of the ancient Near East have been careless in their use of unexamined assumptions about ethnicity. Ethnicity is a slippery ascription which may be said to be appropriate when a people accord it to themselves and are so recognized by others, but the ethnic descriptors show shifting patterns over time and are notoriously difficult to apply to ancient situations (Kamp and Yoffee). In the case of Israel before the monarchy, I think we are looking at "an ethnos in the making." Surely social standing is not to be set off in categorical opposition to ethnicity but is detectable rather as one of the possible, even frequent, components of ethnicity. In early Israel, I judge social standing to have been a significant factor, as the highly probable ʿapiru-Hebrew connections strongly hint.

Fortunately we have a few textual benchmarks (Halpern, 1983). An Israel is mentioned in the Egyptian Merneptah stele around 1220 B.C.E. The exegesis of this text is greatly disputed (Coote, 1990), particularly where this Israel was located in Palestine, its demographic composition, and its social organization. Nonetheless, the Israel of this stele is surely in continuity with the Israel of the early biblical texts. According to Judges 5, by about 1100 B.C.E., Israel referred to a loose confederation of ten parts (Stager, 1988). It is not valid to deny to this pre-state people a term they used for themselves simply because the term was understood by redactors on the mistaken analogy of a nation-state with a culture and religion wholly discontinuous with the Canaanites. We must, however, strive for a contextual characterization of early Israelite people-hood that does justice to its incipient consciousness as a new social and cultural entity.

In my address to the International Congress on Biblical Archaeology, I summed up the ethnicity issue in early Israel as follows, and I stand by that formulation:

> Although de Geus [1976] made considerable progress in describing Israel's Canaan-based ethnicity in terms of ethico-juridical and aesthetic-cultural community processes, I do not think he reached the nerve center of that Israelite ethnicity which erupted with such force at the end of the thirteenth century B.C.E. I believe, on the contrary, that the most fruitful and promising hypothesis is that Israel's dawning self-ascription as a people took place in a precarious social organizational matrix, where peasants and other kinds of producers and providers of services struggled to take command of the agrarian means of production. This was the forge that brought them to extraordinary self-consciousness, as it propelled them into the consciousness and social world of others around them (1985c:44).

Culture and Society vs. Religion as the Locus of Israelite Identity

This topic is intimately related to the ethnicity vs. social standing issue. De Geus and Coote-Whitelam make us acutely aware of how distortingly—indeed shockingly—theologized the history of Israelite religion has become in the hands of its Jewish and Christian exegetes, to the point that it is necessary to do a vast clearing operation just to be able to look at the ritual and symbolism of the first Israelites with fresh eyes.

So what *are* we to do about the religion of premonarchic Israel if it must be totally reconceptualized (L'Heureux; Mark Smith)? If it was not the "everything" that biblical theologians, and even Mendenhall with whom I share so much, have made of it, was it merely the "negligible" or "peripheral" thing that we make of it if we say that, along with no historical reconstruction, we can make no religious reconstruction of early Israel? In our over-reaction to an unhistorical theologizing of early Israel, how can we overlook the premonarchic cult objects and installations that call for some sort of interpretation (Dever, 1983)?

A historical material strategy wants and needs to know what the people it studies felt, believed, hoped, and planned, in other words their "ideology," which includes their "theology." Ideas can and do become material forces when they move people sufficiently. Were they such in early Israel? A look at the premonarchic poetry, not to mention the sagas and laws, of these people is sufficient to show that at least by 1100 B.C.E. a large number of them were adherents of Yahweh. While we need to guard vigilantly against loading later theology onto these texts, whether of a monarchic/exilic Israelite variety or one of our own making, we do need to recognize that early Israel had religious ideology and practice which stand in a direct line of development with later Israelite religion.

Premonarchic Yahwism was probably not a simple unity. It may have both possessed and lacked features of later Yahwism. It may have been the special province of a priestly cadre. It may have displayed close affinities with Canaanite religion. It may have had to struggle hard against alternative cults and ideologies. The chances are great that all these qualifying statements about premonarchic Yahwism are true in some measure. Nevertheless, Yahwism was articulately present and appears to have been shared by several tribal segments of Israel and to have sanctioned the people's social and juridical systems and to have motivated its self-defense (Gottwald, 1979:667–709, 903–13).

I do not see that this religion was a foreign or adventitious overlay on the culture and society. It was precisely an aspect of the culture and society, one of its idioms, and a symbolic binding agent for the social whole. Indeed, as Frick argues by way of Roy Rappaport's anthropological studies, Israelite ritual may have regulated features of the economy (1979:248; see also Flanagan, 1988:312–16), and, as Stager suggests, the priestly ranks may have siphoned off younger sons who could not hope to inherit land (1985:23). Moreover, it appears that the aniconic oddity of early Yahwism was not, as so often thought, an abstracting gesture to remove God from nature and magic, but a power-asserting symbolism aimed at preventing the expropriation of peasant surpluses by priests and rulers (Gottwald, 1986c; Kennedy; Hendel).

So, without foolishly deriving everything Israelite from Yahwism and without surreptitiously reading later Israelite beliefs into the beginnings, we can soberly assess the coordinating and regulating role that Yahwism and its advocates played in shaping the communal life of early Israel. The precise social historical "force" or "weight" of Yahwism in pre-state Israel must of course be demonstrated and not pontificated. In any event, it is a methodological and theoretical error to rule Israel's premonarchic religion out of the picture as if to atone for our predecessors who made altogether too much of it and did so with a too uniformitarian conception of Yahwism from its inception.

To round out my remarks, I conclude with the remainder of the preceding quotation from my 1984 address:

> The social organizational struggle for the control of the political economy also triggered the religious ideology and cult which in turn validated and energized the struggle. It was the mixture of this new political economy and new religion which pulled together peoples of varying previous identities and initiated a new integral cultural development (1985c:44).

Religious Conversion and
the Societal Origins Of Ancient Israel—
A Reply to Jacob Milgrom

ABSTRACT

The contention of Milgrom (1982) that early Israel could not have been constituted by the conversion of non-Israelites, since prior to the Exile one could not "convert" to Israel but only "assimilate" slowly through inter-marriage, is rebutted as a non sequitur. Milgrom's argument is derived from D and P laws which cannot with any confidence be regarded as in force in the tribal period. It is, in fact, prima facie evident that "conversion" of people to membership in the Israelite movement during its initial forma-tion—better described as "recruitment" and "commitment"—will have been a very different phenomenon from the conversion of individuals to an Israelite religious community once it was fully formed.

The social revolutionary hypothesis posits that diverse groups of proto-Israelites—with broadly congruent cultural, social and religious interests—joined by stages in the formation of early Israel as a coalition of agrarian peoples who slowly shaped a distinctive national identity. Studies of the conversion of indigenous Africans to Islam and Christianity by the anthropologist Robin Horton, in which he counters the "theological chau-vinism" of many earlier explanations, are employed to elucidate the complex interplay of cultural, socioeconomic and religious factors operative in the formation of Israel. Finally, two issues prompted by dialogue with Milgrom and Horton are tentatively explored: (1) Once the cult of Yahweh became the dominant unifying religious force in tribal Israel, by what means did newcomers to Israel enter into the practice of the cult as full participants?; (2) Since "new" religions customarily draw in some measure on features of older religions in their environment, what are the possible "triggers" in Canaanite religious thought and practice which may have contributed to the genesis and early entrenchment of Yahwism in Israel?

On the basis of a textual exegesis of how non-Israelites could become Israelites in biblical times, Jacob Milgrom has called into doubt the hypothesis that Israel originated by means of a social revolution chiefly of native Canaanites,[1] as advanced in variant forms by George E. Mendenhall (1962; 1973) and Norman K. Gottwald (1979; 1983e). By focusing on what he takes to be a "tacit assumption" of the revolutionary model, namely, a presupposition that the phenomenon of religious conversion was operative in earliest Israel, Milgrom concludes that "religious conversion is neither attested nor possible in ancient Israel before the second temple period" (1982:169).

In pursuing his argument, Milgrom distinguishes two ways of becoming an Israelite other than by birth: (1) one way was an immediate affiliation to the religion through conversion which at the same time conferred full membership in Israel; (2) a second route was to marry an Israelite and, after some generations, one's descendants would assimilate into full standing in Israel. In substance, Milgrom contends that one could "convert" to Israel only after the Exile, whereas before that one had to "assimilate" slowly through intermarriage.

To fill out a conceptual apparatus for thinking about the subject of conversion and its pertinence for Israelite origins, I want to propose two further understandings of how people might join Israel: (3) a third mode was absorption through territorial conquest resulting in voluntary or compulsory observance of the religion, a mode probably most extensively practiced in the Davidic conquests of previously Canaanite regions adjacent to Israelite tribal holdings; and (4) a fourth pathway was to have lived among the various peoples who joined together in the highlands of Canaan to form the people Israel and to worship the God Yahweh. We can call this primal mode of becoming Israelite "participation in the originative formation of Israel."

Milgrom skirts the mode of absorption by conquest when he dismisses the ḥērem as a piece of historical fiction but does not propose what happened to all those Canaanites who were not destroyed by Israel, other than to allow that many of them, especially in northern Israel, may have assimilated through intermarriage. As for the process by which Israel came into being, Milgrom does not entertain the slightest consideration of the possibility that the "charter members" of earliest Israel, either in sizable numbers or in toto, consisted of people who had previously known other identities and who were now "changing" (converting?) to a new identity.

In this response to Milgrom, I shall argue that he is mistaken to believe that the biblical data he cites on religious conversion to Israel are demonstrably applicable to the recruitment of membership in earliest Israel. On narrow literary and historical grounds, his data are inapplica-

---

[1] Milgrom (1982).

ble to premonarchic Israel because they cannot be shown to be older than the eighth century B.C.E. at best. More tellingly, on broader socioreligious grounds, his data are inapplicable to premonarchic Israel because there exists the prima facie probability that there was a significant socioreligious structural and processual difference between "joining" Israel at its genesis and "joining" Israel once it had achieved a stable and continuing identity. "Conversion" will scarcely have meant the same thing in two such different stages of Israel's development.

The body of Milgrom's claims about conversion and assimilation in biblical Israel consists of an analysis of the P and D legislation on the topic, concerning which he concludes as follows:

1. Contrary to majority scholarly opinion, the Priestly writer treats the *gēr* in a legal status entirely separate from the Israelite. The *gēr* must keep only the prohibitive commandments, so as not to defile the holiness of land and people, but need not keep the performative commandments incumbent on Israelites. Only Israelites were "full citizens" and there was no way provided by P, such as length of residency in the community or catechetical instruction, by which the *gēr* could pass into full citizenship.

2. Deuteronomy speaks about the imposition of *ḥērem* on the Canaanites (7:3) and the denial of admission to the *qāhāl* for bastards, Moabites, and Ammonites. Taken together, the primary intent of these two provisions is to prevent intermarriage with any of the indigenous or neighboring peoples. D is worried that intermarriage with foreigners, far from assimilating them over time to the worship of Yahweh, will instead assimilate Israelites over time to the religion of the foreign spouses.

Surprisingly, Milgrom assumes without demonstration that these P and D stipulations were in force in premonarchic times and that it was only later, in postexilic times, that it became possible for gentiles to convert to Judaism in the sense of directly entering into the worship of Yahweh and enjoying at once the full rights of a Jewish citizen. It is taken for granted by Milgrom that premonarchic non-Israelites could only have been incorporated into Israel via the one route provided in P and D: marry an Israelite, keep a minimum of laws to safeguard holiness, and in time have their descendants become full Israelites. This appears to entail the further assumption that the holiness laws of P and D were observed centuries before the redaction of those legal collections. Furthermore, Milgrom perceives no distinction between individual gentiles converting and groups of gentiles converting, although he implicitly allows for group "assimilation."

By deduction from the foregoing premises, Milgrom is able to dismiss the construct of Israelite social revolutionary origins involving aggregations of "converts."

> Thus, the assumption of the revolt model that the national entity of Israel was formed by mass conversions to its covenantal faith is totally without warrant....It [the assumption of mass conversion] is an anachronism, a gap of one thousand years. Conversion of individuals is not attested until the postexilic age, and the phenomenon of mass conversion not until the Hasmoneans and the advent of Christianity (1982:175).

Milgrom goes on to say that this anachronistic assumption of early mass conversions is "fatal" for Mendenhall's form of the revolutionary hypothesis since Israel was for Mendenhall—apart from the exodus Israelites—composed entirely of Canaanite converts. On the other hand, it is "less fatal," though still very damaging, to Gottwald's version of the revolutionary hypothesis because Gottwald allows for Canaanite "neutrals" (for example, enclaves only later absorbed, such as Shechem and Jerusalem) and for Canaanite "allies" (for example, Gibeonites and Kenites). Therefore, what I proposed as "a secondary vehicle of absorption into Israel" was, in Milgrom's view, the exclusive way by which Canaanites could have become Israelites in early days: at first neutralized as a threat to Israel, they could assimilate over time through intermarriage with Israelites.

The net effect of Milgrom's critique is to expose what he judges to be a fundamental contradiction in the revolutionary model of early Israel. A viable model of Israelite origins must posit the preexisting ethnic unity of Israel from the start, since that is what P and D attest if they are read at face value with respect to premonarchic times. "But, if so," he asks, "in what sense will it be possible to ascribe the formation of Israel to a revolt (1982:176)?" In short, Milgrom is able to account for Israel's initial composition only by the insertion of an extra-Canaanite ethnic entity whose process of emergence and formation he does *not* explore because it is assumed to lie anterior to the "entrance" of this "completed" people into the land. Since the revolutionary model *does* deliberately aim to explore the ethnic formation that Milgrom presupposes, and, moreover, to locate that formation *within the land itself* it is clear that none of his objections pertain to those originative conditions in which Israelite self-identity was coming into being.

Surely we cannot accept P and D legislation as having been binding in premonarchic times without further ado. To be sure, it is widely believed that certain elements of P and D/Dtr preserve features from the tribal period. It is, in fact, critical to my own case for the revolutionary hypothesis that elements of Joshua and Judges, redacted by Dtr, give us clues to the originative formation of Israel which are at striking variance with the overall perspective of the final redaction. It is also my judgment that the tribal social organizational typology displayed in P yields valid information about premonarchic conditions, and in this I share a large measure of agreement with Milgrom who has elsewhere written on the topic (1978).

There is, however, no reason to give carte blanche credence to everything related or prescribed in P and D/Dtr. Each tradition must be independently evaluated, and, in the present instance, Milgrom does not show cause why P and D on "religious conversion" should be taken as reflective of premonarchic conditions.

Moreover, it is not alone the details of the instructions on the *gēr* and intermarriage which must be assessed, but also the overarching conception of the social and religious whole envisioned in these retrospectively redacted documents which must be carefully weighed against the probable social realities of tribal times. The social locations of D/Dtr in late Judahite monarchic conditions of revival and collapse and of P in diaspora and restoration conditions were very different social settings from that of a decentralized coalition of tribal peoples struggling into existence. The commanding notion of tribal Israel as a unitary people already fully formed is constitutive of both D/Dtr, with its view of the tribal formation as a kind of proto-state and of P, with its perception of the tribal union as a cult community in embryo. With disastrous results for the reconstruction of Israelite beginnings, biblical scholars have by and large taken over the D/Dtr conception of Israel as in principle a "nation-state" from the start. Marvin L. Chaney has driven home this sociopolitical blunder with telling effect:

> Proponents of the conquest model have been inconsistent and imprecise in conceptualizing Canaan, Israel, and their mutual antagonism. On the one hand, Canaan is understood to comprise various agrarian city-states with ever-shifting alliances and enmities, while Israel is envisaged as nomadic tribes, invading from the desert. At a more tacit level, however, following the lead of the "Deuteronomistic Historian," the language used to speak of both seems to presuppose the nation-state as prototype...the nation-state in disguise. But if Canaan was a collection of jealous *city*-states, each with its own petty king, the *nation*-state mold fits premonarchic Israel even less well. Prior to its 13th century occupation of the hill country, it had no territorial definition: prior to David, its poor, unfortified towns and villages witness neither centralized political control nor the extraction and redistribution of a significant economic surplus. In short, the tenuous unity of premonarchic Israel, its lack of sharp social stratification, and its enmity for the city-states of Canaan cannot be explained by the tacit assumption of Israel's prior existence as a nation-state in the desert. The "Deuteronomistic Historian" and many moderns notwithstanding, the nation-state is not always the primary category of history (1983:47–48).

Thus, in naively positing premonarchic Israel as a virtual nation-state, Dtr reveals that it does not have the slightest conception of a *complex socioreligious process* by which Israel was formed, just as it lacks *a precisely documented historical account* of the events by which Israel came to power in Canaan. For D/Dtr, as likewise for P, the originative period of Israel is grasped fundamentally as a generative act of God rather than as an accomplishment of people in a particular social history.

For Dtr to manifest this kind of sociohistorical "blind spot" is of course entirely understandable, but it is another matter when biblical scholars, who have access to sociological method and theory, perpetuate Dtr's misperception. Consequently, whatever the merits of Milgrom's textual exegesis, which for the purposes of this paper need not be contested nor confirmed, his attempt to "translate" the results into an assessment of the circumstances of Israel's initial formation must be judged a failure. Fundamentally it is a failure because it mismatches data from *very different social worlds* when it tries to transplant recruitment or conversion criteria from the *nation-state* social construct of D and the *cult-community* social construct of P into the social world of the *associated tribes* of nascent Israel.

The social revolutionary notion of "mass conversion" in early Israel is not really, as Milgrom claims, a "tacit assumption," since its adherents set it forth as an open hypothesis. There is, however, a deep-rooted tacit assumption behind this hypothesis, as is the case with all the other hypotheses involved in the social revolutionary model, and it runs like this: without exception, everything told us in the Bible about Israel's origins is set forth in late redactional frames that give an airily religious version of Israel's beginnings which must be thoroughly "deconstructed" and "reconstructed" into a social historical rendering of human activities.

With respect to the "conversion" theme at hand, as with all other features of Israel's origins, we must posit Israel as a sociohistorical phenomenon that at one time did not exist and then, under particular circumstances, did come into being, at first as loosely linked tribes and eventually as a state. We have much clearer information as to how the Israelite state arose than we possess concerning the emergence of the associated tribes whose beginnings were largely preliterate. The biblical account is essentially folkloric in its format and tone, even when we allow for a greater "history-like" aspect in parts of its "filler" traditions.

This highly schematic traditional account tells us that Israel arose through a call to one man and his family which through natural propagation grew to twelve tribes that entered Canaan from Egypt and conquered the land. The vast majority of scholars concur that this is an artificial construct that does not bear up under scrutiny, for a host of reasons. In this regard Israel's origin stories are much like others the world over that cast the obscure beginnings of a people eponymously in terms of the actions of single persons and small groups that are genealogically related. Often these folkish origin stories leave unexplained gaps in the narration and switch the locale or scope of the subject without clear transition signals. All these features of popular origin stories defy the recognized canons of descriptive history writing (Vansina: esp. 21–24).

For example, consider the hiatus between the end of Genesis where Israel consists of the seventy-odd folk in Jacob's family and the beginning of Exodus where Israelite slaves are "swarming" in their thousands, to the extent that they terrify pharaoh as a threat to Egyptian rule. Add to this the decided evidence from many sources that by no means all Israelites in Canaan, or even a majority of them, were escapees from Egypt. All in all, as Martin Noth's pentateuchal analysis underscored conclusively—however we may dispute him on particulars—the stylized format of the origin themes gives us full justification to focus our attempts to reconstruct Israelite origins on the incremental growth of Israel in Canaan (1972:42–45, 252–59).

From the standpoint of "Israel forming within Canaan," we are best positioned to approach the patriarchal and exodus tradition complexes from the proper perspective, reading them "backward" as it were, since they appear to function primarily as dramatic "root metaphors" which tell us mainly about the vital formative processes and concerns of the highland Israelites. It is probably also the case that these patriarchal and exodus tradition complexes contain valid memories about the fortunes of certain groups who entered into the formation of Israel. The very possibility of extracting such information from them, however, depends upon our first establishing them firmly as literary retrojections produced by Israel as it took shape in Canaan.

For the purposes of our discussion about conversion in early Israel, the preceding understanding of the genesis of the origin traditions is of decisive importance. I am convinced that it is a methodological and epistemological error of major proportions to attribute to "Israel" of the patriarchal and exodus traditions a "completed" and "cohesive" ethnicity which was simply extended unaltered into tribal Israel.

Consequently, behind this "family tree" image of Israel's birth, with the sons of Jacob spawning the closely knit tribes of Israel conceived as a family writ large, we are searching for sociohistoric conjunctures of peoples, and of conditions and processes, that can best explain how Israel came about, if only by initially *delimiting possibilities and excluding improbabilities*. This "explanation" by delimitation and exclusion must include a clarification of Israel's peculiar "tribalism," which we can no longer attribute simply to a prolongation of pastoral nomadism, but must grasp and explicate as something more akin to a "revitalization movement."[2] This "explanation" must also include an integral, socially critical reading of the rich body of literary traditions which speaks so fluently of a complex socioreligious process of popular formation.

At this point the comparative study of Israel's origin stories in relation to the origin stories of various peoples the world over is a most needful and promising research task. This is so because in certain respects, and from case to case, we are more knowledgeable about the genesis of these peoples than we are of the genesis of Israel. Within our grasp is the possibility of controlled comparisons that specify the ways in which the formation of Israel may be judged comparable, and thus be significantly enlightened by, for example, the formation of the Icelandic, Iroquois, or Sioux peoples. By the nature of all the variables involved in such far-flung and diverse social constellations, these comparisons will be delimitation of possibilities and probabilities rather than one-to-one proofs (Wilson, 1984:28–29). In a situation, however, where even though the biblical text and the archaeological data are exhaustively combed for new ideas, various competing explanations of Israelite origins continue in stalemate, such comparative inquiry into the origin stories of known peoples is a largely untapped resource of incalculable worth.

To give but one example, it strikes me as more and more evident that while we cannot yet give a very confident assessment of the historical veracity of the Egyptian sojourn and exodus traditions, we can say quite a bit in terms of the social referents and allusions of those traditions, provided that we understand that those referents and allusions are in the first instance bounded in social conditions in highland Canaan. It is plausible, perhaps even compelling, to recognize in the traditional "portraits" of Moses and the other Israelite leaders definite projections of the type of bicultural risk-takers who, like the "intellectuals of the new order" vital to the leadership of peasant movements in our time (Wolf, 1969:287–89), were the "brains" that joined with the "muscles" of the Israelite rank and file to devise flexible strategies and tactics for building the tribal confederacy as a viable way of life.

The conception of Israel's formation crucial to my argument is that pre-monarchic Israel was a people composing itself cumulatively by a

---

[2] The programmatic essay on this topic is by A. F. C. Wallace. In studies of ancient Israel, apart from my *Tribes of Yahweh*, "revitalization" concepts have been chiefly applied to prophecy and apocalyptic (see R. C. Culley and T. W. Overholt).

new bonding of individuals and groups, all of whom were leaving previous allegiances and identities as they developed their new Israelite identity. Thus it is evident that my actual "tacit assumption" about "conversion" in premonarchic Israel is very different from what Milgrom supposes. I do not assume that early Israel received outsiders into an already very well defined community that in its essential structures and practices was like the community of Israel in later centuries. Nor do I assume that transfer of loyalties to the Israelite community in early days was preeminently for religious reasons by analogy with postexilic conversions to Judaism. In fact, we make no progress in reconstructing Israel's origins as long as we assume close equivalence between social and religious terms in earliest Israel and in later Israel.

Stated positively, my tacit assumption is to expect Israel's originative socioreligious formation to have differed considerably from its later maturing formation, so that all considerations of what it meant to "be" Israelite and to "join" Israel in the two situations must be formulated carefully with full regard for the differing socioreligious contexts. Working out of this assumption, my hypothesis is that Israel was formed in Canaan out of a number of elements of the populace, with differing degrees and kinds of previous identities, and that the "Israel" so formed was not only, or even chiefly, a religious community but an entire social formation, a whole socioeconomic and cultural system, which simultaneously developed a religion of prominence as one major component in the forging of group identity.

Very likely "conversion" is a misleading word for the premonarchic context.[3] "Recruitment" and "commitment" to a risky social project come closer to demarcating the community-building process through which Israel arose. In fact, I did not make much use of the term "conversion" in *The Tribes of Yahweh*, and when I did employ it in one of my key formulations, I put it in quotation marks:

> As to the mode of Canaanite "conversion" to Israel, I have in mind situations wherein city-state rulers and classes are overthrown, thereby freeing elements of the city-state populace to incorporate in the burgeoning alternative social system of Israel (1979:556).

"Conversion" (= recruitment/commitment) in this instance meant entering a social movement that was tending toward a societal formation with its own growing coherence and distinction. To "enter" this movement as a society-in-the-making was to participate in resistance to taxing

---

[3] Rambo, (1982:146–59), provides an extensive bibliographic survey of recent anthropological, sociological, historical, psychological, psychoanalytic, and theological studies on religious conversion.

and conscripting sovereignties and, as the necessary corollary of that resistance, to participate in the building of networks of self-help and self-understanding to replace the rejected "social services" and "cultural interpretations" of city-state organization and ideology.

The primary vehicle in early Israel for providing a new cultural self-understanding was the religion of Yahweh. The formerly powerless of Canaan (the "no people") were becoming powerful enough to control their lives as never before (at last "a people," "the people of Yahweh"). Clearly then religion played a part in these initial conversion-recruitments to Israelite ranks, but we must not be too quick to assume the content or social placement of Yahwism in that formative period. In particular, we must avoid the assumption which Milgrom appears to make, namely, that the shifts in commitments and loyalties involved in the world of Israelite identity-in-the-making are to be equated, even roughly, with those involved in the world of a long-developed Israelite-Jewish identity.

In considering conversion as participation in the originative formation of Israel, we must recognize that this initial Israelite movement and social formation was not a religion or religious group within the categories of a "church/sect" typology, that is, a religious folk who share social, political, and cultural features secondarily or peripherally to their fundamental and separately constituted religious identity. The religious language of early Israelite self-understanding should not deceive us into abstracting and segregating the religion from the total social and cultural formation. The religion of early Israel must be viewed in its sociocultural embededness, whether as a cultural subset or as the symbolic and ritual dimension of the whole culture, for it can be viewed fruitfully from both perspectives. Religious talk and practice in early Israel were emphatic functions of social struggle:

> In Israel the object of the divine activity is an entire people struggling to unify and defend a living space on the organizational principle of equal access to the basic resources for all members (1979:697).[4]

The capacity to hold religion firmly within its largest social and cultural matrix, denying it independent causative or metaphysical privilege in our historical analysis, is easier to sustain in studying religions other than our own. For this reason, comparative study of non-Jewish and non-Christian socioreligious phenomena, including conversion, is likely to be resisted as irrelevant for early Israel at the very juncture where it is most needed to "open up" our understanding.

---

4 For the meaning of egalitarianism as applied to early Israel, Gottwald (1979:798–99 n. 635).

The anthropologist Robin Horton, who has extensively studied the circumstances and conditions of African conversions to Islam and Christianity (Horton, 1971, 1975), has some cogent things to say about the "theological chauvinism" with which some Christian historians and anthropologists have responded to his conclusions. Horton studied the relationship between African native beliefs in high gods and lesser gods, on the one hand, and the incidence of conversions to Islam and Christianity, on the other hand. He concluded that conversions to these monotheistic missionizing religions were most frequent and abiding when the sociohistoric situation had already prompted a shift in the focus of attention within the native beliefs and rituals away from the lesser gods, who deal with immediate details of life, toward the nor- mally more remote high gods, who deal with those larger problems of the society which emerge urgently in times of change or crisis. In other words, a predilection toward Islamic/Christian monotheism was spurred by the threat or actuality of large-scale social systemic change mediated through the monotheizing tendencies in the native religions.

The response of some Christian scholars to this argument was to hold resolutely to the position that religion alone can explain the con- versions and, more specifically, that "true religion," in this case Christianity, is not amenable to non-religious explanations. Horton called these critics of his position, which included Edward Evans- Pritchard and Victor Turner, "The Devout Opposition."[5] In the judg- ment of these opponents of sociohistoric explanation of religious effects, African preparation for and conversion to Islam or Christianity should be interpreted in terms of theological or ecclesial triumphalism. In their thinking, Horton claims, the genetic fallacy is alive and well: if you can explain how deeply religion has been mixed with and moved by secular factors, you thereby weaken religion or show it to be false. Horton sums up Evans-Pritchard's way of sealing off "true religion," and its pagan anticipations, from radical sociohistorical inquiry:

> ...causal explanation is appropriate to illusory beliefs, but not to true ones. For the Christian, all beliefs in spiritual reality, whether monotheistic or polytheistic are at least approximations to the truth. Hence it is fruitless to search for their causal antecedents (1975:396).

In terms of our inquiry into conversion in early Israel, "devout opposition" to a social critical interpretation of Israelite faith sometimes

---

5 Horton (1975:394–97). In sharp contrast to Horton's "devout oppositionists," A. R. Tippett, without recourse to spiritual or theological causes, schematizes the conversion process to Christianity in Oceania with anthropological and sociological sophistication.

takes the direct form of assertions about the privileged and therefore socially unanalyzable priority of the revealed truth of the biblical account. More often, however, the opposition appears in the form of assumptions about Israel as "an unchanging essence" or about Israel's faith as "transcending history." Whatever rough-hewn symbolic value these assertions may have, as mindsets they contribute to halfhearted and inconsistent application of historical method when the sacred history-transcending categories are substituted for rigorous social historical thinking. Although Milgrom does not address these assumptions, and it would thus be inaccurate of me to attribute them to him, it does seem to me that his reluctance or resistance to conceptualizing early Israel in a processual mode rests logically on such essentialist views of biblical Israel. And because this basic orientation is not unique to Milgrom, but is evident in the work of many biblical scholars, it is important that it be surfaced for critical consideration if the day-to-day work of biblical studies is to be clarified and prospered.

If we turn for a moment to consider what did happen in the formation of Israel out of diverse preexistent identities, two issues, prompted by the work of Milgrom and Horton, deserve to be formulated and briefly commented on: (1) insofar as the religion of Yahweh was but one subset of Israelite society, once a cult of Yahweh became the dominant unifying religious force, by what means did newcomers to Israel enter into the formalities of the cult?; (2) since a "new" religion always draws in some measure on features of older religions, and may even be precipitated by elements of the older religions which are suddenly depreciated or brought to prominence in a radically altered way, what are the possible "triggers" in Canaanite religion which may have contributed to the eruption of Yahwism in Israel? Over against spiritualizing abstractions that remove Israel's religion from its social matrix, I have consistently stressed the close fit between religious identity and sociopolitical identity in early Israel. To be or to become Israelite was to acknowledge Yahweh, and at the same time it was to be part of or to enter into a movement of decentralized villagers bent on overthrowing the tributary rule of city-states in the region. To become Israelite was to make a break and to reorient religiously and sociopolitically with life and death stakes.

Nonetheless, internally the "fit" between religion and sociopolitical reality was hardly a simple harmonious one. It appears that Yahwism had to win its way in Israelite circles against considerable hostility and apathy. It also appears that the vanguard Levites formed a propagandizing and organizing cadre for the propagation and consolidation of Yahwism. When this uphill battle of the new cult is taken into account, it is likely that allowance should be made for the possibility that in some cases, varying perhaps by region and over time, people who entered Israel were "on probation," even if that meant no more than that their participation in the cult was approved by Levites after a suitable period of instruction. In that event, people might already be socially a part of Israel and militarily active in its defense before they satisfied all the requirements for participation in the cult. Certain features of the incorporating ceremonies (covenants) in Joshua 9 and 24 may best be understood on the model of probation for newcomers to the religion of Yahweh.

To be sure, consideration of continuities and discontinuities between Canaanite and Israelite religion, along the lines of Horton's exploration of the move from African native faiths to Islam and Christianity, is greatly hampered by minimal evidence as to how the Canaanite cults operated in the lives of those mainly rural highland people who became Israelites.[6] Looking at the decisive sociohistoric pressures on religion, what "filters" would have operated for retaining or rejecting Canaanite religious belief or practice and what impetuses would have encouraged adoption of a new cult?

Israel took shape as an agrarian society that before all else had to master highland cultivation in order to take root and survive. Secondly, it had to be able to defend itself against city-state sovereignties that attempted to dominate it. Thirdly, it had to develop internal self-rule and self-help procedures in order to serve the collective interests of its members. Lastly, it had to develop a way of understanding itself that could be articulated in religious symbols and rituals. How did the first three needs influence the adoptions and adaptations in religion?

It seems that the religious dilemma facing this new social movement was not an easy one to resolve. The Canaanite "high gods" were tied into the city-state system as an ideological support for the hegemony Israel was rejecting. The cults of the Canaanite "lesser gods," presumably the main preoccupation of agrarians, would appeal to the Israelite insurgents as the received sensible practice for cultivators of the soil. The dilemma was twofold: the aspects of Canaanite religion that would prosper Israelite agriculture and the aspects of Canaanite religion that would justify city-state dominion and delegitimate the Israelite social project were so closely linked that they could not be easily separated. It would be difficult "to pick and choose" among the Canaanite religious

---

[6] Gottwald (1983b:32–33), questions whether the theocratic ideology of Canaanite state religion succeeded in permeating popular culture with a common world view.

offerings without in one way or another "buying into" their ideological function in buttressing city-state rule over the countryside.

What was needed was a religion that would prosper agriculture and underwrite a communitarian mode of life. Whatever its source, the cult of Yahweh came to meet this need, but only, it seems, through a complex dialectical contest with Canaanite religion. Yahwism resolved the dilemma by providing a deity who was equally concerned both to deliver his people from tributary dominion to communitarian freedom and to prosper them in their arduous struggle to extract their livelihood from the highland soil. It appears, however, that Yahweh had been in the first instance the deity of deliverance from oppressive circumstances and only secondarily a god of fertility. Consequently, the challenge for Israel, and especially for the levitical devotees and interpreters of this god, was to make firm the link between the history-making and nature-fecundating aspects of Yahweh, and to do this in such a way as to renounce religious legitimation for Canaanite politics and social stratification.

In this process of sorting out the religious *old* and the religious *new*, the generic name for the Canaanite "father god," El, was retained as one of Yahweh's names, while the name Baal, more threatening because of his apparently closer association with agrarian cults, was rejected. Many of the particulars of Canaanite religion, from its mode of producing religious songs to its sacrificial system, were easily preserved by the Israelite movement as long as they could be shorn of their ideological support of the Canaanite city-state. Looked at in terms of resolving a fundamental dilemma in the tension between religion and social structure, the curious twists and turns by which Israel both appropriated and rejected Canaanite religion are more understandable than when viewed solely as religious choices.[7] It is also clear that no once and for all clear-cut decisions in these religious matters could be counted on to prevail, inasmuch as the Levites and the most loyal Yahweh adherents had to

---

7 Hillers (1985) faults *Tribes* for a moralistic negative view of Canaanite religion essentially no different from the judgmental view of the older "biblical theology" advocates. Hillers appears not to have attended closely to my assessment of Israelite theology as a development within a shared ancient Near Eastern "common theology," and, in particular, he has overlooked my extended dialogue with the views of "the Cross school" and W. Brueggemann on the error of nature-history dualism in evaluating Canaanite and Israelite religions as polar opposites pure and simple (1979:903–13). Although compressed, Sperling (1986) has an excellent sketch of the Canaanite-Israelite religious dialectic as a dimension of Israel's formative social revolution.

rely mainly on example and persuasion since, as a decentralized polity, there was no way to compel compliance in a lasting manner.

In conclusion, Milgrom makes one specific objection to the revolutionary hypothesis which merits response because it is a recurrent one among critics of the hypothesis. The objection may be broadly phrased in this way: Israel could not have originated in social revolution because its traditions preserve no explicit or incontestable memory of such a social revolution.

Milgrom's form of that objection is couched in this manner: "A mass conversion of Canaanites during Israel's formative period would not have been ignored by Deuteronomy" (1982:173). Strictly speaking, Milgrom is correct. Had Deuteronomy known of such a phenomenon, it would have been worked into the book in some way, possibly as a one-time exception for incorporating supposedly sincere Canaanites no longer to be allowed because the undertaking had not worked out well.

If, however, the overarching interpretive framework of Deuteronomy does not go back with any certainty beyond the eighth century, why should we think that the actual circumstances of Israel's emergence in Canaan would any longer be clearly remembered in their unique totality? This was, however, not simply a memory "fade-out" over three or four centuries. Major changes in society that are later overturned or reversed tend to be forgotten. We can see quite definite reasons for this "forgetting" in the case of Israel. It was certainly in the interests of those who profited from the reversal of Israel's social revolution to erase that memory insofar as possible.

In fact, the subsequent development of Israelite traditions can be viewed as a contest between those who sought to erase the memories of social revolution and those who sought to preserve and rekindle those memories. The former, commanding as they did substantial political power and literary resources, were able to obscure the memories of social revolution, but they did not succeed in expunging them altogether because the revolutionary roots of Israel lived on in the hearts and minds of others who were able to maintain and nourish aspects of the original communitarian practice within the social structure that resisted the encroachments of monarchic administration and ideology.

After two centuries, Israel became a single monarchic state and then split into two states. Centralized governments require unequivocal stability and solid historical charters. Monarchic Israelite circles derived the state-charter from God via the patriarchs, Moses and Joshua, eventually to be actualized in the dynasty of David. The writers and keepers of the literary traditions were chiefly those under state aegis. To have retained and cultivated the social revolutionary specifics of Israel's

beginnings would have been to place the security of the Israelite monarchy in jeopardy, since a people that began in social revolution might
turn revolutionary against their own kings, and in fact such did happen
more than once, although these outbursts against royal authority were
always subsequently contained within yet another centralized dynastic
structure. When one considers how much of the social revolutionary
thrust and potential of American history has been "forgotten" over two
hundred years of time, even though those tendencies are fully documented, it should not surprise us that the circumstances and the basic
process of Israel's originative social revolution were lost to view.

Since earliest Israel was a folk movement struggling to establish
itself under adverse and spartan conditions, it seems that the main
tradition-building energy went into serving the immediate needs of the
new society by means of liturgies and laws rather than into relating the
past by means of connected accounts of how the revolution took place.
There were narratives no doubt, portions of which survive in Dtr, but
these narratives seem to have been recited at cultic celebrations and thus
were never given a larger historical context. By the time monarchic
traditionists attempted to provide a larger context, the older narratives
had lost their revolutionary edge, either through modification at the oral
stage or in editing by pre-Deuteronomic collectors. Moreover, since
during the monarchy the defense requirements of Israel were met by a
professional army under state command, a social context no longer
existed for the practice of military initiative by a citizen militia which
had been the backbone of Israel's formative social revolution. Therefore,
as Milgrom observes, it is doubtful that Dtr knew of any comprehensive
social revolutionary scenario in which to lodge the older stories, even
though some aspects of that scenario might have been serviceable to the
nationalist restoration of Josiah had Dtr known of it.

Those who, like Milgrom, protest that the origin stories lack revolutionary memory need to be reminded that, when it comes to describing
the actual circumstances of Israel's formation in Canaan, the origin
stories do not preserve *any single coherent perspective* on the spatiotemporal process. The so-called Dtr framework of Joshua is shot through with
vague generalities that naively retroject united Israel as a nation-state in
arms. The Dtr framework does not display Israel as a socially articulated
people, beyond the twelve-tribe device, and does not register a military
strategy nor show a sequence of victories. Strictly speaking the commanding Dtr outlook does not present a developed historically plausible
account of "conquest," "immigration," or "social revolution." It is only
in the diverse "filler" traditions used by Dtr that we find scattered social
organizational and military data which require us to assemble them into

a reconstruction of events, structures, and processes in one form or another. In short, the social revolutionary hypothesis labors under no greater disadvantage than all hypotheses about Israelite origins in the land. "Conquest" or "immigration" only appear to be more valid models because they have been dominant in biblical scholarship and because the monarchic apologists worked so successfully to exclude "social revolution" as an interpretive option.

But, although Israel's originative social revolution is lost as an interpretive frame for reporting the overall process of its establishment in Canaan, the impact and effects of that social revolution show up in many other ways. For example, if Robert Polzin is correct, even in the subtext of Dtr's redaction of Joshua and Judges there is a stress on the disquieting incorporation of "outsiders" into early Israel which may indirectly preserve displaced recollections of Israel's formation out of "mixed peoples" (124–45).

Most significantly, although the precise course of the social revolution that birthed Israel is not described in the Bible, many of the norms and practices of the newly formed society are reported, even if offhandedly and piecemeal for the most part in all the major blocs of biblical literature, ranging through song, narrative, law, wisdom, prophecy, and apocalyptic (Chaney, 1983:67–72; von Waldow). Furthermore, what distinguishes the religion of Yahweh from "the common theology" of the ancient Near East, with which it shared so much (as Morton Smith and Bertil Albrektson, 1967, have convincingly demonstrated), is precisely a theological and ethical gestalt correspondent with communitarian values and practices in opposition to hierarchic privileges and controls (Gottwald, 1979:670–91, see also n. 7 below).

Thus it is not a mere matter of locating "fossils" of the originative social revolution in Joshua and Judges, but it is also a matter of identifying persisting communitarian norms and practices in the infrastructure of Israelite society and religion in subsequent periods, even though these norms and practices were overdetermined by hierarchic rule. There is good reason to believe that the founding Israelite impulse to be self-determining and self-producing contributed to Jewish survival in exile and dispersion under colonial conditions, as also to the confrontation with Hellenistic and Roman overlords and their Jewish collaborators, and finally to the hardy grass roots character of rabbinic Judaism (Gottwald, 1985a:419–56).

Israel's Emergence in Canaan—
an Interview with Norman Gottwald

ABSTRACT

Since an actual abstract of this interview would be a banal disregard for the genre, I wish rather to explain why I have chosen to include a "popular" piece of this sort, so markedly different from the other more academic entries in Part I of this collection. I have included the following interview for a number of reasons: (1) To my surprise, the response of many readers to the interview, scholars as well as laity, has been to report that it gave them a clearer conception of "where I am coming from" in my views on Israelite origins than any of my formal academic writings. (2) While the interview covers many of the same points as my more systematic and detailed exposition in the Prolegomenon on "How My Mind Has Changed or Remained the Same," it does so in a discursive oral form that approximates the give-and-take dialogue of many of my liveliest exchanges with academic and lay audiences, thereby illustrating one of my most characteristic means for communicating ideas and receiving feedback that becomes a part of my ongoing reflection. (3) Furthermore, in this interview, my interrogator adopts an assertive role, not hesitating to pose a number of very common objections to my work—of the very sort that I frequently hear from fellow scholars, though usually more subtly couched—e.g., that I dismiss the historical veracity of biblical traditions, that I make out-of-context comparisons between Israel and other societies distant in time and space, that I discount archaeological data, that I impose ill-fitting Marxist categories on ancient social settings, that I openly reject or tacitly undermine theological truth claims, etc. By having such resistance to my work baldly and forcefully stated, and by allowing me to respond idiomatically, the issues at stake may in fact come to light more vividly than in scholarly papers.

Norman K. Gottwald, W. W. White Professor of Biblical Studies at New York Theological Seminary, is known for his pioneering work in developing and applying sociological and anthropological methods in the study of the Hebrew Bible. Of special interest are his views regarding the vexed question of Israel's emergence in Canaan. For years scholars have debated whether Israel possessed the land by means of conquest or by peaceful infiltration. More recently, Gottwald has extensively developed a third view—that Israel emerged in Canaan as a result of a "peasant's revolt" by a Canaanite underclass. Aspects of his theory have been widely defended by leading scholars, while others have vigorously attacked it as nonsense. In this interview Gottwald modifies his "peasant revolt" theory and describes it instead as a "social revolution." The following interview was conducted by *Bible Review* editor Hershel Shanks.

HS: Norman, I'd like to talk about a central issue in biblical history—the emergence of the Israelites as a people. We can agree that it occurred in the 12th and 11th centuries B.C.E., but maybe that's all we can agree on. There are three theories in the scholarly literature about how Israel emerged. One is called the "conquest" theory—that Israel came in from outside and conquered Canaan. The second is the "peaceful settlement" theory—that the Israelites came in gradually and settled in unsettled areas of Canaan in the central highlands. The third theory is often associated with your name; it is the newest of the three theories. It's called the "peasant revolt" theory—that Canaanite peasants revolted against their overlords. Is that a fair statement of the three theories?

NG: I think it's a fair statement, except I would like to rename my theory the "social revolution" theory and not tie it too closely to any particular theory about a peasant revolt.

HS: Where did the name "peasant revolt" come from?

NG: That came from George Mendenhall, who was the first person to propose this general model. He called it a peasant revolt, using as an analogy the peasant revolts in Germany (in the 16th century).

HS: Did you ever use that term?

NG: Yes, I did use the term.

HS: You've abandoned it now?

NG: It's not my preferred term because it specifies a little too narrowly exactly how the social revolution occurred.

HS: One of the things that confuses me is whether these are mutually exclusive theories, or is there some evidence to support each of them? Isn't there some truth in all of them?

NG: Well, I think there's truth in all of them. There's truth in the conquest model in that there was some military activity that occurred.

There was fighting over territory and cities. And there is truth in the peaceful immigration model in that Israel was composed of various segments at various times. Even though they operated as a group of tribes at any particular moment, it was not always a stable group. Segments were added or fell away. There is evidence that Judah came into the group later than the other tribes. Judah is not mentioned in the Song of Deborah, for example (Judges 5). I still think that the social revolution model is the best organizing model because "Israel" does introduce a new kind of social organization and with it a new religion.

HS: What do you mean by the term "organizing model?"

NG: A paradigm for describing the overall character of events in a situation where all kinds of things are happening.

HS: One of the things that leads laypeople to reject your theory is that it seems to them to be "anti-Bible." But I'm not sure it really is. It does seem to me, though, that you unnecessarily create obstacles for the acceptance of your theory. If you agree that there were a lot of things going on, as you've just told me—that there were some battles, there were different movements of people, some coalescing, some disengaging, some disappearing some being added to—after all, it was a 200-year process—can't you get all this right out of the Bible itself?

NG: Of course, the Bible is our main source of evidence. I'm actually viewed as too "pro-Bible" by those who think we don't have any reliable sources for the period before the Israelite monarchy. There are scholars who say that the biblical text is so late that you can't say anything about Israel before the time of King David (c. 1000 B.C.E.). I feel you *can* say something based on the biblical sources. To that degree I am accepting (of the Bible), more than some other scholars are.

HS: You recognize there's some truth in each theory—there was some military fighting, and, therefore, conquest; there was some peaceful immigration—we can get this from the Bible, can't we?

NG: That's where our basic information comes from. We try to supplement that with information from ancient Near Eastern texts and from archaeology, through comparative studies, by attempting to figure out some situations that are similar enough to Israel's origins to shed some light on the process.

HS: That comparative material can be anthropological, sociological, from various cultures. And that's basically what you've tried to bring to the discussion, isn't that right?

NG: That's correct, yes.

HS: Does your addition to the discussion in any way detract from the biblical materials that indicate that there was a peaceful immigration, and that there was also some fighting and conquest?

NG: I don't think it detracts; I think it illuminates. Every model is trying to make sense out of what is said in the Bible and what isn't said there, and out of the elements that are contradictory in the Bible. Take the model that is closest to the Book of Joshua—the conquest model. Those holding that view acknowledge that the conquest wasn't total. You have traditions assigning the taking of a particular city or region to Joshua, and other traditions—also in the Bible—assigning the same city or region to another figure or group. So there are problems in the text, any way you look at it.

HS: I think that we can all agree that there are problems in the text, and I think that anyone who approaches the text from a modern critical standpoint recognizes that the text has been worked over and often reflects attitudes and outlooks of a later period. It reflects different viewpoints. The details can't be harmonized. But often these different viewpoints simply reflect different aspects of reality that can be harmonized. Do you think that's a fair statement?

NG: That's a fair statement. I take the biblical account and try to throw some understanding on why the Bible presents it in the form it does— for instance, why the Bible presents us with such a total conquest, whereas when we examine the text in detail we see that a total conquest didn't occur. What is the basis of that contradiction? How did the biblical account develop?

HS: In the first twelve chapters of Joshua, we get a picture of a conquest. But then in Judges we get a balancing picture which indicates that the conquest was by no means total, and there was a lot of peaceful infiltration along with piecemeal conquests. This is also supported by archaeological evidence, isn't it?

NG: I believe it is, so far as I understand it.

HS: All right, then, so far as I understand you, you have something to add to that picture. And I'd like to know what it is that you have to add.

NG: Well, I think that what I add is to take into account that the Israelites were human beings, with a certain social organization. Because of our religious interest in the text, we sometimes overlook this. If we were dealing with non-biblical peoples, we would look at their social organization, but because we're dealing with the Bible, there's a tendency not to raise that question. I try to raise that question: What does it mean that they were in tribes, for example? Most everybody would concede that the Israelites were organized in tribes. What were these tribes like? What does that mean in terms of the conditions that prevailed in Canaan at that time? And, then, how does their religion connect to that, since their religion would be part of the way they lived their daily life.

HS: Those are interesting questions, but I think you and I can agree that all serious students recognize that the Israelites were human beings. But when you talk about "social revolution" that's something most people would not get out of the Bible. People have been reading the Bible for thousands of years. But until Norman Gottwald and maybe George Mendenhall a little bit before him came along, no one said that this is a social revolution. And you've said something else. You've said the people who were involved in this social revolution, as you call it, were not people who came from outside of the land of Canaan, but were almost exclusively people from within Canaan. Moreover, you say these Canaanite revolutionaries were a particular social class: they came from the poor underclass. Would you agree that's a fair statement of your position?

NG: Yes, I think that's fair.

HS: Can you tell me what you mean by the social revolution you refer to? Why do you think that these people who became Israelites all came from a local Canaanite underclass, rather than from outside?

NG: Okay. First, it isn't true that Mendenhall and I were the first to see this social revolutionary dimension. I think we were the first to try to present it in relation to a historical/critical understanding of the Bible. But if you go back through the history of the church, you'll discover that again and again groups such as the left wing of the Reformation and various Puritan sects in England in the 17th century picked up on that. In fact, they modeled their notions of a more democratic society on their assumption that Israel introduced a major political and social change in the society that preceded it.

HS: I'm a little surprised to hear you relying on that precedent. Wouldn't you agree that the people who saw Israel's emergence as a social revolution were not looking objectively at the text? They were not trying to find its meaning by exegesis but were in fact reading into the text based on their own social beliefs. They were performing eisegesis—reading into the text.

NG: They were looking as objectively as they could, in the absence of very much critical scholarship at that time. They were looking as objectively as other people were, others who looked at the text and found that it justified kingship and other forms of authoritarianism.

HS: That may be so. But they were both reading into the text something that objectively wasn't there.

NG: I'm not saying that they gave the best interpretation of the text, but it is possible to sense in the Bible a social revolutionary dimension, just as it's possible to sense other dimensions in it. I would agree that now for the first time we have a critical way of advancing that perspective. Now, why do I think that most of the earliest Israelites were internal to the land of Canaan, that they didn't come from outside? I think so because the earliest texts reflect basically an agrarian people who were at home in this land. Even the stories about their being in Egypt assume that they have come down from Canaan and that they then move back to Canaan. Their language shows a continuity with the Canaanite language. It is, in effect, a dialect of Canaanite. There are similarities in customs and literary forms and in religious terminology. The sacrificial system, for example, as has long been recognized, reflects a continuity between Canaanite and Israelite sacrificial systems. It's just as plausible, from this evidence, to conclude that they were there in Canaan for a long time as it is to conclude that they came in and adopted these aspects of Canaanite culture. The usual theory is that the Israelites, after having been pastoral nomads, came into the land and then adopted the Canaanite culture. The argument is that they then adopted a sedentary life, city and village life, agriculture, even the Canaanite language. But that simply doesn't comport with the evidence.

HS: Let's start with something that we can agree on. Beginning about 1200 B.C.E. we have literally hundreds of new settlements in the hill country of central Canaan. Is that a fact that we can agree on.

NG: Certainly there was a growth in the population of the hill country after there had been a sag in the population of that area.

HS: And we can agree that these settlements were Israelite settlements.

NG: All things considered, I think we can, even though we don't find the name "Israel" in inscriptions at the sites and we can't always distinguish sharply between what may have been an Israelite and a Canaanite settlement. But it was in this area that Israel later appears—we know that—so somewhere in there, they're present, no doubt.

HS: And we can also agree that these are farming villages.

NG: Primarily, with a mix of pastoral life, such as you would find even today.

HS: So our problem is to find out where these people came from and who they were, isn't that right?

NG: That's one of the problems, yes.

HS: Just because they're there in farming communities doesn't answer the question of where they came from. It seems to me that you're arguing in a circle. If you're saying they came from Canaan because we know that they are farmers, you're assuming the answer to the question in the question itself!

NG: Well, I think I'm adopting the simplest of all possible explanations. Since you see them looking very much like Canaanites and diverging from them in a new religion and a new kind of social organization, the simplest explanation would be that they have certain things in common.

HS: Is there any way that your hypothesis could be proven wrong? What kind of evidence would contradict your hypothesis?

NG: Hmm...

HS: Is there any way that we could conceivably disprove it?

NG: That is one of the problems. In the early period of Israel, it is very hard to know for sure what could disprove anything. Well, yes, I can imagine what would disprove it: If we had some absolutely authenticated text from that time that told of a large group of Israelites, coming down from northern Syria, that already had their own identity as Israelites and had recognizable religious ideas such as we find in the Bible, and then they appeared in Canaan and invaded Canaan from the north. Or in another version, they came out of the desert. If we had such a text that nobody could reasonably dispute, a firsthand text from that time, that could disprove my hypothesis.

HS: If the only way I can win the argument with you is to provide you with such a text, I must confess that you have a pretty good case. There's no way that I can do that. But it seems to me that you've stacked the deck.

NG: Any of the theories—the conquest theory and the peaceful immi-gration theory included—would need something that solid to disprove it. I don't think I'm putting myself in a privileged place. I'm simply pointing out the difficulty we're all in, since we're dealing with a fairly undocumented period. We're only building up a case for probability, in the absence of a whole lot more information.

HS: I suggest that although we do not have exactly the text that you require, we do have a text that says that there was a people who came from Canaan and therefore must have had some characteristics of the Canaanites. Just because that people—Israel—eventually developed some ideas about God, doesn't mean they didn't use the same kinds of bowls and storage jars as the Canaanites. This text goes on to say that this people went down to Egypt and came out of Egypt and went back where they had previously been. As you've indicated, and I would agree, there was no formal conversion ceremony when they came back, no identity cards saying they were Israelites. But they did come back, and they settled in the hill country of Canaan. And no doubt many people joined them as they journeyed from place to place, finally settling in Canaan. What I've said is perfectly in accord with the biblical text, and I would ask you, first of all, whether you agree with this summary; and if you do, then what does your theory add?

NG: I think it's very probable that one of the elements within the group we call early Israel was an element that had been in Egypt. The text is not as firsthand as I called for in order to prove or disprove particular theories, because the traditions in the text developed over some centuries. But I think the biblical text does have considerable power to it. What I add is to stress that the really decisive formation of Israel occurred in the land itself whatever else may have been contributed to it from the patriarchs or from a Moses group that came out of Egypt. Where we really see Israel taking shape and coming to express itself religiously is in the context of the land of Canaan itself. Egypt actually claimed that Palestine was within the territory of its empire at this time. Egypt in the biblical text is the symbol of oppression that the underclass is experiencing from the city-states in Canaan and later from the Philistines. All of these forms of oppression are concentrated in the liter-ary symbol of the Exodus. You could well have had an actual historical Exodus, but its meaning was enlarged and enriched in the same way, for instance, that the Pilgrim fathers in this country serve to illuminate American beginnings. Even though the Pilgrims were only one colony, their experience becomes rich as a symbol of many other colonization experiences along the Atlantic seaboard. We are all in a way connected with the Pilgrim fathers, even though most of us actually came as immigrants from other parts of Europe and Asia. It's really a question of how you put the elements in the Bible together. Most scholars have long had problems with the idea that all of Israel was in Egypt, especially if you accept the numbers—600,000 armed men.

HS: I think we can agree that's an inflated number. There are some people who would translate *ʾălāphîm* (generally translated as thousands) as a small population unit. If we have 600 units of people, whatever those units were, that makes the size of the army a little more plausible.

NG: That was Mendenhall's idea, and I tend to agree with him, which would give an army of 5,000 or 6,000 men. You asked about social revolution. By that I mean that there was an actual change in the mode of production in the sense that Israel rejected the idea of having a king and of paying taxes and doing conscripted labor. "We have no king but Yahweh," was the new cry. They were withdrawing from the rule of the city-states or resisting the attempts of the city-states to control them. And that represents a revolution socially. Now some of that was brought about by military action, some of it was probably brought about by the weakness of many of those city-states at the moment. They couldn't force themselves upon Israel. Israel then organized itself in another way, as a free agrarian society. Instead of relying on kings, they had a citizen militia; and instead of relying on the religion of El and Ba'al, they adopted their own faith, a faith in the God of this independent people, the people who had been no people, but who now became a people; and that includes having an integral existence as a social reality.

HS: According to the Bible, this devotion to Yahweh is something that they had before they entered the land. Would you disagree with that biblical picture?

NG: In the Bible it's presented as having occurred at Sinai.

HS: But if it was given at Sinai or developed at Sinai, it would have been developed outside the land. Your model, as I understand it, is that there was no Israel before the social revolution in Canaan.

NG: I don't believe that there was an Israel, as we've come to recognize it, apart from this formation of the tribes in Canaan. But as to where a particular feature of their belief comes from, there was so much communication in the ancient world, it wouldn't surprise me if the first use of Yahweh occurred outside Canaan, though I don't think we can be certain of that.

HS: That raises a broader problem I have with the way you express some of your positions. What you've just said seems to me to reflect a too-extensive skepticism. Of course we don't know for sure what happened. We can never be sure of these things. But if we discount some of the details of what the Bible says—it is, after all, a theological book and not a history book, and it does reflect the perspective of later periods—but if we discount for that, then we still have a core. And no matter how much we discount, we have a tradition that Israel's devotion to Yahweh developed outside the land, before they came into Canaan. I sense in you a kind of skepticism, as if "Well, that could happen, but it's no more likely than otherwise." If you have a core of tradition in the Bible, why can't you say that that's the most probable factual situation?

NG: Exactly. The question of course is what is the core and how to perceive the core. To grant a strong possibility that the specific Yahweh cult developed outside the hill country of Canaan among some Israelites—or people who are going to become Israelites—is still consistent with the main formation of Israel in the land. This in turn is expressed in the tradition itself, which says that those Israelites who came out of Egypt came originally from Canaan. When Moses tries to understand this, and asks "Who shall I tell them sent me?" he is told to tell them that a God with the new name Yahweh, who is supposedly the God of the fathers, sent him (Exod 6:3). That does not conflict with the fundamental insight that it's a Palestinian formation and that Yahweh was known there. Some of these folk are presented as coming down into Egypt and then coming out. That's still, to my mind, a movement within Canaan itself and not an outside entity or an outside force serving up pastoral nomads to people the land. We used to deal with the question by saying the Israelites had a nomadic culture, and thus Canaanite culture was newly introduced to them only when they arrived. But it seems to me they belonged to Canaanite culture even if they practiced some pastoralism. In short, pastoral nomadism isn't available, as it was once thought to be, to explain the emergence of Israel.

HS: The emergence of Israel does require some explanation, though, doesn't it? After all, we do have hundreds of their villages that weren't there before. They had to come from somewhere. Where did they come from?

NG: In my view there was a waxing and waning of population over the centuries. Historians have sometimes tended to over-stress the notion that the waxing must be due to people coming in from outside. We now question that. It's an open question in any given case whether the increase is due to an immigration from outside. It may or it may not. There may be a population growth coming from nearby areas. I think, in the case of Israel, there was some flight from the lowlands out of the Canaanite city-states toward the Israelite hill-country. Part of the growth can be explained by population increase due to improved agriculture. Under the stress of circumstances, people began to cultivate the highlands in a more intensive, organized way, so that it could sustain a larger population. And I wouldn't rule out the possibility that there were some elements coming from abroad to join the new movement.

HS: It's as if you said—at the very end of your explanation, "Well, the biblical explanation may also be a strand in the truth." But that's sort of the tail end of your explanation, a kind of add-on.

Let's start with the agreed fact that we have these hundreds of new villages in the central highlands of Canaan and that they had to come from somewhere. If we start only with that datum, there are a number of possible explanations—at least theoretically. There could have been a population increase. These people could come from the cities in the lowlands of Canaan. That's looking at the situation theoretically. But we have another piece of evidence, which you bring in only at the tail end of your explanation and that is that the Bible says they came from outside. And there is another bit of evidence, from another very distinguished scholar, Larry Stager at Harvard, who says that the amount of the population increase at this time is so dramatic that, based on his population studies and his examination of the sociological evidence regarding the increase in population, these people could not have come just from inside Canaan.

NG: There are really a couple of questions here. One is where these people came from. But to me the most important question is who they are, regardless of where they came from.

HS: Can we first concentrate on the "where from" question? I repeat: Where did these people come from?

NG: From within Canaan. Some of them may have come much more recently than others, and some of them may have been through an experience of bondage in Egypt, which provided a strong impetus to a whole movement once they got into the land.

HS: How do you explain the fact that the biblical text records only one tradition—that is that the Israelites came from Egypt, where they were slaves. That's a denigrating, vile origin, which ancient peoples would hardly be proud of. So that's reason to think that if it's there, it's true.

We know that on many issues the Bible contains varying, sometimes conflicting, traditions, but on this issue there's only one tradition: that they came out of Egypt. There's little, if anything, in the text saying they came from the city-states in the lowlands of Canaan.

NG: I wouldn't agree that there's little, if anything, in the biblical text saying they came from the city-states in the lowlands of Canaan. But I would agree that the dominant tradition is of their having been slaves who came out of Egypt. What might surprise you is that that provides much of the foundation of my argument; that is, the tradition tells us Israel finds its origins in bondage. And to me those origins mean bondage not simply in Egypt, which may well be the case, but also in Canaan, which was then part of the Egyptian empire. They may have been enslaved in the city-states of Canaan, or threatened by the Philistines. This "slavery in Egypt" becomes the metaphor. I think that the enslavement in Egypt has in fact become the dominant literary and theological metaphor for a wide-ranging experience of bondage.

HS: What is the evidence in the biblical text for the bondage in the city-states of Canaan?

NG: In Joshua and in Judges, we have stories about the overthrow of kings. We see the denigration of kingship, as, for example, in Abimelech's attempt to become king, with the people rejecting him (Judges 9). We see Joshua putting his feet on the necks of conquered kings; we see Israelite resistance to any domination in any way and specifically a resistance to the idea of having a king.

HS: There was a lot of turmoil in the world around 1200 B.C.E., not only in Canaan but practically all over the world. Isn't that right?

NG: Yes.

HS: And a lot of different peoples were forming about this time, coalescing and emerging. Is it your view that there were no great migratory movements that accounted for the formation of these new peoples?

NG: Obviously, there were some movements going on. The Philistines were a part of a movement of Greek-speaking people who came out of the Aegean. They were driven eastward through the Hittite empire. I'm not denying there were movements.

HS: I was, of course, thinking of the Philistines. Here they are on the coast of Canaan, and you don't deny that they came, in a major migration, from outside.

NG: I'm not saying migrations don't happen, but I think we have to examine each case on its own.

HS: And you're saying that when you examine the evidence concerning the Philistines, you find that they did come from outside but when you examine the evidence for the Israelites, they didn't come from outside. Is that your position?

NG: Right.

HS: How do you distinguish the Philistines from the Israelites, especially in the face of the Bible, which says the Israelites did come from outside?

NG: The initial movement of the Israelites, according to the Bible, was just small groups of patriarchs; so if there was a movement, it was just a very small group. This group went to Egypt, but they came from Canaan. Their beginning point was Canaan, and they went back to Canaan. In the case of the Philistines, on the other hand, we have contemporaneous texts, we can trace their movements. We have more strands of evidence for the Philistines than we have for the Israelites.

HS: Can you tell us who the ʿapiru (= Habiru) were? What part, if any, did they play in the emergence of the early Hebrews or Israelites?

NG: The ʿapiru are mentioned in texts over several centuries from all over the Near East. There are a fair number of texts from this period—from about 1450 to 1300 B.C.E., just preceding the time of Israelite beginnings. They tell about a people who seem to be socially marginal, who organize themselves in groups, who offer their services to various governments. Sometimes they are agricultural workers. Sometimes they are military mercenaries. Sometimes they are brigands, organized robbers. Sometimes they get captured. The interest in them in connection with Israelite origins arose because of the similarity of ʿapiru to the Hebrew word ʿibrî or "Hebrew."

HS: Is there a semantic connection between the two words?

NG: Apparently there is a semantic connection. They seem to be cognates. I'm not a linguistic expert, but there's a very strong feeling that there is a cognate relationship between the two words. The Israelites in certain ways represent that kind of movement, a breaking away from the existing city-state structure and developing alternative modes of existence.

HS: Weren't the ʿapiru outside of Canaan?

NG: No, they're inside as well. All over.

HS: Doesn't the evidence from the Amarna letters [diplomatic correspondence from the 14th century B.C.E., found at Tell el-Amarna in
Egypt] place them outside of Canaan?

NG: No, no. Inside as well as outside. The references in the Amarna
letters to ʿapiru place them as far south as Jerusalem.

HS: As far south or as far north?

NG: As far south. Most of them are in Syria, Lebanon, down into what
would be Israel today. As far as Jerusalem.

HS: But the Amarna letters were discovered in Egypt.

NG: Yes, but they were written from locations in Palestine.

HS: So that the ʿapiru the Amarna letters speak of were in Palestine.

NG: Right. Some of them were captured and were taken to Egypt.
There are references in these texts to their posing threats to various city-
states. What this probably means is that they were hired troops that one
city-state was using against another.

HS: Do you contend that the ʿapiru support your theory?

NG: Broadly so. I don't agree with some scholars who feel that all of
the Israelites were ʿapiru. I think probably what happened is that a
sizable part of Israel, as it formed, was made up of some members of
these groups of ʿapiru. But I think a majority of Israelites were peasant
folk. Israel was a composite, including peasant folk who hadn't previously been organized: ʿapiru groups, artisans, perhaps Rechabites who
were metalworkers, priests from other places, some religious leaders in
the tradition of Moses. It's a composite. That's why I don't think we
should adhere too strongly to "peasant revolt" language. That language
overlooks the fact that there were other groups who made up early
Israel, even if most of them were peasants. In short, I think many, but
not all, ʿapiru became Israelites; but not all Israelites had formerly been
ʿapiru.

HS: What did it mean to be an Israelite in the 12th or 11th century
B.C.E.? If we read the Bible, it meant devotion to the Israelite God
Yahweh. It was a religious connection. George Mendenhall, to whom
you trace the source of some of the theories we've been talking about,
disagrees with you—and very vociferously so in regard to the organizing, driving force that connected the people we call Israel. According to

Professor Mendenhall, the driving force behind this coalescence of all kinds of people was a religious ideology, Yahwism, the notion of a unique God as described in the Bible. You disagree with that, don't you?

NG: I disagree with Mendenhall's formulation of it. I think the issue is whether the religious impact or influence is independent. For Mendenhall, it's as though the religious ideas create the people. My argument is that the religious ideas take place within a social formation that is in the process of coming into being. The social, economic, political, cultural, and religious factors all belong together. These people are able to be religious in a particular way because of all these other factors. And they are able to sustain all of these other factors because of their religion. So I would say that their religion was a very important ingredient in this formation. For example, people rejecting a centralized government often have trouble organizing. They have difficulty being unified. They can't get together. They know what they are *against;* it is more difficult for them to concur in what they are *for.* That these people, Israel, could get together and stay together can be attributed, in my view, very considerably to their religious faith. But the initial reason they wanted to be together was based on more than simply religious concerns. They had social, economic, and cultural concerns. They wanted to be a people with their own significance, free of foreign powers. So that it's all one ball of wax.

HS: But what you're talking about now refers only to those people who may have come to be part of Israel from the Canaanite cities in the lowlands.

NG: No, what I'm saying refers to everybody, even if they came from outside. They came to be part of Israel because they'd been kicked around.

HS: In your sociological analysis, Norman, how do you account for the emergence of this unique religious revolution?

NG: Sociologically, I would account for it by saying that you have people here who were in readiness for a new perspective that values horizontal relationships among people, as opposed to authoritarian relationships. They value family and community, without hierarchal leadership and without giving away their life's substance to some overlord. The religion of Yahweh appears to have had this character, affirming the life of the people: Yahweh is always the God of Israel, Israel is always the people of Yahweh. And this religious perspective introduces communal togetherness and communal responsibility, an ethic that is binding upon all the people, a mutual responsibility for each other rather than giving special powers to a king or priest. Moses' role as a leader—and that of the other leaders—is closer to the people than any of the contemporaneous kings or the kings that later develop in Israel.

HS: But the kind of aspirations you describe are common to all people. All human beings want this. Why this people? Why did this religious revolution happen to this people at this time?

NG: Actually, I don't know why it occurred to this people at this time. There's a mystery in history. Why did the Greeks develop tragedy and philosophy, instead of somebody else? You can point to many particulars that made it possible, but what immediately precipitates it is another question. As a believer, I would say something theologically. I would say, "Of course I believe that God is behind this." But I can't give an account of that sociologically. I can't translate that belief into a sociological theory. What I can do sociologically is try to describe it.

HS: Where does theology fit into the picture? What do you do with the fact that the Bible says God had a hand in this.

NG: Well, as a believer I agree. In what way does God have a hand in it? That's what we're trying to figure out. The Bible certainly doesn't have a God who's physically present doing it. There may be a manifestation of God, but God isn't walking around doing it. So in some way it's being done through human agencies—sometimes through the Egyptians, sometimes through Moses, sometimes through the people themselves. I don't hesitate to say I think God had a big hand in it. But how the hand of God works is something Jews and Christians have tried to understand in various ways. And that's what we're trying to do in this case. That doesn't take away from God. It isn't as though God only explains what can't otherwise be explained, because in one fashion or another you can explain almost everything. If God only explains what can't otherwise be explained, you wouldn't have much room for God. Rather God is the basic reality behind all explanations. We only want "to explain" because God is the underlying premise of all order in the world. What was God's method in forming Israel? As a believer that would be my ultimate question. There's no way to prove sociologically that God had a hand in it. You can't even prove that out of the Bible. The Bible claims, but you still have to believe the Bible. You still have to have something in your own experience to think that the Bible's interpretation is believable.

HS: Some people are suspicious of your work because it is openly Marxist. And for many people Marxist means Communist. Can you tell us about your Marxist beliefs?

NG: I'd be glad to. I do use a Marxist methodology. To use an analogy, it's like using a Freudian methodology in psychology. Marx worked out, in effect, a road map for identifying how social and economic forces work together to create contexts in which social change occurs. I don't regard these changes deterministically, however. There is always a range of possibilities within limits.

HS: Do you depart from Marxism in that particular respect?

NG: I am one of the flexible Marxists. There are Marxists and Marxists and Marxists. Some are very rigid, so-called vulgar Marxists. I would be more what is often called revisionist or neo-Marxist. To me, Marx's theories are an aid, just as Freud's ideas are an aid, though not a final answer. Freud probably missed a lot of things. Marx missed a lot of things. So to me his ideas are a tool, like any of a number of other tools. It's more or less accurate if it answers the evidence. You know, does it appear to help or not?

HS: Some people say you explain so much in economic and revolutionary terms because of your Marxist orientation. And conversely you ignore the ideological and the religious. How do you answer this?

NG: I don't think that's correct. The Marxist method points out that everybody must produce in order to live. In other words, everybody has some economic interests. You simply look to see how that's working. The Marxist method doesn't require that in every situation there is a revolutionary change. For long periods, there are sometimes no observable or significant changes. You have to look at the evidence. Marxists and non-Marxists alike can look at the evidence: How much of a change does there really seem to be? What is the nature of the change? Someone may say "Well, that's not enough change to be revolutionary." But at least we focus on the question.

HS: All scholars who perform sociological analyses have to say to themselves, "There are economic forces at work here; there are social forces at work." But that's not enough to make them a Marxist. What makes one a Marxist?

NG: Because you look at the way the whole thing fits together in furthering or inhibiting social change.

HS: Doesn't everybody do that?

NG: No, they don't. They tend to keep things separate. They develop a lot of studies that are solely political history or solely religious history. Everything else is just kind of general background. It seems to me that all these dimensions of life impact one another. In other words, I would say that the particular force and strength of Yahwism is connected with there being a peasant people in the hill country eking out an existence, fighting off the city-states, struggling to survive, knowing how to conquer what's really a wilderness to them. That kind of analysis is just now opening up on a large scale. It's almost like the early experience of Zionism. You can't understand the early history of Zionism without the material reality that the early Zionists were facing—as well as their faith. If you take the Zionist ideology alone, it doesn't make any sense; and if you just take the physical business of rescuing the land, it doesn't make sense either. You've got to put them together. So it seems to me it's the vital, interactive connection of those things, the material and the spiritual, that must be put together.

HS: But Marx rejected the spiritual, didn't he?

NG: He rejected the spiritual as an abstraction; that's true. And his own religious sensibility was not great; that's certainly true. To my mind, however his particular view on religion is far from the last word. By using his own system, we can make corrections for his views about religion.

HS: If I understand you correctly, what you're saying is his system is simply looking at all kinds of factors and seeing how they interact together. The social, the economic, the political, the ideological. Is that correct?

NG: That's correct. But not so "simple," because grasping the interaction of factors is a complex task.

HS: I myself wouldn't call that Marxist. Maybe you would.

NG: I would. I would because I see it mostly not being done by sociologists, who simply pursue a single line of analysis.

HS: Isn't that taking an unnecessary burden on yourself—to defend yourself as a Marxist?

NG: No, because I'm really not defending myself. I'm just describing where I got the idea to analyze Israel as I do. The results speak for themselves.

HS: What do you say to the people who associate Marxism with Communism?

NG: I say, well that's like associating Hegel or Kant with the German Kaiser or with Hitler. You can connect various philosophies that have gotten tied up with various political movements, but they don't necessarily have to go together.

HS: Is Marxism a mainstream sociological theory today?

NG: *Yes*, it is. Very much so. Very strongly.

For me, the Bible is not diminished in any way by the kind of analysis I perform; it's enriched. Every theory involves some way of interpreting what is in the Bible. I think my analysis really helps us recover some of the concreteness, the earthiness of what happened. We see our ancestors more concretely.

HS: Thank you very much, Norman.

B

---

*Prophecy, Monarchy
and Exile*

Were the "Radical" Prophets also "Cultic" Prophets?

ABSTRACT

The longstanding debate about whether and how canonical prophets were connected to the cult was approached sociologically in an exchange of views by Peter Berger and James G. Williams in the 1960s. Prompted by that exchange, this lecture was an attempt "to step back" from detailed argument about particular prophets and to sketch prophetic options for working within Israel's religious institutions, drawing on general anthropological, sociological and social psychological knowledge. The argument is presented as a series of hypothetical options, together with the delimitation of factors that would have prompted prophets who had fundamental differences with institutional practice and ideology either to stay in cultic service or to depart from it. The two cult prophetic roles of liturgist and consultative specialist are considered in the calculus of the willingness and ability of radical prophets to continue as cult personnel. Finally, the continuity/discontinuity in role performance between a cult prophet and a radical prophet who departed the cult is estimated, as well as the likelihood that a prophet outside the cult could gain a serious hearing. This schema of hypothetical options and outcomes facing prophets with cultic connections, taking into account factors conducive to one or another option preference, can be viewed as a set of methodological lenses through which the data on any particular biblical prophet may be assessed. The approach taken resembles in nucleus some of the more extended anthropological and sociological studies of the prophets subsequently published by Burke Long, Thomas Overholt, and Robert R. Wilson.

In articles on the social location of prophecy, Peter Berger (1963) and James G. Williams (1969) concur that religious innovation is not restricted to social marginality but may occur as well at the heart of regnant religious institutions. Where they sharply disagree is whether the radical or classical prophets of Israel are likely to have held official positions in the established cult, with Berger favoring a positive conclusion and Williams a negative one. Moreover, the two interpreters frequently draw their opposing viewpoints from the same textual evidence.

In my view this vexed question can best be approached by closely examining the assumptions and implications of radical prophetic participation in or separation from the cult.

1. A formal separation should be made between the message or ideology of a prophet and his social role. In terms of the question posed in this lecture, a prophet with a highly radicalized message (i.e., a strong and even all-encompassing rejection of existing institutions), need not be assumed to have severed himself from a social role that he already held in the institution he attacks, nor need he be assumed to have reached radical conclusions exclusively from an outsider position.

2. Similarly, a formal separation should be made between the form of the prophet's message and his social role. In terms of the question posed, a prophet who expressed his message in literary genres drawn from institutional matrices (e.g., cult, judiciary, royal court, army), need not be assumed to have held a role in the institution that supplied the speech and thought forms he employed. The institutionally shaped genres do require that he have been a member of the society and therefore exposed to knowledge of the institutions. The degree of his exposure is not directly equatable with a role in the institutions, since people are often strongly affected by the actions and thought modes of institutions in which they are not role participants. The cultic forms of radical prophetic speech do not by themselves inform us as to whether or not the radical prophet had a role function in the cult.

3. In exploring the possible links between radical prophecy and cult prophecy, we should recognize that radicalization is a process that could alter the views of cult prophets. We may posit that a cult prophet who arrived at a radicalized rejection of existing institutions would not necessarily have left his position voluntarily, even under great pressure. What, we need to ask, would motivate a radicalized cult prophet either to stay in or to leave his position in the institution?

The factors prompting a radicalized cult prophet to leave his position will have included: (a) recognition of the inconsistency, experienced either as conceptual hypocrisy or as moral guilt, involved in acting within an institution he rejected; (b) awareness of the need to strike against the institution not only by speaking against it but by separating himself from it and by possibly building counter-institutional alternatives; (c) the personal discomfort and public shame of attacks from his fellow institutionalists and even threats against his life. In principle, we can easily imagine a radicalized cult prophet withdrawing from the cult for reasons of ideological and moral consistency, practical implementation of his principled rejection of the institutions, or pressure by the institution portending the prophet's expulsion from office.

The factors prompting a radicalized cult prophet to stay in his position will have included: (a) the belief that, since his message was radically judgmental, his most effective platform was within the institution where he had a "captive" audience, i.e., both in the sense that in this manner he would reach the maximum relevant audience and in the sense that as a participant in the institution his criticism might be understood as serious and not frivolous or personally deviant; (b) the belief that the transcendent judgment would take effect upon and within the institutions, where "the action really is," and that he had an obligation as the spokesman of radical judgment to stay at the heart of institutional conflict; (c) lack of any alternative social role, either because none was available or because he did not see the possibility of building a counter community along institutional lines in the face of the institutional monopoly on public discourse; (d) temperamental and ideological resistance to being silenced by those who, from the prophet's perspective, most needed to hear what he had to say. Thus, in principle we can conceive a radicalized cult prophet staying in the cult for reasons of immediate effectiveness, long-range impact, absence of a viable alternative, and stubborn resistance to harassment.

4. The practical impediments to a radicalized prophet continuing long as a cult prophet (or of becoming one) are nonetheless at once evident: (a) every time such a prophet conducted his cultic function, he would be faced with the choice of performing it according to institutional norms or of using the role to criticize the institution in ironic reversal of the cult ideology with its aims of public assurance and stability; (b) since the defining mark of a radicalized prophet was speaking out radically, and not merely entertaining radical thought privately, the prophet's every action in the cult would open him to the charge of malfeasance or dereliction of office. All the institutional norms and sanctions would face the radical prophet as implacably as he opposed his judgment to the institution. Whatever a radicalized prophet's hopes might have been to remain a cult prophet, his radical message and his socially accommodating role in the cult were so sharply contradictory that the institution could scarcely view him as anything but "a bone in the throat." Consequently, while we can imagine cult prophets in various stages of radicalization, it is not very plausible to imagine a fully radicalized cult prophet being indefinitely tolerated as a functionary in the cult he lambasted.

5. To reach more exactitude in assessing the circumstances in which radical prophecy was voiced in the cult or driven from it, we would

have to know a good deal more than we do about the actual roles of the so-called cult prophets. The subject is a vexed one, but we do possess a fair amount of information about these cult prophets. Prophets, other than those whose names attach to biblical books, are referred to at many points in the Hebrew Bible. They are distinguished from other religious functionaries such as priests, seers, diviners, elders, etc., but at times the prophets are associated with these other figures and appear to share some activities with them.

Recurrent features among many of these prophets may be noted, although none are sufficiently present to characterize all prophets without further ado: association in bands or guilds, connection with cult sanctuaries, group excitation or ecstasy, derivation of message from direct inspiration rather than from received tradition, intercession and healing, proclamation of judgment on offenders against Israel's God, specialization in oracular "observations" or "predictions" about the near future. It has proven impossible thus far to bring all the descriptions of functionaries called prophets (or related terms such as men of God or visionaries) into any convincing single model of office, or even into a number of models that can be confidently distinguished from one another. "Prophet," and closely related terms, seems to have been used to designate various kinds of activities associated with the notion of Israel's God speaking immediately to situations of human need and crisis, and in many instances the term may be anachronistically or impressionistically employed in the traditions.

Insofar as the prophets are described at work within religious institutions, they most frequently perform the following functions: inciting to or proclaiming victory in Israel's wars, admonishing and chiding sin and announcing judgment on particular sinners, interceding to avert the communal consequences of sinful acts, and giving counsel when approached by individuals for disclosure of the future or for healing.

These functions can be recognized as falling into at least two major roles within the cult: (a) the role of liturgist, in which the prophet at stated points in the public ceremonies declaimed victory or prosperity, denounced sinners, and interceded with God to avert communal suffering due to sin and evil; (b) the role of consultative specialist, in which the prophet was approached by individuals, from kings to commoners, to provide oracular revelations of future events, to help solve practical problems, to heal sickness and otherwise avert bad fortune. This way of relating clusters of functions to certain cultic roles is admittedly an ideal construct for which there is no single adequate profile in the biblical texts. The construction is synthetically arrived at by critically culling many texts and searching for common elements. Nevertheless, it appears to be a reasonable hypothesis and it will assist us in considering more exactly whether and how a radicalized cult prophet might continue to function in a cult role.

6. We may refine our inquiry a little more exactly if we propose that the radicalized prophet would have found it easier to continue to function as a consultative specialist than as a liturgist.

As liturgist the prophet declaimed fixed pieces or, at any rate, had limited choices in the themes and speech forms he could employ while still being faithful to his charge within the institution. Departures from the prescribed themes of assurance and welfare for the social whole, permitting judgment only on particular sinners, would have drawn immediate notice and objection. Opportunity for the prophet to maneuver on middle ground where he might mitigate the most offensive aspects of his liturgical radicalism could have been rapidly foreclosed.

As consultative specialist, however, the prophet had more freedom. The inquirer brought an immediate question or problem for prophetic insight or solution. The prophet had a range of possible responses. There was always the chance that the inquirer was already either radicalized or susceptible to radicalization so that the prophet's word to him could be "subversive" of the usual words dispensed in such a situation. Also, the prophet as consultative specialist was not so instantly open to public scrutiny of his words. In short, he had some room in which to maneuver so that his routine function could be given radical content without necessarily raising hackles every time he spoke.

7. Significant continuity in role functions between cultic prophets and non-cultic prophets is apparent. Prophets who withdrew or were expelled from cultic service continued to work with the same skills and functions, the difference being that they were no longer attached to shrines or assigned duties by the official religious leadership. As liturgists they preached their radical messages in the streets wherever they could find an audience that would listen, and as consultative specialists they gave their private oracles to anyone who came to them. Short of imprisoning or killing these radical prophets, they could range at large, now without cult sponsorship—doing what they had always done. While openly severed from the official religious institutions, they were joined in a love-hate relationship to those institutions, in fierce competition with their prophetic counterparts in the cult.

8. Once severed from their cultic roles, were not the radical prophets doomed to ineffectiveness and irrelevance? Decisive in our answer to this question is the way in which prophetic radicalization operated ideologically within society. Their emphatic criticism of exist-

ing institutions was grounded in a normative conception of those institutions as intentional instruments of the community's proper end under the sovereignty of Yahweh. In this fundamental respect they shared the very communal self-understanding of the cult they criticized, and at the same time they participated in a broad consensus of opinion among a majority of Israelites. Israel was answerable to Yahweh and had recognized obligations to fulfill. The issue at stake was the content of the obligations and the adequacy of their discharge in the present.

The ideological relevance of the radical prophet was in his commitment to clarify for the people the true meaning of their existence under Yahweh. Because of the shared initial religious premise, which was also a social premise, the prophetic iconoclasm could not be dismissed without pause as psychic or social deviation or temperamental idiosyncrasy. It had to be faced, accepted or rebutted, in terms of common Israelite traditions and values. In what way does Yahweh exist for Israel? In what way does Israel exist for Yahweh? How do the institutions of communal life at all levels, cult included, implement or obstruct the ends of the community under Yahweh? The prophetic radicalization of those questions casts familiar terms and values in a new light, effecting an ironic reversal of viewpoint in which communal assurance gave way to communal self-criticism. As a result, even when cut off from institutional roles, prophets could find a hearing in the community in proportion as their fellow Israelites also became critical of the institutions whose powerful effects upon their lives could not be escaped. The "freedom" of the radical prophet to speak out was a stand-in for the "freedom" that most Israelites did not have, and for this he might be envied, resented, admired or followed—but not disregarded.

One further ideological element in Israel gave support to noninstitutional prophecy. From earliest times, Israel had the belief that God was its immediate sovereign and that all human leaders were instruments of deity. God could raise up leaders, sometimes through existing offices, but often ad hoc to meet new situations. This conception lay behind the periodic rise of military "judges" and of earlier generations of prophets. Even though the contemporary institutions might expel prophets, traditional thinking in Israel was saturated with the background memory of how God works sometimes in defiance of leaders supposedly representing him. While it certainly would require much empirical evidence and considerable courage to move an eighth-century Israelite to see Amos or Hosea as God's voice in his era, in the face of the authoritative claims of kings and priests, this traditional belief in Yahweh's veto power over Israel's leaders was a potent facilitator of receptiveness to the radical prophetic message. Given this ideological saturation of public life in Israel, in moving out of the sanctuaries and into the streets, radical prophets were contributing to a counter-culture which claimed to be the proper embodiment of Israelite faithfulness to Yahweh.

9. The above attempt to establish some bench marks for exploring the relationship between cult prophecy and radical prophecy is no more than a sketch of formal possibilities in which the full range of historical data about prophecy has not been exhaustively employed. In particular, certain aspects of the problem have not been touched, e.g., whether one of the prophetic functions in the cult was to proclaim apodictic law as covenant terms, namely, the prophets as "law-speakers" or "covenant-mediators"; whether so-called "court prophets" such as Nathan were a distinct group or simply particular cult prophets singled out by the king as close advisors; whether prophets operative in the cult could produce messages on their own initiative rather than wait to be consulted; and whether there are any indications that radical prophets went beyond forming provisional microcosmic embodiments of the true Israel to try to build counter-institutions.

The pursuit of these and other issues will enrich and complicate the sketch so far offered. Yet they do not appear to overturn the main outlines of our characterization of prophetic options in Israel's institutional framework. The primary challenge to further progress is how to reduce the diverse and often fragmentary data, especially concerning a profile of prophetic "office(s)," to comprehensible models which will do justice to the variegated and sprawling historical phenomenon of Israelite prophecy. An inescapable aspect of this grappling with the data will be a close examination of each prophet, without constricting prejudgments of what his message, speech forms and social location are "supposed" to be according to previous assumptions that cult prophecy and radical prophecy, like oil and water, never mixed.

CHAPTER 9

The Plot Structure of Marvel or Problem Resolution Stories in the Elijah-Elisha Narratives and Some Musings on Sitz im Leben

ABSTRACT

This lecture analyzes prophetic marvel stories in 1 and 2 Kings according to their function-components in keeping with V. Propp's method for analyzing the plots in folklore. On the basis of the analysis, eighteen marvel stories are classified according to whether they combine instrumental instructions and instrumental actions in eliciting the marvel, or exhibit only one or the other of those two function-components. The full form is found to convey "restoration" marvels, while the abbreviated or fractured forms relate "innovative" marvels. The core features of marvel stories, together with their optional elements, suggest a process of generating stories that was relatively free and inventive, both at the level of the individual story and at the level of the compilation and redaction of stories. The plot structure analysis tends to corroborate the hypothesis that it was circles of Elijah's and Elisha's followers who told these marvel stories to memorialize the wonderful power of Yahweh at work through the prophets. Collaterally, there are indications, especially in 2 Kgs 8:4–6, where we meet a marvel story within a marvel story, that this genre sometimes functioned as testimony in advocacy hearings before authorities to secure the socioeconomic entitlements of Israelites who had been unjustly treated. This accords with other evidence that material and ideological support was exchanged between the prophetic communities and sectors of the agrarian populace in mid-eighth century northern Israel.

One way of discerning narrative patterns in particular biblical literary genres is to note the constant and variable function-components in the structuring of plot. In attempting to discern the narrative structure of a series of marvel stories in 1 and 2 Kings, I shall employ a modified version of Vladimir Propp's scheme for analyzing the linear sequence of elements in folkloristic texts (1968: esp. 19–24). In adopting Propp's analytic method as a heuristic device, I make no attempt to evaluate his theories about folklore, nor do I enter into an assessment of how the biblical stories compare with extrabiblical folklore.

The Seven Function-Components of the Marvel Story

1. *Specification of the Actors* (coded A in my analysis). The dramatis personae are introduced, sometimes with time and place details.

2. *Introduction of the Problem* (coded B). The problem or complication requiring resolution is introduced.

3. *Instrumental Instruction* (coded C). One or more instructions are given which sets in motion a line of action leading toward resolution of the problem.

4. *Execution of the Instruction* (coded D). The instructions are carried out, sometimes with ineffectual results.

5. *Instrumental Action* (coded E). An action is performed which contributes instrumentally to resolution of the problem.

6. *Culminating Statement* (coded F). A statement is made which culminates the instrumental instruction and/or the instrumental action.

7. *Marvelous Resolution* (coded G). The problem presented is marvelously resolved.

Subtypes of Marvel Stories According to Function-Components

In what follows I indicate in code the sequences of function-components in the Elijah-Elisha marvel stories, grouping them into the three subtypes that emerge from the analysis. Occasional use of an asterisk (*) is explained below under "General Observations," #6.

I. *Marvel Stories Containing Instrumental Instruction/Execution of Instruction (C/D) and Instrumental Action (E):*

1. 2 Kgs 2:19–22 (purification of water): A + B + C + D + E + F + G.
2. 2 Kgs 4:38–41 (purification of stew): A + B + C + D* + E + F + G.
3. 1 Kgs 17:17–24 (raising of a widow's son): A + B + C + D* + E + G + F.
4. 2 Kgs 4:18–37 (raising of a woman's son): A + B + C + D + E + G + F.
5. 2 Kgs 6:1–7 (retrieval of axhead from river): A + B + C + D + E + G + F.

6. 2 Kgs 1:1–17 (king dies of injuries and his troops are killed by lightning): $A + B + C + D + F_1 + E + F_2 + G$

II. *Marvel Stories Containing Only Instrumental Instruction (C) and Execution of Instruction (D):*

7. 1 Kgs 17:2–7 (prophet fed by ravens [bedouin?] and drinks from brook during drought): $A + B^* + C + D + G$.
8. 2 Kgs 3:4–17, 20 (water supplied for army on campaign): $A + B + C + D + F + G$.
9. 2 Kgs 4:8–17 (barren woman is granted a son): $A + B + C + D + F + G$.
10. 2 Kgs 4:1–7 (widow's children saved from debt slavery): $A + B + C + D + G_1 + F + G_2^*$.
11. 1 Kgs 17:8–16 (replenished meal and oil): $A + B + C + F + D + G$.
12. 2 Kgs 4:42–44 (meager food feeds many): $A + B + C + F + D + G$.
13. 2 Kgs 5 (a leper is healed by bathing): $A + B + F + C + D + G$.
14. 2 Kgs 13:14–19, 25b (delivery of Israel from domination by Damascus): $A + B^* + C_1 + D_1 + F_1 + C_2 + D_2 + F_2 + G$.
15. 1 Kgs 18:17–46 (rain comes to break drought): $A + B + C_1 + F_1 + D_1 + C_2 + D_2 + F_2 + G_1 + G_2$.

III. *Marvel Stories Containing Only Instrumental Action (E):*

16. 2 Kgs 2:23–25 (jeering boys killed by bears): $A + B + E + G$.
17. 2 Kgs 13:20–21 (a prophet's bones raise a corpse): $A + B + E + G$.
18. 2 Kgs 8:1–6 (woman's land rights restored): $A + B + G_1 + E + G_2^*$.

General Observations

1. The indispensable function-components in all the marvel stories are $A + B + G$, together with at least one additional component that moves the action from the problem stated in B to its resolution given in G.

2. The fullest form of the marvel story employs both instrumental instruction/execution of instruction (C/D) *and* instrumental action (E) to resolve the stated problem (six examples under subtype I). More frequently, the problem is resolved only by instrumental instruction/execution of instruction (nine examples under subtype II), and less often solely by instrumental action (three examples under subtype III).

3. The relative simplicity of the marvel story plot secures a fairly regular sequence in its function-components. The one component that

tends to "float" is the culminating statement (F), which is accounted for by the variations in its content, since the culminating statement sometimes announces or interprets the resolution in advance and sometimes punctuates the resolution after it has occurred by means of exclamation or further command. The appearance of a problem resolution in the middle of story #18 is a special case to be discussed below.

4. Function-components sometimes appear twice in a story to mark discrete events or provide emphasis. These instances are marked in the above analysis by the numerals 1 or 2 attached to the function symbol (e.g., C_1, C_2). The repetitions of the problem resolution component (G_1 and G_2) in stories #10, #15, and #18 are of particular interest since they illustrate the convolutions of form that can result when the genre structure is stretched. In story #15, G_1 refers to the fire from heaven that consumes the offering to Yahweh and G_2 refers to the coming of torrential rains that break the drought. In this instance, G_1 can be construed as one of the instrumental actions that makes G_2, the climax of the story, possible. Story #10 is very similar, where G_1 is the greatly expanded supply of oil that makes possible G_2, the payment of debts to spare the children from slavery. The difference is that the sale of the oil and payment of debts appear as a command of the prophet whose fulfillment is presupposed but not stated. In story #18, G_1 is highly anomalous, since it is a reference to a problem resolution from one story cited within a second story (to be further discussed below).

5. Under each of the subtypes, I have arranged the marvel stories from the simplest and most regular examples to the more complex and "disordered" specimens. Thus, the examples that occur toward the end of each list of subtypes are "boundary" cases that strain the basic marvel structure in various ways. My reasons for retaining these as instances of the marvel story genre are discussed below.

6. In a few cases, the marvel stories are so compact and terse that strictly speaking a particular function-component is not stated, but the unfolding of the story presupposes that the function has occurred "off stage" as it were. These ellipses are marked by an asterisk in the analysis above (e.g., B*, D*).

Reflections on the Marvel Stories as Analyzed

1. The contention that there is such a genre as a "miracle story" or "wonder story" has been criticized as inadmissible because the determination of what constitutes a miracle is said to be a matter of content or subject matter, and thus necessitating a subjective judgment of the inter-

preter not necessarily shared by the biblical narrator. The discussion over content easily falls into a thicket of debate about what is and what is not a miracle, according to criteria that may be extraneous to the stories.

In my judgment, the above analysis substantiates the existence of a marvel story genre based, not upon content subject to arbitrary assessment, but upon a functional progression in the story line from problem to resolution. The collocation of function-components stamps such a story as formally distinguishable from other stories.

Without a doubt the resolution of the problem in each marvel narrative is conceived by the narrator as *extraordinary*, as a denouement that came about against heavy odds and that could not have been predicted. But the point is that our identification of this extraordinary event is not derived from extrinsic criteria, i.e., what we take to be extraordinary, but what the storytellers judged to be unusual as specified by the actual structuring of the plot into a determinate series of function-components which highlight the unexpected and remarkable outcome. To minimize the intrusion of extrabiblical theological and philosophical notions of miracle into the stories, I prefer to call them "marvel stories" in preference to the label "miracle stories." We might go a step farther and designate them "Problem Resolution Stories," or even stories about "Resolution of Problems by Spectacular Means."

I grant that some of the more loosely structured examples, where other modes of narration have entered in to complicate and partially obscure the genre, may leave us in doubt about the formal criteria for demonstrating a marvel. For example, is the king's restoration of the woman's land a marvel (#18)? Is Joash's three-fold defeat of Damascus a marvel (#14)? While there are atypical features in both of these stories, it appears to me that the function-component criteria are sufficiently present to confirm that the culminating events described are conceived under the mode of "marvelous resolution of problems."

2. The question naturally arises why an apparently fuller form of the marvel story in which instrumental instruction and instrumental action occur is not more frequently represented. My analysis has identified six fully formed examples, while the remaining twelve are abbreviated, nine with instrumental instruction alone and three with instrumental action alone.

I regard the marvel story with combined instrumental instruction and instrumental action as the prototype, the full form of the genre, for the reason that all five instances are so internally coherent. In every case the instrumental instruction calls for something to be done or some object to be brought that sets the stage for the prophet to enact a marvel.

Therefore, I am strongly inclined to view the specimens with fewer function-components as abbreviations or truncations of the fuller form, rather than to conceive of the fuller form as a secondary combination of two independently developed story types. There is, however, a basic difference between the instrumental instruction subtype and the instrumental action subtype which we must now explicate.

The reasons for the elimination of the instrumental instruction from three of the marvel stories are understandable. With respect to #16, the account is a virtual "negative marvel story," in that it does not accomplish a beneficent resolution of the problem presented by the specified actors but a destructive, death-dealing resolution instead. It is true that story #6, the other "negative marvel story" among our examples, does include instrumental instruction, but the instruction is not addressed to the chief protagonist, as in other marvel stories, but to the king's messengers in the form of a rebuke and announcement of judgment to be delivered to the king. In the usual marvel story there is a trusting and receptive, often expectant, person or persons to whom instructions can be given that will contribute directly to the resolution. To the contrary, the boys who jeer the prophet and the king who faithlessly seeks Baal-zebul for healing are not in a position to execute prophetic instructions.

In the case of #17, the marvel element is so vastly heightened that the mere bones of a prophet fortuitously raise a dead man to life. The prophet is deceased so he cannot give instructions. The funeral party has no awareness of an impending marvel and thus has nothing to say, nor indeed anyone to whom to say it, since the one who will unwittingly experience the marvel is himself a dead man.

As for #18, although it reports a restoration marvel, the appeal of the woman to the king for restoration of her land has taken the place of instrumental instruction. The novel situation of the judicial hearing before the king has produced other anomalies in this marvel story. In an unexpected twist, the instrumental act of the king in appointing an official to expedite the restoration of the woman's land incorporates a command to the official which amounts to an instrumental instruction to carry out the marvelous resolution. We observe also that the actual resolution is not reported, although it is obviously taken for granted.

The reason for the elimination of the instrumental action in a majority of the examples is not so obvious at first glance. There is, however, an important clue in the fact that all specimens of the full marvel story, except for the idiosyncratic "negative marvel story" in #6, are "restoration marvels," i.e., they restore the status quo ante: water (#l) and food (#2) are purified, an axhead is recovered (#5), the dead live again (#3–4). By contrast, among the examples of the abbreviated story without instrumental action, only #13 and #14 appear to me to be restoration marvels (to be treated below). All the others are what might be called "innovative marvels" or "evocative marvels" in that they bring a new situation into being either by providing what is not present (food and drink for a prophet in #7, water for a thirsty army in #8, a son for a barren woman in #9, reprieve for children from debt slavery in #10, and rain after drought in #15), or by indefinitely extending or expanding something that is present but in insufficient quantity (oil in #10, oil and meal in #11, bread and grain in #12). Interestingly, #10 combines the two types of innovation, G_1 being a marvelous expansion of oil supplies and G_2^* being the creation of a new economic status of freedom from debt.

In the innovation marvels of the first sort, where an absence must be corrected by a virtual *creatio ex nihilo*, it is understandable that an instrumental act by the prophet is not included. He gives appropriate instructions that set up the situation in which God acts directly rather than through human agency. Such an explanation seems adequate for marvels which "start from scratch" because the fully absent must be brought into being. In these instances it may be said that the prophet has nothing to act upon.

But in innovative marvels of the second kind, where it is a matter of overcoming an insufficiency rather than supplying what is absent, we may well ask why the prophet does not perform an instrumental action. As I view it, the dynamics of these stories of multiplication or expansion of materials already present are such that a specific instrumental action is unnecessary on the prophet's part. The requisite trigger for the marvel in these "insufficiency stories" is that the person suffering the lack has to treat the meager food supply available as though it were ample. The instrumental instruction is to begin eating it or to begin storing it in vessels. The execution of the instruction becomes the medium for the marvel to occur as a "natural" extension of the ordinary line of action. Doubtless there is also present in this kind of story a strong faith element, a believing in the absurd and audacious word of the prophet that there is more present than meets the eye.

Story #18 is a very particular reshaping of the marvel story genre because, while the prophet's servant sets up the situation in which the woman is given a hearing before the king, he does not transgress upon the legal and administrative powers of the king either by instrumental instruction or instrumental action. The king must authorize restitution for the woman and, when the king appoints an official to deal with her appeal, the instrumental action is virtually collapsed into the marvelous resolution which becomes such a foregone conclusion that it need not be reported but can simply be assumed to have transpired. I see this text as a purposeful refraction of the marvel story genre that achieves much of its dramatic effect by its overt linkage to the preceding marvel stories involving this same woman of Shunem (#4 and #9).

Story #13 is a rhetorically inflated marvel story, the longest of all our specimens, in which a major intent of the telling is to underscore Yahweh's power through his prophet in a most flagrant and didactic manner. Elisha addresses Naaman only through a messenger and he insists that Naaman be cured by the commonplace but demeaning act of washing in the Jordan River. Naaman feels he is entitled to a face-to-face instrumental action by the prophet, but the story treats this "remote control" healing as exceptional in Israel. The aim of Naaman's offhanded and unceremonious healing is to teach him a lesson in humility. The crucial point is that Naaman reluctantly follows instructions he finds to be ignominious and insulting from his perspective as a high official from Damascus. The aim of this extreme humiliation is to teach him the vast power of Yahweh to heal, even "at the flick of a finger," a lesson so well learned by Naaman that he converts to Yahwism. It is also noteworthy that Gehazi, Elisha's servant, is portrayed as unfavorably in this story as he is favorably pictured in #18.

Story #14 has the character of a "restoration marvel," since it relates how king Joash was empowered to recover Israelite territory lost to Damascus. But if we are to view it formally as a restoration, the scope of the restoration is far beyond anything covered in the other restoration stories. In those cases, the prophet dealt with a single spring, a single pot of stew, a single axhead, a single dead youth, etc. Here the restoration involves large regions of Israel to be regained by military conquest. The contributory symbolic actions are provided for by instructions which the prophet gives to the king. The king shoots an arrow and strikes the ground with arrows as commanded. There is nothing for the prophet to do; the king, as commander in chief of the army, performs the symbolic acts. Of course there is the further factor that the events take place while the prophet is on his deathbed and this too may have discouraged the narrator from assigning an instrumental action to the prophet.

3. Recent studies of narrative forms (e.g., Rofé, 1970; Wilcoxen, 1974) have identified basic plots in the storyteller's repertory which may be elaborated in various ways in the course of telling and retelling stories. The above analysis shows the marvel story to be one instance of such a basic plot structure which is capable of multiple adaptations, both in its formal arrangement and in its content. Larger sequences are built up by joining as many as three marvel stories around a single motif or actor (e.g., in 1 Kgs 17:2–24 the connecting thread is the famine motif

and in 2 Kgs 4:8–37; 8:1–6 the common denominator is the person of the woman of Shunem).

By observing the several permutations in the arrangement of the function-components, in the terseness or expansiveness of particular functions, and in the openness of the genre to features from other narrative modes, we observe that the basic marvel story plot, simple enough in its outline, was malleable, even to the point of splintering and dissipating as it entered into concourse with other narrative forms.

We have already noted some of these artful modifications of the marvel story genre, such as #13 where the healing of the leper is used as a platform to project two motifs which have nothing to do with the marvel story as such: the conversion of an aristocratic foreigner benefitted by the marvel, and the mendacity and greed of a prophet's servant. In story #7, Yahweh replaces the prophet as the marvel worker. Likewise in story #15, probably the most "distorted" of all our examples, Yahweh is the marvel worker since strictly speaking there is no instrumental action that brings the rain, but by challenging and defeating Baal on Mt. Carmel the prophet sets the stage for Yahweh to send the rain as he pleases. In story #8, the prophet is loath to facilitate any marvel for the king of Israel but finally does so for the sake of the king of Judah who is a partner in the military campaign against Edom, and in stories #14 and 18, the king as commander in chief and supreme judicial officer, respectively, takes the role of the executor of the marvel. In all these instances it is evident that political and social factors have entered in to modify and stretch the marvel story genre. But that all these examples remain within the orbit of the marvel story genre is clear when we compare them with stories such as 1 Kings 20 and 2 Kgs 9:1–13 in which prophets are intimately involved in military and political affairs, but without recourse to marvels. While Yahwistic jargon is used in the latter narratives, with "holy war" as a controlling ethos of the actions, the role of the prophet is to facilitate "normal" military and political processes rather than to intervene with extraordinary resolutions.

4. It does not appear that the analysis of function-components in the marvel stories reveals anything certain about their assignment to oral or written stages. Gunkel's claim about a tendency to move from shorter and formally purer to longer and formally more disintegrated specimens of a genre may well be true in some circumstances and might explain some features of the stories we have examined. It is doubtful, however, that such a tendency is the whole truth. There is no sustained correlation between purity of form and story length in these marvel stories. Some of the formally skewed stories are as brief as some of the complete specimens, and a number of the longest stories retain most of

the function-components. There are two difficulties with Gunkel's apparently logical dictum: (1) if storytellers worked with basic plots from which they spun particular stories, their freedom to vary length and tighten or loosen the form may not have been as rule-governed as often assumed; and (2) once we accept that the stories have been recast editorially when incorporated in larger books, in our case Kings, nothing precludes that the writer/editor may have shortened some longer stories in his sources and lengthened some shorter ones, adhering at times closely to a conventional marvel form and departing from it at other times according to the larger interests of his overall narrative.

Consequently, I am inclined to think that the relative tautness, fullness, or integrity of genre vs. looseness, abbreviation and dissipation of form is less a matter of lapsed time or a shift from oral to written medium than it is a matter of function: namely, the precise concerns that the writer/editor of the stories as they now stand wanted to express in including them. As one instance of this factor, the full form of the marvel story fits the "restoration marvel" which prophets apparently performed in their shaman role. The abbreviated and fractured forms, whatever their length, fit the "innovative marvel" and the various contexts in which the prophet was not simply dealing face to face with a single suppliant's request that could be dealt with by itself but in which a larger world of political, social, and religious actors was involved. And it is equally likely that a similar flexibility in use of the marvel story genre was operative in the oral stage of their development.

Musings on the *Sitz im Leben* of Prophetic Marvel Stories

Assuming that these stories were not simply fabricated by the Deuteronomistic Historian, but arose in their main outlines during the careers of Elijah and Elisha, there are a few indications of *Sitz im Leben* within the stories themselves. Von Rad (vol. 2: 14–32) and Steck (146–47) suggest, in the light of texts such as 2 Kgs 4:38 and 6:1, that the prophetic conventicles around Elisha were the probable setting for the initial production and preservation of Elijah stories. That similar genres and motifs link the Elijah and Elisha stories implies that followers of Elisha made similar collections of stories about him. We could hypothesize that a major reason for telling these stories was to memorialize the wonderful power of these prophets in the service of Yahweh, and that the immediate audience was the company of prophetic followers of the master. At the same time, the interaction between prophets and the array of persons who play roles in the marvel stories implies that there would have been a wider audience for these stories among those sympathetic to the prophets. According to several of the stories, the prophets in fact depended in considerable measure on material and moral support from lay Israelites.

A more precise clue to the possible settings and uses of these stories appears in 2 Kgs 8:4–6 where the telling of one marvel story (#4) is part of the plot in another marvel story (#18):

> Now the king was talking with Gehazi the servant of the man of God, saying, "Tell me all the great things that Elisha did." And while he was telling the king how Elisha had restored the dead to life, behold, the woman whose son he had restored to life appealed to the king for her house and her land. And Gehazi said, "My lord, O king, here is the woman, and here is her son whom Elisha restored to life." And when the king questioned the woman, she told him the same thing. So the king appointed an official for her, saying, "Restore all that was hers, together with all the produce of the fields from the day that she left the land until now."

Interestingly, the context for telling the marvel of the raising of the woman's son is an advocacy hearing concerning the woman's legal right to her house and lands which, during her seven years' absence from the country, had been taken over by another (confiscated by the crown?). The teller of the raising of the woman's son is a prophet disciple who appears as a witness or ombudsman to support the woman in her cause. The marvel story thus related serves to legitimate and reinforce the woman's socioeconomic rights. The logic for telling a marvel story within a marvel story appears to be this: if it can be shown that Yahweh has intervened spectacularly on behalf of someone through the person of his prophet, such an intervention constitutes collateral support for that person's just claims on a later occasion.

We must of course be cautious both about the veracity of the socioreligious information preserved in the Deuteronomistic History and about drawing generalizations concerning other marvel stories based on this one instance. But even if the interlocking of stories in the woman of Shunem series is secondary, and thus the creation of a collector of the stories, there is no good reason to doubt that the literary device chosen reflected a known practice of telling marvel stories orally in a setting where legal claims were presented and argued. While the king's request, "Tell me all the great things that Elisha did," has an impromptu innocence about it that is characteristic of the marvel genre, the fact that the royal request "happens" to coincide with the entrance of the woman into the king's presence shows otherwise. It is reasonable to infer from this text that, in the course of his hearing grievances and legal claims from subjects, the king was accustomed to entertaining stories of what prophets had done on behalf of petitioners. Recitation of marvel stories for the purpose of legitimating the rights of needy and aggrieved folk would also fit well with the provision of ample oil for a prophet's widow that enabled her to settle her debt (#10).

To note that one marvel story was used on one occasion as legitimation for threatened or deprived socioeconomic rights is of course not to show that all marvel stories were so used or that such was the only use of the marvel story genre. We have already alluded to the likelihood that the primary locus for the assembling and telling of these stories was the prophetic conventicles presided over by Elisha and probably continuing to exist after his death. A closer examination enables us to establish a link between the origin of the stories in the prophetic communities and their use on occasion to give support to socioeconomic entitlements.

More than one commentator (e.g., Jepsen: 58–83, 143–90; von Rad, vol. 2: 14–32) has viewed the Elisha prophetic groups as religious formations which stood at the lower fringe of society, perceivable as socioeconomic refuge points (possibly connected with asylum at sanctuaries?). Here the impoverished members of society, now less protected by a weakened tribal organization, found a rallying point, a means of physical sustenance, and a bracing ideological elixir. Within this support network, spearheaded by prophetic groups, the socially needy could also find advocacy for their claims insofar as they could be pressed upon the judiciary and the royal court.

Moreover, we note that among the circles of admirers and supporters of the prophets were families with properties still intact who helped to sustain the prophetic communities (note the man who brings them provisions, 2 Kgs 4:42). Communication between the prophets and the royal court, as well as frequent prophetic access to government officials, is stated in a number of the stories. This relationship between prophets and state officials, while always tenuous and at times openly hostile, provided a channel for the prophetic communities to publicize and advocate the customary socioeconomic rights that the mainstream institutions of Israel were infringing. What these socially marginal prophetic groups lacked in immediate political clout they made up for in grassroots support and in ideological sharpness by developing a fund of stories that, in addition to their venue within the prophetic circles, supported the rights of the socially weak and the economically impoverished—stories that showed what great things Yahweh had done for them through his prophet.

The Rise of the Israelite Monarchy—
A Sociological Perspective

ABSTRACT

At the outset of an SBL program unit on Sociology of the Monarchy, the following remarks were made as part of a panel presentation intended to propose directions and issues to be pursued in a sociological study of monarchic Israel. The focus of my remarks was on the transition from tribes to state, no longer to be conceived as an instantaneous and sweeping transformation of Israel but as an incremental development. Material and social conditions in tribal Israel that were conducive to political centralization are identified, a slow and uneven introduction of the full panoply of state institutions is argued, and a protracted process of conflict and accommodation between central government and tribal society is proposed. Areas for future research are outlined, including the sources of state revenue and methods for circumventing customary land tenure. It is suggested that a necessary long-range structural and conflictual view of monarchic-tribal relations will profit from comparative sociological data.

Political analysis of the monarchy has generally operated with a number of presuppositions that cry out for reexamination. Among the assumptions with widest currency are the following: that the impetus to kingship was largely or entirely due to outside forces, that the transition from tribal order to statist order was achieved in a single step, that the tribal order quickly disintegrated in the face of the state apparatus, and that the polarity of charismatic vs. dynastic leadership (the former term not very sociologically delineated) adequately frames the dynamics of the transition to statehood.

As we launch our consultation on the Sociology of the Monarchy, I propose to make a start toward rethinking our models of transition to monarchy by raising three questions.

1. *What internal as well as external forces contributed
    to the adoption of the monarchic option in early Israel?*

Customarily the superior political and military organization of the
Philistines is credited as the primary factor in Israel's move to monarchy. I see no reason to doubt that this was the main external pressure at
work, although there remain many questions about Philistine social
organization and exactly how the Philistines were related to their Egyptian political predecessors in Canaan and to the Canaanites whom they
came to dominate over large sectors of the land. On the other hand,
social science alerts us to the reality that major institutional change is
prepared by internal as well as external factors and that, unless a society
is conquered outright and institutional changes crudely imposed, the
internal factors prove crucial in shaping what changes will occur and
how they are brought about.

What then were the internal developments in the tribal organization
of Israel that contributed to the emergence of monarchy? The aim of the
tribal institutions to achieve and maintain an approximate social equality among the landed families of Israel was not easily realized. Elitist
practices and habits of mind had to be challenged and held in check. It is
appropriate, therefore, to look for indicators that the rise of the state in
Israel was facilitated by survivals and by fresh outcroppings of elitism
that welcomed monarchy as a way to strengthen and legitimate privilege among those with material and social advantage under the tribal
system.

Potential evidence for sketching the manifestations of premonarchic
elitism may be seen at a number of points in the biblical record. Gideon
is offered the kingship (Judg 8:22–23) and his son Abimelech attempts to
establish a dual petty kingdom based on Shechem, a Canaanite city at
peace with Israel, and involving at least his own tribe of Manasseh
(Judges 9). Nabal of Judah is pictured as a man of wealth in flocks and,
judging by his wife's gifts to David, probably of agricultural holdings as
well (1 Sam 25:2–3, 8). The same Nabal, in reacting to David's
"protection racket," speaks derisively of many servants who have lately
broken away from their masters (1 Sam 25:10), and this comment accords with the report that among the four hundred distressed and dis-
contented men who gathered to David at the Cave of Adullam were
those in debt (1 Sam 22:1–2). This calls our attention to indications that a
fair number of premonarchic persons are said to have had "servants/
slaves." The challenge to understanding such allusions lies in the ambiguity of the Hebrew term ʿăbādîm, which appears to embrace a range of
statuses: slaves by purchase, debtors pledged to working off their obli-

gations, persons without family or kinship backing who attach themselves to and work for powerful households, as well as wage servants.

Eli's sons are pictured as grossly abusive of priestly privileges (1 Sam 2:12–17), and Samuel's sons are said to have taken bribes and perverted justice (1 Sam 8:1–3), although Samuel himself offers an oath of denial of any such anti-social behavior on his part (1 Sam 12:1–5). The monopolization of leadership positions by some families would tend to shield such abuses from scrutiny and censure.

It is probable, given the discrepancy in material resources from subregion to subregion within Israel, that there was an objective basis for certain families and tribes to make a claim to dominant social power based on their greater prosperity and enlarging regional influence. The Joseph tribes and Judah, owing to a combination of fertile land and relative insulation from political and military pressure, appear to have advanced significantly beyond the productive levels achieved by tribes in Galilee and Transjordan. Even before Saul and David contended for state power, the Josephite and Judahite power bases that supported them were doubtless solidifying, their rivalry heightened by the rapid rise of Judah following its relatively late entrance into the Israelite confederation. It is likely that the constituencies of Saul and David were privileged families who saw the struggle for dynastic control over the state apparatus as a way to consolidate and improve their standings in Israel far more assuredly than under the tribal system with its decentralization of power. With the incursion of the Philistines into the Israelite heartland, the security of all the powerful families, north and south, was threatened. One of the advantages enjoyed by David lay in his cunning and masterful manipulation of the Philistines while he was in exile. His adroitness in this matter eventually commended him, even to those who had previously supported Saul, as the leader who could best protect their interests against the Philistine menace.

2. *How rapid and even in development was the transition from tribal to monarchic social organization in early Israel?*

The usual historiographic strategy is to look for some decisive point in the reign of David when the Rubicon of full statehood was crossed, complicated of course by the difficulty that we have a better notion of some of the accomplishments of Saul, David, and Solomon than we have of the chronology of their reigns, and thus of the trajectories of growth for the various state institutions and policies.

Because our information about the rise of monarchy is preserved in a Deuteronomistic framework that reads intentions and meanings into the accounts from the vantage of centuries of later experience with kings, a focused effort is required to refine our methodology of study by considering whether various elements that went into the state structure in Israel may have been introduced experimentally, even accidentally, and developed unevenly. Rather than to conceive of a "leap" into monarchy, we might more accurately imagine state institutions as "creeping up" on Israel by increments. Also to be considered is whether some measures tried for a time later fell into disuse or were deliberately sloughed off because of their ineffectuality or because their renunciation was the necessary price to insure the continued loyalties of the general populace or of key social sectors on whom the state depended for support.

Looked at functionally, it appears that an effective state will have existed in Israel when a group of political specialists could command popular resources through a bureaucratic apparatus and were able to perpetuate their control dynastically. Also, the state will have been effectively in position when attempts to abolish it, in contrast to merely changing particular rulers, were suppressed and it was generally accepted that *someone* should be head of a permanent state. In these terms, Buccellatti's (125–30, 195–212) and Ishida's (151–86) stress on the importance of dynastic succession for any functionally significant notion of kingship seems to be well-taken in contrast to Alt's problematic use of a charismatic notion to conceptualize the disorder in the northern kingdom resulting from the inability of any one royal aspirant or social sector to hold the throne commandingly before the rise of Omri (1966a).

Renewed attention needs to be given to the sources of state income. What resources were commandeered through taxation and in military and corvée labor? What revenues were generated in international trade? How were taxes assigned and collected? What was the approximate tax rate and did it vary markedly over time? What effects did tax policies have on agriculture? After Solomon's ill-fated indulgence in corvée labor, how extensively and regularly was conscripted labor employed during the divided kingdom? It is probable that hard data on many of these questions about the state economy are not to be found, so that a comparative study of state economies elsewhere in the ancient Near East and in comparable state structures elsewhere in the world will be necessary to "fill in the blanks" with informed estimates.

It may also be argued that a state is in secure power when its patronage system is able to reward the major social groups in its territory. Samuel's warning about the effects of monarchy seem to allude to such a system (1 Sam 8:10–18). Saul refers to it when he suspects that David is using promises of patronage to win away his followers (1 Sam 22:7–8). David and Solomon made such appointments, at least some of which were accompanied by property holdings. Whether such holdings were regarded as personal possessions of the grantee or were attached to the office and transferred subsequently to each new occupant is another issue to be pursued. At any rate it can be hypothesized that the patronage system strongly benefitted the chief families of Judah and the Joseph tribes. The split of the kingdom into two political entities was precipitated by a combination of peasant opposition to the corvée and resentment by leading northern families that the house of David was not assigning them a large enough share of political patronage.

3. *How successful was the state in replacing or suppressing the tribal order, and did it have to accommodate itself to certain tribal realities that constrained its powers?*

The normal model in biblical studies is to think mainly of monarchy replacing tribalism except for survivals in religious beliefs and nostalgia for past social life. Given the Deuteronomistic and Chronistic penchant for treating kings as the principal actors in national history from Saul onwards, coupled with a corresponding sparseness of information about happenings at the grassroots, the disappearance of tribalism as a factor in monarchic history is tempting to concede. But certainly we have been mistaken in this glib assumption. Social scientific reflection tells us that monarchies are of many sorts and that central governments must adapt to the continuing forms of socioeconomic life among the populace who are always not only subjects of the state but also members of a civil society with its own social practices and values that the state must come to terms with. Many facets of Israel's monarchy can only be properly understood if we posit a process of conflict and accommodation between state and tribe. I have in mind the breakup of the united kingdom, the patterns of state administration, the sociopolitical location and bias of prophetism, religious reform movements, the formulation of foreign policy, land tenure and fiscal policies—to name only a few of the more obvious phenomena of monarchic times.

Probably military organization was the sphere in which monarchy won its quickest and most lasting victory in the shift from a citizen volunteer army to a standing professional army, what Max Weber called "demilitarization of the peasantry" (55–56, 100). Judicial organization, by contrast, seems largely to have remained in tribal hands, with the likely addition of special jurisdictions for government officials and crimes against the state. In the late monarchy, the Deuteronomic Reformation attempted to centralize the judicial system.

The place of state and tribe in economic organization is a tangled question. Currently there is a wide-ranging debate over the peculiar joining of strong central state and backward rural economy represented by the imprecise term "Asiatic Mode of Production." From that debate it may yet be possible to derive some clearer conceptual tools for analyzing the political economy of ancient Israel. For the moment, it appears that the great mass of agricultural production remained in peasant control, with the state introducing manufacturing and mining on a relatively small scale and sponsoring or closely regulating trade as an aspect of its fiscal policy. It is obvious, however, that by means of taxation the state could transfer varying amounts of the agricultural surplus to its coffers and redirect it into the hands of the leading social groups supporting the monarchy.

What is not so clear is how the notions and practices of land tenure were affected by monarchy. As far as we know, tenure in land was formally held by extended families and was recognized de jure under the monarchy, i.e, we know of no formal repeal of the long-standing tribal conventions of land tenure. However, it is evident that the integrity of the land holdings and consequent economic security of families were seriously breached by one or another circumvention of the traditional barriers to amassing wealth at the expense of weaker members of society. Whatever the legal niceties, commercialization of property with attendant right of transfer for a price introduced debt procedures that seem not to have been prevented by the courts, although perhaps legal fictions were employed to give the appearance that traditional procedures were being honored. If royal decrees ever did confer legality upon the commercialization of property, we are uninformed of it, although it should not be forgotten that we do not possess any specifically royal law in the biblical text.

At any rate, given the moral condemnation of prophets and Deuteronomists, expressed somewhat randomly and episodically toward state incursion into the tribal economy, it is easy to assume that this trend toward commercialization of property was extensive and irreversible. Nonetheless, the telling fact that tribal notions of land tenure served as the basis for rural resistance to commercialization of property down to the very end of the monarchy does make it evident that the state and the social strata who prospered by alienating land did not, after all, have so swift and complete a victory. They may have moved warily for long periods of time and probably were unevenly triumphant in different regions of Israel. Mettinger argues that the

accrual of crown land in ancient Israel was achieved mainly by conquests, appropriation of vacant land and purchases from non-Israelites
rather than by the direct expropriation of tribally validated family
holdings (1971: 80–85). Of course we must not exaggerate the significance of such a "benign" government policy, since it still leaves open
various extralegal or quasi-legal devices for the powerful to seize and
break up family holdings. The point is to recognize that the attack of the
powerful on the rural population was not a single catastrophic blow but
took many forms and made uneven progress which prompted strong
rural resistance throughout monarchic times.

So, as we embark on our project to explore the sociology of the
monarchy, we have our work cut out for us. Biblical and archaeological
data for reconstructing the Israelite monarchy in its full socioeconomic
and religiopolitical dimensions are insufficient. It is imperative in the
circumstances that comparative anthropological and historical sociological studies be enlisted to help us form operational models of state societies erected on earlier tribal or retribalized foundations. Among the
potential analogues for this purpose are pre-classical Greece, pre-repub-
lican Rome, African tribal societies, Amerindian societies, and Islamic
states. A recent comparative study in this vein by Marfoe sketches how
the emergence of the Israelite state might be conceptualized and more
adequately analyzed when it is placed within the history of national
states in southern Syria from prehistoric through Islamic times. His conceptualization is oriented around the contrast between steppe kingdoms
and highland kingdoms and is based on his field work in the Biqa Valley
of Lebanon. The temporal and spatial reach of comparative sociological
studies of this sort, together with their conceptual categories, are tools
that have been largely lacking in "straight" political histories of ancient
Israel. It is our task to learn how to hone these tools in order to deepen
and extend our understanding of developments in monarchic Israel
which simply cannot be grasped solely by collecting and classifying
textual and archaeological data.

A Hypothesis about Social Class in Monarchic Israel in the Light of Contemporary Studies of Social Class and Social Stratification

ABSTRACT

A historical material analysis of social class is the most productive method for understanding the dynamics of Israel's society during the monarchy. To provide orientation to the often elusive concept of "social class," a survey of recent social theory about class in contemporary societies leads on to a specification of class in pre-capitalist societies, particularly in the ancient Near East, where the so-called Asiatic Mode of Production (which I have subsequently come to designate as Tributary Mode of Production) was marked by absence of private ownership of land, self-sufficient village communities, and a highly centralized state in a commanding social role. The trajectory from village self-sufficiency to state sovereignty in Israel is traced, and an inventory of social classes in monarchic Israel is proposed. The non-producing classes extracted surplus labor value from producers by a two-fold cycle of taxation and indebtedness. The paper includes a plea for closer attention to the peculiar Israelite dynamics of social class conflict in a relatively weak version of the Asiatic state interfaced with a tenacious tribal infrastructure possessed of strong religious ideology.

Introduction

In this selective survey of social scientific studies of class and stratification, the organization is as follows: (1) a brief sketch of the shape and direction of class studies in contemporary societies; (2) a closer look at class studies of antiquity; (3) problematics in our understanding of Israelite monarchic society raised by the foregoing. The paper moves from reporting selectively to ruminations and conjectures and on to a schematic of mode of production and a hypothesis about social class in monarchic Israel.

Class in Contemporary Societies

I begin with a sketch of current class studies because it is only from the position of having recognized classes in present capitalist societies that the notion of looking for classes in pre-capitalist societies has arisen. Our desire to be as objective as possible in discerning classes in antiquity seems best served by fully recognizing that the way we view class in our own situation deeply affects how we view class in antiquity. This acknowledgment opens up the space to distinguish similarities and differences in class formation in the situation of the observer and in the ancient situation observed.

The three broad routes followed in the study of social class continue to be those charted by Marx, Weber, and Durkheim (Barber; Lipset; Giddens and Held: 3–11), as they are likewise decisive for social scientific studies of the Bible (Mansueto). In the Marxian historical materialist analysis, social class is specified by location in the mode of production, and the conflict of classes is the moving agent in social change. In the Weberian interpretive analysis, social class shares space with strata defined as status groups and parties and the sum of the strata is only one of a number of variables in social change. In the Durkheimian functionalist analysis, social class is an aspect of the division of labor, more or less mirroring the needs of society at any given time, and as such is generally harmonious or homeostatic in its function.

In general, historical materialists prefer the term *class,* while interpretive and functionalist advocates favor *stratum,* but usage is far from invariant, some Marxian studies employing strata synonymously with classes and many non-Marxian studies doing the reverse. The key differences in the approaches are not satisfactorily caught by a single term, since they involve how classes/strata are articulated in the social whole and what determinable effects they have on social change. My own view is that the Marxian framework is comprehensive and incisive enough to make room for valuable elements from the other perspectives while offering more fruitful explanations of social dynamics and social change (Gottwald, 1979:622–42).

In recent years Marxian class studies have been greatly influenced by the approach of Althusser who stresses that the mode of production is the economic aspect of the total social formation which includes political and ideological aspects, each of the zones being "semi-autonomous." Each class has its "place" within these aspects but also a particular "position" that varies at each "conjuncture" of social circumstances. N. Poulantzas views each class, including the ruling class, as sufficiently diverse that sectors of the class may align themselves variously with other classes at particular conjunctures. The state has a relative autonomy from class in that, while it serves the long-term interests of the ruling class, it may oppose short-term policies or pressures from sectors of the ruling class. E. O. Wright picks up on the fluidity of "class boundaries" to argue that some classes, notably the petty bourgeoisie (composed of white-collar and technical workers as well as owners of small businesses), are in objectively contradictory places in the class structure. R. W. Connell criticizes Althusserian schemas as too formalistic and functionalist to allow for the precise analysis of real life class conflict (Giddens and Held:93–147).

H. Braverman studies how the division of labor under monopoly capitalism alienates workers through fragmentation of tasks and loss of overall grasp of the work process and goal. His account corresponds in some ways to Weber's trajectory of increasing bureaucratic stultification. A. Giddens takes issue with Braverman's neglect of the unevenness of capitalist application of scientific management and of the continual fightback of workers against their alienation. Giddens notes the paradox of a new middle class that frequently shows its class awareness by denying class under the impetus of careerist individualism. F. Parkin brings a Weberian protest against overplaying mode of production and stresses professional qualifications and credentials as equally important with control over property in the formation of class (Giddens and Held:148–86).

How do capitalist elites rule in and through the corporation and the state? One theory has it that ownership and control in corporations have been separated to such a degree that real control is now in the hands of managers. M. Zeitlin responds that ultimate control lies with the owners who remain generically a propertied class no matter who manages their property day to day. G. Therborn subordinates the question of who has power to the question of what is done with power to shape a given social order. Thus, we should analyze the influence of state power on the continuance of the regnant mode of production. C. Offe, V. Ronge, and B. Frankel examine the role of the state in sustaining a comprehensive social institutional order in which capitalist mechanisms can function optimally. To do this, the state mediates class antagonisms of all kinds. While it is not active in capital accumulation, the state depends on capital accumulation for its revenues and thus has a vital interest in supporting conditions that favor accumulation. The unimpeded march of bureaucratic rationalization projected by Weber is challenged by the dislocations and tensions that are constantly produced both in the productive process and in state rule (Giddens and Held:189–276).

With respect to technology, labor process, and labor markets, S. A. Marglin, in a study of the move from guild manufacture to the putting-out system and then to factories, argues that the hierarchy of labor discipline introduced was not simply a function of technical efficiency but more importantly of the desire of capitalists to gain control over the work process in its entirety. E. P. Thompson shows how the clock more than the power machine distinguishes the industrial age. Task-oriented labor as an aspect of daily life was replaced by timed labor separated off from the rest of life, with time itself becoming a scarce resource. D. Stark, J. Rubery, P. Doeringer, and M. Priore take up the impact of the labor market on class formation and consciousness, an issue neglected by Marxists because it seems a Weberian preoccupation. Worker resistance has in fact been a major obstacle to imposing greater work discipline, but that very resistance has produced divisions among workers. Labor becomes segregated into primary and secondary sectors, vital "firm-specific" jobs and peripheral dispensable jobs. Workers in the former category do not readily support the struggles of workers in the latter category. Therefore, the effects of labor market on class consciousness and action must be treated not only technically but also strategically in terms of managerial goals to fragment and weaken the position of all workers (Giddens and Held:279–350).

Concerning class consciousness and ideology, there has been a challenge to the simplistic view that people either do or don't have class consciousness on the grounds that there are gradations or types of consciousness. D. Lockwood develops a typology of working class images of society: the traditional or proletarian worker, the deferential worker, and the privatized worker. M. Mann contests the Parsonian and Althusserian views of an ideological consensus in society. Shared values are not always interpreted in the same way, and people may acknowledge an order of things pragmatically that they do not accept normatively. What counts in social order, says Mann, is not that all classes share common beliefs but that the dominant class or classes do so, in the face of which workers with different views may feel compelled to accept coexistence of viewpoints because lack of power gives them no alternative. N. Abercrombie and B. S. Turner observe that alongside ruling class ideology there exist oppositional cultures and ideologies which resist bourgeois individualism and moral prudishness, to give but two examples. At the same time the ideas of the ruling class are themselves "fractioned" without jeopardy if they display enough unity to secure the coherence of their class position as a whole (Giddens and Held:353–416).

The place of gender and race in class analysis has prompted a wealth of studies which at first seemed antithetical to Marxism but subsequently has involved considerable work within a Marxian framework.

The one Marxist classic on gender produced by Engels is now recognized to have used some very faulty 19th century anthropological theories, but the essential correctness of his argument is still a matter of controversy. E. Garnsey, H. Hartmann, and J. Humphries have tried to uncover the precise interrelations of class and gender oppression. Garnsey underscores the vital role of women in socially necessary labor both in the family (unpaid) and in secondary sectors of the labor market (low paid). Hartmann argues that preexistent patriarchalism was vastly strengthened by capitalism which increased male dominance in the economic and political realms. Both Marxist and feminist analysts have tended to view the family negatively, noting how surplus labor value is indirectly extracted from the unpaid work of the housewife and fed back into the process of surplus value creation in the economy at large. Humphries, however, pictures the working class family historically as an essential source of support for workers, not only socially and emotionally, but in direct material assistance. Kinship ties remained the one social relationship that workers could control (Giddens and Held:419–92).

Ethnicity, like gender, introduces a further complexity into class studies. R. Blauner uses models of colonialism and immigration to show how American Indians, blacks, and southwestern Hispanics were incorporated into U.S. society as subject peoples through forced labor rather than through voluntary immigration which characterized European ethnics. The result is a concentration of white ethnics in manufacturing and state administration and of non-white ethnics in mining and transport with very limited opportunities for upward mobility. E. O. Wright's statistical study of black and white incomes in the class categories of managers/supervisors, petty bourgeoisie, and workers shows that blacks receive less income than whites in all categories. On the other hand, the differential between the pay of white and black workers is very much less than the differential in income between all workers and all employers. Wright argues that capitalists do not directly foster racism, but that they benefit from racism in two ways: the extraction of surplus labor value from non-whites takes place at a higher rate than with whites, and racial divisions among workers weakens the position of all workers and strengthens correspondingly the position of capitalists as a whole (Giddens and Held:495–544).

A final dimension of class studies is the inquiry into whether or how socialist societies, particularly those in Eastern Europe, have abolished, altered, or masked class structure. Those who argue that class has not been abolished under socialism include advocates of a "convergence" thesis according to which industrial societies, capitalist and socialist, tend to become similar over time, but the perpetuation-of-class thesis is also held by Marxists who claim that Eastern European societies never really broke with capitalism. The alternative view is that the socialist societies abolished private property and thereby gained greater political control over economic life than has capitalism, although neither the state nor division of labor has disappeared under socialism. The consequence is that class is less prominent in state socialism than in capitalism. Closely related is the issue of the status of the communist party either as new ruling class or as powerful elite. In support of the former it is argued that the party initiates central planning of production and thus makes decisions about surplus value that has been extracted from all others who work. In support of the latter it is pointed out that party officials cannot make private capital investments or inherit wealth and that the democratic centralism of Soviet management theory attempts to combine initiative from below with centralized policy formation (Giddens and Held:567–644). Following B. Rizzi and A. Carlo, U. Melotti advances an exceptionalist interpretation according to which Eastern European societies are now under "bureaucratic collectivism" which is a *sui generis* formation, a new breed, that cannot be assimilated to capitalism or socialism and will be able to move on toward socialism only if the workers can get control over the collective property that is now de facto owned by the elite (Melotti:141–53).

Class in Pre-Capitalist Societies and Particularly in the Ancient Near East

When we turn to ancient history to make a class analysis, we necessarily have to choose theories and models of some sort, for it is not sufficient merely to compile extensive descriptive data about a phenomenon we have not clarified in its essential features and interrelationships with other phenomena. This need for specifying and clarifying models is not grasped even among many who work on the social history of antiquity because they work chiefly as specialists in the humanities. When students of ancient social history begin to draw on data for cross-cultural comparison, the failure to examine models in making choices is further complicated. For this reason, use of anthropology to clarify ancient societies may confuse as much as it helps. To get anywhere, one must begin with a clear model which can then be discarded or modified as one attempts to find meaningful patterns in the data viewed through the model. Thus, because aspects of ancient society exhibit "tribalism" or "peasantry" is insufficient basis to employ any or all anthropological studies of tribes and peasants without first thinking through very carefully the relevant points of comparison through modeling experiments.

Anthropology itself is in ferment over model-making, and in very diverse ways has taken up class/stratification as an object of study. Political anthropology has concentrated on the typology of band, tribe, chiefdom, and state formation. Extensive work on gender and ethnic stratification has tended to proceed without reference to stratification due to production. Sometimes anthropologists use stratification to refer to any form of social inequality, and sometimes they restrict it to inequalities involving society-wide strata. Nevertheless, some of the topics in anthropological treatment of stratification relate closely to issues in the treatment of class as a force in historical societies and in relation to mode of production. For example, the assumption that the emergence of a surplus over subsistence needs triggers the emergence of rulers has been much examined and other intervening variables have been identified, such as "social surplus" determined as desirable for public good and delegated to leaders to manage for the community, or "population aggregation" in which population size and density press for social control that requires specialization of office and power (Cancian). Potentially valuable as anthropological materials are for the study of class in antiquity, anthropology itself no more gives us an automatic model for when and how to use its data than does the cluster of methods used in historical study.

So we have a situation where the object of our study, class formations in early historical societies, involves various kinds of inquiry that have hitherto been scattered among the disciplines of history, sociology, and anthropology in such a manner that no one of these disciplines is sufficient for our inquiry. Yet nothing is gained from becoming interdisciplinary until we choose the conceptual analytic frame within which we will draw on all the disciplines as appropriate. And what is "appropriate" use of the contents of the respective disciplines is only arguable on the basis of some model.

A model adequate to study class in historical antiquity, or in any period for that matter, must meet the following criteria: (1) it must be broad enough to view the whole course of human history and prehistory as a social continuum; (2) it must be precise enough to discriminate changes and differences that have occurred over the course of human social history; (3) it must offer analytic concepts that disclose the basic workings of social life both in its dynamic integrity and in its changefulness. If all these criteria can be met, we are then in a position to draw from history, sociology, and anthropology in order to make comparisons between societies and between epochs within any society.

My option for the Marxian model of social reality can be put this way: while the Durkheimian and Weberian models pass muster on the first two criteria, they are insufficient on the third criterion. The Marxian model alone gives us analytic concepts of sufficient exactitude and complexity to enable us "to bite into" the social data so as to discriminate social metabolism and social change and to periodize the successions of social forms in time and space. This is not to say that Weber and Durkheim make no contributions to our knowledge of societies; it is only to say that their schemas lack the richness and dynamism necessary to a model of how societies function and dysfunction.

A further word about the status of the analytic concepts in the Weberian and Marxian models. In my view the Weberian analytic concepts, known as ideal types, are not strictly analytic concepts but only loose characterizations of types of social behavior which are useful in making comparisons of large sweeps of social history, but they remain too much on the surface of events or too mired in the subjective meanings that social actors entertain. They have value in "pre-digesting" mountains of social historical information but they are not tools that get to the core of the workings of society. Ideal types don't exist anywhere in a specific social situation; they are at best ways of perceiving the data preparatory to analysis. By contrast, the Marxian analytic concepts are abstractions that point precisely to relationships among people in actual social formations and specify where and what to look for in the social interaction. Of course, this is not to say that we can always find the data at once, or perhaps in many cases ever, nor does it mean that the model is an automaton that quantifies and weighs all variables. It simply means that we have a regular and reliable way to look at socially interactive humans in patterned structures and sequences that are shaped and modified in broadly determinable ways.

Also, the Marxian analytic concepts can be operationalized so that hypotheses about specific segments of social life can be tested. I have elsewhere noted that when Swanson operationalizes hypotheses about the social circumstances in which beliefs in high gods arise, he understands that he has vindicated Durkheim and undercut Marx. In fact, occupying ground that Durkheim and Marx share in their common perception that religious ideology is correlated to social reality, what Swanson has done is to operationalize that broad perception by moving in a characteristically Marxian manner to specify more precisely which social aspects are most important for which religious effects (Gottwald, 1979:625–27, 639–41). With greater theoretical clarity, Katherine S. Newman, in an effort to clarify the evolution of law, uses standard ethnographic resources and statistical measurements to verify her hypothesis that "the greater the development of the forces of production, social relations of production, and social stratification, the more complex a society's legal institutions" (117). In doing so, she operationalizes all the analytic concepts in her hypothesis for testing purposes. And she concludes by stating exactly why her hypothesis is congruent with the Marxian model as against the Durkheimian and Weberian models about legal evolution. It is not *un*differentiated social complexity that brings legal complexity, nor is it *any* sector of social complexity such as technological sophistication or developed political institutions that brings about legal complexity. It is, so far as she can determine through her tests, precisely the *interaction* of *three* developing sectors (forces of production, relations of production, and social stratification) that produces legal complexity (204–14). Finally, as staunchly as she defends the Marxian specificity of her conclusion, it should be noted that Newman disclaims any belief that all aspects of law can be accounted for by economic factors.

It is not possible here to rehearse the entire Marxian historical materialist body of analytic concepts. For those who want fuller reference, particularly where Marxian analysis touches historical studies and anthropology, one can hardly do better for sharp and succinct statements than to turn either to this study by Newman or to the work of Melotti.

For our purposes in the study of class in ancient and biblical societies, the key Marxian analytic concepts are *class* as determined by relation of people to the *mode of production* understood as a combination of the *material forces* of *production* (including human physical and mental powers) and the *social relations of production,* the latter meaning the way that producers (and non-producers where there is class) organize their work and appropriate the labor product. Class is seen to exist when some people live off of the labor product of others.

This living off the labor product of others is called *exploitation* in the objective sense that the value of one laborer's production, over and above that laborer's needs for subsistence, is appropriated by someone else. This labor product beyond the subsistence need of the laborer is called *surplus product* which is also *surplus value* because the exploiter consumes or exchanges the "good" of the object produced, thereby denying the producer the use or exchange of the object that embodies the producer's labor. In the first and last instance, this "exploitation" is not a *moral evaluation* but an *objective description.* Whether the extraction of the surplus value is viewed as good, bad, or a matter of indifference, the transaction actually occurs. Similarly, then, *class conflict* is not a moral evaluation but an objective description in that producers and non-producers struggle to increase, diminish, or arrest the appropriation of labor surplus.

The surplus labor product may be appropriated in various ways and it may be distributed in various ways. The surplus value may be reserved exclusively for the non-producer who extracted it, or it may be dispensed to other non-producers who provide various goods and services to the extracting non-producer, or it may be used for public works in defense or in ceremonial and religious activities, or it may be employed to improve the conditions of production so that there will be a larger surplus value to extract at a later date.

While I have stressed that this generation of class is not a moral judgment but a social fact, it is usual for non-producers to develop explanations that legitimate their extraction of surplus value, either as a matter of ancient custom, service to the public good, or divine right. Especially when class conflict becomes visible and intense, moral arguments arise both among the exploiters and the exploited. The exploiter does not want the appropriation of another's labor to appear as an arbitrary intervention based on brute force but wants it to be seen as a transaction that is good for the social whole and in keeping with the will of the god(s), these arguments of the general and highest good also corresponding with a claim of personal merit on the part of the non-producer. The producer feels otherwise and may come to formulate counter-arguments to the effect that it is a moral and religious good, as well as a matter of the laborer's merit, that the rate of appropriation of surplus labor should be lessened or that the appropriation should stop altogether.

This, I think, is the nub of the Marxian understanding of class, exact enough to be recognizable but protean enough in its possible forms and complex enough in its connections with other aspects of social life to require a careful delineation of its workings in each instance. Interestingly, the Weberian approach allows for class as one form of stratification, characterizing class as inequality in "life chances." That characterization is good so far as it goes. At the same time Weber rejected the theory of surplus labor value and sharply relativized class struggle. In doing so, I cannot find that he made any direct refutation of Marx's analysis. The main thrust of Weber's overt objection is one that is very widely voiced: Marxian class theory doesn't allow for many other important social facts and influences. The objection is mistaken because Marx, like all the rest of us, knew very well that there are all sorts of social relationships and influences. The class-generating mode of production is *not the only* set of social relations but it is the *single most important* set of social relations for understanding how societies operate. And it is at that level that the discussion of the Marxian model should be pitched, or, rather that is where it should be pitched if one is satisfied that class as described does exist.

If one concludes that the whole analysis of class in relation to mode of production is wrong, then there is no point to go further with the Marxian model. If it is seen to describe correctly one set of social relations, then one can ask if it does have singular importance and try to establish the range and flow of its importance in relation to all the rest of social interaction. I would contend that one is working within the Marxian frame as long as one is examining and testing the singular importance of class and mode of production, but in order properly to test the singular importance of class one has to "try on for size" as it were the possible singular importance of other social relations. So to this point one may be only at the threshold of the model. One is fully within the model when one sets out to trace the configurations and flows of social interaction as they articulate around the mode of production and begins to specify these configurations in specific societies, generating hypotheses and testing them as best one can. None of this precludes "dropping out of the model" from time to time to see if it still works adequately and, even while working within it, using the results of one's detailed studies to sharpen or refine the model.

But in order to examine class in ancient society through the Marxian model, we have to distinguish the appropriation of surplus labor value in its capitalist and pre-capitalist forms. In the *capitalist* mode of production there is a constant drive toward turning the labor surplus into commodities for exchange with a view to enlarging the stock of capital through accumulation, and, at the same time, the laborer is "free" to sell his/her labor to any capitalist of choice, labor itself having becoming a commodity for sale. This capitalization process is progressively separated out of the body of other social relationships into an autonomous sphere that seems as other and as determined as God. Civil society is seen to stand apart from the production process and to have no responsibility for it, while government from time to time may help it along with laws and revenues or slap its wrists when the social damage from economic practices is extensive. The inexorable quasi-mystical workings of the production process (noticeably like the mysteries of God) stand more and more over against the privatized person who may choose among the many possibilities in civil society, culture, and religion just as s/he chooses among employers. The appropriation of the surplus labor value is "hidden" behind the veils of free labor, consumer goods, democratic rights, and "acts of God" notions of economics.

In the *pre-capitalist* modes of production, class society had a less differentiated productive center in two respects: there was a less elaborate division of labor, and the economic dimension of life was more fully entangled in the other aspects of social life. The family was the typical unit of production. The surplus value existed as a potential stock of capital but only potentially. The surplus did not have free reign; it was not loosed into growing markets nor accumulated as a constantly mobile and mounting force that sent shock waves of change through the whole society. The surplus was consumed by the exploiter, or exchanged in trade that passed largely over the heads of the laborers who operated mostly by barter, or it was used for public works, only a fraction of which would directly benefit the laborers. While the production process was embedded in the social fabric, the actual appropriation of the surplus was not hidden as it is in capitalism. People knew their surplus was being taken from them and used by others. As under capitalism, religion justified this expropriation, but the exploited did not face the ruling class as private individuals nor did they worship as voluntary joiners of religious societies. They were members of social solidarities that were not yet threatened with attenuation and dissolution by capital accumulation and free labor.

But were all instances of pre-capitalist class-based production of a similar type, or were there sufficient differences that we should discriminate among them? If the latter, how should they be characterized? And how were they related to one another? Were they unalloyed unities sharply set off from one another in every time and place they appeared? Are these modes of production to be arranged serially and unilinearly on the view that all societies pass through all the stages of pre-capitalist modes of production? Or are they to be articulated as more or less simultaneous multilinear routes that various societies follow?

In *Manifesto of the Communist Party* (1848), Marx and Engels set forth what was widely understood as a unilinear scheme of five modes of production and types of society:

1. the classless primitive community;
2. the slave-based society of classical times;
3. the feudal society based on serfdom;
4. the modern bourgeois society based on the capitalist mode of production;
5. the classless society of the future.

In subsequent elaborations, extensions and illustrations of their schema, Marx and Engels developed sharply away from whatever unilinearism they may once have entertained. In particular, they stressed that the modes of production of non-European regions might be special cases that would require greater study and reflection. There is ample evidence in their work, all the more clearly so as their full writings have slowly come into print, that they held open the probability that human societies were coming to capitalism along different routes and that the feudalism of Europe and Japan was only one of these routes. From the mid-1850s on to his death in 1883, Marx first advanced and then developed at some length the notion of an Asiatic MP as an alternative route to capitalism that much of the globe outside of Europe and Japan had trod (Bailey and Llobera; Krader).

Before discussing various ways of articulating the Asiatic Mode of Production (hereafter AMP) in relation to the other modes, I want to confront the persisting misconstruals of the mode of production schema as a rigid unilinear straightjacket or as some kind of substantialist teleo-logical or vitalistic force that "determines" history rather like the God of some theologies. Many dogmatic Marxists have so construed the schema, and, were they right, then the analytic power of the Marxian model would be lost, and we should have little more than a collection of brilliant and audacious insights and guesses about history, in any case untestable.

Conceding that Marx nowhere fully fleshed out the totality of his multilinear conception of the modes of production, in part because its full import dawned slowly on him and in part because of his method of writing, Melotti helps us to see how for Marx the schema could be both global and multiform:

> When the dominant mode of production changes, society itself is changed in every aspect. In other words a new social-economic formation is created....The process affects every man [sic] and every society in the world. That is not to say that it takes place simultaneously and completely every-where, in the same way. It is rather that the progress of social-economic formations also implies a gradual drawing-together of separate societies into closer mutual contacts and bigger units, which prefigure the coming of a future integrated world society (Melotti:5).

As for the idea that Marx saw the production schema as represent-ing a predetermined and inexorable plan "laid on humanity," observe his protestations about history as some grand design apart from people in motion:

> *History* does *nothing*, it possesses *no* immense wealth, it wages *no* battle. It is *man* [sic], real living man that does all that, that possesses and fights; "history" is not a person apart, using man as a means for its own particular aims; history is *nothing but* the activity of man pursuing his aims (Marx in *The Holy Family*, Eng. trans. 125, quoted in Melotti:7).

Orthodox Marxism has adhered doggedly to a unilinear five-stage schema that has no place for the AMP: Primitive MP, Classical MP, Feudal MP, Bourgeois MP, and Socialist MP. Thus, the history of the treatment and mistreatment of the AMP is deeply intertwined with practical politics in the socialist and communist parties. It would take us far afield to go into all the circumstances and reasons, but I will note that the English language collection of essays by Soviet Assyriologists edited by Diakanoff, which contains valuable data and theorizing, is seriously marred at the level of conceptualizing the Mesopotamian MP by a total rejection of the AMP in favor of efforts to fit Mesopotamia into a slave or a feudal MP (Diakanoff). I also note that among some Marxists who have rejected the notion of an AMP, there are flexible-minded neo-Marxists who find the conception demeaning to the third world and overly Eurocentric (Amin; Mansueto:30–34), while other Marxists equally sympathetic to the third world have concluded that, to the contrary, the AMP removes Europe from its position of privilege in the schema (Melotti:101–27).

Among Marxists accepting the AMP, there have been at least three conceptions of how it fits in the total scheme, and two of these are still operating within a basically unilinear schema:

1. *The AMP in a "Bilinear" Model: Plekhanov and Wittfogel*

This view sharply distinguishes the AMP as a "dead-end" development out of the primitive commune, arising from the need for massive irrigation works, and mechanistically conceived as perpetually static, unable to develop to any other stage. This assigned the AMP to a vestigial position and left only the one route to capitalism by way of feudalism.

2. *The AMP in a Neo-Unilinear Model: Godelier; Chesneaux; Tökei*

Here the AMP is incorporated as a stage falling between the primitive community and classical society. The effect of this is to produce strained efforts to find signs of AMP in pre-classical Europe and signs of classical and feudal MPs in non-European settings. Sometimes additional MPs are included, such as Godelier's distinction between classical and slave-based MPs and his introduction of a Germanic MP prior to the feudal MP.

3. *The AMP in a Multilinear Model: Rodinson; Hobsbawm; Melotti*

A multilinear model sets the class-based pre-capitalist MPs side by side as different routes emerging out of varied forms of the primitive commune and proceeding in diverse ways toward the Capitalist MP (see chart in Melotti:26). In this schema, foreign influence from the Germanic barbarian invasions and from colonial penetration into the third world have had significant effects in shaping the movement from one MP to another. Multilinear representation of the MPs helps to bring out the role of superstructural factors (military and political interventions) in altering MPs, as when the primitive Germanic communes collided with the Roman slave-based society to cancel out both and initiate feudal society and as when western colonial trade and Japanese invasion of China catapulted that land out of the AMP into socialism.

> It deserves emphasizing that this model is very closely in line with Marx's thought. Contrary to the usual belief, although he was concerned to distinguish carefully between Asiatic, classical and feudal society for the purpose of specific analysis, Marx repeatedly treated them as being on an equal footing, at least in certain respects. And the reason for his doing so is that the corresponding modes of production, taken as particular forms of landed property, all differ from one another far less than the feudal mode itself differs from capitalism—which, of all the forms he analyzed, was the only one truly "superior" to the rest. Only capitalism, in Marx's view, constituted a real quality jump in the process of man's historical development, by breaking the stranglehold of nature . . . (Melotti:27).

If then the ancient historical societies of the Near East are conceptualized as instances of the AMP, what was their basic character? It consists of three principal features which mark it off both from the capitalist MP and from the related pre-capitalist classical MP and feudal MP: absence of private ownership of land; a system of self-sufficient village communities; and a highly centralized state in a commanding social role.

Absence of Private Ownership of Land

Land in the villages is possessed and used both by individual households and commonly for grazing purposes but the land is not owned by the villagers. Ownership, not necessarily spelled out directly in law, is in the hands of the state as sovereign and landlord. The index of state ownership is the right of state officials to collect tax (rent) on village lands and to do so on the basis of representing the state in its public function. This is in definite contrast to rent in the classical MP, which is based on private ownership of lands and persons, as it is also in contrast to rent in the feudal MP, which is based on private ownership of land but not of persons. Consequently, the owner in the classical MP is the landholder and slaveholder; in the feudal MP the owner is the feudal lord; and in the AMP the owner is the tribute-collecting state. "Rent" in the different conditions must not be confused for in each case it represent a different scope and meaning of "ownership."

To say that absence of private ownership is a feature of the dominant MP is not to exclude that private ownership may here and there appear within the AMP, but only as a subordinated feature that does not succeed in bursting the integument of communal ownership vested in the state and symbolically projected onto the god(s). The question of whether we see elements of private ownership during the Israelite monarchy is a subject open to empirical investigation, notably with respect to the role of trade and usury in the society.

Self-sufficient village communities

The AMP has as its base agrarian, pastoral, and handcraft pursuing villages which constitute self-sufficient units of residency and production. The consequence was that together the primacy of the village and the absence of private ownership of land insured an exceedingly weak form of urban life, what Marx called "a kind of indifferent [undifferentiated?] unity of town and countryside" (1857/8, The Pelican Marx Library, 479). The "cities" lacked a truly urban ethos and a genuinely productive basis. They were centers of state administration and trading locations that were parasitical on the villages. By contrast, the cities in the classical MP were headquarters for the landed proprietors and eventually centers of commerce that had far-reaching productive effects, and the feudally situated cities progressively emerged in conflict with the feudal lords, generating commerce and private property outside the manor system that finally burst the feudal MP asunder. It can be said that the city in the AMP "is the manifestation of a pathological gap between the despotic court's conspicuous consumption and actual productive capacity of society" (Melotti:65).

Highly Centralized State in a Commanding Social Role

Under the AMP the political superstructure is decisive in land ownership and in the extraction of surplus value from the villages and thus in the development of public works such as irrigation systems, defense works, administrative and religious structures, and storage of large quantities of food. The contrast in this regard with the feudal MP is manifest, for in the latter the state has no important economic and political functions which are diffused by assignment to the feudatories and it does not engage in public works. Also, in the AMP land tends to be scarce and labor abundant, so that land registers may be kept, while in the feudal MP land is plentiful and labor scarce, so that serf censuses are preserved. The contrast with the classical MP is not so clear-cut, in large measure because the classical MP is obscurely conceptualized (Finley). The Roman Empire, as the culminating political structure of that MP, was a vast military administration that both taxed and built public works, but its outward extent and might disguised an instability and disjuncture with the underlying relations of production which were of different sorts, since within the empire were combined the old heartland of the classical MP along with Germanic and Slavic communes at the frontier and societies under the AMP in Egypt and the Levant. The law and administration of the empire guarded private property, which proved not to be productive when cultivated as large estates, so that, as the empire eroded at the frontiers, trade and agriculture wound down. In other words, the dominant slave-based MP coexisted precariously with subordinate modes, with the result that the state under the classical MP was less stable and enduring than the state within the AMP where the social relations of production were more homogeneous and better integrated with the political superstructure as a whole.

Special Problem of Class under the AMP

Lively debate has surrounded the question of whether the state is the exploiting class in the AMP or whether it serves as the arm of other or additional expropriating classes such as landlords, merchants, skilled artisans, priests, etc. In my view, the state in its tribute-collecting function was the primary, and perhaps even exclusive, expropriator of the subject classes. Yet it would be ridiculous to contend that one person, the king, could be the sole beneficiary of such massive extraction of surplus labor value. Civil servants, military leaders, professional troops, merchants, artisans, and priests, in their capacities as state functionaries, were also beneficiaries of the extracted surplus. Themselves non-productive, except for the artisans, they lived off the village surplus product.

There arises here the issue of possible independent non-governmental expropriators, particularly in the development of commerce and in the practice of money-lending. This is far from certain. In our study of biblical society, it is frequently—even customarily—assumed that the merchants and money-lenders acted on their own as entrepreneurs and thus, in these instances at least, private property was recognized. We should not, however, jump too quickly to this conclusion in the light of the peculiar character of the AMP. It appears that the bulk of trade, especially the trade involving full-time specialists, was state-controlled and state-sponsored, which made it one outlet for the expenditure of the tax-rent collected from the villages, e.g., oil, wine, and wheat in exchange for luxury goods and vital building materials. Tolls on transit trade would also be state revenue. The role of the money-lender under the AMP is less clear, but even in this instance the loans at usury are understandable as loans on surplus value derived from taxes or from crown lands assigned for the support of state officials. Just as tax-collecting was farmed out under state administration, so it is likely that money-lending was a state-administered activity assigned to persons benefitting from the public treasury. In this way, the very tax-rents of the villagers were returned to them at high interest rates.

Of course, precisely through a "personalizing" of the activities of trading, tax-farming, and money-lending, it is likely that private property could begin to arise and constitute a ground of struggle between the state and independence-seeking officials. When the central government was weak this would have been an attractive maneuver for dependent officials to attempt. This would have been precisely the phenomenon which Weber characterized as the effort of prebendal officeholders to convert their status into that of patrimonial officeholders who could inherit wealth. We face a certain dilemma in our assessment of this form of fractional struggle within the ruling class between the crown and the crown's appointees. I would state the dilemma in this way: if creditors were making loans on public funds, then it might be expected that defaulted loans would convert ever more village land into crown land, but such a development is not attested in the biblical texts at any rate; on the other hand, if the defaulted loans were yielding more and more village land into the private ownership of the lenders, then the scale of private holdings in Israel would have mounted far beyond what we normally see in the AMP. The way out in this case might be, however, that the creditor—precisely as representative of the crown which in principle owned all land—was entitled to take "custody" of the encumbered lands, which continued to be conceived within the use domain of the villagers even though the former "users" of the lands were now debtor slaves, tenant farmers, or refugees from their own lands.

That land was being encumbered and "bled" over and above the regular tax system, whether as private property pure and simple or as custodianship, amounted to "raiding" the villages in a manner that threatened the base of regular state revenues due in tax-rent. This would constitute objective ground for state-initiated reforms such as those carried out in the Mesopotamian debt waivers and by Josiah in his reconstitution of the flow of revenues to Jerusalem so it bypassed the intermediaries who siphoned off excessive shares of tribute (so Claburn). This whole matter of how ruling class fractions operated during the monarchy and the ways they found to extract surplus value over and above the regular tax-rent, and through what legal instruments, is a matter requiring urgent attention in social study of the Bible. For unless we consciously correct ourselves, we are disposed to read the ancient terms as if capitalist legal forms were fully in force. Think of all the biblical commentators who have assumed that because Jeremiah "bought" the field from Hanamel and even sealed a "deed," he now "owned" the field in the Greco-Roman or capitalist sense of ownership—often to the point of forgetting about biblical customary law that views the prophet's action as a restitutionary or protective act on behalf of the family patrimony.

The manner in which trade and usury can operate on a considerable scale while still remaining fettered by the larger constraints of the AMP is expressly noted by Marx:

> Trade will naturally react back to varying degrees upon the communities between which it is carried on. It will subjugate production more and more to exchange value....However, the dissolving effect depends very much on the nature of the producing communities between which it operates. For example, it hardly shook the old Indian communities and Asiatic relations generally....But capital arises only where trade has seized possession of production itself, and where the merchant becomes the producer, or the producer mere merchant (1857/8:858–59).

> Usury works revolutionary effects in all precapitalist modes of production only so far as it destroys and dissolves those forms of property which form the solid basis of the political organization, and which must be continually reproduced in order that the political organization may endure. Under the Asiatic forms usury may last for a long time, without producing anything else but economic disintegration and political rottenness. Not until the other pre-requisites of capitalist production are present, does usury become a means of assisting in the formation of the new mode of production (1867:597).

Melotti acknowledges the tendencies toward and first expressions of private property in the AMP, while also showing how decisively the development was held in check :

> One can even go further than Marx and find in it a fairly developed class structure without impairing the validity of the model's explanation. It can be admitted that—as suggested by recent historical discoveries [referring to Wittfogel on land in China]—as well as state officials and peasants, there were landed proprietors who had illegally appropriated land at times when the central authority was weak, and there were sometimes immensely rich bankers and merchants, yet such admissions do not fundamentally conflict with the model we have described. The historically specific feature of Asiatic society implied in the model is the fact that even those classes never managed, under a suffocating state power, to gain for any length of time that degree of social and political power or ideological and cultural free-dom that in the West opened the way to capitalism (Melotti: 103).

Historical Societies Exhibiting the AMP

Melotti has assembled a list of the countries which Marx denoted as "Asiatic," reminding us that not all of Marx's instances are in Asia nor are all the countries of Asia designated "Asiatic": in the Far East (India,

China, Java, Dutch East Indies), in central Asia (Tartary), in the Middle East (Egypt, Mesopotamia, Persia, Arabia, Turkey), in pre-Columbian America (Mexico under the Aztecs, Peru under the Incas), and in Europe (Etruscans, Spain under the Moors and Russia [termed "semi-Asiatic "]). Later typologists of the AMP have included additional regions: Cambodia, Vietnam, Ceylon, Japan (for Marx feudal), prehistorical Greece and Minoan Crete, though one or another are often viewed as marginal instances of AMP. Various typologies of the AMP by Wittfogel, Godelier, and Dhoquois distinguish in one way or another between stronger/weaker or fuller/less complete forms of the AMP (Melotti:73–95).

Typology is relevant in asking if Palestine in biblical times fell under the AMP and, if so, with what strength or completeness in its display of the basic features. Neither ancient Palestine nor the Levant are designated under the AMP by any of the typologies I have seen. Because of the small size of the political units in Palestine for much of its history, and perhaps also because of the apparent presence of private property instanced in the Bible, biblical scholars in particular have frequently described ancient Palestine as "feudal." It seems much more to the point to view Palestine under one of the weaker variants of the AMP typified by a significant degree of localized agriculture that does not depend on extensive public works. It needs also to be considered whether the classical or slave-based MP is important for Palestine even as early as Hellenistic times (Belo:60–86).

Class Within the AMP of Biblical Israel

In the light of this review of class studies especially focused on the AMP, certain problematics of ancient Israelite society can be formulated both as a way of characterizing what we know of that society and of posing additional research and theorizing to uncover further data and to conceptualize matters ever more clearly.

1. Is the *Israelite monarchic society a form of the AMP?* Can we characterize its *mechanisms as a totality?* Does the examination of biblical and extrabiblical evidence suggest a centralized state living parasitically off the village communities while it provides certain public works and services to the villages? Can the administrative structure of the state be reconstructed in some detail? Do we know which public works and services it did and did not supply? Can we picture the process of tax-rent collection with some precision, including possible tax-farming systems, methods and kinds of surplus payments, differentiation of

revenues for particular aspects of government, and the forms of funding for the religious establishment and how the funding may have been divided between state cult and village cult (cf. Crüsemann)?

2. Can the *tax-rent payable to the state* be specified according to the *kinds of surplus* taxed and the *rate of extraction* of the surplus? We begin to see the outlines of this surplus extraction when we see that it puts a premium on readily collectible, storable, transportable, and exchangeable items, which ranks olive oil and wine high in value, cereals in the middle, and animals last of all, to which is added the demand for regularity of tax payments. The kinds of surplus called for strike destructively at the risk-spreading and labor-optimizing economy of the villages, while the demand for regularity of payment conflicts with inevitable fluctuations in annual harvests (Hopkins, 1983, and, more fully, 1985). Thus, it is not merely that the state took part of the surpluses as they would "naturally" emerge from the village economy. More seriously for the peasants, the tax-rent demand worked to *restructure the ratios of kinds of surplus produced,* thereby undermining the diversity of crops and herds that carried the peasant through difficult times even as it ignored the fluctuations in harvests by constancy of demand for payment in the face of which the now less-diversifying peasant was all the more vulnerable.

The situation was thus "development" at the peak of the economy and "under-development" in the subsistence sector for the agrarian producers. Taking this dynamic in surplus extraction into account, can we develop estimates of the rate of extraction in its impact on the producers over the course of the monarchy? And can we do this in comparison with other monarchies at the time and in comparison with the premonarchic and postmonarchic eras? (Premonarchic would include not only the Canaanite states from which Israelites broke away but also the free agrarian MP of inter-tribal Israel since the tribes had to designate some portion of the surplus as "social surplus" for purposes of common defense, worship, etc., even if that was not a matter of very deliberate joint planning).

3. Can the *class composition* of the extractors of the agrarian surplus be specified *in relation to the state and legal structures?* This appears to be so far very obscurely understood, in part because the problem has not been very clearly formulated. In an effort to conceptualize the issues, I cite the fullest schema of forms of surplus extraction and of social classes and fractions for biblical Israel of which I am aware (Mansueto: 34–35):

I.   Forms of Surplus Extraction:

   a.   taxes and tithes imposed by the indigenous Israelite monarchy and priesthood;

   b.   tributes imposed on the Israelite ruling classes by foreign oppressors...both during the periods of dependent monarchy and provincial administration.

   c.   rents extracted by the growing numbers of latifundaries, who further stood in diverse and complex relations with the various Israelite dynasties, foreign states, trading partners, etc.

II. Social Classes and Social Fractions (Sub-divisions of classes):

   a.   ruling class groups: the Israelite royal houses, during the monarchic period, together with priestly sectors, dependent on taxes and corvées from the peasant communities; the metropolitan ruling classes of the various empires which dominated Israel, dependent on tributes levied on the population and collected by the indigenous ruling classes or imperial administrators; and latifundaries, dependent on rents from more or less private estates.

   b.   middle layers: craftsmen, functionaries, and lower clergy dependent on benefices which do not provide income sufficient to maintain an aristocratic style of life, and independent craftsmen and merchants,

   c.   exploited classes: two principal kinds of peasantry

      •   peasants protected by redistributional land tenure and other community guarantees,

      •   tenant farmers on the estates of latifundaries; and marginated rural people who have no regular access to the land.

Mansueto notes the diachronic dimension in this schematic when he adds, "The relative importance of these classes and class fractions varied over time; some, such as the royal house, disappeared entirely, while foreign ruling classes and the priestly sectors, together with latifundaries, became increasingly more important. Generally speaking, we can expect a secular trend toward latifundialization and disintegration of the peasant communities" (35). If we juxtapose Mansueto's schema for ancient Israel with what was earlier said about the special problem of class under the AMP, we readily identify three points in Mansueto's formulation which hone in on the "slippery" issues in characterizing class. The first is the reference to "diverse and complex relations" between latifundaries and the state (I.c above); the second is reference to latifundaries who draw rent "from more or less private estates" (II.a above); and the third is reference to peasants "protected by redistributional land tenure and other community guarantees" in contrast to peasants who are not so protected (II.c above). Taken together, these specifications stake out the position that latifundaries in the ruling class were accruing private property from peasant lands, but an element of uncertainty is expressed in the qualification "more or less private estates."

Now it is this "more or less private property" which we noted as constituting a particular problem of conceptualization under the AMP. Does *all* of the extraction of surplus occur under direct state auspices or does *some* of the extraction occur beyond the immediate control of the state structure and in what sense is that extra-state exploitation recognized legally? And what is the stance of the state toward this economic activity outside of its aegis? I suggest that the problem is composed of at least two parts: (1) the communally recognized form of land ownership during the *premonarchic free agrarian period;* and (2) the communally recognized form of land ownership during the *monarchic tributary peasant period.* I am arguing that we must consider the forms of communal recognition of land ownership in both periods.

Communal Recognition of Land Ownership in Premonarchic Israel

Here I take for the base line that early Israel broke away from state sovereignties and legal claims when it *de facto took its lands out of the tax-rent system.* The break occurred at the politico-military and ideological level and did not involve any attempt whatsoever to argue Israel's case within the jural structures of the state societies (whatever legal forms those states may have had to legitimate landholding). It appears to me that Israel took de facto control of the land into the hands of the agrarian producers as it asserted Yahweh to be ultimate owner of the land in place of the Canaanite city-states. *No de jure formulation of this expropriation of the domain of the states occurred* at a comprehensive conceptual level, and for two reasons: (1) Israel did not have to justify this "use-ownership" because the Canaanite states would in no case entertain such justification; Israel had only to defend what it did by force of arms; (2) Israelite "law" was customary and precedent-oriented, so that the internal protection of use-ownership of land called, not for generalized statements about free agrarian ownership, but for specific stipulations about how the patrimonies were to be protected through mutual aid and the prevention of usury.

Communal Recognition of Land Ownership in Monarchic Israel

With the rise of monarchy, at least from Solomon on, *Israel returned to the tax-rent system through the internal development of its own state formation.* Nonetheless, this was not a simple return to the status quo ante obtaining under Canaanite city-states, for the reason that much of the infrastructure and most of the culture and ideology of the Israelite people had been built up on free agrarian grounds. The Israelite state that could take political and military command, and thus enforce the tax-rent, was contested by an alternative culture and ideology. I posit that we should also *expect that contradiction to show up in the way the state extraction of surplus took place and how it was rationalized* whether by formal legal instruments or otherwise.

In accounting for the rise, vitality, and endurance of the Israelite free agrarian forms of life and ways of thinking, a multilinear conception of the development of the modes of production enables us to explore the possibility that the intertribal free agrarianism of early Israel represented a "survival" or "reemergence" of the primitive commune and to consider which of the different versions of the primitive commune (as identified, for example, by Melotti:28–33) best approximates what we encounter in Israel. Space being limited and the topic being strictly speaking tangential to this paper, I will not carry the thought very far. I note only a very terse and conceptually fuzzy reference by Marx to the Jews as a primitive commune analogous to pre-state Greece and Rome. How Marx viewed the Jews in this respect is not developed beyond a quotation from Niebuhr, the historian of Rome, who states that all the law-givers of antiquity, Moses above all, founded their success on securing hereditary possession of land for the greatest possible number of citizens (1857/8:476).

In the larger context of his discussion of the primitive commune, Marx appears to understand the village community under the AMP as retaining features of the older communes in their internal organization and regard for the land as a communal possession. A further ingredient is added to our reflection by Melotti's amplification of Marx's view of the Germanic commune in which widely scattered people came together in assemblies so that their communalism was mediated through periodic gatherings. If Israel was in some sense an expression of the primitive commune, it may have added to and infused the agrarian inertness of the ancient Near Eastern village with a covenanting practice that mobi-lized and linked otherwise separate communities and made room for newcomers to the community. While this is a study for another time and place, it may not be amiss that some of the most persisting analogues to aspects of early Israel's tribalism have come from Icelandic society and culture which was part of the broad Germanic and Scandinavian pre-state experience (Njardvik; Kristjánsson).

In keeping with my speculations about the severe limitation of private property under the AMP, I now formulate a hypothesis about how the collision of state extraction of surplus and free agrarian resistance was rationalized by the ruling class in monarchic Israel. The ruling class in monarchic Israel extracted surplus in two ways that were systemically connected: a state tax-rent, compounded by foreign tribute, was the initial and dominant method of extraction, which in turn spawned a credit/debt system that was formally outside the state administration, but that was necessitated by the peasant hardship that the state generated via the tax-rent (see the accompanying chart). The class fraction that lived off the tax-rent was made up of state functionaries and the class fraction that lived off the debt payments was made up of latifundaries, who probably for the most part had a base in state administration which gave them command of resources enabling them to extend credit to peasants. At the same time, I hypothesize that the state legitimated the tax-rent as payment due to Yahweh's servants who protected the patrimonies of the free agrarians, and the latifundaries explained their taking possession of indebted lands as the work of "custodians" or "keepers" of the patrimonial shares of those who fell hopelessly into debt.

In short, I suggest that this hypothesis helps to explain several features of the surplus extraction process, the class structure, and the ideologies operative in monarchic Israel.

1. It shows how the tax-rent initiated a process of surplus extraction so disruptive of the peasant economy that it necessarily generated a secondary means of extraction by credit-debt payment.

2. It shows how the ruling class was differentiated into the two fractions of state functionaries and latifundaries who, though differing in the way they extracted surplus, were united in sharing benefits that were mutually reinforcing and that could not be independently derived apart from the complete system with its interlocking "moments" of tax-rent surplus extraction and credit-debt payment surplus extraction.

3. It shows how the ruling class could articulate an ideology that explained these two forms of surplus extraction as doing service to Yahweh by protecting the patrimonies of the villagers, thus interpreting the monarchy as a faithful servitor of the independent village communities and the social revolution that had freed them from Canaanite city-states. This cast the peasants of Israel into a defensive position which demanded a fundamental rethinking of Yahwism in relation to the objective situation in which they found themselves as objects of a double surplus extraction system.

To keep this inquiry within bounds there are many aspects of the mode of production and the superstructure in monarchic Israel that I have not considered, such as crown land, trade, the specific forms of debt, funding of the cult, forms of theology (royal, prophetic, popular). I have, however, provided a framework within which those questions can be pursued and thus a theoretical structure that can move our social scientific studies forward. At the same time it is a hypothesis about social class in monarchic Israel that can be operationalized, tested and revised, even discarded if we find a better one.

RULING CLASS EXTRACTION OF SURPLUS DURING ISRAELITE MONARCHY

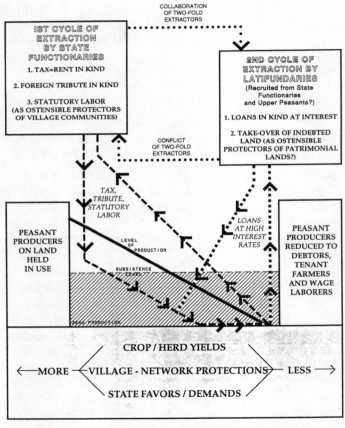

Chart by Eva Mahoney

The Book of Lamentations Reconsidered

ABSTRACT

This address to Korean Old Testament scholars represents a return to a scrutiny of Lamentations more than thirty years after my doctoral dissertation on that subject, in which I take the measure of new literary, tradition-historical, redactional, and sociological contributions to an enriched understanding of this tightly constructed collection of acrostic/alphabetic poems. A controlled dialogical interplay of voices—poet, Zion as a grieving mother, an anonymous suffering "man," the citizens of Jerusalem and Judah—simultaneously expresses grief and shock at the fall of Jerusalem and struggles toward a new ethical and spiritual foundation for community. The central problematic is this: how are we Judahites to rebuild community after a catastrophe that, although in large measure deserved, has proven excessive and indiscriminate in its far-reaching effects, stretching far beyond all moral calculations? Prophetic, priestly, Deuteronomic and wisdom concepts and counsels flow together in a "social existential" commitment to shape a more just and faithful community in the confidence that Yahweh will honor and sustain this undertaking.

More than thirty years ago, I began my scholarly career with a doctoral dissertation on the book of Lamentations, which was published in revised form (Gottwald, 1962). Returning to the same study in the light of major shifts in biblical studies over recent decades (Gottwald, 1988a), I am pleased to discover new literary, tradition-historical, and sociological perspectives which both alter and enrich my earlier conclusions.

In this lecture I shall comment first on the acrostic and form-critical structure, followed by attention to composition and redaction. After a chapter by chapter examination of the flow and interaction among the parts of the book, I shall conclude with remarks on the sociological and theological setting.

Acrostic and Form-Critical Structure

Lamentations consists of five closely constructed poetic compositions on the topic of the destruction of Jerusalem in 586 B.C.E., poems
that both evoke the sense of catastrophe and give voice to the psychic,
social, and religious trauma of the survivors. It shares a pervasive
lament idiom with Psalms, Job, and the prophetic books of Jeremiah,
Ezekiel, and Second Isaiah.

The outstanding structural feature is the acrostic device that
distributes the entire Hebrew alphabet of 22 letters in sequence
throughout each of the first four chapters. The final chapter echoes this
device by using 22 short lines. The acrostic structure is uniform within
each lament but shows variation from poem to poem. In chapters 1 and
2, each three-line strophe opens with one of the letters in alphabetic
sequence. Chapter 4 follows the same pattern but is shortened to two-
line strophes. Chapter 3 achieves a denser acrostic form by beginning
each line with an acrostic letter, producing three ʾaleph lines, three beth
lines, three gimel lines, etc. Each of the first three laments has 66 lines,
whereas the last two laments combined yield only 66 lines.

The most notable literary effect of this acrostic design is to constrain
the choice of vocabulary and word sequence within each line, and to
break each lament into 22 subunits that produce cameos of grief tersely
expressed. The compactness and conciseness of the literary form impose
an economy of speech on otherwise boundless grief and shock. The
effect is to heighten emotion in the reader or listener.

The tendency for acrostic artifice to break the compositions into
fragments is countered by skillful shifts in speaker and point of view,
creating continuities of description, emotion and thought that span
several acrostic strophes in pleasingly varied ways (Lanahan). The shifts
in speaking voice correspond closely to the linguistic conventions of
recognizable genres: the funeral song, the individual lament, and the
communal lament.

Influence of the funeral song shapes the speeches by the poet-
observer who bewails the fall of Fair Zion[1] (or Daughter of My People)
as a city personified. No typical funeral is in view, however. Although
Zion is likened to a widow and bereaved mother, her "husband" is not
dead (only remote and hostile), nor are all her "children" dead since
some have survived to remember by composing and reciting these very
laments.

---

[1] The translation of bat ṣiyyôn as "fair Zion" is indebted to the discussion of
Hillers (1972:xxxvii–ix).

Contours of the individual lament are adopted when personified Jerusalem speaks as a suffering woman. This "Mother" Zion incorporates all the pain and anger of her Judahite "children," confessing their collective sins and calling on God to mitigate or terminate the horrible and extreme suffering. We are made acutely aware that this woman is an imaginative figure who both embodies and stands apart from particular Judahites whose sad condition she reports and bewails. The personification admirably succeeds in infusing mass suffering with the personal meaning that only specific human sufferers can give it (Mintz).

The individual laments of chapter 3 are a special case. They are not framed or marked as personifications; they derive their collective reference in part from association with the surrounding chapters and more directly from their juxtaposition with an enclosed communal lament (3:40–47). Read by themselves, the cries of the unnamed "man" of 3:1–24, and of one or more "I" speakers in 3:52–66, are typical individual laments of anonymous sufferers so plentiful in the Psalms.

Communal lament becomes the vehicle for the last chapter. There is no separated voice of the poet-observer and no personification of city or people. Judahites speak in a united voice which, from a literary point of view, erases many earlier ambiguities and brings dramatic closure to the troubled book. This powerful literary "closure" does not, however, offer either an emotional-psychic or theological "closure."

Composition and Redaction

Lamentations was almost certainly written and collected in the sixth century B.C.E. to commemorate the destruction of Jerusalem by the Neo-Babylonians in 586. Its stock of lament language was, by that time, already richly developed in Israelite religion. Moreover, the overarching genre of lament over a destroyed city probably owes much to ancient Mesopotamian tradition and practice that continued unabated down to late biblical times (Gwaltney).

The first four laments share vocabulary and stylistic devices, modulation of speaking voice, genre structures, and acrostic scheme. These similarities imply, if not a single composer, at least a group or "school"/"guild" of lament traditionists. On the other hand, each lament is self-contained formally and displays marked individuality of expression and focus. Since there are no conspicuous signs that the laments were written at one time as parts of an intended single work, it seems best to argue for their independent composition, followed by later compilation/redaction. It is possible that the compiler/redactor was author of one or more of the laments, most likely the last of the series, and that minor modifications were made in the text during the course of redaction.

The separate laments were probably created for recitation at annual fast days observed on the site of the ruined Temple during the Exile (Zech 7:1–7; 8:19; cf. Jer 41:5). The compilation and redaction of the whole may have been occasioned by a notable event such as release from Exile and anticipation of rebuilding the Temple. This notion has been questioned by some interpreters because there are no traces of release from Exile or of Temple rebuilding in Lamentations. Nevertheless, the Mesopotamian practice of using just such bleak laments on the occasion of cleansing and rebuilding a temple site (Gwaltney) suggests that the somberness and restrained hope of the exilic compositions might have been regarded as suitable reminders of the dark past, even though at the time of redaction the situation had already changed for the better.

Is there a redactional design in the arrangement of the laments? The short, technically non-acrostic chapter 5, speaking in single genre, functions well as the conclusion. It is imaginable as a possible opening lament, but this would make the book more didactic than it is and would end the collection on a more confident note than at present. Chapter 3 as centerpiece is the linchpin of the redaction, whose enigmatic voices and assertions of veiled hope serve as a meta-commentary on the other laments. Many commentators have seen a chiastic arrangement in the correspondences between chapters 1 and 5 (generalized "emotionally distanced" descriptions) and between chapters 2 and 4 (detailed "emotionally involved" descriptions). Such pairing of these chapters oversimplifies the evidence, since chapters 1 and 2 are closest in terms of the speaking voices and chapters 4 and 5 are closest in their inventories of the suffering subgroups within Jerusalem/Judah. No unequivocal linear progression of thought is apparent, but the cumulative effect of reading and rereading the laments, with chapter 3 shedding its qualified light over the whole, shows a slowly dawning understanding of the trauma as something both to learn from and to live beyond.

Chapter by Chapter Examination

The first lament of poet and lady Zion (chapter 1) divides equally between these two speakers. Fair Zion, at first merely the object of lament, gradually gains voice to speak of her own suffering. The note struck by the poet and confirmed by Zion is that the city is bereft of comfort from any source. Zion voices the incomparability of her pain and pictures the angry assault of Yahweh. Although confessing fully her rebellion, Zion cites mitigating factors in her punishment that merit Yahweh's reconsideration, at least in providing for the punishment of the city's destroyers who have "overdone" it in their fierce cruelty. Uniquely in the Hebrew Bible, Lamentations identifies a past event with the Day of Yahweh as the time of judgment. Zion now asks that this Day will also fall on the arrogant enemies (by inference Babylonia, whose ally Edom is named in 4:21–22).

The second lament of poet and Lady Zion (chap. 2) differs from the first in significant manner. Fair Zion has much less to say, while the poet grows more articulate and reflective, directly addressing Zion and struggling with her to grasp the enormity of the events she has experienced. The poet moves into close emotional and ideological empathy with Zion. To be sure, the poet finds God's judgment on Zion deserved; nonetheless, the means chosen to punish are bitter and hard to accept, especially the abrasive taunts of the enemy and the death of children by famine. Zion responds with grief-stricken and horror-driven reflexes: Look what you have done, Yahweh! Look at those to whom you have done it, the dying children!

The anonymous individual lamenting that follows (chap. 3) breaks sharply with the preceding poet-Zion dialogue: "I am the man who has seen affliction by the rod of his wrath" (v 1). Nonetheless, the language and tone of this chapter operate with the same problematic as chapters 1 and 2: How are we survivors to understand and live with a merited punishment that has produced shocking and excessive results that generate new injustice?

The major difficulty in interpreting this chapter is the veiled identity of the speakers. This problem may not have existed when the lament was recited as a solo piece in the cult, since intonations in delivery, explanatory directions, even different speaking voices, may have clarified the issue. The shift to a written text created a new context of meaning, less immediate and more dependent on the eye and experience of the reader. The redactor appears to have left the speakers in anonymity as an artifice to deepen reader involvement in the suffering expressed. As this chapter stands in its five-chapter matrix, it seems to be asking: what do we learn about *national* suffering when we see it through the lens of *individual* sufferers who have attained a measure of hope and faith amid all their adversities? That we should see this sort of interplay between national and individual suffering is corroborated by genre structure: enfolded within faith-affirming and hope-engendering "I" speech, we find groping and frustrated "we" speech in the form of a quite traditional communal lament.

In the third lament of poet and city (chap. 4), Zion personified as a woman does not speak, although she is referred to by the poet. In place of the Fair Zion speeches of chapters 1 and 2, the city expresses itself in a communal lament (vv 17–20). The individualized presentation of Judah's suffering, characteristic of chapters 1–3, gives way here, as in chapter 5, to overt communal discourse by the collective body of sufferers.

Chapter 4 as a whole lays bare the physical, sociopolitical, and moral fragility of the upper classes. Political and religious leaders failed equally. Perfidious prophets and priests are rejected as though they are lepers. The lamenting populace acknowledges their misplaced trust in political allies and in their own king. The prophet-like announcement of the end of Judah's punishment (4:21–22) vindicates the hope expressed in chapter 3 and is to be read less as superficial jingoism than as a renunciation of all false hopes (cf. Isa 40:2).

In the concluding communal lament (chap. 5), we come face to face with economic hardship, social disorder and political restrictions among inhabitants of the Babylonian subprovince of Judah. The harrowing descriptions are meant to elicit divine intervention, but with careful qualifications.

Significantly, the lament of chapter 5 holds to the paradox disclosed in chapter 3 and sustained by the poet voice in chapter 4: Judah has both sinned and been sinned against. This time, however, the insight is internalized and expressed by the whole people. The community owns up to its own sins (5:7, 16) and at the same time appeals for its disgrace and oppression to be relieved (vv 1, 17–20). In a closing appeal to Yahweh, the people seek a restored relationship with their God (v 21), but with a caveat.

A troubling final question escapes their lips, "Or have you utterly rejected us? Are you angry with us beyond recall?" (5:22). Has Judah learned its lesson too late? Does God still honor a relationship with the people or is it broken off irrevocably? The unclouded confidence of the "I" voice in chapter 3 is not yet firmly within the people's collective grasp. Even so, the overarching sense of trust situated at the center of the redaction in chapter 3 will in time prevail among those who mourn Jerusalem by praying these laments to Yahweh.

Sociological and Theological Setting

What were the sociological and theological contexts of these lamentations? To what traditions and to which social actors and spokespersons do we attribute this book? In past interpretation, there has been an overly simple search for a single source. In my original work on Lamentations, I too one-sidedly connected the book with Deuteronomic theology and morality (Gottwald, 1962:50–52). In challenging my view, Albrektson just as one-sidedly identified Lamentations with the Davidic-Zion theology (1963:214–39). Once authorship by Jeremiah was dismissed, scholars have placed the book in one or another of several familiar streams of tradition: prophecy, Deuteronomistic thought, kingship traditions (Davidic/Zion), priestly theology, or wisdom teaching. In truth, however, no single tradition adequately accounts for the book, because, in the riptide of national collapse, the streams of tradition were commingling and clashing, forcing new channels of thought and action.

Lamentations shares with prophetic and Deuteronomistic thought the firm belief that Judah's sins precipitated the collapse of its national institutions. This belief is dressed out in the prophetic image of the people as a faithless defiled woman. In accord with critical prophets, Lamentations condemns the superficial assurances of "false" prophets who also joined corrupt priests in murdering innocents. The prophetic belief in judgment on the nations as well as on Judah is firmly attested in these laments, as is the necessity of contrite confession and wholehearted conversion.

The wisdom affinities of Lamentations appear prominently in 3:25–39, a text in which the transcending mystery of God is declared, suffering is seen as disciplinary as well as retributive, the long-range justice of God is affirmed, and patient waiting on and hoping in God are inculcated.

Royal traditions associated with the Davidic dynasty and with the security of Zion are most evident in the astonished outcries of passersby who thought Jerusalem to be impregnable, and in the communal lament of those who trusted naively in their king as "the anointed one of Yahweh." The poet joins the personified Zion in expressing shocked disbelief at the enemy's violation of the sacred Temple. These references in context suggest that all the special privileges of David and Zion, which depend ultimately on the faithfulness of Judah to divine requirements, have now been justly canceled.

It is true, as many commentators have observed, that Judah's political leaders are not unambiguously condemned. Nevertheless, the censure of priestly and prophetic complicity with civil rulers presupposes censure of the latter. Moreover, in my judgment, the assertion "our fathers sinned and are not" (5:7; cf. 2:9) refers in all probability to the political leadership swept away by death and exile. The focus of Lamentations on faulty *religious* leadership may be due to the post-destruction reality in which the defaulting *political* leadership is no longer in power. In addition, old style priests and prophets, who escaped the city's fall, may still be vying for control of the reconstituted religious life in Jerusalem and, in the process, they threaten the status and credibility of the Lamentations traditionists who speak for a "reformist" line of thought and practice.

In sum, anyone holding rigidly to the conventions of a single theological tradition could hardly have woven the sophisticated web of poetic argument in Lamentations. Strict prophetic and Deuteronomistic adherents had good reason to regard the covenant with God as decisively broken off because of Judah's sins. Followers of traditional wisdom tenets had little precedent for grappling with the sociopolitical and religious ramifications of the city's fall. Ardent Davidic-Zion loyalists could not tolerate the idea of a breach of the unconditional promises to the holy city, its Temple, and the Davidic dynasty. Those who considered Judah's government and society to be as just, or even more just, than those of other nations would not have understood or sympathized with the notion that corporate political, social, and religious "sins" explained Judah's sad end.

For the social setting of the Lamentations traditionists, we must look to the ritual practice on the ruined Temple site, where fasting, prayer, and sacrifice were carried on with the presumed permission of the Babylonian overlords. The poets and the compiler/redactor of Lamentations prepared these texts separately and collectively for public recitation. In that sense they were "priests," cultic personnel, but it does not follow that they had been born or appointed priests within the pre-destruction Jerusalem temple cultus. The destruction of Jerusalem shattered the former priestly establishment as cataclysmically as it shattered the political establishment. The Lamentations traditionists may formerly have been prophets or government servants, of the sort that gathered around Gedaliah's administration at Mizpah (Jer 40:5–12). Or, they may have been former lower order Temple priests or priests from non-Jerusalemite locations unaffected by the Deuteronomic centralization of worship at Jerusalem. Nor do we know on whose authority the Lamentation traditionists wrote and performed these texts. Political authority had passed from an independent monarchy in Jerusalem to Babylonian provincial administration in Mizpah. The monarchic oversight of the

Jerusalem cult was abolished. Probably struggle for control of the improvised cult in post-destruction Jerusalem was intense and the Lamentation traditionists were among the contenders for ideological and ritual power who succeeded. Unless the Babylonian administration provided it, they probably served without stipend and in that regard were "laity" who had to find livelihood on their own.

Lamentations in its final form exhibits a striking and innovative amalgam of prophetic, Deuteronomistic, and wisdom motifs that subordinates and neutralizes the acknowledged Davidic-Zion traditions without rejecting them outright. This theology of active engagement with national crisis is the work of poets and pastoral/priestly leaders who communicated directly and persuasively with the demoralized Judahite survivors of 586 B.C.E. In doing so, they undertook a critical project of corporate "grief work" by which they bridged the gap between primal grief and outrage at the fall of Jerusalem and the ethics and theology by means of which their people interpreted public events and oriented their lives. So successful were they in linking the idioms and concepts of the lament genre to a major historical crisis that Lamentations provided a paradigm for later generations of Jews and Christians to struggle with the meanings of corporate calamity and to work out strategies for living through world-shaking catastrophes, reaching even to the wars and massacres of the 20th century.

C

Canon, Theology, and Teaching
Hebrew Bible

CHAPTER 13

Social Matrix and Canonical Shape

ABSTRACT

Social matrix and canonical shape are assessed as complementary and reciprocal contexts for viewing the development of biblical literature and for appropriating scripture hermeneutically. The substance of social scientific and canonical critical methods and conclusions are characterized, on the basis of which it is argued that each methodology is constructively aided by the insights of the other. Social critical method works with a literature growing toward and eventuating in canonicity, while canonical critical method works with a canon whose contents and final shape are produced in a social process. Both ways of perceiving the Bible are integral to a proper theological hermeneutic.

The catch phrases "social matrix and canonical shape" suggest the relationship between social scientific criticism and canonical criticism in Old Testament studies. In particular, I want to stake out the intrinsic compatibility of their respective concerns, and even the necessity of their collaboration, in order properly to fulfill what each approach hopes to achieve. In the process, I will offer a critique of certain inadequacies and dangers in the formulations of both types of critics.

I

Social scientific criticism, also known as sociological criticism or biblical sociology, starts from the premise that biblical writings are social products.[1] They were written by people shaped by and interacting within institutional structures and symbolic codes operative in the primary sectors of communal life, such as economy, family, government,

---

[1] On social scientific methodology, see the essays by Bruce J. Malina, Norman K. Gottwald, and Gerd Theissen in Gottwald (1983a:11–58). For bibliography, see Gottwald, 1983f:168–84; 1992:88–89.

law, war, ritual, and religious belief. These Israelite-Jewish social networks, always in flux and full of tension and contradiction, supply an indispensable context for grounding other insights of biblical studies, including the results of historical critical methods and the newer literary methods, as well as canonical criticism itself. The guiding question for social science approaches to the Bible might be framed in this way: What social structures, processes, and codes are explicit or implicit in the biblical literature, in the scattered social data it contains, in the overtly political history it recounts or touches on, and in the religious beliefs and practices it attests?

Social scientific criticism is many-faceted, proceeding along several fronts or axes of inquiry and employing a variety of methods and theories. For example, it works along a continuum from limited inquiries into particular offices, roles, and institutions toward more inclusive analyses and reconstructions of the larger social system. At times, it operates with synchronic analysis of social realities at a particular historical juncture or in a posited representative moment that gives a cross-section of social life. At other times, it operates with a diachronic analysis of how the social phenomena, of whatever scale, developed over time. Typically, it organizes the inquiry and the results into the rubrics supplied by the social sciences, but it may also bring a social scientific perspective into exegesis that follows the discursive form of the biblical texts.

Social scientific criticism, in addition to drawing on archaeology, cautiously employs comparative method for studying social formations cross-culturally in order to theorize about the social history of Israel, since it is well known that the biblical texts are frequently too restrictively religious, too fragmentary, or too anachronistic to be able by themselves to give us a balanced picture of Israelite society. All in all, in contrast to past erratic or undisciplined efforts, there is currently good reason for confidence in proposing controlled hypotheses about Israelite society. Granted that important social data are lacking for ancient Israel, we can nonetheless formulate testable models for conceiving the society, models that are necessary for interpreting the knowledge we do have and suggestive of additional research needed to refine and revise our tentative mappings of biblical societies.

Insofar as the whole of biblical societies is the object of study, global social theorists such as Karl Marx, Émile Durkheim, and Max Weber are key influences and guides. The use of Marxian, Durkheimian, and Weberian tools of analysis and synthesis is often highly eclectic. What is especially important in the work of these theorists is that they held broad and coherent perspectives which, in varying ways, viewed the components of society as multi-dimensional and interactive, giving rise to contradictions in society that fuel social change. Furthermore, after a long era of reaction against crude social evolutionary schemes of the nineteenth century, neo-evolutionary social theory is being cogently applied to ancient Israel, allowing as it does for different rates of social change from society to society, for leaps in stages or retrograde developments, and for calculations of trends or tendencies in terms of probabilities instead of heavy-handed determinisms.

I do not hesitate to claim that social scientific criticism completes the task of historical criticism by providing more or less detailed social referential readings of the biblical texts. Admittedly, these texts differ greatly in their accessibility to social analysis. One might generalize that laws and prophetic texts have been somewhat more amenable to social scientific exegesis than have imaginative narratives, such as sagas and legends, and wisdom genres. Yet it is fair to state that some headway is being made in the social interpretation of texts composed of all the major genres of biblical literature.

A word should be said about where I see my own study of premonarchic Israel falling within this description of social scientific criticism. In *The Tribes of Yahweh* and subsequent studies (1979; 1983e; 1985a), I propose in considerable detail that the body of literature identifiable as probably premonarchic is most satisfactorily explained as the creation of a social revolutionary movement, largely of a peasant populace, carving out its own material and cultural living space in the highlands of Canaan in a trans-tribal, village-based revitalization process that consciously broke with centralized government in the Canaanite form of city-state hierarchy.

The religion of these Israelite folk arose coterminously with their social and political struggle and was both the ideological propulsion for and the most distinctive cultural expression of their movement. This social organization, along with its religious ideology, continued as an active force throughout the changing conditions of later Israelite and Jewish social history. In my recent overview of the Hebrew Bible, I attempt to trace the social organizational and conflictual threads that run unbroken throughout biblical history and literature (1985a).

My hypothesis is comprehensive and many-stranded, and it is comparative. It also includes major efforts at sociological exegesis of texts, especially in Joshua and Judges. The hypothesis stands or falls on the sum total of evidence it appeals to in biblical and extrabiblical texts, material culture, and comparative studies. Of course, this "evidence" is not piled up and counted, so to speak, for it has to be interconnected, weighed, and prioritized, which necessarily leaves considerable room for differences of interpretation, even among those who share my broad perspective. It is also to be expected that the hypothesis will have to be modified, enlarged, and corrected over time. Also, while this whole approach raises critical questions about our own religious faith, the truthfulness of my hypothesis is not determinable by whether it suits piety, church tradition, theology, or politics.

II

Canonical criticism has set for itself the task of showing how the biblical text was shaped and interpreted as scripture and what that means for properly understanding it in its own setting and in properly appropriating it in our settings. While social scientific criticism draws upon a body of methods and theories developed in the social sciences, canonical criticism has a less sharply demarcated set of analytic tools.

Canonical criticism draws mainly on aspects of literary theory and hermeneutics in order to push beyond redaction criticism's interest in single books and series of books to an examination of the final form of the text as a totality, as well as the process leading to it, and to raise issues of theological authority and hermeneutics in a manner that grows organically out of the historical literary description of the canonizing of scripture. But precisely where the emphasis falls in canonical study, and how the elements at work interact, is heatedly discussed among canonical critics. For instance, does the emphasis fall on the final shape of canon or on the shaping process that culminates in canon?

The most prolifically published representative of canonical criticism, Brevard S. Childs, focuses heavily on "the canonical shape" of the final form of the text conceived as determinative for historical and theological interpretation (1972, 1977, 1979). The actual role of historical criticism in the canonical task posited by Childs has been the subject of much controversy. I conclude that, in practice, Childs builds regularly on historical critical insight, but that in his theoretical formulations he often appears to denigrate historical criticism per se, which is either outright self-contradictory or, more likely, a miscommunication on his part, since he may be meaning to say that historical criticism is necessary but not sufficient to canonical criticism. More problematic and crucial to his enterprise is exactly how the final shape of the canon is normative for interpretation.

In the main, Childs' canonical shape seems to be the final redactional stroke that disposes the contents in certain ways and thereby accents or interconnects motifs and perspectives that control the overarching reading of the text. Examples of this canon-controlled structuring are intricate arrangements of judgment and salvation patterns, and oscillating movements between past, present, and future in the operative hermeneutic of the final hand (redactor/canonizer?). I credit Childs with an acute, intuitive eye for seeing redactional constructs, especially in the prophetic literature. For me, the most original and perceptive aspect of his work is redaction critical, in which he advances toward a phenomenology of canonical form.

In his recent canonical analysis of the New Testament, Childs tends to replace the earlier term "canonical shape" with "canonical form," and he offers a section on "Methodology of Canonical Exegesis" (1985:48–53). Canonical exegesis seeks for "traces either of how the author intended the material to be understood, or of the effect which a particular rendering has on the literature" (49).

Among the signs of canonical shaping are the following features: (1) the overall structure of the book; (2) prescripts, conclusions, and superscriptions; (3) assignments of historical setting for the book; (4) the relation between the author's stated vantage point and the probable audience of the document; (5) the function of the addressee; (6) the function of indirect authorship or pseudonymity; (7) the effect of putting certain books side by side so that material is dropped, added, or separated. I should also add that, with this new book, Childs removes all doubt about his emphatic rejection of literalistic, univocal, fundamentalist readings of the canon.

James A. Sanders, in distinction from Childs, does not give excessive or privileged stress to the final form of the canon. What interests him is the canonical process operative through all the stages of Israel's literary history (1972, 1976, 1980, 1984). The canonical process was a trend toward repeating communal values and resignifying them in textual form. Furthermore, the various ways in which biblical writers repeated and resignified these values along the trajectory toward the final canon provides us appropriate canonical hermeneutics for our own reading of the Bible. Scripture is seen as "adaptable for life" throughout its entire course from initial composition and collection down to its present appropriation.

Gerald T. Sheppard attempts to nuance and refine Childs' approach, which he prefers to call "canon contextual criticism." He does so by trying to include all the compositional and redactional moments in the development of Scripture within the paradigm of the "final" canonical perspective (1974, 1980, 1982). For Sheppard, canon contextual reading sees the final text dimensionally and includes a careful delineation of numerous ways that Scripture comments on Scripture. Sheppard seeks to overcome a narrow theory of intentionality (Childs' inclination), but also to contest the assumption that theological exegesis simply imitates the technical hermeneutics of biblical writers (Sanders' inclination). For example, Sheppard describes three forms of inner-biblical exegesis that represent different expressions of canon consciousness: (1) midrash, in the sense of reemploying set phrases in an anthological manner; (2) "canon conscious redaction," which relates one canonical book or part of a book to some other canonical book or collection; (3) thematization of historically disunified traditions under the canonical rubrics of Law, Prophets, and Wisdom (1982). It may be added that Joseph Blenkinsopp's work on prophecy and canon argues a particular case of canon-conscious redaction in the sense that the Law and Prophets have been accommodated to one another, notably in the inter-textual formulation of the conclusions to Deuteronomy and Malachi.

III

Suppose we now undertake a conversation between the two forms of criticism, chiefly but not exclusively with Childs as the voice for canonical criticism. It is acknowledged that I speak primarily as a practitioner of social scientific criticism, but I do so as one who takes canonical criticism's concerns seriously and who respects what it aims to accomplish even when dissenting on the presuppositions and conclusions of certain of its advocates. Immediately, we can recognize a systemic drive and a comprehensive impulse in canonical criticism that is analogous to the systemic drive and comprehensive impulse in social scientific criticism. Each can be conceived as total in its aims and formulations. Each attempts to resolve the multiplicity of the texts into common denominators, whether the common denominator of social matrix, which birthed the texts and is more or less reflected in them, or the common denominator of canonizing consensus in the religious community, which put its stamp of approval on the present scope and form of the texts and which urges us to locate particular texts within a body of texts viewed as an authoritative theological complex.

So the question arises: Are these two "totalisms," these comprehensive canonical and social scientific methods, irreconcilable and exclusive of one another? Is either of them mistaken from the outset? Or are they schemata which can each get at something important, leaving us with the problem of how to relate them in a historical understanding of ancient Israel and in a contemporary appropriation of the literature?

It seems to me that, while they are totalistic in methodological thrust, the two methods are not intrinsically "totalitarian," by which I mean that I cannot see anything in the essential enterprise of either form of criticism that excludes the other on principle. Nevertheless, to carry through a methodology properly, all the way to its limits so that it gives maximal yield, means that a single-mindedness must be applied. This does not mean that the advocate of the method, much less the whole community of scholars and interested people at large, necessarily accepts that this method alone yields truthful and valid results. It only means that the results achieved by this method are significant and must be addressed. The overall significance of such a comprehensive method, and especially its precise relation to other valid methods, is hardly assessable prior to the results of detailed inquiry and certainly not by fiat of single scholars, including those most committed to the new method and those most opposed to it.

One way of exploring the contact points between social scientific criticism and canonical criticism is to examine what happens when the essence of the claims of each is carried into the territory of the other.

To begin with, what has canonical criticism to say to social scientific criticism? When assertions about canonical process and shape are brought into play, what is their legitimacy and pertinence for social scientific criticism? Through the categories of sociology of literature, ideology, and symbolic interaction, it is at once obvious that canonical criticism poses a set of issues altogether proper to social scientific criticism.

Consider canonical process for a start. The Pentateuchal themes, by way of example, are selective and highly arbitrary in their accents. Narratives, poems, and laws are brought into an ordered design around key nuclear themes or motifs. At the earliest stage of Israelite tradition-ing, there was a stylizing and patterning impulse at work that con-densed, expanded, juxtaposed, interwove, and prioritized elements in the tradition without any strict regard for actual spatio-temporal relationships. This tendency systematically centralized the experiences of diverse groups in early Israel as if they had happened to a united Israel. The centralizing manipulation of the traditions gives them, at an early stage, the character of "canonical traditions" (Gottwald, 1979: 35, 40, 63, 92, 111–83 passim).

Consequently, we can say with confidence, and precisely as an aspect of the sociology of Israel's literature, that from Israel's beginnings as a tribal confederation in Canaan an ordering transmutation of histori-cal events and social processes was decisively at work, doubtless because this revolutionary people relentlessly asked for its own mythos, its own foundation charter, its own objectified validation for being what it was and what it was struggling to become in a sociopolitically alien environment. Thus something like a "canonical process" was indeed operative as a basic communal activity at an early date, and this very tendency or process had a social matrix.

It is more difficult to form a judgment about canonical shape, if only because its various literary and theological dimensions have yet to be sorted out and the status of canonical shape seems to mean somewhat different things to different canonical critics. Immediately, however, it must be acknowledged by social scientific critics that late biblical society produced a canon of set books and that the adoption of this canon was highly significant of and for the direction that early Judaism took. A social reconstruction of postexilic Israel that ignored the emergence of "the religion of the book" would be truncated and inadequate social description and social analysis.

Both canonical process and canonical shape are ways of underscoring the ideological component of Israelite society and religion. The scripturalizing tendency in Israel brings its symbolic world front and center as part of the agenda of social scientific criticism. In a recent article on Old Testament theology, Walter Brueggemann points out that the radical social equality of Israel and its embrace of the pain of the oppressed and the deprived has its counterpart in a radical deity who affirms the oppressed and embraces their pain. He goes so far as to say that the struggle between a severe contract theology and a theology of pain and oppression is internal to God as "a question of God seeking to present and represent himself as taking all of these data into account" (1985b:43). For the social study of religion as ideology, it is certainly a datum of importance that the picture of God in ancient Israel has this characterization of a deity who struggles to overcome conceptions of gods as endorsers of social inequality and despisers of the underclasses of society. Israel's characterization of God contends with exactly the points of a just and humane public order that Israel contends with.

For the sake of a social understanding of Israel, it is appropriate and necessary that biblical theology should examine carefully what is said about the thoughts, feelings, and actions of this Yahweh. There is, for instance, solid ground for social symbolic reflection in the discovery of Raymund Schwager that, while there are no less than 600 Old Testament passages about instances of violence that are condemned by Yahweh, there are a full 1000 cases that display Yahweh's own violence (summarized by North:14–15). I contend that this is a social datum because it correlates both with the forms of violence that Israel suffered and that Israel practiced, as it also correlates with Israel's ambivalent assessments of and copings with violence. I would, therefore, argue that theological and social inquiries into biblical violence are greatly limited when they are separated and that correspondingly they gain depth and explanatory reinforcement when associated (Gottwald, 1979:592–607, 667–709).

What now does social scientific criticism have to say to canonical criticism? When the assertion that all religious expressions have a social context and a social counterpart is brought into play, how does this impact our discernment of the canon?

To begin with, there is the question of the positions of various social groups with respect to their preferences for and their interests in this or that canonical shaping of the literature. It is not sufficient to speak of an undifferentiated "communal mind or will" as the stimulus to canonical process and the arbiter of canonical closure. Literature, especially canonical literature, is not disinterested. Every text has its social matrix and represents one or more social interests, whether we can easily identify them or not. And the final act or series of acts that fix a canonical boundary and content have a social matrix and interest as well.

Childs refers to social factors in the shaping of the canon but in little more than a formal way, with little specificity, and never—as far as I can see even in his most recent work—in such a way as to grant that the very act of canonization, conceived as the ultimate religious act in a literary mode, is itself a thoroughly social act conditioned by a social locus in which this particular canon won out over other possible canons or over against resistance to canonization itself.

As Sanders concedes, and Sheppard and Blenkinsopp more explicitly recognize, social scientific criticism helps us to grasp the tensions and conflicts expressed in the inclusion and exclusion of texts and in their articulation in relation to one another. Without this sensitivity and method, canonical criticism may lapse into harmonization that simply accepts a communal decision to validate a collection and arrangement of literature as somehow overcoming, flattening out, and resolving all the prior and continuing socioreligious struggle in the community. In the absence of social scientific criticism, canonical criticism may obscure the reality that the mere assertion of what has been affirmed as canon does not tell us precisely enough what the force and thrust of the canonical decision actually was for the canonizing community, and thus derivatively or analogously what its force and thrust might be for us.

Blenkinsopp has put this social ingredient of canonical studies very well indeed:

> The biblical canon cannot be taken as an absolute, in the sense of providing in a straightforward way a comprehensive legitimation or normative *regula*

fidei. For the canon itself arose out of the need to resolve conflicting claims to authority in the religious sphere and the resolution did not come in the form of a final verdict. These claims, moreover, can be traced back to the prophets whose language about the nature and activity of God simply rules out the idea of a canon as it is generally understood....in the last analysis we cannot dissociate religious authority from personal experience (142–43).

The idea of a canon, in particular, would call for examination as an aspect of social history, implying as it does claims to authority and comprehensive attempts at legitimation on the part of different groups and individuals. For the most part this work still remains to be done, and it is no wise derogatory to the religious claims being made to insist that it needs to be done (148).

At this point, a word of caution to both parties in this dialogue of criticisms is advisable. All comprehensive methods and forms of criticism, including theology I should add, can go awry by turning into dogmatism and positivism and dead-ending in a sort of methodological fundamentalism. The same can happen with social scientific criticism and canonical criticism, and it is most likely to happen when critics of one persuasion talk only or mainly among themselves.

Social scientific fundamentalism results when one lapses into thinking that a social matrix can be conjured out of thin air, or that knowledge of a social matrix directly accounts for a text in all its features, or that everything in a text that is not immediately traceable to a social rootage is inconsequential.

Canonical fundamentalism results when one lapses into thinking that the religious community's authority-affirming fiat floats transcendently above history and society, or that the canonical decision gives us an indisputable clue to meaning that can shortcut the inquiry into the entire history of the text and its changing shapes, or that from the canonical form of the text we can directly read off prescriptions for our situation in the absence of information and sensitivities about what is at stake in their and our social contexts.

Both forms of methodological fundamentalism can produce flat or monolithic readings of texts that ignore individualities in the growth and functioning of texts in the communities where they were at home, and in particular may miss the special complexity of language in its relation to social and intellectual history, both in biblical times and in our own socioreligious situations.

Semiotics or sociolinguistics will be increasingly vital both to a proper social criticism and a proper canonical criticism. How do the special interests of groups get articulated and how are they given compelling currency in particular genres and aggregations of texts? What is the social status of texts that seek to give large-scale interpretations of the origins, meanings, and obligations of communities? Why do some texts make more direct allusions to social data and others more indirect allusions and some no allusions at all, at least in any denotative sense? What are the different kinds of socially perceived texts signifying, *really* signifying: that one should do or not do certain things, think or not think certain thoughts, obey or not obey certain leadership claims, side with or oppose this or that interest group, social tendency, or governmental act or regime?

If we make a distinction between penultimate canonical process and a culminating canonical shaping, what in fact happens when the meanings of texts are re-signified along the way and in the final closure, sometimes *sharply* re-signified? Certainly, the way we should understand canon will be affected by what we understand the function of these canonical texts to be as signifiers of particular meanings to the canonizing community. For example, are the significations from earlier stages of canonical process carried over into the "canonical intentionality" so-called? Or are the earlier significations abolished or altered so that a higher order intentionality cancels out, heightens, spiritualizes, historicizes, or subordinates the preceding significations of texts as they functioned in prior contexts? Childs seems to be arguing some form of the latter but his results to date, while suggestive and at times even brilliant, are impressionistic and appear far from definitive. A "final shape" that is supposed to be determinative of our interpretation ought to be demonstrable according to widely agreed criteria.

At issue is not only how significations may change through stages of literary development, but also the question of the status of language offered as authoritative language. What did the canonizing community think it was commending when it singled out this particular literature? This may seem a relatively easy question to answer when the language is directly prescriptive of particular ritual or social behavior. Even in that case, however, we observe prescribed behavior that may no longer have been doable or may not have been of much relevance to the canonizing community's preferred repertory of behavior. When it comes to language of celebration, admonition or warning, or history-like narratives, the authority claimed is especially problematic. The intended and actual results of conferring authority on these texts may have been manifold: to secure particular kinds of ritual or social behavior, to strengthen internal unity or consensus in the community, to give an identifying stamp to membership in the community, to insure obedience to authorities whose entitlements to be obeyed or whose interpretations, instructions, and policies were in dispute, or simply to preserve cherished stories.

Much the same questions about what authority of the canon specifies apply equally wherever later generations have affirmed this canon as their own. New social factors and new comprehensions of language continuously reshape the range and quality of authority which the ongoing communities assign to the canon. In our own time, how do changing notions of the relation between the oral and the written, between factuality and interpretation, between literal and symbolic meanings, and of the very import of language as metaphor—how do all these intellectual and sociocultural developments give different colorations to what is signified by accepting a canon? Then and now, *how closely* and *over what range* were and are behaviors and meanings in the community expected to be regulated by this normative literature? What sanctions, if any, have been applied for violating the canon? An astute canonical criticism, informed by social critical awareness, should be able to help us with such questions.

IV

To sharpen the dialogue, I conclude with a focus on the canonical closure of the Law to bring out the agreements and differences in the ways that Childs and I approach the issues. The shared ground between Childs and myself can perhaps best be seen by noting our criticisms of the biblical theology movement. Walter Brueggemann has made a most interesting, if fleeting, association between my attitude toward biblical theology and Childs' attitude toward the same subject.

> Gottwald has found a way (even if he is not interested in it) of giving substance and credibility to the now discredited "mighty deeds of God" construct. As is well known, Childs saw the problem: "Mighty deeds of God" is a way of speaking that seems to float in the air without historical basis. The approach of Wright and von Rad had not solved the problem of "actual" history and "sacred" history. The recital of sacred history appeared to have no rootage in historicality. Gottwald has found a way for those who will speak in terms of "mighty acts." But now it must be faced that the recital is an ideological articulation of a radical social movement. Obviously the implications for doing Old Testament theology are acute (1980:445).

What Brueggemann correctly notes is that Childs and I are looking for a way to anchor biblical theology in something broader and deeper than a series of confessional statements abstracted from biblical texts and communities. Childs' manner of doing this has been to lodge biblical theology in the broad contours of the scriptural collections as designed and affirmed by a canonizing community which serves as our authoritative ancestor in the faith. For Childs, the canon itself as a total content becomes an enlarged confession of faith whose accents and proportions are to be determined by a continuous reading of the whole.

On the other hand, I choose to locate biblical theology in its metaphorical range of reference to Israelite socioeconomic, political, and cultural life by showing how the basic assertions of that theology correspond to socioeconomic, political, and cultural interests and desiderata in ancient Israel. I claim that anything experienced or claimed with respect to God has a counterpart experience or claim with respect to human life in the concrete Israelite community.

So what is at stake between these two views of biblical theology? The difficulty I find with Childs' way of anchoring biblical theology, broader gauged though it is by far than the acts of God theology, is that it rests in the end on the narrow base of the canonizing community. It overlooks the special pleading of that community and misses the tremendous social systemic tensions and conflicts integral to the final outcome of the community's canonical decisions, of the sort initially explored in the work of Burke O. Long and Paul D. Hanson. Moreover, the canonical appeal tends not only to negate, or at least slide over, the social problematic of the canonizing community, but also to obscure the social problematic of the interpreting communities in which we are discerning the ancient canon's applicability to us. That Sanders to a degree, and Sheppard and Blenkinsopp more explicitly, are open to the social placement of the canon, implies that canonical criticism *need* not be, and I would say *should* not be, as "a-social," even "anti-social," as Childs makes it out to be.

Let me now illustrate these issues with respect to the canonical closure of the Law. I begin with the widely held view that the thrust of the community in canonizing the Law was to achieve order, stability, and fidelity to established priestly leadership and interpretations, assuming for the moment that P-like tendencies were principally at work in the scripturalizing of the Law. If that was the social matrix of the canonizers of the Law, does that not already orient us, the interpreters, toward an ordering and stabilizing purpose in our use of Scripture? What then are we to do with the challenge and threat to order and stability in our own social and ecclesial milieus and in many parts of the biblical canon itself? (Likewise, is not the sharpness of radical prophecy toned down by engulfing it in the moderating and comforting wrappings of the redacted collection of the prophets?) Does it not seem likely that a canonical criticism uncorrected by social scientific criticism, and not greatly concerned with historical criticism, will "stack the deck" toward a kind of biblical theology that is ecclesially circumscribed and committed in advance to preserving and reinforcing the current churchly and academic privileges and outlooks of contemporary official interpreters?

It is true that at a number of points Childs attempts to guard against this kind of circular exegesis and theology. But by accenting the surface structure of the finished text and by underplaying history and society, much the same kind of hypostatizing or reifying of the canon can result as occurred with the elevation of confessions of the acts of God to normative rank. I detect just such a dangerous leaning in some of Childs' remarks, especially where he excludes from consideration social factors that were not in the conscious minds of the canonizers or which they deliberately expunged from the text. For example, Childs says:

> It is clear from the sketch of the [canonical] process that particular editors, religious groups, and even political parties were involved....But basic to the canonical process is that those responsible for the actual editing of the text did their best to obscure their own identity....Increasingly the original sociological and historical differences within the nation of Israel were lost, and a religious community emerged which found its identity in terms of sacred scripture. Israel defined itself in terms of a book! The canon formed the decisive *Sitz im Leben* for the Jewish community life, thus blurring the sociological evidence most sought after by the modern historian. When critical exegesis is made to rest on the recovery of these very sociological distinctions which have been obscured, it runs directly in the face of the canon's intention (1979:78).

A little later, Childs speaks of "'a canonical intentionality' which is coextensive with the meaning of the biblical text" (79).

To the contrary, it seems to me that only through recovery of "sociological distinctions which have been obscured" by collectors, redactors, and canonizers can we get a true sense of the pluriformity of the canon, and thus give a full hearing to its various voices in relation to all the factors at work in our own situations as interpreters.

By way of recovering these lost dimensions of canonical politics, we can identify two sets of vested interests at work in the canonizing of the Law, one from outside the restored Jewish community and one from within it.

1. The Demotic Chronicle from Egypt discloses the Persian initiative in commanding the priests of Egypt to codify the ancient laws of the land which then became Persian provincial law. Precisely the same Persian intervention makes sense as the governmental instrument by which the reforming Jews from exile were able to make the Torah both

the distinctively Jewish religious and civil charter and the Persian provincial or district law honored in Judah.[2]

2. Secondly, the curious combination of P Torah in Genesis through Numbers with D Torah in Deuteronomy probably signifies that the priestly establishment favoring P had to make concessions to other groups who favored D, such as Levites and prophets, in order to effect a broad enough coalition of forces to make the new law persuasive and enforceable. Thus, the first stage of canonization can be seen to have produced a "new consensus Torah" (Sheppard, 1982:25; see also Wilson, 1980:305–6).[3]

If we grant social conflictual origins to the canon, Childs is not very convincing or self-consistent when he says:

> The canonical interpreter stands within the received tradition, and, fully conscious of his own time-conditionality as well as that of the scriptures, strives critically to discern from its kerygmatic witness a way to God which overcomes the historical moorings of both text and reader (1985:51–52).

In my judgment, neither the sociohistoric process of canonization nor the requisites of theology itself give warrant for using the Bible "to discern...a way to God which overcomes the historical moorings of both text and reader." As far as I can see, *the canon* is very historically and socially moored, and *I as interpreter* am very historically and socially moored, and *the God shown in Scripture* is very historically and socially moored. Childs may here be confusing the capacity of widely separated historical contexts to address and inform one another with a severance from historical moorings altogether.

V

As I view the future of canonical criticism, which I take to be a bright and promising one, it will not lie along the route of collapsing the meaning of the biblical text into what the final canonizers made of it. It will have to embrace all the varied fought-over meanings and their social settings, from the beginning, and not excluding the canonizers. To

---

[2] S. Dean McBride, Jr., has so far offered the fullest account of this Persian intervention in Jewish canonization (lecture on the Pentateuch and the Law of the Temple in Ezekiel 40–48, Yale Divinity School, February 1977; to my knowledge McBride has not published on the subject); see also Geo Widengren in J. H. Hayes and J. M. Miller (515), indebted to Egyptologists W. Spiegelberg and F. K. Kienitz.

[3] Gottwald (1985a:103, 106, 436–37, 459–69) elaborates on the impact of the conjunction of Persian intervention and Judahite political compromise on canonization and social history.

capitulate to the obscuring process of the canonizers in effacing the identities and conflictual stances of editors, religious groups, and political factions, would be to default both as historians and as theologians.

Theology does have truth at stake, including the truth of how theologies have arisen in our past (Gottwald, 1983d). A moment's reflection tells us that one of the prime reasons for obscuring the identity of those who advocate authoritative decisions and interpretations is to make their judgments look unquestioned and ancient, even timeless, and certainly descended from divine authority. To overlook this psychosocial reality of ideology and mystification in religious assertions, canonical assertions included, is to deliver theology into an uncritical subjection to the unexamined self-interests of canonizers and contemporary interpreters. This, in turn, leaves us vulnerable to unconscious captivity within our own horizons, at a loss for a critical perspective by which the Bible could tell us anything we did not already know or by which it could come to bear tellingly on thought and practice today.

I conclude with the confidence that canonical criticism is not inconsistent with social scientific criticism, provided that each sees the element of the other that is intrinsic and necessary to its own enterprise. As Sheppard concisely formulates it, the two criticisms belong together:

> Better theological exegesis requires a recognition that all the words of scripture are human words, historically conditioned, and contextually relativized in service to a larger theological claim upon a later believing community (1985b: 31).

A social hermeneutic open to the social locus of original texts and canon and to the social locus of interpreters will have both a linguistic canonical sensibility and a sociological bent toward uncovering the self interests, past and present, through which the divine interests are asserted. In plain truth, in biblical traditions, every assertion of divine interest is also someone's human interest. The collaboration of canonical criticism and social scientific criticism will improve our chances of discerning, focusing, and critiquing the admixture of divine-human interests which form the content of biblical revelation.

CHAPTER 14

Max Weber and Yehezkel Kaufmann on Israelite Monotheism—A Review of Irving M. Zeitlin, Ancient Judaism: Biblical Criticism from Max Weber to the Present

ABSTRACT

This review critiques the work of an accomplished sociologist who, on entering the realm of biblical studies, abandons his best theoretical and methodological insights for understanding Israel's social history. He replicates Max Weber's once ground-breaking, but now outdated, reading of ancient Israel, which he further confounds by accepting Y. Kaufmann's concept of an unchanging monotheism from Moses onward. The result is an undigested amalgam of social commentary and idealist ruminations on the religious ideas that one-sidedly produced Israelite history. The aniconic thrust of Israel, which Kaufmann and Zeitlin perceive as a metaphysical a priori, is better understood as the historical material resistance of Israel to the socioeconomic and political domination of tributary state power, legitimated and facilitated by religious cults and symbolized by the idol whose insatiable appetite "consumes" human production. (On the historical material/socioeconomic significance of Israel's prohibition of idolatry, see now Kennedy, 1987, and Hendel, 1988–NKG).

In this brisk and readable volume (Oxford: Polity Press, 1984), an accomplished and widely published North American sociologist from the University of Toronto tackles the thorny issue of the social origins of ancient Israel, taking the pioneer work of Weber (1952) as his point of departure. Irving Zeitlin's undertaking is an instance of a crossover genre in which scholarly experts in non-biblical fields turn their attention to Jewish origins. From psychologists have come works by Sigmund Freud, Theodor Reik, and Erich Fromm, and, more recently, from social scientists have issued volumes by Morris Silver, Aaron Wildavsky, and Michael Walzer.

Zeitlin begins with the premises of Weber's "historical-sociological method," i.e. to examine how the religion of Israel arose and functioned in its social context. This is achieved by using abstract ordering principles or concepts (ideal-types) in order to grasp the subjective meanings that the Israelite social actors assigned to themselves, their world, and their faith (*Verstehenssoziologie*). What the author hopes to do is to update and correct Weber's conclusions in the light of sixty years of subsequent biblical scholarship. The ensuing scholarship which Zeitlin regards as relevant is work in archaeology (valuable but not decisive on key questions), the tradition-historical labors of Alt and Noth (unproductive except for some of Alt's observations on patriarchal religion), and the theories of Yehezkel Kaufmann (which he accepts in toto). So much is Zeitlin's dependence on Kaufmann the heart and soul of his book that it would have been more accurately sub-titled "Biblical Criticism from Max Weber to Yehezkel Kaufmann." Inevitably, then, one's assessment of Kaufmann's theories will determine one's basic responses to Zeitlin's project.

So complete is Zeitlin's endorsement of Kaufmann's views—and yet so little does he clarify or criticize those views in the broad context of the history of biblical scholarship—that something must first be said about Kaufmann if one is to understand the gist of Zeitlin's argument as well as its decided limitations. Kaufmann was a Russian-born Jew who lived for some time in Germany before emigrating to Palestine. His initial scholarly work was in Jewish history and sociology. He wrote a two-volume work in Hebrew, *Exile and Alienation: An Historical-Sociological Study of the Jewish Nation from Ancient Times to the Present* (1928–1932), before turning to biblical studies and producing his multi-volume and better known *History of the Religion of Israel* (1937–1956), likewise in Hebrew. Considerable portions of the latter have been translated into English (1961, 1970), but the earlier sociological study remains untranslated.

Exile and Alienation is a complex, richly nuanced, work deliberating on the future of the Jewish people by trying to assess the relative weight and interplay of religion, culture, and politics in the origins and history of the Jews. It is my own view that this sociological study of the history of the Jews, although practically unknown outside Hebrew language scholarship, will outlast Kaufmann's biblical studies in its fertility of insight. Simply put, Kaufmann concluded that religion had played the primary role in giving cohesion and endurance to the Jews. In advancing this thesis, Kaufmann broke sharply with the premises of various cultural-political Jewish revival programs favored by Eastern European Jews to which Kaufmann had been fully exposed as a Jew of Russian origin. It is within these polemics over the proper direction for contemporary Jewish life that Kaufmann's vehement "overstatement" of the uniqueness and priority of Israelite religion must be understood. In fact, his turn to biblical studies was an attempt to buttress his "religion above all" thesis by spelling out precisely the determining force of Jewish monotheism from earliest times.

Kaufmann thus came to the Hebrew Bible not so much to see what Israel's earliest religion was like but to show that it was monotheistic from the start just as it was monotheistic when it served to bond the Jewish people from the Exile onward. What had been, in his sociological study, a religious factor of great importance, but interacting with other factors complexly, now became a monolithic essence that sprang full-blown from Moses and never deviated thereafter, nor seemingly did it ever develop or vary in any respect that merits our consideration. This primal Mosiac monotheism is not so much argued as a hypothesis as it is flatly affirmed and tirelessly reiterated as an axiom.

The biblical interpretation of Kaufmann is noted for two features: his peculiar understanding of idolatry and his arbitrary and eccentric use of literary and historical criticism.

Concerning pagan idolatry, Kaufmann insisted that the early victory of monotheism in Israel was so overwhelming that Jews lost all living knowledge of foreign religions. This meant that Israel mistook idolatry for fetishism instead of a visual representation of gods who were conceived as alive in their own right while indwelling the idols. He undertakes contorted explanations to convince us of Israel's ignorance of living polytheism and of Israel's absolute imperviousness to ideas and influences from these cults apart from crude fetishism which made no impression whatsoever on Israelite faith. Few close readers of the Bible have been able to believe that the pagan religions were such a dead issue for Yahwists, or so uncomprehended by them, nor have they been able to conceive the monotheism of biblical Israel as a single intuition and system of belief that underwent no development through the centuries. The undoubted distinctiveness of Israel to which Kaufmann validly pointed, even its religious uniqueness, is not at all grasped by such a conceptually rigid approach that turns Israel into a truly insular people, "in" the ancient Near Eastern world but not "of" it, and such a reading in the end does violence to the "historical-social" illumination of the Jews that Kaufmann and Zeitlin intend.

With respect to historical critical method, Kaufmann's vagaries are a constant puzzle. He granted the method in principle and accepted several of the major conclusions of modern biblical criticism, including the recognition of pentateuchal sources. While disavowing biblical literalism, at every crucial turning point in his argument he employed biblical materials as though they presented a reliable historical account. What the Bible says about Moses, exodus, and conquest is accepted by Kaufmann as more or less straightforward history. Oblivious to the oblique ways that non-historical literary genres reflect reality, he had no use for Noth's genre and tradition analysis nor for Noth's immigration theory of the Israelite settlement. For Kaufmann the neat biblical scheme of periodization that moves in an unbroken line from patriarchs to Joshua was largely unproblematic. Consequently, the literary and historical foundations of earliest Israel were as unclouded as its religious origins.

It should be stressed that Kaufmann's case is mounted with enormous energy and erudition, and it remains well worth the reading, if only because along the way, almost as sideshows to the main event, there are rich and fascinating observations that hint at other, far more radical, lines of interpretation. Kaufmann has won virtually no followers on his main points among biblical scholars because of what strikes them as his unwarranted adoption of biblical literature as a seamless garment directly attesting historical events. As I see it, although he certainly hoped to close the gap between idealist and positivist biblical histories, Kaufmann constructed a curiously split-level interpretation of Israel that is idealist in its view of the religion while positivist in its view of the events recounted in biblical literature.

By opting for Kaufmann's angular reconstruction of Israel's religion, Zeitlin of course falls heir to all the liabilities of Kaufmann's position. It might be hoped that Zeitlin would bring fresh evidence and new argumentation as an historian, or that his perceptions as a sociologist would at least introduce new perspectives and correlations that could offer another way to support Kaufmann. Alas, with minor exceptions, this is not the case.

The closest that Zeitlin comes to breaking fresh ground is in his astute treatment of the solidarity of Jewish slaves as the matrix for monotheism, particularly through Nietzsche's category of *ressentiment*, in which justice and salvation for the underdog are fueled by experience of bondage (93–94). He also sees, uncannily, that the great inhibitor to this solidarity was envy and divisiveness among the oppressed (78, 97). Yet, because the Moses traditions are read as literal history, Zeitlin misses the opportunity to explore the social processes involved in Israelite emergence from oppression as a phenomenon not restricted to a historicist reading of the content of the stories. These processes may be seen not only operative in Egypt but more broadly in Canaan as the tribes came together and likewise during the monarchy as Israelite peasants struggled against their own monarchy. In this respect, the political scientist Michael Walzer has a better grasp of the social processes of oppression and liberation among these early Jews than does Zeitlin, and probably for the reason that Walzer is looking at the Jewish uprising as a prototype of later political revolutions in the West, whereas Zeitlin is awkwardly trying to think sociologically about the disembodied monotheism preconceived by Kaufmann. Even Wildavsky's study of Mosaic patterns of leadership is more sociological than Zeitlin's work because its categories manage to escape the literal reading of the stories toward which Wildavsky tends.

The upshot is that in spite of his Weberian wish to demonstrate that the "spiritual" and the "real" were inseparably joined in ancient Israel (xi, 137), Zeitlin produces the opposite effect. The ethical monotheism he envisions from Moses on has a docetic cast: it is simply posited as a given, encasing the Israelites in "a bullet-proof shield" against all harm. The obverse of the caricature that these Yahwists believed the "real" idols to be pagan gods pure and simple is the caricature of Yahweh as the "spiritual," wholly transcendentalized God. A reifying split between the spiritual and the real opens up and widens, uncorrected and out of control, once Zeitlin makes the initial decision to work with Kaufmann's versions of the ideal-types of "polytheism" and "monotheism."

With Kaufmann, Zeitlin simply overlooks the alternative possibility that a form of belief in one God for Israel arose early but developed only through great struggle and permutation as it was concretized and re-concretized in changing social organizational conditions over the centuries. As it is, only the original linkage of monotheism and social bondage in Egypt is necessary: once monotheism is released autonomously into history, the later social settings do not greatly matter since those settings are overpowered and infused by the monotheistic passion which neutralizes their novelty and serious impact on Jewish life and thought. Only once can I see that Zeitlin shows a glimmer of recognition about the possibility of grave struggle, and then only to grant "a bitter struggle" over monotheism in the desert wandering which had to await the next generation to be settled once for all (103). In fact, so disconnected is Zeitlin's appropriation of Kaufmann from the actual discourse of biblical scholarship that he spends energy rebutting the view that the eighth century prophets created monotheism, apparently unaware that one has to search hard these days to find *any* biblical scholar who would argue that outmoded position.

Perhaps one reason that Zeitlin has been able to adopt Kaufmann with an untroubled mind, indeed without qualification, is the datedness of the biblical scholarship he has consulted. Although some items in his bibliography are as late as 1983, the works cited in footnotes generally do not reach beyond the 1960s, and of course his sparring partners are primarily Wellhausen, Alt, Noth, and Albright. Of literary critical work on Joshua-Judges, for example, he takes no account of the studies of Richter (1963), Mowinckel (1964), or Auld (1980). With respect to social scientific treatments of Israel's origins from within biblical scholarship, he cites only an early article of Mendenhall while ignoring *The Tenth Generation* (1973), and there is no sign that he has read de Geus, *The Tribes of Israel* (1976) or Gottwald, *The Tribes of Yahweh* (1979). Moreover, Zeitlin's omissions of practically all contemporary biblical scholarly works that have employed sociological and anthropological theory severely limit the pertinence of his book. Among the obvious oversights may be mentioned Morton Smith on religious politics in Israel; Robert Wilson, Burke Long, and Robert Carroll on the sociology of prophecy; Paul Hanson on the sociology of apocalypticism; and John Rogerson on the uses of anthropological theory in biblical studies.

Lest I be seen as carping without proposing alternatives, I shall comment on one of the missed opportunities in Zeitlin's approach. A sociologist of Zeitlin's stature, notably one with his grasp of Marxian tradition, might reasonably have been expected to ask basic questions about the social function of idolatry in the ancient Near East: How did idolatry work socially? Who benefitted when people practiced idolatry, and who benefitted when they ceased to practice it? There is, I suggest, a straightforward answer to those questions.

Since the idols were focal points of ceremonies in which enormous amounts of foodstuffs and other goods were offered to the gods, thereafter to be turned over to the state and temple officials for consumption or conversion into other forms of usable wealth, it can be said that political and religious hierarchies were directly reproduced and legitimated by idolatry. Renunciation of idolatry meant, therefore, that precisely in the "religious" act, peasants and herders were simultaneously refusing to reproduce and legitimate the prevailing hierarchies. The "unseen God" of Israel, receiving the "tribute" due, turned it back in large measure to the people who produced it. "Mono-Yahwism" (a less abstract term than "monotheism") was the religious facet of tribal independence turned sharply against idolatry as the religious facet of hierarchic domination.

The inner bond between social organization and religion, in the two modes described, gives "historical-social" specificity to idolatry precisely as a form of material and social domination. Here is the concrete mediation between monotheism and social history which Kaufmann and Zeitlin are at a loss to supply in their one-sided preoccupation with religious ideas. This mediation also brings out vividly the social revolutionary character of Israel in tandem with its religious revolutionary character. When it is further recognized that this social revolutionary thrust of Israel can no longer be explained as a spill-over from pastoral nomadism but represents a village-based agrarian movement, we are on the way to grounding the origin of monotheism in dialectical connection to its sociopolitical environment.

Why has Zeitlin missed this mediation altogether, in fact not even searched for it? It is a direct result, I believe, of his settling for Weber's (and Kaufmann's) subjective meaning of social action theory to the exclusion of Marx's theory about the primacy of objective social relations in all subjective interpretations of action.

How then should one read Zeitlin's work? This is certainly not the book to read either to understand Weber's analysis of biblical Israel or to evaluate Weber's contribution in that field. Nor is it the book to read to see how a sociologist uses his own theoretical insights and methodolological controls to make a fresh study of ancient Israel, although *that* is surely the book Zeitlin could most ably have written. Rather, it is a book to read for a restatement of Kaufmann's position about Israelite monotheism, to which the author has added some elaborations and nuances, none of a fundamental nature. In a more limited way, it is a survey of the history of Israelite religion to be set alongside the more balanced studies of Vriezen (1963), Ringgren (1966), and Fohrer (1972).

In a significant earlier work from which I have greatly profited over the years, *Ideology and the Development of Sociological Theory* (1968; 2nd edition, 1981), Zeitlin argued convincingly that we can best understand the classical social theorists of the nineteenth and early twentieth centuries if we see that they were "in debate with Marx's ghost." In *Ancient Judaism*, Zeitlin has given us "the ghost of Kaufmann" minus the "debate" necessary to convince us that Kaufmann's idiosyncratic interpretation of biblical monotheism is the key to understanding Israelite religion as a social phenomenon. If, in the future, Zeitlin should open up that debate, in full conversation with the latest social scientific biblical criticism, it is probable that he could contribute measurably to clarifying the issues and formulating the ground rules for social scientific discourse about ancient Israel. I, for one, would enthusiastically welcome such a debate.

On Integrating Multiple Truths in Biblical Texts—A Review of Walter Brueggemann, David's Truth in Israel's Imagination and Memory

ABSTRACT

This review of a literary and theological study of the role of David in four bodies of biblical traditions applauds the attempt to inter-read congeries of texts that have differing perspectives on the same subject. The difficulty is that overly sharp typological distinctions among the "truths" of David— conceived as the truths about "tribe," "man," "state," and "assembly"—are abstracted from tradition history and social history in a rather arbitrary manner. The resulting "snapshots" of David lack "the moving picture" of David's own time and of the later moments when he is invoked in certain ways. The integrative social hermeneutics that Brueggemann aspires to will require a clearer delineation of forces at work in and around each text and in and around each interpretive act as we read biblical texts for their contemporary import.

Walter Brueggemann here writes another of the sort of book on the Old Testament that has become his trademark, what might be called an "integrative hermeneutical" genre (Philadelphia:Fortress Press, 1985). In this genre the results of biblical scholarship in several of the methods (always the most up-to-date) are assembled and set in interplay by means of interpretive frames informed by contemporary hermeneutical theory. As with the author's other works, the angle of approach is fresh and the insights penetrating, forcing the reader into engagement with the argument, and often triggering further lines of thought and alternative ways of associating the numerous elements introduced into the discussion. In the end, however, this reviewer finds that Brueggemann has yet to take the additional steps required to round out his method so that his undisputed brilliance as an interpreter can be seen to exhibit a fully adequate and definitive hermeneutic with established controls.

Following on the florescence of studies in the David traditions (among them, e.g., the author's "David and His Theologian" [1968]), Brueggemann sets forth four "truths" about David as articulated in the diverse biblical sources about this archetypal king of Israel. The truths are so formulated in each instance that they associate with particular literary devices and sensibilities and with certain social locations and functions, as well as constitute integral theological constructs. The interplay of these literary-social-theological "truth-sets," in Israel and in contemporary church, becomes the lively agenda of the book.

Diction and style are part and parcel of Brueggemann's argument and of the effect it makes in the reader. His language is allusive and figurative, "teasing out" the subject matter, and it must be carefully followed—sometimes decoded—lest one jump to premature conclusions about his meanings. "Circling" speech, connoting as often as it denotes, keeps open the hermeneutical circulation, so that no single chapter is simply finished, nor does the book as a whole come to a single secure resting point.

The first truth of David. The narrative of "The Rise of David" (1 Sam 16:1–2 Sam 5:5) is said to express "the trustful truth of the tribe." By this Brueggemann describes how David, the chief aspiring to be king, is the one who embodies and leads the marginalized Israelites in their struggle for social power and security. The narrative is brisk and single-minded in its survival thrust and unconscious of moral and political ambiguity.

The second truth of David. The "Succession Narrative" (2 Samuel 9–20; 1 Kings 1–2) is explained as "the painful truth of the man." Here the private failures and abuses of the king are shown to have public consequences; the literary portraiture is subtle, neither cynical nor maudlin, and communicates apprehension about power when wielded by leadership as calculating and egoistic as David's.

The third truth of David. The accounts of David's consolidation of power and of Yahweh's covenant with the new king (2 Sam 5:6–8:18) are interpreted under the rubric of "the sure truth of the state." In these texts, religious ritual and covenant ideology buttress the burgeoning Israelite state hierarchy. As literature, the traditions are flat and tedious compared to the lustre of the two preceding biblical sources, for they either coolly describe imperialist politics or they legitimate Davidic state power in the high-flown language of oracle and prayer. The rule of the king is equated with the rule of God.

The fourth truth of David. The royal liturgical promises (Psalms 89, 132; Lam 3:21–27; Isa 55:3) and the ecclesial sketch of David

(1 Chronicles 10–29) are understood to project "the hopeful truth of the assembly." David is construed as the prototype of Jewish dynastic renewal (or a "democratized" form of Jewish independence) and as the model of the pious temple worshipper. Here the predominance of liturgy and pious reflection over narrative excises the blunt and problematic truths about David so visible in the first two bodies of traditions.

There is no doubt in my mind that Brueggemann's inter-reading of the literary, social, and theological dimensions of texts is the direction that biblical interpretation must take, and his pioneering work is to be applauded. All the more reason that we should examine the pitfalls and deficiencies of such an approach which must be overcome before we can attain a full-bodied cross-methodological reading of texts that will have hermeneutical force and precision. Thus, to attend to the "snags" in Brueggemann's work is to attend to the problems faced by all of us who attempt integrative textual readings and reconstructions.

Brueggemann's categorizing of the units of study raises problems. In some respects the divisions of the subject into the four "truths" chosen are made too sharply, and the literary, social, and theological alignments within each "truth" are too neatly drawn. The literary contrasts between the "Rise of David" and the "Succession" narratives seem overstated, and the assorted texts grouped under the third "truth" do not form a stylistic or conceptual unity. On the social plane, the distinctions as made among "tribe," "man," "state," and "assembly" tend to mask or blur important issues. In particular, the typology obscures how the tribal David passes imperceptibly into the statist David, and also how really "political" the assembly's David is insofar as he images either the civil or ecclesial autonomy of the restored community. Likewise, the claim that the Succession Narrative offers a truth about the man that does not serve state ideology is not convincing, since the strong case for the text's apologetic political function is not rebutted. It may be seriously doubted that we see any "man" David who is not also the David of "tribe" or "state" or "assembly."

Moreover, the characterization of the sociopolitical entities of tribe, state, and assembly, while adroit, becomes so typologically elastic— almost metaphorical—that the lines of connection from the sociopolitical world to its literary and theological counterparts are left largely unargued and undeveloped. Much of the text is literary and theological commentary, assuming or implying social grounding, but not directly showing it. By renouncing a historical framework from the start, Brueggemann declines the one path that might have yielded a fuller picture of the way David and his traditions were grounded and how they functioned in the ancient Israelite political economy (cf. Gottwald,

1986b). Likewise, no particular socio-literary theory or method, such as those of Terry Eagleton or Fredric Jameson is employed for sketching how social reality makes itself felt in various literary genres, as much by what is "absent" from the text as by what is present in it. This also means that the materialist inter-reading of texts, as practiced by Belo and Clévenot, is neither taken up nor evaluated by Brueggemann.

As for ultimate hermeneutical criteria, Brueggemann reminds us forcefully that truth is "polyvalent," even the truth of history, so that we must ask of all the modes of truth concerning a figure like David: which David? or whose David? In the face of persisting positivist tendencies among biblical historians, the author mounts a very necessary case. Once it is established, however, he goes on to urge that none of the several "truths" is sounder than or preferable to the others, leaving us with a subjectivism that does not comport with many of the judgments within the book. Brueggemann signals that some of the truths are nearer to the historical David than others and his assessment of social and political oppression, ancient and modern, implies that he wants to give some priority or "edge" to the truths about David that see him critically. But exactly what "edge?" In what situations? By what interpretive criteria? Brueggemann does no more than imply the controls for assessing and appropriating David's truths vis-à-vis our truths as interpreters.

Just as we cannot locate the biblical David in his multi-traditioned context apart from a careful analysis of modes of production and of the development from tribal through statist to colonial Israel, so we cannot make sense of David's truths for ourselves apart from an analytic grasp of our own political economy—our place within it and how our ideas on all matters are related to it. Of course it would be unreasonable to expect Brueggemann to have written the full history of political economy in a book of this kind. Nonetheless, we have not done our work until we can show how the fulcrum point of political economy is operative in the text and in the interpreter.

If integrative hermeneutics is to be truly social, it must be able to identify concretely the distinctive and always changing juncture of forces at work in and around each text and in and around each interpretive act. The "truth" of the text, amid its multiple meanings, emerges relationally in the particular way it interacts with and contributes to what we feel, think and do in our world. Much more inquiry and hard thinking is needed to identify the conjunctions of determination and freedom in which biblical texts were generated and in which they are grasped and re-enacted in our own truth scenarios, in imagination and in deed. That Brueggemann's work thrusts us uncomfortably to this hermeneutical boundary situation is a tribute to its energetic reach for what it does not yet attain. Meanwhile, his zest and daring make joy of the ongoing quest.

CHAPTER 16

Literary Criticism of the Hebrew Bible:
Retrospect and Prospect

ABSTRACT

In this paper, originally invited by the Biblical Criticism and Literary Criticism Section of the Society of Biblical Literature, I was asked to assess the achievement of newer literary criticism of the Hebrew Bible from the viewpoint of one who works primarily with other methodologies. Accordingly, I laid out three methodological practices—literary, social, and theological—noting that they tend to work autonomously but must be drawn into closer collaboration if we are to derive the full benefits of each for clarifying the fullness of ancient Israel as a people speaking in literature, associating in social concourse, and generating religious meaning. I go on to comment on "meeting points" or "synapses" between three different pairings of these methodologies. By beginning with literary texts, we can extend our appraisal to social and theological worlds by means of a Marxist literary theory of the type practiced by Terry Eagleton and Frederic Jameson.

As an informed and sympathetic outsider to the biblical literary critical guild, I have been invited to assess the achievements of literary criticism of the Hebrew Bible, particularly in terms of its bearing on biblical studies as a whole. At the same time I shall be noting feedback from other forms of biblical criticism which may prove instructive for the literary critical task. This is a daunting undertaking which requires me both to choose a large enough frame for the presentation to set forth a point of view and to select and focus my "case studies" concretely enough to be pertinent to the actual work we do as biblical interpreters.

My basic argument is that there exist a number of coordinate dimensions to biblical texts which carry equal weight for interpretation and imply their own methods of disclosure. While these coordinates securely possess their own integrity, they nonetheless imply and require one another to interpret the fullness of the texts. I shall divide my discussion into three parts:

1. I shall specify three coordinates under the rubrics of "literary," "social," and "theological," and underscore how the history of the development of the different types of criticism has emphasized the autonomy of each coordinate while paying little corresponding attention to the ways they imply and require one another.

2. Taking the literary coordinate as the principal interest, I shall indicate some of the points in current research where the literary coordinate and its appropriate methods encounter the other coordinates and their methods, with the result that new opportunities arise to sharpen the work of each critical practice and to invite collaboration in forwarding the complex task of biblical interpretation. These "points of meeting" will be set forth as a series of "examples" or "case studies" in the inter-reading of the coordinates.

3. Finally, I shall raise the issue of a satisfactory literary theory which will be able to frame and give intellectual warrant to the inter-reading of the literary, social, and theological practices. The work of the literary theorists Terry Eagleton and Fredric Jameson will be proposed as one way of plotting and interconnecting the coordinates.

Literary, Social, and Theological Critical Practices

In recent decades, literary and social critical practices have arisen alongside—and at times in opposition to—the older historical critical practice, while the much older theological approach has undergone revision in step with the new complexity of biblical inquiry. These critical practices have been pursued with unrelenting vigor and with enough payoffs to have attracted enthusiastic practitioners and to have shaken up the way the field is construed and divided up for working purposes.

In the main these critical practices have proceeded along highly independent lines, appropriate to their corresponding coordinates and often with the overt or tacit assumption that they are not only different but incompatible mappings of the biblical terrain, so radically dissimilar in starting points that their findings cannot be expected to meet other than disjunctively. After a brief look at the circumstances and grounds of this presumed incompatibility of critical practices, I will contend that amid and beyond all the pronounced disjunctions that separate the literary, social, and theological worlds of the Bible, they do in fact converge toward a hermeneutical horizon where all are complementary and mutually enriching aspects of a single biblical landscape. Moreover, I shall urge that the convergence of these perspectives and practices does not come simply at the end of study, as a final moment of integration, but informs the entire process of study, since each of the criticisms uses data and raises questions that call the other forms of criticism into play (Gottwald, 1985a:6–34, 596–609).

Literary Critical Practice

It is virtually impossible to overstate the scope and impact of the explosion of literary studies of the Bible. Biblical scholars have at long last come to employ the full arsenal of literary criticism and not merely its genetic aspects related to source criticism, form criticism, tradition criticism, and redaction criticism. As Leonard Thompson puts it, drawing on a phrase of Robert Penn Warren, there opens before us "a more fantastic country," the realm of structured and structuring speech which need not serve immediate historical and social reconstruction or distill theological truths to be a plausible and compelling world. This fictive world can be explored, as Edgar McKnight notes, according to any or all of four literary elements: the work itself, the author of the work, the universe imitated in the work, or the audience receiving the work.

Now in order to bring this literary world fully into the consciousness of biblical scholarship as a legitimate object of study, it has been methodologically and psychically necessary to open wide the gulf between the literary coordinate and the history and society associated with it and the theological constructs expressed in it. This emphatic declaration of independence by biblical literary critics has been productive in authorizing their undertakings and carving out a recognizable space for their work. Once the sphere of literary critical practice is securely established, however, the question of the long-range status of literary criticism vis-à-vis the other types of criticism emerges with growing insistence. How are the literary findings to be communicated to other kinds of critics and how are literary critics to receive feedback from specialists in the other critical practices? Unless this problem of communication and collaboration is faced, literary criticism may settle into balkanized dogma, isolated from the larger body of biblical scholarship.

Social Critical Practice

Studies of the social coordinate in biblical interpretation have followed a course very much like that of literary studies. Social inquiry into biblical traditions has been able to uncover the contours of social organization and social change which underlie and pervade the checkered political and religious history of ancient Israel. The dike restraining social scientific criticism from a full engagement with the Bible has been breached at so many points that we have passed irreversibly beyond compiling social data as random realia to a deepening clarification of how biblical people lived as social beings and how their social struggles, self-interests, and utopian aspirations are expressed directly and indirectly in the texts. Here too, alongside the literary world, unfolds "a more fantastic country," the social world of a people who were not simply speakers or writers on religious subjects but also producers and reproducers of a determinate social existence which encompassed all aspects of life. Just as literary critical practice has removed forever the uncritically read text, so social critical practice has taken away for all time the uncritically assumed society, whether of wandering nomads or of religiously preoccupied students of sacred texts.

In order to validate the systemic examination of the Bible's social fabric, it has been necessary to sharpen the gulf between social structure and process and what is written both in its literary form and in its theological content. The favorite label for this maneuver by those who don't like it is "reductionism," generally not noticing the "reduction" practiced by their own methods. This assertive declaration of independence, analogous to the situation in literary criticism, has laid new foundations and fashioned new tools for recovering the conflictual social world previously dissipated into history and culture narrowly or fuzzily conceived. But exactly as in the literary fold, so too within social critical practice there looms the threat of stagnating dogma unless the social critical results can find their way into the give-and-take of commonly addressed hermeneutical and exegetical tasks.

Theological Critical Practice

The study of the theological coordinate has developed differently than studies of the literary and social coordinates. After all, theological methods of inquiry into the Bible have been at work far longer than the full-bodied literary and social practices. By instinct, theological critics want to be the integrating and synthesizing interpreters of the Bible. That task was difficult enough when theology had to wrestle with the results of historical criticism. With the eruption of new critical practices onto the biblical scene, theology faces a disorienting array of choices. On which of the critical practices should it draw and in what depth and over what range? Should it try to stand back from the thick of the fray in the other critical practices, wary of being trapped in fads? But if it does "stand back," on what material content will its theological reflection stand? The main historic roots of theological criticism of the Bible are in the classical theological and philosophical traditions which do not offer ready means to appropriate the literary and social understandings deeply and substantively. Thus, theological criticism must run "to keep up" with its own object of study.

Where recent theological criticism of the Hebrew Bible has been strongest is in laying hold of the expanded literary dimensions of historical critical practice by turning form criticism, tradition criticism, and redaction criticism to its purposes. Yet it cannot be said that "stream-of-tradition"/trajectory theological constructs or canon critical schemes are closely in touch either with literary or social critical practices as they are now carried on with rigor and sophistication. While theological criticism hopes to take advantage of the new openings, it has great difficulty with the elusive imagination of the literary coordinate and with the cold secularity of the social coordinate. Unless new theological discourse can bridge the chasms between it and the other critical practices, theological study of the Hebrew Bible may more and more resemble notions from past ages of biblical scholarship uninformed by a vital engagement with the full range of our current ways of recovering the richness of the Bible in its several facets.

The Ground of All Critical Practices

But what if the literary, social, and theological coordinates are so autonomous that there is no way to overcome their differentia as separate subject matters? Why, we necessarily ask, is there reason to believe that these types of criticism can cooperate and cohere in a larger project of biblical interpretation? The "reason" I advance may seem deceptively commonsensical and possibly so truistic that it amounts to little. I believe, however, that it is the bedrock from which we start any form of critical practice.

At bottom the three critical worlds we have surveyed do share a common ground and currency, even though that ground is not directly accessible to us. In the critical practices associated with the three coordinates are disclosed the simultaneous expressions of human beings who lived in communities of a certain social character and who wrote their thoughts and feelings in texts of certain types and who found meaning in their life together through religious categories of a specific sort. These literary, social, and theological "worlds" which we split for analysis were inhabited by real people for whom those worlds were dimensions of their lived experience and shared meanings. The three coordinates which we are trying to bring together coexisted in their collective lives and interpreting minds, filtered through linguistic and cultural socialization processes.

To be sure these worlds are separable and distinctive with respect to their particularities as speech, as social patterning, and as religious symbol and practice, and they require separable treatments according to varying methods. Always, however, the analysis begins from and returns to the unifying ground of a people speaking, associating, and generating religious meaning. What we are challenged to attempt is a way of seeing the literary, social, and theological artifacts in their specificity and in their ensemble, synchronically as function and diachronically as process. So the "trick" in critical practice is to keep the distinctions that matter while seeing the assemblage of dimensions and elements at work in the whole social formation. The test of whether this holistic approach is more than a slogan and self-deception is to be able to negotiate the interconnections among the coordinates as they appear in texts, without lapsing into detached piecework or vaulting into uncontrolled abstractions. This means to pay attention to the kind of information that can be productively passed from coordinate to coordinate at the "synapses" between them.

Where the Critical Practices Meet

It seems to me that the way to work toward better covering theory, able to overarch and intercommunicate among the different critical practices, is to attend to the "joins" or "synapses" at the points where the practices do or may touch one another. As it stands, the varying critical "answers" are usually presented as incommensurates, or, if in some way on the same plane, regarded as rivals in an uneasy truce or stalemate. Instead, we need to inquire as to exactly what these literary, historical, social, and theological "answers" consist of, the "questions" they do and do not address, and whether the interfacing and interreading of these various "answers" teaches us anything that can sharpen the practice of each and that can lead on to collaboration because we come to see exactly why and how the subject of study in all its complexity truly requires more than the one critical practice we are best at.

Since our orientation for this discussion is the literary coordinate, I shall note some of the ways in which the results of literary criticism present themselves at the boundary points, the "joins" or "synapses" between the coordinates, interfacing and prompting dialogue with historical, social, and theological criticisms and new kinds of inquiry internal to literary criticism which this encounter provokes. In choosing my examples or case studies, I have drawn freely from different types of literary criticism, such as the study of biblical rhetoric or poetics, structuralism, and deconstruction, without any attempt to adjudicate among them on literary critical grounds.

The Meeting of Literary and Historical Practice

First, I call attention to the meeting points between literary critical practice and recognizably older forms of historical critical practice. With respect to the endeavor to write a history of ancient Israel, one devastating effect of literary criticism has been to undermine the positivist tendencies of the historical critical approach, and perhaps even to throw into doubt the possibility of writing more than a sketch of most periods of biblical history insofar as the Bible constitutes the primary or sole source of information. For example, recent literary analysis of the two accounts of the war of Deborah and Barak against the Canaanites in Judges 4–5 (Murray; Hauser) and of the Succession Narrative of David in 2 Sam 9–20 and 1 Kings 1–2 (Whybray, 1968; Gunn) caution severely against reading these texts as eyewitness accounts, since literary compression, expansion, and transposition of events are underscored in all the texts and since the aims of the texts were far afield from what we take as documented historiography. I have no doubt about the wisdom of this caution.

On the other hand, this literary "de-composition" of presumed historical sources may give us useful units of historical reflection. If the literary materials yield certain themes or programs, such as "Yahweh's use of weak women to confound strong men" in Judges 4–5 or of "David's giving and grasping" in family and political affairs in the Succession Narrative, we may ask if these construals of the original events accord with other information about them, and also what connection obtains between the events of the times of the judges and David and the situations in which the literary profiles were created. This may seem a very "weak" form of historical reconstruction, but, provided we acknowledge its indirection and imaginative ingredient, this too is an aspect of history as "the past remembered in a certain way."

In my judgment there is also an overlooked direct contribution of the newer literary criticism to source criticism proper, even though this may come as a surprise to literary critics who have generally distanced themselves from source critical questions for understandable reasons. We now have a substantial body of work, notably by Robert Alter (1981) and Meir Sternberg (1985), which sets forth nuanced descriptions of literary techniques in biblical narrative, for example, forms of characterization and types of repetition. Much of this work has been done precisely in the pentateuchal narratives regarded as constituent of the J, E, and P sources. Would it not make sense to apply these newly refined literary criteria to the designated pentateuchal sources in order to determine if differentia in characterization, repetition, and other literary devices do or do not support the classical divisions of the text into sources? As far as I know, no one has taken up this task.

The Meeting of Literary and Social Practices

The location of the "synapses" between literary critical practice and social critical practice may be more tenuous and problematic, since these two practices are relative newcomers to the field in their present developed forms. By the nature of the case there are a good many "blanks" or "gaps" about social history and social change that we are trying to fill in because they are not directly addressed in the texts. At the same time, literary criticism is far from having adequately treated all sections of the Hebrew Bible.

Let me first speak of the possibilities in comparative literary studies, which may turn out to be a heuristic aid that will increase precision in both the literary and the social critical practices. I will illustrate with the historylike saga genre, whose sociohistorical context we find hard to pin down to the particularities of any one period, either with respect to the oldest horizons the stories contain or in respect to the times of their final composition. These double horizons of *oldest reference* and *time of composition* are presently distributed by various scholars over a span of 1500 years from the Early Bronze Age to the Exile. It seems to me that to make progress on this issue we need to look to places outside Israel where we have a body of sagas that is more closely controlled by attendant historical and social data than is the case in ancient Israel. I believe that a likely place to begin the search is with the Icelandic sagas and their parallel chronicles within the setting of the history of Iceland's settlement by Norwegian peoples who were fleeing the introduction of kingship in their homeland and who retained a loose tribal structure for many centuries (Njardvik; Kristjánsson). Once we have determined, if possible, what sorts of historical and social conditions are coordinate with the literary features of the Icelandic sagas, we may have some controlled grids for reexamining the pentateuchal sagas in Israelite history and society. It may also be worth looking at recent advances in the historical and social clarification of the circumstances surrounding the King Arthur legends for similar comparative literary and social controls possibly applicable to the sagas in ancient Israel.

Another promising boundary-confronting aspect of literary practice is the manner in which structuralist or formalist analysis of narrative programs in the Israelite sagas yield semantic themes that are fraught with connotations alluding to or issuing from the social formation. In Joshua, for instance, Robert Polzin claims that the "first" Deuteronomistic voice of authoritarian dogmatism shows us a unified people of one origin and status, while the "second" voice that speaks for critical traditionalism attests to a miscellaneous assortment of peoples, the majority of whom are in one way or another "outsiders" to the male assembly of "true" Israelites: Rahab and her family, Gibeonites and their allies, women, children, resident aliens, Levites, etc. Polzin sums up: "As the narrative describes Israel-the-community settling within Israel-the-land, it never ceases to emphasize how much of the 'outside,' both communally and territorially is 'inside' Israel" (145).

Rather similar issues about who is "in" and who is "out," as well as who is "in control," are suggested in David Jobling's analyses of the narrative programs of Numbers 11–12 (1978:26–52) concerning murmuring and rebellion in the wilderness, and in Numbers 32 and Joshua 22 (1980a) concerning the disposition of tribes on either side of the Jordan. In the former case, the program has to do with getting through the wilderness safely to Canaan. A leading semantic theme is the people of Israel arranged in a hierarchy which, from top down, runs like this: Moses, Aaron, people, Miriam, rabble. The corresponding semantic theme concerns provision of true knowledge of how to get through the wilderness, which is guaranteed by obedience to the instructions of Moses and Aaron at the top of the hierarchy. In the latter case, the program has to do with getting the tribes properly arranged on either side of the Jordan without splitting apart in distrust and alienation. The semantic themes are the unity of Israel, the proper scope of Israel's land, and the place of women and children and the coming generations in securing the unity of the people in the land. There is a great deal of "touchiness" about the full Israelite status of the Transjordanian tribes.

As an aspect of the structuralist analysis of the texts in Numbers 32 and Joshua 22, Jobling attempts to test the appropriateness of the immigration and revolt models of the settlement of Palestine as clarifiers of the structuralist literary data. He does not succeed in coming to a firm conclusion. Instead, the patterning of the dealings among the tribes is analyzed with the aid of conflict resolution theory from social psychology so that various scenarios of avoidance and of procedural resolution of conflict are seen at play within the accounts. Little is made of the wider import of such an analysis, but it might be promising to undertake a conflict resolution analysis of groups of stories in the Hebrew Bible in order to see if preferences for particular strategies typify particular literary traditions, historical periods, or levels of social and political organization. Somewhat along these lines, William Herbrechtsmeier attempts to correlate the original stratum of Deuteronomic legislation with types of third-party adjudication construed according to a theory of evolution of law correlated to levels of political organization (drawing on Newman).

In short, I am arguing that the social structural and conflictual impli-cates of these narrative programs bear careful examination, not in a narrow historicist sense but in terms of broad patterns which can be cautiously assessed in terms of approximate historical periodization. For instance, does the "touchiness" about Israel's composite and compro-mised origins stem solely from collective insecurity in a late monar-chic/exilic Deuteronomistic horizon, or does it reach back to memories of the premonarchic formation of intertribal Israel out of diverse groups of previously unrelated peoples?

My boundary-breaching examples between the literary and social coordinates have so far been taken from narrative genres. I wish now to mention the covenant or treaty genre as a stellar instance of the same phenomenon. The notion that Israel's covenant form is an adaptation of the suzerainty treaty from imperial politics is widely championed among biblical scholars, although many see this model as primarily Deuteronomic and not at all characteristic of earlier Israel. It so happens that the literary evidence for the suzerainty model is so fractured and scattered in the Bible—probably because of the reshaping of liturgical texts and literary redaction—that the decision of the comparativist to collect it all into a typical or modular form of suzerainty treaty is highly arbitrary.

It is possible, however, that this "literary" question may also be approached by another route, namely, through comparative sociology and politics. If we compare the sociopolitical organization underlying the suzerainty treaty in the ancient Near East with the sociopolitical organization of premonarchic Israel, the likelihood is strengthened that the suzerainty treaty was *not* the model of the premonarchic Israelite covenant except insofar as it may be an "antimodel" by which Israel cancels out imperial politics as a realm without any claim on its thinking and on its manner of life. I mean by this that the suzerainty treaty presupposes autonomous long-existing states that enter relations at narrowly specified points, leaving the rest of their existence untouched, and who do so as a normal part of international politics concerning which there is no cause for exceptional comment. By contrast, Israel has only recently been constituted a people, and its "treaty" between God and people, and among the peoples themselves, is in fact a "constituting instrumentality" which creates its own sovereignty de novo, in a manner that breaks sharply with the way "covenants" are conceived among the nations. Thus we may conclude that there was some justification for Israel to think of itself as unique on specifically sociopolitical and religious organizational grounds (a point treated theologically by the doctrine of the chosen people).

The Meeting of Literary and Theological Practices

Lastly, I will mention some meeting points of literary critical practice and theological critical practice which appear to be instructive in generating research possibilities that will refine the literary conclusions and the theological conclusions. I want first to comment on the tendency of some literary critics, beginning at least with Erich Auerbach, to round out their detailed literary analyses with attempts to explain the literary features of the Bible as a product of the religion or theology of Israel. Robert Alter, for instance, attributes the literary power of the Bible to the monotheistic belief of Israel, and Meir Sternberg sees the biblical literature as shot through with and shaped by an ideologizing of history. At times, perhaps because the theological treatment is far briefer than the literary, these explanations read almost like "spontaneous generation" theories, the faith, as it were, directly producing the literature so that the literary and the theological cease to be coordinates and the former is subsumed under the latter.

Alter at least has been quick to admit the impressionistic character of his suggestion so that it more nearly amounts, I think, to a question to pursue than it constitutes a satisfying answer. Others have noted that it is odd, if Alter and Sternberg are right, that it was just when the monotheistic and ideologizing forces grew strongest in Israel, namely in the Exile and restoration, that the literary power of the narratives waned. It seems that some other mediating terms are needed between the high levels of theology or ideology and the literary expressions. I suggest that we look at sociopolitical forms, especially the conflictual wrenching from Egyptian-Canaanite servitude to tribal freedom to independent monarchy and return to servitude under Assyria and Babylon, as the likely matrix and resource for developing crisp and laconic stories that are highly contentious and materially bound to issues of immediate communal crisis. In this connection, it is relevant, I think, to attend to the suggestion of one scholar in regarding the short story as a virtual creation of the Yahwistic revolution at the beginning of Israel's intertribal social and religious formation, "designed to portray the radical effect of a new and great commitment upon the part of a new people who were once not a people....The literary form was new, the people were new, the purpose was new" (Campbell, Jr.:8–9). In a broad sense this construal of the Israelite short story fits with Alter's attribution of the narrative skill to a religious source, but it does so not by the invocation of something so general as "monotheism" but by a correlation of the social features of the early Israelite movement and the earthy themes of the stories coincident with Yahwism of a certain type specific to the premonarchic period, which we probably do well not to call monotheism.

I mention here only one other mediation candidate in accounting for the lapidary narrative art in early Israel. I refer to the notion that early Israel, like early Greece, stood in a creative tension on the boundary between an oral culture and a rapidly developing literary culture, a tension which is aesthetically very creative (Innis). Of course this oral-written passageway needs to be looked at in terms of its sociopolitical and religious correlates.

A tentative summary of the interaction of the coordinates in producing superb narrative might be as follows: when Yahwism was spawned in conjunction with intertribal sovereignty and prevailing oral genres, and then extended under monarchic sovereignty that nurtured writing, the narrative power was generated and sustained, but as sociopolitical sovereignty and religion were disjoined from the Exile on, the narrative power to synthesize the social-theological combination lost much of its earlier force and edge.

To illustrate, let me cite an instance of a literary-theological "synapse" where the structurally analyzed narrative contradictions parallel theological contradictions. A vivid case in point is an actantial analysis of Genesis 2–3 according to which Yahweh is the initial sender/giver of the human cultivator Adam as object to the whole created earth as receiver, in order to till its waiting soil (Jobling, 1980b). The program is compromised, however, and nearly destroyed, with Yahweh "coming off" as a deceptive giver, a folkloristic villain, since he in fact withholds the human cultivator from the whole earth by keeping him in the garden as a personal attendant. The original program can only be carried out by Yahweh appearing in a second role as helper when he creates the serpent and the man-woman pair out of the undifferentiated human. The serpent by tempting and the human pair by succumbing to temptation together become the subjects/protagonists who facilitate the blocked transfer of the human being as cultivator of the soil to the outside world. In the process, however, Yahweh must take on a third role as opponent who punishes the man in such a way that he enters the outside world as a greatly impaired cultivator since the soil will now produce poor yields.

This fascinating structural reading gives what amounts to a narratized transformation of the theological enigmas that have plagued interpreters of the story over the centuries and constituted major debating points within Christian theology. Yahweh's conflicted roles of sender, helper, and opponent are ways of alluding to the unresolved problems about divine justice, goodness, and power and about human freedom, guilt, and responsibility which are posed by the prohibition and the punishment for its violation. It can be said that we have a theological puzzle because we have a narrative program in which Yahweh appears to have put himself and the human pair in a "no win" situation hedged by a "double bind." Message one reads: "Don't eat the fruit! Stay here in the garden. But of course then you will not 'know' and human life in the real world will never begin!" Message two reads: "Eat the fruit! Gain knowledge and start living in the historical world. But of course you will live a frustrated and limited life lacking the social harmony and physical abundance of the garden!"

In short, if this account is looked at as an actual transcript of the first human events and of the mind and behavior of God assumed to possess the attributes assigned him in many later theologies, the story is out of joint. If, however, it reflects some of the major contradictions of human experience and does not hesitate to involve God (not necessarily here congruent with later notions of deity), the literary, social, and theological "faces" of the story will be less a puzzle to us and more a revelation of how certain contradictions of corporate human life were imagined in certain contexts in ancient Israel.

What form should theology take if it is to attend to literary critical practice? It seems to me that a proper beginning point for a theology of the Hebrew Bible is to take account of everything that the Bible says about God, everything that God says, and everything that people say to God. This would be to follow radically and faithfully the course of the text. It would be an enormous task of registering and grouping the data. Unless and until this is done, however, theological criticism will continue to build very selectively on narrow bases of God-talk and perhaps often with assumptions about how that language functions which a fresh look might alter. Of course a mere adding up of all the theological formulations according to some classification system will not produce theology, but interpretation would, I think, be better founded and more consistently answerable to a wider range of data than is now the case.

A Literary Theory to Encompass the Critical Practices

How shall we conceive and give theoretical formulation to the interplay of the coordinate critical practices? It will have to be theory that does justice to all the practices as truthful ways of uncovering aspects of textual meaning. When I say that the literary, the social, and the theological are coordinate dimensions and coordinate critical practices, I mean that they are of equal rank and importance as specific "moments" or "instances" within an interpretive process that links or coordinates them as indispensable aspects of recovering meaning.

I would, however, like to stress that coordinate in rank and significance does not mean coordinate in the sense that any and every possible way of proceeding to interrelate the coordinates is advisable or productive. I take it, for instance, that literary criticism has effectively established that we begin with the text and we begin with it as a whole, from which point the literary genetics can be traced and the social and theological coordinates can be brought into play at every stage in the synchronic and diachronic literary treatments. This assumes that we are practicing literary, social, and theological criticism of a text called *Bible*. It is appropriate, and sometimes necessary, to supplement critical practices on the text with study of the social history or of the history of theological thought, etc., and then a first step would not necessarily be to consider the texts as wholes.

If, however, we attempt to convert the strategic first place of the literary coordinate in textual study into an assumption about its priority in rank and significance, we overstep the coordinating frame and truly "reduce" everything to the closed world of the text. We must have a theory that explains how the widest realities of life generate meanings in the text—how the text is open in certain ways to penetration and formation by the limits and conditions of history, society, and theology/ideology.

Simultaneously, we must recognize that the social and theological worlds enter the text through mediations of a complex sort. As we cannot let all the meaning of the text collapse into a self-constituting structure impervious to the rest of life, so we cannot rupture the aesthetic integrity of the text by making it a mere veiled set of signs about external conditions and happenings. No projection or mirror theory claiming that history, society, or ideology simply "toss off" or "exude" textual meanings will possibly do. The sui generis character of linguistic activity within the whole of human action must be respected and specified as a special way of rendering meaning that is in itself inseparable from the human life activities it refers to. So, an adequate theory of the coordinate critical practices must leave space to specify this oblique relation of literature to life, while also eschewing the impression that literature is free-floating from life and unqualified by it.

Among contemporary literary critics known to me, Terry Eagleton and Fredric Jameson come closest in my judgment to meeting the above desiderata. I comment only on some of their signal emphases. Eagleton locates a text within wider and narrower frames of constraint. The wider frame is the predominant mode of production interacting with the prevailing ideology. The narrower frame is the literary mode of production and ideology associated with a particular aesthetic ideology which is given a twist by the specific authorial ideology of the writer. The result of writing within these frames is a text with its own ideology. This text is not a mere passive product of the mentioned constraints but a particular formation in the force field which works so as "to actively determine its own determination," thereby presenting an ideology unique to the text. The ideology of the text does not preexist the text but is coexistent with the text, as it constitutes a peculiar expression of the general ideology or of some oppositional ideology locked in contest with the prevailing ideology.

When we take our stance within a work of fiction—and I would say also within a biblical historylike genre as well—whose relation to the historical is not straightforward, we discover that part of the text's very ideology as text is to present itself, as it were, outside of history or, at best, to be a reference to a general human condition uncluttered by historical specificity. This feature, which Eagleton calls "the pseudo-real" of the text, is an aspect of its guise as literature and in this act of self-hiding we see the text's ultimate residual connection to history.

> The text, we may say, gives us certain socially determined representations of the real cut loose from any particular real conditions to which those representations refer. It is in this sense that we are tempted to feel that it is self-referential, or conversely (the twin idealist error) refers to "life" or the "human condition," since if it denotes no concrete state of affairs it must denote either itself, or states of affairs in general. But it is precisely in this absence of the particular real that the text most significantly refers—refers not to concrete situations, but to an ideological formation (and hence, obliquely, to history) which "concrete situations" have actually produced. The text gives us such ideology without its real history alongside it, as though it were autonomous....If it seems true that at the level of the text's "pseudo-real"—its imaginary figures and events—"anything can happen," this is by no means true of its ideological organization; and it is precisely because that is not true that the free-wheeling contingency of its pseudo-real is equally illusory....The truth of the text is not an essence but a practice—the practice of its relation to ideology, and in terms of that to history....Like private property, the literary text thus appears as a "natural" object, typically denying the determinants of its productive process. The function of criticism is to refuse the spontaneous presence of the work—to deny that "naturalness" in order to make its real determinants appear (73–74,101).

Jameson, following Althusser's notion of "history as absence" and reworking Greimas's binary oppositions as a way of mapping the "ideological closures" that texts achieve, has developed sophisticated analyses of how the limits of the social and ideological worlds of the author are mediated or refracted into limit situations in the fictional works. Much of his attention is given to what the text excludes in its way of seeing the problematic of the story or in its way of recognizing live options for the characters. His tracings of these "ideological closures" in Balzac and Conrad are elaborately done and succeed in bringing out the historical and social ground while also accenting the distinctive shape of the plot and characterization, unique in the very moment that they manifest the history which is strictly absent from them. Jameson thus tries to show how the conflicts of the text, especially what it excludes or omits as possibility, have a significant correlation to what is experienced and deemed as centrally disputed, actual, possible, or impossible in the lived fabric of the society experienced by the writer:

> History is *not* a text, not a narrative, master or otherwise, but, as an absent cause, it is inaccessible to us except in textual form, and our approach to it and to the Real itself necessarily passes through its prior textualization, its narrativization in the political unconscious....Ideology is not something which informs or invests symbolic production: rather the aesthetic act is itself ideological, and the production of aesthetic or narrative form is to be seen as an ideological act in its own right, with the function of inventing imaginary or formal "solutions" to unresolvable social contradictions.... History is therefore the experience of Necessity, and it is this alone which can forestall its thematization or reification as a mere object of representa-tion or as one master code among many others. Necessity is not in that sense a type of content, but rather the inexorable *form* of events; it is therefore a narrative category in the enlarged sense of some properly narra-tive political unconscious which has been argued here, a retextualization of History which does not propose the latter as some new representation or "vision," some new content, but as the formal effects of what Althusser, following Spinoza, calls an "absent cause." Conceived in this sense, History is what hurts, it is what refuses desire and sets inexorable limits to individ-ual as well as collective praxis, which its "ruses" turn into grisly and ironic reversals of their overt intention. But this History can be apprehended only through its effects, and never directly as some reified force. This is indeed the ultimate sense in which History as ground and untranscendable hori-zon needs no particular theoretical justification: we may be sure that its alienating necessities will not forget us, however much we might prefer to ignore them (35, 79, 102).

To date, the explicit use of literary theoretical mappings of this sort in biblical studies has been minimal. In conceptualizing Deutero-Isaiah and Lamentations for teaching and writing purposes, I have employed Eagleton's categories and am impressed by their "utility" in forcing clarity of questions and in compelling careful and frequent interreadings among the coordinates. Only more recently have I become aware of Jameson and have yet to fully "cash in" on the points where he seems to advance beyond Eagleton. A recent "Jamesonian reading" of Psalm 72 by David Jobling does a skillful job of opening up the "differences" in a royal psalm so as to show how the operation of political centralization and the tributary mode of production in Israel effect the very structuration of the psalm as a literary work (1992).

Finally, let me add that nothing I have said is intended to lay out flatly this sort of boundary crossing as a project for every literary critic, or for every biblical critic of whatever stripe. What I am contending is that the community of literary critics—and all the other critical communities—must include these boundary searching projects with agendas that challenge and stretch the rest of us. We must encourage and support colleagues who venture on this course by offering them our constructive criticism. And of course, in so complex and heady a work, nothing can prevent results that are slipshod or nonsensical, some proportion of which must be tolerated for the sake of the health and productivity of all the critical practices which depend upon the lively interchange among them.

CHAPTER 17

Teaching the Hebrew Bible:
A Socio-Literary Approach

ABSTRACT

This description of my way of structuring a first-level course on the Hebrew Bible, requested for an anthology of the Modern Language Association, articulates the aims of my textbook, *The Hebrew Bible: A Socio-Literary Introduction* (1985a), and shows how I use its organization of the subject matter in classroom instruction. The interconnections of historical critical, literary critical, social critical and theological methods are specified and illustrated.

This essay describes the way I orient and structure a course called "Introduction to the Hebrew Bible" and my rationale for what I call a socioliterary approach. According to my experience and the accounts of other teachers and students, the first-level course is notoriously demanding on the learning skills of students and the curriculum-designing and instructional skills of teachers. Although intended as preparation for more advanced offerings, the introductory course is in fact often the only course in which many college and university students will ever study the Hebrew Bible.

Developments in biblical studies over the last two decades have greatly complicated the task of teaching the Hebrew Bible. In addition to the explosion of new archaeological and textual data, a wealth of new methods has arisen, without replacing valuable older methods, thereby enlarging the scope of what might reasonably be included in a beginning course. Facing an expanding and unsettled field, the teacher must make painful and sometimes confused decisions about what the course will and will not cover. Such curricular choices are usually influenced by the existing traditions of biblical instruction at the college or university in question, by the instructor's understanding of the field and expertise within it, by the available and manageable textbooks, and by the knowledge, expectations, interests, and needs of students.

Three main considerations govern my decisions about the shape and content of the course.

To begin with, the Bible is always studied from a point of view. The number of points of view has increased as new methods of study have developed and as the Bible has been used and interpreted in various religious and cultural contexts over the centuries. In my judgment, it is advisable to acquaint students with the broad phases of the history of biblical interpretation including divergences in Jewish and Christian views. I do this by a brief overview illustrated with a few texts. In any particular class, students will nearly always express a variety of views, which underscores the crucial role of perspective and presupposition in biblical studies. I point out that my own presuppositions and the role they play in shaping the course are logically and pedagogically distinguishable from those of others in the field and from those of the students.

One aim of the course is to help the student identify presuppositions, recognize how they function, and come to reasoned judgment in holding to or in changing presuppositions as they bear on the content of the course. This orientation runs so much against the grain of notions about education as objectively imparting uninterpreted knowledge that it is not enough merely to state it at the start of the course. Instructor and students need to remind themselves that, while they examine a shared text, they do so from various angles and often with differing assumptions. Thus the course "Introduction to Hebrew Bible" must examine not only the content of the Bible but the assumptions and interpretive processes of the involved readers.

A second consideration is that the actual study of the Bible is a study of content according to some method or methods. Enough of the content of the Bible must be studied so that students gain firsthand knowledge of what is really in it and, often even more to their surprise, what is not in it. Simultaneously, sufficient methods must be used to bring out the growth of the Bible in its total setting so that students grasp the biblical content as an intelligible multidimensioned whole. This recommendation leaves ample scope for numerous defensible choices of particular contents and methods and of varied ways of articulating them.

In whatever combination and sequence, it is the interplay of content and method that sets the course in motion, gives the study its pace and liveliness, and offers students a way into the text that will have lasting value after the course is ended. In the absence of a fruitful engagement of content and method, biblical instruction tends to drift into one or the other of two deadening patterns: either a reading and summarizing of biblical texts according to an unexamined agenda, or a recital of methods and their results disconnected from texts and their sociohistorical settings.

Finally, decisions must be made about content and method. Choices of the biblical contents to be studied require well-considered criteria. My chief criteria are these: (1) regard for the general shape of the Torah, Prophets, and Writings, so that the "story line" (where there is one) is grasped and so that students are exposed to the main literary genres; (2) attention to the likely preunderstandings of students, so that there is a good mix of familiar and unfamiliar materials and so that students can "unlearn" some of the stereotypes they have about the material they "know"; and (3) focus on a smaller group of texts that are useful for demonstrating the fruitfulness of particular methods by actually showing how they work on "model texts."

Decisions about the methods to be employed require equally well-considered criteria. At least every other year, I try to think through carefully the range of methods and their accomplishments, their scope and limits, their interrelationships, and the best way to introduce and illustrate them in a beginning class. My aim is to acquaint students with the major results of the methods, provide them a measure of skill in practicing one or more of the methods, and help them develop criteria for evaluating results that appear to conflict or to be unrelated.

To encourage critical reflection about presuppositions and methods, I structure the course not as a collection of serialized data but as a set of routes (methods) through specified terrain (biblical contents) that provides intelligible and reproducible patterns of movement between and among the wholes and parts of the subject matter. This general movement consists of three specific types of movement that are functionally separate but that must conjointly feed into one another for a satisfactory understanding of the Hebrew Bible. First, there is a literary movement within the stated contents of the Bible between and among its "framing" wholes and its "nesting" parts, together with the process by which the interlocking wholes and parts reached their present form. This is the immediate and obvious object of biblical studies. Second is a sociohistorical movement between the literary contents of the Bible and their wider cultural, historical, social, and religious referents. These referents include direct allusions in the biblical text and broader social and historical phenomena either implied in the text or presupposed by the text. Last, there is a hermeneutical movement between the Bible in its ancient context, as seen by the preceding two movements, and the meanings and uses of the Bible as appropriated and practiced by contemporary readers. This hermeneutical movement reflects on the extent of consonance and dissonance between biblical meanings in their original context and biblical meanings construed as authoritative or suggestive for contemporary life.

Some may object that I have omitted a religious-theological movement. I prefer to treat the religious-theological aspect of the Bible as an integral dimension of the other types of movement. Theological statements are both literary and sociohistorical; they are also hermeneutical since they call for decoding and reinterpretation in the movement back and forth from ancient world to contemporary world. I have no objection to distinguishing a specific religious-theological movement provided it is not regarded as an abstracted realm pulled loose from its literary, sociohistorical, and hermeneutical matrices. Precisely because the theological sphere has so often been either ignored or elevated abstractly above all other biblical considerations, I consciously distribute religious and theological matters throughout the other forms of movement so that they can neither be overlooked nor idealized.

In the organization of my book *The Hebrew Bible: A Socio-Literary Introduction*, each segment of the Bible is treated according to literary and sociohistorical perceptions, while matters deemed theological are frequently discussed in connection with one or the other of these rubrics. In the conclusion, I suggest a graphic format for mapping some of the major interconnections of the literary, social, and theological sectors when viewed chronologically throughout biblical times. Moreover, the hermeneutical movement between "then" and "now" is highlighted at the beginning of the text as at the end, while the influence of the interpreter's stance is brought out at many points in between. The structure of this textbook corresponds fairly closely to the format of the introductory course as I have developed it in recent years.

The older historical critical methods, which I used exclusively when I began to teach thirty years ago, are well attuned to sharp analysis of the biblical "parts." The newer literary, canonical, and social-scientific methods, which I have added bit by bit to my teaching, are valuable and necessary means for assembling the parts into meaningful "wholes." Nonetheless, most teaching of the Hebrew Bible has yet to find a satisfactory way to bridge the gap between studying the parts and grasping the wholes.

Nowadays I am moving toward a more integral "part-whole" deployment of the various methods, though it is far from smooth and finished in all respects and certainly not yet a synthesis of all the methods. This consolidation has been possible for two reasons: on the one hand, a number of biblical scholars who are practiced in differing methods have begun to take steps toward constructive correlations among them. On the other hand, I have found that students, lacking strong vested interests in any one method, can appreciate the contributions of the various methods and even work out tentative combinations or associations so that the methods do not seem to work against one another. Even when the results of different methods do not readily assimilate into a single grand interpretation, students often find it challenging to live with the ambiguities of this methodological explosion.

In interweaving the literary, sociohistorical, and hermeneutical movements so as to incorporate a range of methods suitable to specific biblical contents, I am now experimenting with the following approach to introducing students to the Hebrew Bible, consisting of a series of closely interlocked and cumulative steps:

1. Identify the Hebrew Bible as a subject matter of study governed by the hermeneutical starting point that the Bible is a cultural classic and a religious scripture. Draw on the history of interpretation to specify some of the ways that the Bible has been and is "seminal" or "authoritative." At this point brief reference may be made to the canon and to enough of the history of biblical translations to orient students to the most widely used contemporary translations.

2. Specify the precise subject matter of the course as that literary whole consisting of Torah, Prophets, and Writings (using literary and canonical criticism), and characterize the contents of the Bible in various ways, including its topics (what it talks about) and its literary genres (how it says what it says). At this stage, the defining whole is discriminated illustratively according to some of the kinds of parts that compose it so that the whole is recognized to be richly variegated (use results of certain historical critical methods such as history of religion, form or genre criticism, tradition-historical criticism).

3. Specify the context or surround of the Hebrew Bible as a sociohistorical whole consisting of the communities of Israelites and Jews amid other ancient Near Eastern peoples (use historical criticism and social-scientific criticism). Differentiate "sociohistorical" by referring to all the levels and aspects of community life, such as family, village, tribe, state, social class, cult, religious enclave, and so on. Indicate that this sociohistorical world is sometimes referred to in the Bible (e.g., tribal data in the early books) and at other times only implied or presupposed if we are to make the fullest sense of the text (e.g., nationalist reform and expansion under Josiah as the context of the first edition of the Deuteronomistic history). Geography, archaeology, and ancient Near Eastern history may be judiciously included at this point.

4. Bring together the literary and sociohistorical wholes, viewed as processes, by sketching the literary growth of the Bible from its smaller parts to its final form in interface with the social history (understood as including political, religious, and cultural history). In this way the phases of the literary growth are contextualized with reference to the corresponding phases of social history. At one point or another, such an "inter-reading" of the literary and the sociohistorical worlds draws on contributions from the entire arsenal of methods.

5. Move to particular segments of biblical literature and characterize or exegete texts. Interrogate these sections of the text by all the historical-critical methods, but, instead of stopping with the historical critical maneuvers, carry the results of the specific textual studies back to their contexts in the literary and sociohistorical wholes. If, for example, one has exegeted Judges 5, where does it fit in the growth of biblical literature: in the book of Judges, in the Deuteronomistic History, and in the whole canon? With its celebration of peasant warfare against Canaanites, how does the song reflect the society of early Israel, what did it communicate to the society of the time of Josiah when taken into the Deuteronomistic History, and what did it mean for those who canonized Joshua-Judges?

At this stage, one faces opportunities to test the contrary claims of literary critics who insist on taking the text as a self-contained entity and literary critics who admit of the relevance of describing the growth of the text and the text's relation to sociohistorical reality. Having, for example, studied Judges 5 from various angles, students can discuss what is gained and lost when the Book of Judges is treated as self-contained, on the one hand, and when it is treated as an evolved literature with sociohistorical reference points, on the other. Students can also consider whether these two perspectives are in some way compatible (by way of illustration, see my presentation of Joshua and Judges, 1985a: ch. 6, secs. 23–24, or that of the Moses traditions in ch. 5, secs. 20–21).

6. Complete the full round of study by returning to and evaluating the hermeneutical starting point from which the approach to the Bible began, in step 1. As a result of the orienting maneuvers in steps 1–4 and of the exegetical-contextualizing work of step 5, students will have a solid grasp of some texts that they can apply to their situation as contemporary interpreters. How, for example, do they now view Judges 5 and other "holy war" texts in comparison with their initial understanding when they began the study? How does what they have learned qualify the contemporary cultural and religious understandings of these holy war concepts?

The structured and structuring movement outlined above describes both the overall progression of the course and the typical style of study within the subdivisions of the course. The oscillating part-whole movements on the three levels (or four, if one treats the theological dimension as a separate movement) are undertaken repeatedly with respect to all the contents studied so that they eventually become second nature to students. My description may appear overelaborate and unduly self-conscious, but my experience is that, as the students become practiced, the pedantic specification of each step can be abbreviated or dropped, except as someone raises questions or as the class encounters striking or anomalous texts that present special problems.

This socioliterary hermeneutical approach to the Hebrew Bible uncovers its chief structures and dynamics, is instructive concerning modern use and abuse of the Bible, and is congruent with the way we actually learn deeply and lastingly about anything. Finally, the course orientation and structure I have detailed accord with a view of the Hebrew Bible as an open-ended "question-answer book," for we may say of the Bible what Carlos Fuentes has said of the novel:

> The novel is a question that cannot be contained by a single answer, because it is social and society is plural. The novel is an answer that always says: "the world is unfinished and cannot be contained by a single question" (cited in *The New York Times Book Review*, 2/16/86).

Part II

THE HEBREW BIBLE IN
OUR SOCIAL WORLD

A

Social Critical Theology

C H A P T E R   18

The Theological Task after
The Tribes of Yahweh

ABSTRACT

Socially and theologically, early Israel was embedded in its ancient
Near Eastern world, but its distinctive mix of social organization and faith
stood out as a critical variation of the general environment. The sociological
method of *Tribes* contributes to a present theology that understands the
"God-talk" of the Bible as symbolic representations of a totalizing and
directive sort that are not to be confused with sense perceptions or cognitive concepts.

Theological representations are developed through critical reflection
on active faith in the social sites where believers struggle with the realities
of daily life. Such representations provide an "onlook" or orientation
toward social theories, analyses, and strategies. Theological representations
cannot be dissolved by sociological criticism of the Bible or of present
society, but must nonetheless continually reshape themselves in the light of
fresh understandings of the social sites where they appear.

The theological task, once sensitized to sociological criticism, is to
review and rework Jewish and Christian history as an interplay between
faith, theological representation, and social practice. The recovery of an
organic theological curriculum of study entails the disciplined exercise of a
theory-practice "loop" that links biblical tradition to the present through
the mediation of Jewish-Christian history in all its religious, theological and
social aspects.

The title could be heard to strike a pretentious note, as though I were
proposing that my sociological study of early Israel now made possible
an entirely new theology. The intention rather is to indicate how I
believe the theological task is affected or shaped by a thoroughgoing
application of sociological criticism to biblical texts. Some readers of
Tribes have thought either that I announced the end of theology or that,
whatever my intentions, no theology would be possible on the basis of
such deconstructed reading of the Bible.

By deliberation *Tribes* did not undertake a new theological construction in method or content. Instead, I stated that "I do not present a new theology so much as the *preconditions* for a new theological method which would employ the biblical records as ideological products and instruments of the social formation of Israel" (668, emphasis added). How then does one begin to spell out the theological implications of the hypothesis of the social revolutionary origins of Israel and of the method and theory by which that hypothesis is reached?

Theology in Ancient Israel

An important premise of my argument in *Tribes* is to locate ancient Israel in its social matrix and to identify the social structural and developmental-conflictual features which have hitherto been described largely as "religious" or, more broadly, as "historical" or "cultural." In doing so, I pose a total social formation which includes religion and culture, and which clearly has its own history (although many of the details are inaccessible), but which encompasses the whole constitution and experience of Israelites as determinate human beings who engaged in concrete activities to bring their society into being and to preserve and develop it. A village-based retribalizing movement broke away from city-state control, and in the course of that historical project to enable economic and political emancipation through self-defense and mutual aid, the movement created its own culture (210–33, 323–37, 464–85, 489–97, 584–87, 592–602, 611–18, 894–900, 903–13). Central to that culture was the religion of Yahweh with a sharply etched symbol system and a centralizing cult practice. This religion was a key factor in achieving unity and perseverance in the historical project of economic and political emancipation (63–71, 493–97, 592–607, 618–21, 642–49, 692–703, 901–3).

The socioreligious system of early Israel may be analyzed from as many angles as there were elements that composed it and as there are means for tracing the interactions among the combining and interacting elements. We may, for example, focus on the crops and agricultural technology that formed the base for the solidifying of the movement in the hill country, and go on to clarify the economic impact on residential patterns, forms of governance, and religious cults and symbols (650–63). We can also focus on the peculiar "retribalized" social structure of the Israelite movement and its adaptive relationship to the economic, military, and cultural priorities of the movement (293–341, 611–18). Or we can just as legitimately begin with religious symbol and cult and trace how the specific material environment and the forms of social organization came to expression in the religion (618–21, 660–63). What we can no longer do in good conscience is to isolate the religious factors from the total social setting as though, once the historical and social "accidents" are noted as "background," we are free to move on to the self-contained religious essentials.[1] For theology, this is of utmost consequence, not only because of the socially embedded nature of the subject matter in biblical texts, but because of our position as socially situated and conditioned believers and theologians.

In the last section of *Tribes* I try to develop a profile or cross-section of the theological structure of earliest Israel both in its congruence with ancient Near Eastern theology and in its distinctiveness (670–91).

It is my judgment that ancient Near Eastern and early Israelite religion participated in or shared a common structure in certain key respects:

1. The high god (either sharing power as one god among others, or as the highest for a given purpose or moment, or as the exclusive deity) is individuated, given personal attributes, and elevated as the comprehensive generative or engendering power behind all that is, or all that has momentary relevance.

2. The high god is active in the world of nature, history, social order, and often in a moral order as well.

3. The high god is conceived by natural and human analogies, which come to expression in titles, iconic symbols, and expressions of the feelings and expectations of worshipers. These analogies include natural elements, atmospheric and meteorological phenomena, topographical features, animals and plants, and familial and sociopolitical roles.

4. The high god is manifested or experienced as powerful, just, and merciful, and likewise effectual in enacting or assuring power, justice, and mercy in human affairs past, present, and future.

5. The high god is in bond with a people, organized in a particular sociopolitical, territorial, and cultural formation, and this relationship tends to be reciprocal—even contractual—in the sense that god and people know what to expect of one another. The god frequently imposes sanctions on the people.

6. The high god is interpreted by human representatives who occupy recognized social roles in accord with the kinds of social organi-

---

[1] Gottwald (1979:592–607) presents critiques of the pronounced tendency of biblical interpreters to abstract Israel's religion from its society, as exemplified in the work of John Bright, George E. Mendenhall, and Georg Fohrer.

zation typical among the worshipers. The relation between god and people is interpreted according to "punishments" and "rewards" which are code-concepts for concrete gains and losses in the natural, historical, and social domains. In times of social conflict and political turmoil, the interpreters of the same god may disagree in their readings of the will or message of the god.

Amid this common theological structure of the ancient Near East, Israel at its inception introduced new developments that marked it as exceptional:

1. The sole high god usurps the entire sacred domain, calling for the exclusive recognition of one deity in the life of the people. The hyper-individuation of Yahweh can be traced in the rhetorical modes of expression concerning divine qualities and doings, in the domains of life where the god is involved, and in the behavior prescribed or prohibited by the deity.

2. The sole high god is alone active in the world. Where ancient Near Eastern polytheism tended to diversify, fragment, and disperse human experience, Yahweh's singularity tends toward a more integrated and coherent assertion of the totality of meaning in human experience. Where certain realms, such as death or sexuality, are not immediately penetrable by this sole god, they are nonetheless denied to any other divine powers. Symbolic reflection on *the* activity of *the* one God is encouraged, although it falls short of some alleged single divine plan until apocalyptic times.

3. The sole high god is conceived by egalitarian sociopolitical analogies, by which I mean that the representations of Yahweh are chiefly those of a warrior-leader who brings the distinctive intertribal community into existence and defends it. Of course one cannot properly speak of equality between Yahweh and people, since Yahweh is the superior leader and also creator who benevolently rules human community. The terms chosen to characterize deity, however, show Yahweh to be establishing equality among people by creating Israel. The concretization of El as Yahweh (Yahweh is probably an epithet of El that means "the one who creates the armed hosts of heaven and of Israel" [Cross, 1973:65–71]) defines the special sphere of divine societal reconstruction as an intertribal network of peoples. By contrast, analogies from nature and narrowly cultic analogies diminish.

4. The sole high god is coherently manifested or experienced as powerful, just, and merciful. The content of the revelation is formally very similar to the content of ancient Near Eastern religious revelation in general, but the faithfulness, reliability, and consistency of the deity in dealing with the people is greatly stressed—to the point that Israel gives

much thought to how power, justice, and mercy are interconnected, believing them to be established in one divine ground and thus not at variance with one another. There is an emphatic expectation that all parts of human experience in community will mesh and interact intelligibly and supportively.

5. The sole high god is in bond with an egalitarian people, an intertribal formation. This people is Yahweh's special manifestation, which to misconstrue would be to misconstrue Yahweh. This people is not a land, region, or city; not a descent group formed by actual kinship; not an occupational group or privileged caste; not the protector of single needy persons separated from the whole community. Women share in this equality as members of equal households, and women figure prominently in early Israelite traditions. Yet it seems a chiefly male-led society and the dominant analogies for Yahweh are male, although in many respects it seems as appropriate to refer to Yahweh as "she" as to call Yahweh "he" (685, 796–97, 913).

6. The sole high god is interpreted by egalitarian functionaries. Consistent with a people of equality is the interpretation of Yahweh by various leaders whose roles are circumscribed and contained within the whole tribal system such that monopolies on priestly or lay leadership are checked. No central government is operative, and social stratification is intentionally de-structured. The priestly establishment is sharply contained.

This theological structure of premonarchic Israel can be "demythologized" according to its socioeconomic and communal-cultural referents, in contrast to the usual program of demythologizing into states of existential or mystical consciousness.

> "Yahweh" is the historically concretized, primordial power to establish and sustain social equality in the face of counter-oppression from without and against provincial and nonegalitarian tendencies from within the society. "The Chosen People" is the distinctive self-consciousness of a society of equals created in the intertribal order and demarcated from a primarily centralized and stratified surrounding world. "Covenant" is the bonding of decentralized social groups in a larger society of equals committed to coop-eration without authoritarian leadership and a way of symbolizing the locus of sovereignty in such a society of equals. "Eschatology," or hope for the future, is the sustained commitment of fellow tribesmen to a society of equals with the confidence and determination that this way of life can prevail against great environmental odds (692).

Several of the most baffling aspects of Israel's religion are illuminated in terms of their critical social functions. Yahweh's exclusivity and abnormal jealousy correspond to the singularity and excessive passion of the Israelite social revolutionary movement. Yahweh's purposive neglect of the underworld and rejection of sexual commodity fetishism deny elite rulers the power to manipulate people's fear of death and hunger for sex as tools of oppression. The limited socioeconomic demands of the priesthood prevent a theocratic political monopoly over the people. The "popular" historiography of early Israel shows that the people, and not a few privileged heroes, make history. The salvation paradigms of early Israel (exodus, wilderness wandering, seizure of power in Canaan) are ways of showing that the decisive feature of historical events is social struggle.

Theology Today

On the basis of my reading of the theological structure of early Israel, in correlation with the people's material-social organizational-cultural structure, I offered in *Tribes* the following brief sketch of what theology is not and what it is:

> In our attempt to position the socioreligious nexus of mono-Yahwism [the sole high god belief] and egalitarian Israelite society within the context of a larger contemporary understanding of religion, it is necessary to take our cue from the methodological insight that religion is the function of social relations rooted in cultural-material conditions of life. This entails a rejection of forms of theology that separate religion from theology and that abstract religious beliefs from the socially situated locus of the religious believers. The uniqueness of the Israelite religious perception lay in its discovery through social struggle that the concrete conditions of human existence are modifiable rather than immutable conditions. . . .

> There is but one way in which those ancient religious symbols can be employed today in anything like their full range and power, and that is in a situation of social struggle where people are attempting a breakthrough toward a freer and fuller life based on equality and communal self-posses-sion. Even then it is a risky business to "summon up" powerful symbolism out of a distant past unless the symbol users are very self-conscious of their choices and applications, and fully aware of how their social struggle is both like and unlike the social struggle of the architects of the symbols (701).

In the light of the sociotheological understanding expressed in *Tribes*, I wish to expand briefly on three aspects of the theological task today: the nature and limits of theological representations, the social setting or site of theologizing, and the revitalization of the theological curriculum or encyclopedia.

Theological Representations

Theological representations or symbols, such as the representations of God as an actor in or a shaper of human affairs, are a special kind of thinking which arises at the immediate level of faith but leads on to critical reflection, both because nontheological experience and knowledge press for an accounting from theology and because faith seeks clarity about itself.[2] Theological representations are general ideas that do not give sense data or cognition such as directly represent the world or directly guide our action within the world; they cannot be operationalized. Theological representations are formed out of tradition, and are strongly internalized psychosocially, but they do not replace practical knowledge of all kinds. They are not simply a knowledge alongside other bodies of knowledge but a way of looking at environment and human agency and at the meanings and values associated with various kinds of knowledge. Theological representations are thus totalizing and directive without being exhaustive or prescriptive. They orient and dispose us toward certain kinds of relational perceptions and values and they move us in practical directions, although they are by no means the sole source of totalizing and directive meanings and values.

There are many aspects to the proper comprehension of theological representations. There is the striking inner-biblical tendency to construct, deconstruct, and reconstruct representations of God and of the divine will for people. We also encounter the imperative of analogical or metaphorical limits to our theological representations. Every analogy drawn upon to assert a likeness to God is at the same time qualified by its unlikeness in that God is negatively qualified as one who escapes every analogy. We need especially to recognize how our understanding of theological representations follows on Kant's distinction of ideas such as soul, world, and God as belonging to a different grounding category than sense perceptions and theoretical or operational concepts. Moreover, we need to go on to show how ideas evolve cumulatively and relationally in history (our debt to Hegel), how they ground and function conflictually in a material social base (disclosed by Marx), and how they reverberate intrapsychically (discerned by Freud). The evident universals of the Kantian ideas are seen to be malleable within the strictures created by a developing psychic and social history.

Theological representations belong in a family with art and literature and with ideology conceived as a kind of prevailing "onlook" toward

---

[2] My discussion of theological representations is greatly indebted to Alfredo Fierro (182–256, 305–62).

reality, a set of apparent a prioris or preunderstandings which have to be continually raised to consciousness and critically reflected upon. Thus, the theological representations call for incessant movement from first order statements of faith to second order coordination of these statements in themselves and in relation to other orders of experience and thought. Theological representations give an "onlook" toward praxis, as unreflected forms of behavior are self-corrected through intentional commitment and activity in daily life, gathering the behavior that appears to relate to the theological representations into some kind of coherence and relating it to other behaviors which may have their coherencies from other sources. While these theological representations do not operationalize into specific behavior they give an "onlook" toward concepts whose theories can be operationalized.

The Social Sites of Theological Representation

Theological representations are the thoughts of people in a particular context. Faith and critical reflection on faith are activities in a given social site. The pertinent site, from which we start and to which we return, is our own social location whose specificity must be felt and analyzed as a determinate one with its own history, special pressures and possibilities, and its own movement toward a future which we consciously or unconsciously help to shape. Past theological representations, rising out of ancient Israel and mediated and enriched through Jewish-Christian history, are totalizing and directive toward our present social sites. Theological representations, far from being "free-floating" universals that give us solutions to problems in every time and place, are rather "engaged" images or models that orient us either to thinking or unthinking life in the here and now. This is because the social world, in which theological representations are formed and communicated, is a humanly constructed world structured by power relations and by power-determined distributions of goods, privileges, ideas, and meanings. The theological representations of biblical Israel are highly political in their scrutiny of social power and the ends for which it is used.

Every way of articulating and prioritizing the theological representations is conditioned by a material base in which people actually produce and reproduce their lives according to certain limits, some of which may be immutable but many of which are changeable. These theological representations express particular social interests which in one way or another are negotiated or imposed. The theological representations can serve to cover over these power realities by denying them or can assist in bringing them to light to justify them or to contest for their change. In the process, the theological representations dispose us toward one or another set of theories and operations for dealing with power realities.

Theological representations, like art, literature, and ideology, sensitize and motivate us to deal with power relations in certain ways, but they are not themselves the precise tools for treating power relations, which must rather be theories and methods more exactly tailored to institutional and operational application. We may, for example, entertain a "functional" theory that explains inequality as a rough approximation to people's actual merits, or as the precondition of a social system working at all. Or, we may espouse a "conflict" theory that understands inequality as a forceful or duplicitous imposition of one set of interests on another set of interests without regard to merit.[3] We may accompany functional or conflict social theory with psychological theory that explains how people either necessarily crave mastery and subordination or have been culturally induced to internalize their powerlessness so that they more deeply fear the risk of change than they desire its potential benefits (Schneider). In our own social sites in capitalist United States, although functional theory is very strong, the impact of the theoretical and methodological currents flowing from Marx and Freud are deepening and widening, precisely because they offer us a leverage on problems that long seemed to be insoluble mysteries, and before which theological representations alone are helpless and even dangerously obfuscating.

Now it is evident that the wielders of theological representations can try to mark off areas of social and psychic life as tabooed ground and thereby resist new theories and methods for a priori reasons. Or they may so rush to embrace new theories and methods that they naively equate theological representations with those theories and methods (for example, the much-too-facile strategy of making Christianity and Marxism mean exactly the same thing), failing to observe the proper ground and limits of theological representations. Or theological representations can be recognized to have no special power to dispose over theory and method but rather a critical negative function of summoning and voicing the interests, meanings, and values that any theory or method will serve or disserve. Both the autonomy and conjuncture of theological representations and of theories and methods must be observed.

---

[3] Michael H. Best and William E. Connolly offer trenchant analyses of the functional and conflictual explanations of economic inequality.

In *The Tribes of Yahweh*, I have carried through a radical socioeconomic and religiocultural deconstruction of early Israel without leaving any remainder to save traditional theology by means of the ever-convenient "god who fills the gaps." I have done so by turning theory and method upon the genesis of theological representations in ancient Israel. What I have not done, and could not possibly do by such a project, is to undo the theological representations, both because they are given there in the history and because they inhere in a living tradition today. Just as sense data, theory, and method do not replace art, literature, and ideology, so theological representations coexist with theory and method in the world of praxis. The viability of theological representations rooted in faith and opened to critical reflection is, however, tested by being called upon to give an account of how theological representations relate to their material base and social sites over the whole course of Israelite-Jewish-Christian history.

No mere pasting together of "history of theological ideas" with "history of religious institutions" can possibly accomplish this deconstruction of the history of theological representations in the context of Jewish-Christian praxis within the wider social world from biblical times to the present. The project of *Tribes*, restricted to premonarchic intertribal Israel, needs to be carried forward through all the phases of biblical history, as George V. Pixley (1981) has initially sketched and as Fernando Belo has attempted for the Gospel of Mark. At the same time, the material and social base of theologizing throughout the whole of post-biblical Jewish and Christian history must be relentlessly pursued. Simultaneously, the theory and method by which we analyze and reconstruct the social sites of theologizing must be constantly evaluated, corrected, and enriched. It is clear that both Marxist and Freudian traditions are undergoing great ferment in themselves and in interaction with one another. The fertility of the theories and their applications is shown precisely in their capacity to reflect upon themselves and to improve their analytic and operational powers.[4] In this way, around the rubric of the interface between theological representations and social sites, all the disciplines of the theological encyclopedia can be gathered.

The Theological Curriculum/Encyclopedia

In a recent article, Edward Farley tackles the forbidding topic of fundamental reform in theological education as a theological task. The

---

4 See, among others, Bruce Brown, Stanley Aronowitz, and Alan Gilbert.

theological task is understood by him not as the elevation of traditionally defined dogmatic theology over all the other branches of the curriculum. Rather, the theological task is to grasp the unity of knowledge and understanding requisite to the church and its ministry. I believe that Farley's desiderata for theological reform of the curriculum are met by the following formulation: it is the theological task of the church to grasp the theological representations in their social sites and praxis settings throughout Israelite-Jewish-Christian history and to focus all that critically re-worked content on a self-critical praxis of the church and its leadership here and now.

The Reformation, Farley notes, offered a kind of theological vision that grounded the branches of the theological encyclopedia in a unitary study of divinity in which there was a clear movement out of the biblical revelation and the confessions of the church through history and into the ministry of the church in word and sacrament. Modernity has undermined that unitary study of divinity. Science as the theoretical feeder of technological applications has penetrated the theological structure, sapped the primacy of biblical revelation and confessional authority, and reshaped the dismembered branches of the curriculum into professional specializations with their own independent self-justifications, now busily trying to recover the vision by separate enterprises of "bridging the gaps."

Farley believes that the bridgings, redivisions, and rearrangements of curriculum won't work without a new grasp of the theological task. No doubt he is right. But where does one grasp the nettle? A theological curriculum of theory-praxis as the axis of every discipline absolutely requires a substantial base in the church and a faculty fully committed to it. At the moment the main power in the churches and seminaries does not lie in the hands of those who want to revision theologizing, church mission, and the process of leadership education. In short, our current social site favors utter amnesia and mindlessness toward critical thought and action. Nonetheless, the failures of the churches are so colossal, the urgencies of social crisis so insistent, and the resources of a critical social theology so available that new opportunities for deep-going rethinking and re-acting of Christian faith may be forced by our very desperation.

To bring theological representations into unabashed and total interface with material base and social site calls for the most unrelenting restructuring of consciousness. Theology really ceases to be higher knowledge, as it also ceases to be the arcane elaboration of a privileged faith that stands apart from worldly experience and meaning. A renewed theological encyclopedia of this sort could only come from

Christians with a radical regard for their tradition and with radical trust and courage to commit themselves to the conflictual and open-ended task of restructuring themselves and their world (Herzog). Just such radical regard, trust, and courage impelled the first Israelites, and it is in part for this reason that they entice and disturb us, making it worth our while to study them so intensively and comprehensively that they might be rescued from the platitudes and dogmas that have nearly cut them off from us (Gottwald, 1979:700–9,901–3).

Human Sacrifice and Religious Scapegoating—A Review of Hyam Maccoby, The Sacred Executioner: Human Sacrifice and the Legacy of Guilt

ABSTRACT

This review of a provocative book on the attitude of Judaism and Christianity toward human sacrifice focuses on the way the death of Jesus is understood in the New Testament and calls into question the social psychological and religious reinforcement of group stereotyping and scapegoating stemming from some of the basic Jewish and Christian "myths."

In *The Sacred Executioner* (New York: W. W. Norton & Co., 1982), Hyam Maccoby contends that a current ambivalence about the human sacrifice practiced at "founding" or "critical" moments in ancient societies has imbued religious myths with such a high charge of contradictory gratification and guilt that the myths have reinforced—even caused—the use of unpopular minorities as scapegoats.

Mr. Maccoby, who is the librarian of the Leo Baeck College in London and has written previously about the revolutionary Jesus and Jewish-Christian disputations in medieval Europe, argues that while Judaism overtly renounced human sacrifice, Christianity has paid it a concealed tribute by asserting God required his Son to be killed. Consequently, some of Jesus' contemporaries had to be "Christ killers" to fulfill God's plan. But a stigma falls on the unfortunate human agents, so all the killers' descendants—considered to be the Jews as a whole— are eternally guilty and liable to whatever punishment is dealt them.

In short, the Jew is Christendom's sacred executioner, doing "the dirty work of the Christian community" by performing God's will and then suffering cruelly for it. So bald a statement of Mr. Maccoby's thesis may make it difficult for the Christian reader to confront it openly. A brief summary also passes over the many levels and interconnections of arguments that range from myth and ritual in prehistory, through the Old and New Testaments and Hellenistic religions, to later attitudes in the Christian church toward Jews and the connection of these to persecutions of Jews right down to the Holocaust. The book has an especially startling account of how the Virgin Mary cult occasioned a shift in popular Christian belief in the Middle Ages, from the concept that the adult Christ is physically eaten in the mass to the idea that the infant Christ is eaten. Mr. Maccoby argues that this change directly exacerbated the slander that Jews killed and ate Christian children.

Not all of the far-ranging textual and historical interpretations in this informed and fiercely argued book are equally convincing—nor need they be for major aspects of Mr. Maccoby's argument to carry force. Complex discussions of the sacrificial features of the Old Testament stories about Cain, Lamech, Noah, Abraham and Isaac, and the circumcision of Moses' son are accompanied by fresh translations and speculations of some daring. But the means for evaluating the discussions are not easy to come by, since most of these texts do not overtly speak of human sacrifice, although Mr. Maccoby assumes that it lies "beneath" their surface.

Mr. Maccoby's treatment of the New Testament is more problematic. There the historical substratum is not quite so inaccessible as in the stories of Genesis and Exodus. He has some fascinating proposals, a few helped along by bits and pieces of later Jewish and Christian tradition. He says Barabbas, simply another name for Jesus, was fabricated as a second prisoner to hide the fact that the Jewish crowd wanted Jesus released. Judas, the betrayer of Jesus in a late tradition incorporated into the Gospels, was actually a brother of Jesus and historically no betrayer at all. In a most unnuanced fashion, Mr. Maccoby sees Paul as the first Christian anti-Semite and the Gospels as saturated by Pauline conceptions of theology. Any active opposition of Jews to Christians in the first century is greatly, and probably inaccurately, minimized.

Mr. Maccoby's method, which he takes from traditional Christian exegesis of the New Testament, generally validates his thesis, but his own interpretation of the New Testament takes the edge off that thesis by making its implications more easily evaded than they ought to be. The conflicting biblical figures come off too much like cardboard characters, the Jews looking "good" and the Christians, except for Jesus, looking "bad." In this manner, the myth of the sacred executioner in Christianity is made to look so arbitrary and perverse that its only explanation is that it is a survival of human sacrificial thinking.

The full horror of the tenacity of the social and religious use of scapegoats emerges when we see that the Christian myth of Jews as Christ killers arose out of a situation of intense conflict involving "good people" like ourselves. The author misses the opportunity to say that even if Jews contributed to the death of Jesus the Jew, that is no justification for people's trying to settle old scores by victimizing the descendants of those Jews.

Mr. Maccoby says it is important to know the social grounding of a myth, "especially the conditions in which it first originated." But the major weakness in his historical analysis is a failure to take full account of what the Jewish biblical scholar Samuel Sandmel has aptly said— "Earliest Christianity was a movement in Judea, of and by Jews, for a Jewish purpose." Most New Testament language about Jews, including Paul's, was spoken by Jews in the midst of intense religious and political family fights. The grim turn toward the victimization of Jews emerged slowly once Jews and Christians separated and after Christians gained the political power to abuse the sacred executioner. That history does not change the end result Mr. Maccoby so brilliantly reveals, but it does make important our perception of how history and myth mix, sometimes without malice at the start, to produce ultimately baleful consequences.

Critical to an assessment of the historical death of Jesus is a precise understanding of his politics, and that remains a matter of heated dispute. In his earlier book, *Revolution in Judea,* Mr. Maccoby argued that Jesus, believing himself to be the Messiah, led a revolt against Rome in which He expected God to intervene victoriously. That is one defensible viewpoint. It is, however, more likely that Jesus, acting Messianically without claiming to be the Messiah, focused on the Jewish temple establishment, which enriched the priesthood and collected taxes for Rome, as an oppressive institution to be immediately overthrown in a popular uprising. If that plan had been successful, it would have brought confrontation with Rome, but the plan was nipped in the bud.

Who, then, opposed Jesus, thereby contributing to his death? Mr. Maccoby wants to restrict the Jewish opposition to a handful of high priests and supporters of King Herod who collaborated with Rome. Certainly those groups were the hard-core opposition. As the dangers of a popular uprising became clearer, however, it is probable that many Pharisees (popular lay leaders) were alarmed, as well as artisans and merchants who were dependent on the temple economy. Rural followers of Jesus were confused and, without leadership, vacillated at the critical moment.

The "sacrificing" of Jesus to prevent political turmoil and intervention by Rome need not have required a Jewish trial. (Mr. Maccoby, along with some others, thinks there was only a Roman trial.) All that was required was that enough Jews, by silence and inaction, lend support to the insistence of the high priests and Herodians that Jesus was a dangerous agitator. In a New Testament passage not cited by Mr. Maccoby, the high priest Caiaphas bluntly proposes that the Jewish leaders must facilitate the execution of Jesus because "it is better for one man to die for the people, than for the whole nation to be destroyed" (John 11:50). That is probably very close to the reasoning of those who delivered Jesus the disturber of public order to the Romans, and it requires no theological explanations.

It is most likely that Jesus was a political sacrifice to avoid a greater evil. The transformation of the original event into a cosmic drama of divine satisfaction for sin, occurring as it did within a religious community split off from its Jewish origins, froze the historical parties into types of ultimate good and evil. To confront and root out of ourselves the displacing mechanism of the scapegoat, with its heinous consequences, it is necessary to see that any kind of acute struggle over basic interests lends itself to "blaming myths" that enable us to escape guilt and build popular unity by means of psychosocial projections.

It is evident that the daily run of domestic and foreign policy among nations is carried on in this frame-work. There is nothing like a "good" war against "evil" people to forge at least momentary national unity, especially if the war is quick and successful. Pertinent here is the somewhat similar analysis of human sacrifice as the base of all religions by the French critic René Girard in *Violence and the Sacred*. In later works, Mr. Girard argues that the actual story of the death of Jesus should explode all scapegoat myths, including the Christian versions.

Mr. Maccoby makes a strong case for the maturity of Judaism in facing and repudiating human sacrifice more directly than Christianity has. What he does not do—it would not be reasonable to expect it in a single book—is look for the Jewish myths that have reinforced the use of a scapegoat and other forms of special-privilege thinking and behavior. Two myths he mentions in passing would yield much insight under the sort of analysis he has given the sacred executioner. One is the divine grant of land to the Jews, and the other is the expiation of their sins through exile. The former has served to justify aggressive Zionist policies for returning to a land despite the histories and beliefs of other people who have also lived there, and the latter has served to pacify Jews who felt their oppression had some basis in sin against God, even if not the sins and crimes alleged by their oppressors.

On precisely the grounds Mr. Maccoby cites, many Christians find the traditional formulations of the sacrificial death of Jesus abhorrent and inhuman, while many Jews repudiate the traditional formulations about a chosen people and a promised land. Yet it is probably too much to expect the Christian and Jewish religious establishments to rework their Scriptures to eliminate all the materials that encourage recourse to scapegoats and rationalizing on the basis of Christian and Jewish exceptionalism. They could do so only with a deep shaking of the foundations. One wonders what Christianity would look like if it did not have its offended God the Father sacrificing his Son or what Judaism would look like without its divinely chosen people and promised land taken from a less deserving people.

There is no assurance that the use of scapegoats would stop even if there were such a transformation, because it is fed by sociopolitical and psychological sources as well as theological ones, as its presumed foundation in human sacrifice clearly implies. But if millions of Christians and Jews went through such a self-purging, there might be a strong check on the use of scapegoats throughout the world. Such are the radical limits toward which Mr. Maccoby's unrelenting analysis pushes us, and a book that can challenge us to a fundamental rethinking of the inhumanity at the heart of our inherited religions is itself a kind of sacred executioner of cherished myths.

The Politics of Armageddon—Apocalyptic Fantasies, Ancient and Modern

ABSTRACT

Literalist "dispensationalist" schemes for interpreting biblical apocalyptic, virulent in sectors of Protestantism, are detailed in correlation with their reinforcement of reactionary domestic politics and bellicose foreign policy. These literalizing misreadings of biblical apocalyptic are exposed as totally arbitrary in their pasting together of a rigid timetable of history's end, in their disrespect for the symbolic status of biblical end-time thought, and in their failure to see that the social typing in apocalyptic thought would, in the modern setting, cast the United States as one of the major world empires destined to be destroyed for its arrogant oppression. A positive reading of apocalyptic construes it as an art form, comparable to science fiction and political cartoons, whereby social and political values and commitments can be emotively captured. The apocalyptic art form, however, must be informed and checked by social analysis and social ethical judgments independently pursued.

One of the signal features of the Religious Right is its insistence that it is biblically based. Nowhere is this more resolutely demonstrated than in its vision of the end of history known either as *eschatology*, i.e., its doctrine of the last things, or as *apocalyptic*, so named after the highly lurid symbolic accounts of history's end in the biblical books of Daniel and Revelation. This aspect of the Religious Right is highly appropriate for a seminar on social history and theory because it has more direct and ominous import for political discourse and policy making in this country than at any previous time in our history.

My presentation is an attempt to show that there are inner-biblical controls on apocalyptic thinking by which we can critique its use in the political life of nations. I shall take as my starting point the present rightward shift in U.S. society and politics at least among those commanding the media and setting the public agendas. In particular, I call attention to the way that arms development, belligerence, and risk-taking in foreign policy are morally reinforced and ideologically legitimated by the end-of-history notions of the Religious Right.

The eschatological or apocalyptic scenario of the Religious Right is known more technically as *dispensationalism,* the main features of which I shall shortly characterize. The convergence of apocalyptic dispensationalism and right wing Ramboism is evident not only among the fundamentalist public but also in the inner circles of government, reaching even to the presidency. It is therefore more than a matter of dabbling in the arcane when we grapple with the bizarre details of the dispensational scheme.

There is no need to lay out the full story of the origins and content of fundamentalist dispensationalism (see T. P. Weber). Alternative scripts in the overall dispensational frame will be found in books by dispensationalists (Lindsey and Carlson; Robertson and Slosser), as also in works by evangelical critics of dispensationalism (Ladd; Graham). Of particular interest to us is the story of how Reagan and key administration figures have been influenced by and have adopted much of the dispensationalist way of thinking (Jones and Sheppard).

For our purposes it is sufficient to show the main features of the dispensationalist scenario which consist of tightly forged links in a divinely ordained and implemented chain of events reaching from biblical times through the present to their culmination in the Second Coming of Christ in the not-too-distant future. Few apocalyptists will specify a date for the end of history, but most of them believe that certain recent world events are clear signs that history is now hastening with ever increased tempo toward its denouement. The prophetic and apocalyptic books of the Bible are seen to contain coded references to this chain of events, and as each is regarded as fulfilled or about to be fulfilled, the end is discerned as that much nearer.

What then are the steps in the dispensationalist scenario of the apocalypse?

1. The reestablishment of a Jewish state is the initiating event in the final run toward the end of history. This took place with the founding of the modern state of Israel in Palestine in 1948.

2. The full and proper restoration of the Jewish state occurred in 1967 when reunification of Jerusalem brought the entirety of the holy city within the political control of the Jewish state.

3. Alignments of world powers and their allies in the Middle East will set the stage for a catastrophic end-triggering war. These alignments are taking place now, with the United States backing Israel and the Soviet Union and Arab states opposing Israel.

4. Israel will be invaded from the north and east headed by *Gog of Magog* as described in Ezekiel 38–39. The Soviet Union and its Arab allies will perform this role.

5. This aggression against Israel will lead to the destruction of the invaders by a divine intervention, possibly by earthquake or other natural catastrophe, or, as increasingly expected, by nuclear war. In the view of some dispensationalists this will be the *Battle of Armageddon* mentioned in Rev 16:16, while others place that battle later in the chain of events.

We note that the effect here is to see war as inevitable and attempts at peaceful settlement ultimately useless, since there can be no peace, only armed truce, until Christ establishes the proper conditions following world-wide destruction. The implicate of this viewpoint for many dispensationalists is that the U.S., as the opponent of the Soviet Union, has a biblical mandate to go to war on Israel's behalf and will in effect be helping to carry out the divine plan by doing so.

6. The decisive defeat of the enemies of Israel will lead to a seven-year *"tribulation"* on the earth, which will purge Israel and lead to a recognition of Christ by the Jews who survive. Anti-Christ will come into world power as a pretender and will kill Jews on a vast scale as well as many others who do not confess Jesus as Christ.

Israelis who accept the political support of dispensationalists are well aware of the dubious and backhanded moral and ideological nature of this support since it anticipates mass slaughter of Jews and their ultimate survival only by the conversion of a select number to Christianity.

7. At some point in the ordeal of tribulation, Christians will undergo *"the rapture,"* which will transport them bodily from earth to heaven, leaving only unbelievers on earth in mass confusion and subject to death. Dispensationalists differ as to where the rapture fits in relation to the tribulation. Some place it just prior to the tribulation, others locate it in the course of the tribulation, and yet others position it at the end of the seven years of tribulation. In any case it will have a "happy ending." Christians will either escape the suffering altogether, be saved from the midst of it, or survive it in the end.

This of course means the dissolution of all nations as they now exist, including the United States. The assumption that generally goes with this view is that because there are so many believing Christians in our country what is good about the U.S. will be preserved in large measure through the salvation of individual American believers by the rapture, whereas the atheistic Soviet Union will suffer great loss since only a remnant of Russians, namely its Christians, will be raptured.

8. The tribulation will culminate in the last great war of human history just before the return of Christ to earth. For some dispensationalist interpreters this will be the *Battle of Armageddon*, and nuclear weapons will probably be involved since the nations will fight with whatever means they have. The rapture will of course save all Christians from the dire effects that fall on the godless.

The assumption, often directly underscored, is that Christians need not fear the consequences of a nuclear war, whether they are employed in the first battle to repel the invaders of Israel or in the last battle among the godless nations.

9. Christ will then return to earth triumphantly, accompanied by all the previously raptured Christians, and he will rule the world for one thousand years: the so-called *millennial kingdom*, which will be a direct theocracy.

10. Finally, God will destroy this world and bring into being a new heaven and new earth.

The resulting mindset in this scenario is to create a sense of overwhelming catastrophic events determined by moral and theological factors out of human control. At the same time there is instilled the confidence that, no matter how much destruction the earth and its people experience, the world itself will *not* be destroyed until after the thousand year reign of Christ. The practical consequence is this: Don't worry about war in the Middle East or about nuclear war! All is in God's hands! Thus, while purporting to eschew politics in favor of otherworldly interventions, both catastrophic and salvific, the dispensationalist apocalyptic stance has far-reaching political implications. It converges ideologically and moralistically with American imperial triumphalism, assuring us that our military power and moral rightness are in line with the inexorable will of God for the fulfillment and termination of history.

George Otis, a dispensationalist supporter of Reagan, writing in 1974, explained the fulfillment of the Gog of Magog prophecy as follows:

> The Bible clearly says that this troop movement will still take place one day in the near future. When will this be? Could it be during "War Number Five" coming up against Israel? The early percolating of War Number Five has already begun (quoted in Jones and Sheppard:17).

Foreseeing the U.S. coming to the rescue of Israel, Otis adds, "America will be blessed for her sacrificial role during Israel's crisis hour" (quoted in Jones and Sheppard:17).

In 1983 President Reagan remarked to a pro-Israel lobbyist as follows:

You know, I turn back to your ancient prophecies in the Old Testament and the signs foretelling Armageddon, and I find myself wondering if—if we're the generation that is going to see that come about. I don't know if you've noted any of those prophecies lately, but believe me they certainly describe the times we're going through (quoted in Jones and Sheppard: 17).

Later that same year Reagan amplified his remark in this way:

...Theologians...have said that never, in the time between the prophecies up until now has there ever been a time in which so many of the prophecies are coming together. There have been times in the past when people thought the end of the world was coming, and so forth, but never anything like this (quoted in Jones and Sheppard: 17).

A full critique of this triumphalist convergence of American world power and dispensationalist apocalypticism would require an exhaustive study of all the biblical texts appealed to and a historical retrospective on the place of religion in American politics, with particular attention to religion's role in reinforcing and inhibiting various tendencies in our national self-imaging and in our government policies and decision-making. Let me simply indicate the main lines of the necessary critique.

1. The elements and patterns of the variegated biblical accounts of the last times are treated arbitrarily in dispensationalist apocalypticism. To construct the dispensationalist timetable, materials are culled from many biblical books which themselves represent widely scattered literary and historical contexts. The assumption underlying this arbitrary assemblage of texts is that a single literal revelation of how the world will end is encoded in the Bible by its divine author.

Some texts are ignored and others are taken out of context. In this regard it is interesting that not until Darby advanced the idea in the 1830s that Christians would be raptured before the tribulation had Christian interpreters supposed that such was the intent of the Book of Revelation, and yet today this is the most commonly held dispensationalist view, taken as "gospel truth" by its adherents. In short, the manifold scenarios and idiosyncratic details of the biblical portraits of the end times are thus wilfully cut and trimmed, brazenly bowdlerized in order to produce a single inexorably unfolding scheme believed to represent the divine blueprint for concluding human history. If, however, this initial premise is ungranted and, instead, the rich variety of biblical materials is examined on its own terms, the entire dispensationalist scheme collapses into a compulsive fantasy put together out of a mishmash of biblical texts.

2. The symbolic imaginative tenor of biblical apocalyptic discourse is simply bypassed by the dispensationalists who, wrenching it from its own literary and social historical world, project it grandiosely as world

historical destiny or fate for our time. The approach of the Religious Right to the biblical imagery is historically positivist and scientistic, producing exactly the result that would come from reading science fiction as a literal description of what will happen willy-nilly in the future instead of seeing it, as Ursula LeGuin argues in her preface to *The Left Hand of Darkness*, as fictionalized reflections on present realities and tendencies of human life. The multivalent pictorial language of the Bible is flattened into futurist formulas and objective happenings that are viewed as inescapable even as they are "escapist" in drawing attention away from human responsibility for our present world.

The failure of innumerable preceding attempts to predict "the end"—either by exact date or general time period—based upon close readings of the signs of the times in correlation with the biblical "predictions," does not deter each new generation of eschatological literalists from another try. Time and again the self-evidently time-bound nature of the imagery in the Bible is flagrantly violated, as when the sixth-century B.C.E. Anatolian hordes of Gog of Magog so fearsome to Ezekiel are turned into modern-day Russians. In this very sleight of hand we remember all the other candidates for Gog's fulfillment over past centuries, and we know full well that in the future the Soviet Union will be replaced by whatever nation becomes the latest bête noire in the dispensationalists' political world.

3. More subtle is the way that the dispensationalists overlook and contradict the social location and thrust of the value system and the specific sociopolitical biases and advocacies of the apocalyptic literature of the Bible. In plain fact, the Religious Right turns those values and advocacies upside down. Literature written by and for the marginalized and oppressed is turned into triumphal propaganda for the vindication of the marginators and the oppressors. While studies of the exact social location of the apocalyptic literature produce disputed results, it seems as a whole to speak for powerless and hardpressed people. The makers of world history do not speak in this literature but are characteristically spoken against. It is not they who are vindicated; it is rather they who are overthrown as they are shown in Daniel's image to have "feet of clay." The idea that the United States, as one of the major oppressing world powers, should not only be left out of judgment in the dispensationalist scenario, but should come off "clean" as the instrument of God in the final judgment is a clear warning signal that something vital has been missed in the transfer of biblical apocalyptic into contemporary apocalyptic. If we are to ask for a contemporary social and political placement of apocalyptic discourse approximating its biblical placement, then its use among ethnically and socioeconomically depressed

and excluded groups is far and away more resonant with the Bible than is its employment for a religious "whitewash" of Western hegemony.

4. Because of their confidence that they have decoded the divine plan for terminating history, dispensationalists of the Religious Right foster an uncritical self-righteousness and a dangerous adventurism in the use of this nation's power to push forward its interests in the world. They see no difficulty at all in perceiving American interests as congruent with the interests of God, and at the same time as unfailing in their realization as are the deity's plans. Ironically, it is this very self-delusion of the world powers which apocalyptic imagery highlights repeatedly. Growing out of the prophetic criticism of arrogant and unrestrained power, the apocalyptists posited the downfall of these powers precisely because they were self-blinded and overreaching historical "anomalies," pictured often as beasts, and not even as normal animals but as misshapen "monstrosities" which had lost any clear sense of their own limits and felt no longer accountable to anyone. God will bring them to account.

Our dispensationalists of the Religious Right do not appear to see that anything needs to be accounted for in this nation except the individual moralistic and pietistic infractions of its citizens who don't think as they do about personal morals. Thus, in grasping some of the details and the moral indignation of the apocalyptic mode of discourse, the dispensationalists have entirely missed the major point amid all the trivia that detain them. That point can be stated in this way: big and powerful nations like the U.S. tend toward self-serving and abusive actions on a large scale which are terribly damaging to their own people and to others they impact; consequently, these self-justifying powers, being none the less answerable to God and to the people of the earth, will be greatly surprised when their final reckoning comes.

Is it possible and desirable to construe biblical apocalyptic as a mode of discourse or imaginative symbolics which has a constructive role to play in our contemporary situation? Or is it even worth the effort, given the gulf between the biblical world and our own and the horrific abuse and misuse apocalyptic thinking has suffered at the hands of the Religious Right?

Yes, I think it is possible and worth attempting a positive construal of biblical apocalyptic, and for two reasons. First, apocalyptic is a part of the Jewish and Christian canons of Scripture, and we can be certain that it will continue to be read and interpreted, even if shoddily and to baleful effect. Therefore, if only to counteract and neutralize misguided readings in church and synagogue—not to mention the dire interpretations of the dispensationalist Right—we need to offer a constructive hermeneutic of apocalyptic. Second, the truth is that we ourselves think and feel about politics and the course of history in terms of pictures and images. This is so even if we have no particular taste or affinity for the flamboyance of apocalyptic rhetoric. What political and social power can and should do is constituted in our sentiments and judgments as much by scenes and images of power in action as it is by rational and technical formulations. Politicians understand this, and we shall remain endlessly vulnerable to their manipulation of images unless we have subjected those images to careful scrutiny to determine what it is they actually denote and connote both in their original settings and when transplanted and variously interpreted for our situation.

I have two propositions to advance concerning apocalyptic as a political instrument in our context.

1. Apocalyptic is most accurately thought of as a kind of art form that focuses and mobilizes emotional resources and reservoirs of energy for sustained critical resistance to uses of power experienced as humanly oppressive and destructive. It does so by showing the experienced wrongs in vivid caricatured forms and by showing the expected triumph of just power in similarly vivid manner. Biblical apocalyptic imagery is close in its medium to political cartoons and poster art and likewise to commercial advertising. There can be no denying its power of appeal and its aptness of expression. It gives us striking pictures of power gone wrong and power redirected to the right means and ends. It is pictorial thinking about the political actual and the political possible conceived in the light of moral responsibility and ultimate beliefs about the destiny of corporate human life.

2. Since it is art, apocalyptic does not and cannot replace other kinds of discourse absolutely necessary to an assessment of the uses of power. In particular, it cannot take the place of ethics, social analysis, and political strategy, all of which are independently necessary for reasoning out why things are the way they are in the world and in what respects they ought to be different and can be made different by cooperative human endeavor. What are the crucial structures determining the misuses of power, by what process can they be changed, and how can I best contribute to that process? None of these critical questions can be answered by apocalyptic imagery per se, for biblical apocalyptic itself depends on certain presuppositions about ethics and theology and even about society and politics. Thus the proper level on which to address the Religious Right is on the level of its conception of ethics, theology, society and politics. It is not simply that the Religious Right makes an uninformed wooden reading of the Bible to which I object. It is their fundamental notions of human nature and the human good that I find

objectionable, for it is these preunderstandings about humanity and about God which lead them astray into what I understand to be in the last analysis a truly unbiblical national idolatry and historical fatalism.

Suppose then that we posit very different ethics, social analyses, and political strategies than does the Religious Right, whether we conceive those alternatives as liberal, humanist, radical, socialist, or the like. Suppose, too, that we refuse to accept biblical apocalyptic as a timetable for world history. With these presuppositions, in what situations might apocalyptic imagery fuel the imagination in order to mobilize and energize people toward the social and political ends we favor?

Let me suggest five situations or conditions in the process of social and political struggle where apocalyptic has performed constructive functions and will probably continue to do so for many people, although not necessarily for all.

1. **Situations of daily struggle to survive.** By this I mean situations where people are systematically deprived, oppressed, and even killed off by institutions and structures, so that in order to live from day to day they are driven to eke out self-subsistence, to fashion means of self-defense, and to fight back for their very lives as best they can.

2. **Situations of prolonged struggle.** These are conditions where the obstacles to the redress or overturn of systemic injustice are enormous and so deeply entrenched that the struggle must be long and hard and ultimately dependent on collaboration among those whose immediate interests are self-survival, and thus where the human resources for resistance and commitment to the goal of deep-seated change must be constantly generated and renewed from within the struggling community.

3. **Situations of world-breaking and world-making crisis.** These are the moments of crisis when decisions must be made to risk much—even all, because the world of things as they are cannot go on, and the breaking and remaking of that world is just within reach—and thus a moment when calculation and courage must be delicately balanced.

4. **Situations of actual or imminent self-implication in the abusive use of power.** Most of us, as people of relative privilege, may not find the preceding functions of apocalyptic to be very pertinent to our experience. After all, by and large we have not suffered that much. But now the plot thickens, because we may in fact be so involved in the institutions and structures that are depriving, oppressing, and killing others that we are seriously implicated in the wrong being done. The functioning of apocalyptic is such that it not only consoles and fortifies the oppressed, but it warns the forgetful functionaries of power and calls them to the bar of communal conscience. It may jar us into attend-

ing to sensitive points where we participate in the abuse of power in any number of ways:

- because we are profiting personally through income or investments derived from abusive uses of power;
- because we are among the political decision-makers or implementers of policies that oppress;
- because we are paid managers or servitors of the system, "idea men and women" whose intellectual production is used in ways we did not imagine or intend;
- because, although seeing some unjust application of power, we are too frightened to stand out and oppose it.

5. **Situations where emotion and ideology become blinding forces.** In such conditions we are so close to the source of the wrong, so implicated in it, so habituated to it, so confused or intimidated by emotion and jingoism that we find it difficult to stand back and assess the power used by us or presumably on our behalf or in our name.

In other words, I am suggesting that coupled with incisive ethics, social analysis, and political strategy, apocalyptic imagination can not only strengthen the resistance to social evil and lead the way toward justice among those most severely deprived in our world, but it can also sensitize the conscience and rally the flagging spirits of those who, though knowing better deep within themselves, have tasted just enough privilege and advantage that it is all too easy for them to forget how others suffer.

Looked at as a whole, biblical apocalyptic pictures the world powers—and by implication the institutions and structures that constitute them—in a predominantly negative way. While sometimes doing good, more often than not these wielders of power are doing ill. Babylon in the Hebrew Bible and Rome in the New Testament are the symbols for political power that runs away with itself, using its overweening strength in any way that is self-evidently profitable and can be gotten away with, and in the process claiming even to be God or to have God on its side unequivocally.

Therefore, transferred by broad analogy into our world, the strictures of biblical apocalyptic on great world powers apply as much to the United States as to any other world power. Accordingly, the naive exemption of the U.S. from the judgment of God is the single most distorting feature in the current dispensationalist appropriation of biblical apocalyptic. This glaring transvaluation of the biblical scale of values

disqualifies dispensationalist eschatology as inaccurate biblical interpretation and cripples it as irrelevant politics, since it allows no space to
assess the social and political structures and operations of the most
powerful nation on earth.

Yet, so tempting is it to worship the great beast, to bow before the
idol of Ramboism, that we find it very hard to think straight and think
large when we face emotion-laden issues such as international terrorism,
the Arab uprising in Israel, the Nicaraguan contras, drug traffic, and
minority crime.

Our tendency to reason almost instinctively in terms of the narrow-
est self-interest, and to accept the information and interpretation given
us by the powers that be, bespeaks the extent to which the ideology of
triumphant power may have infected us against our best intentions, so
that our responses become those of the wounded beast, the beast astride
the world that has hurt others terribly but bridles when it is even
slightly wounded, even to the extent of having its sovereign judgments
and benign motives questioned. Do we fail to think and feel about
things in a big enough frame, because we have become so accustomed to
living accommodatively with the beast of our own overgrown power?

In periods of the decadence and corruption of world powers, we
may indeed have reached such an adjustment to the banality of evil that
apocalyptic imagination speaks a recognizable truth when it announces
that only exceptional interventions from "beyond" history, or should we
say from the depths of history, can change the dire course of events. This
stark image of human helplessness gains plausibility when it no longer
seems that the people who could do something about it, perhaps ourselves included, have any idea of what to do, or any will to do it because
good and evil no longer seem to be social and political categories, inasmuch as what happens is out of control and beyond anyone's
accountability.

In such a world apocalyptic thinking cannot be prevented, for it will
be fertile ground both for self-deceiving solace and for imaginative resistance. Apocalyptic will speak most cogently to us when we discern not
only its obvious message that evil is out of control but its twin assertion
about the good for which we are personally responsible but which, in
order to become historically effectual, must find its embodiment in political ethics, imagination, and design. On this latter point, the earthiness
of biblical prophecy corrects and balances the drift toward otherworldly
fantasy in biblical apocalyptic.

The Exodus as Event and Process:
A Test Case in the Biblical Grounding
of Liberation Theology

ABSTRACT

Latin American liberation theology has been faulted for its selective and imprecise exegesis of the Bible. The present essay argues that, to the degree this indictment is true, it is not because liberation theology has overstated the liberative dimensions of the Bible but because it has not sufficiently pursued the "twists and turns" in the biblical struggle for liberation in all their literary, social, and theological complexity. The much-appealed-to "Exodus" theme is examined both as a specified historical event and as a social critical process symbolized in the event. Four biblical horizons for viewing Exodus are characterized: the standpoint of the hypothetical participants in the original event; the standpoint of Israelite social revolutionaries and confederates in intertribal Canaan; the standpoint of monarchic traditionists in a stabilizing Israelite state; the standpoint of Judahite restorationists in a religious and cultural community shorn of political independence. In various ways, the multivalency of the Exodus theme was malleable to shaping by cultic and political factors that "de-historicized" the liberative political dimensions of Israel's birth. The Exodus theme can be "re-historicized" by a careful reading of this inner-biblical process and by an identification of the present interpreter's social location.

On an extended visit to Latin America, subsequent to writing this paper, I discovered that there is a considerable body of social critical biblical studies published in Spanish and Portuguese that has not found its way into translation, and I was also reminded that the material resources for keeping Latin American biblical scholars in touch with colleagues elsewhere in the world are not plentiful.

It is characteristic of liberation theology to seek its biblical rootage in broad themes that it takes to be constitutive and regulative of Christian faith and practice. Among these preferred themes, the exodus of Israel from Egypt has held paramount sway.

In his groundbreaking *A Theology of Liberation*, Gustavo Gutiérrez underscored the biblical exodus as one of the keystones for constructing an integral notion of salvation capable of canceling out and transcending the older "distinction of planes" model, which left Christians ineffectually torn between "profane" this-worldly and "sacred" other-worldly preoccupations. The exemplary status of the exodus is described by Gutiérrez in this way:

> The liberation of Israel is a political action. It is the breaking away from a situation of despoliation and misery and the beginning of the construction of a just and comradely society....The Exodus is the long march towards the promised land in which Israel can establish a society free from misery and alienation. Throughout the whole process, the religious event is not set apart. It is placed in the context of the entire narrative, or more precisely, it is its deepest meaning....The liberation from Egypt, linked to and even coinciding with creation, adds an element of capital importance; the need and the place for human active participation in the building of society....The Exodus experience is paradigmatic. It remains vital and contemporary due to similar historical experiences which the People of God undergo (1988:88–90).

It would not be difficult to find similar statements of the foundational significance of the exodus in the work of other liberation theologians. In particular, the centrality of exodus has been elaborated by J. Severino Croatto (1981) and George V. Pixley (1987).

Is Liberation Theology Sufficiently Biblical?

At first glance, liberation theology's appeal to the Bible may seem straightforward and unproblematic, for it unquestionably draws upon central scriptural themes and has recovered a vivid sense of biblical faith as praxis in the service of justice. Nonetheless, the use of the Bible in liberation theology has not gone uncriticized, not only as we might expect by its opponents, but likewise by its supporters. Those dismissive of liberation theology find its employment of the Bible either too "arbitrary" or too "political." There is no point in detailing or responding to these hostile criticisms, for my own orientation is supportive of the perspective of liberation theology. It is appropriate, however, to evaluate liberation theology's deployment of scripture in terms of its thoroughness and adequacy, and in the process of doing so, to clarify some matters that may ultimately help to blunt the force of criticism from the detractors of this theology. My chief interest in this assessment is to deepen and enrich the work of liberation theology exegetically so that its already enormously productive influence will be extended and multiplied into the future.

For my point of departure, I refer to the work of the Spanish theologian, Alfredo Fierro, who argued more than a decade ago that, in order for the noteworthy promises of liberation theology to grow in explanatory power and to fuel social change in church and society, they must be developed in a more comprehensive, self-reflective, and rigorous manner. Although Fierro's criticisms are by now somewhat dated, it is nonetheless my conviction that the fundamental challenges in his evaluation are still valid and that liberation theology can only profit in the future by paying heed to his sympathetic strictures.

Fierro claims that liberation theologians have tended to waver between "first order" statements of faith and "second order" reflections on faith, and, when brought into question, have been inclined to shift from one level of discourse to the other without answering sufficiently to the criteria of consistency and coherence of discourse. This shows up especially, he believes, in the way that liberation theologies typically regard Marxism, on the one hand, and the Bible, on the other. Although appealing to Marxism as a more or less suitable, even necessary, method of analysis, liberation theologians have frequently refused to engage Marxism as philosophy, social theory, and political strategy and, to the degree that they shrink from doing so, they lapse from being theologians, in the judgment of Fierro. Similarly, although invoking biblical symbols of liberation, these same theologians seldom plumb those symbols all the way to their sociohistorical foundations—or at least they do so incompletely—so that we miss a concrete analysis of the inner-biblical strands of oppression and liberation in all their stark multiplicity and contradictory interactions.

Consequently, the danger to which Fierro appears to point is not that liberation theologies will be too radical or too critical and thus lose a hearing, but that they will not be as radical and critical as they claim and intend to be, and thus will lose the interest and respect that they initially awaken. He laments that a thinness of social structural analysis and theory and a thinness of biblical analysis combine to give many articulations of liberation theology the look of devotional and polemical tracts. In effect, he fears that shallowness of penetration into the subject matter may issue in an "*un*hermeneutical circle" in which neither the biblical "then" nor the contemporary "now" is adequately illuminated.

Of course I recognize that to summarize Fierro's criticisms so briefly lends them an excessive and pontificating ring, whereas proper justice can be done them only by reading his entire text in which he is at pains to cite and quote particular works rather than to issue untargeted broadsides. In any event, Fierro's own constructive contribution toward deepening and sharpening liberation theology is devoted to the programmatic sketch of a materialist theology that would engage Marxism and anticommunism head-on. He has far less to say about strengthening the biblical dimension of liberation theology, and it is precisely the biblical aspect of his criticism that I wish to take up in this essay.

In the liberation theology of Latin America, Fierro observes, the main biblical approach is to dwell upon certain "exemplary" themes such as exodus, the prophetic criticism of society, and Jesus' confrontation with authorities (129–81). Critical exegesis is tapped rather meagerly in most cases, and there is virtually no effort to penetrate biblical social structure and social history in detail. Although this lack of depth in biblical exegesis is being gradually corrected, it seems to me that Fierro is basically correct in his discernment: because liberation theology vociferously claims that the Bible has been misread by dominant theology, it has an obligation to offer specific, detailed corrections of these misreadings. Moreover, the very cogency of liberation theology, in considerable measure, depends upon its being able to demonstrate, and not merely to premise, more socially precise and accurate readings of the Bible than "unliberated" biblical exegesis has been able to produce. Why, we must ask, in contrast to materialist exegesis in Europe and feminist theology in North America, has Latin American liberation theology lagged behind in this important work of "setting the exegetical record straight"?

It seems to me that there may be three contributing factors to the sparseness of in-depth biblical exegesis in liberation theology. First, there is the strong appeal of this theology to a devotional regard for scripture in the ecclesial base communities that displays a predisposition to accept the Bible as authoritative for liberation without extensive demonstration. This, in turn, seems to contribute to overstatements of the liberative dimensions of scripture, without adequate attention to its reactionary currents. Secondly, Latin American biblical scholars have been for the most part only marginally involved in liberation theology. Doubtless one reason for this is that, in spite of its intentions otherwise, liberation theology has not been able to overcome the curricular divisions of the academy that maintain a radical separation between biblical studies and theology. Another factor in the relative marginalization of biblical scholars from liberation theology is the apparent reality that post-Vatican II attitudes toward the Bible are not as widely represented among Latin American biblical scholars as among Latin American theologians. Thirdly, because of the suspicion of Latin American liberation theologians toward First World theology, there has been a concomitant "blocking out" of the recent contributions of First World biblical scholars from the consciousness of Latin American theologians when they do their biblical appropriation. This means in practice that, against their own wishes, the liberation theologians are at times working with an older and inadequate biblical exegesis that weakens, or at least fails to do full justice to, their own case.

It is striking that the literature of liberation theology, with some notable exceptions, is largely uninformed by sociocritical biblical scholarship stemming from North America. As a case in point, it is symptomatic that my *The Tribes of Yahweh* has rarely appeared as a biblical resource in the major works of Latin American liberation theologians, at least in those so far translated into English. This oversight of the theologians is all the more curious since *Tribes* is used in Portuguese translation as a resource in the teaching programs of the Brazilian base communities and a mimeographed Spanish translation circulates among liberation-oriented biblical scholars in Latin America. This neglect of highly pertinent sociocritical biblical analysis leads to anomalous and contradictory social and cultural accounts of early Israel, which are often oddly "out of step" with the theological outlook brought to the biblical text as well as with the theological conclusions purportedly drawn from the text.

To illustrate my point, alongside claims about the liberation of slaves from Egypt, one finds naive remarks in liberation theology about the Israelites as "nomads" or about the "conquest" of Canaan that proceed as though the initial biblical social revolution broadly posited by liberation theologians does not require us to reformulate our views of the sociocultural formation of the Israelite tribes and of their connectedness with the people of Canaan. In other words, a careful critical reconstruction of the political economy and social organization of tribal Israel is largely lacking at the very point in their work where the method of liberation theologians mandates that it be present, for how are we to make sense of the religious ideas of early Israel if they are not integrally grounded in the praxis of the actual Israelite communities that took shape in Canaan? Likewise, the imprecision of liberation theologians about tribal Israel is duplicated in frequently sketchy or erroneous social descriptions of monarchic, exilic, and postexilic Israel.

Exodus as Historical Event and as Socio-Historical Process

The exodus may be understood as event, or a series of events, or it may be understood as a process—as a complex of events exhibiting certain recognizable features. As *event*, the scope of the exodus may be more or less broadly defined. Narrowly, the term is used to designate the exit of the Israelites from Egypt in their crossing of the sea. More extensively, exodus designates the whole complex of events described in the Book of Exodus, from oppression in Egypt to law-giving at Sinai, and—even beyond—to encompass the events of Numbers through Joshua, as far as the relocation of the Israelites in Canaan. As *process*, exodus refers typologically to the movement of a people from a situation of bondage to a situation of freedom, from a collective life determined by others to a collective life that is self-determined, and this movement is understood to be a venture in the face of risk and uncertainty as to the consequences of making "a break for freedom." This entails the possibility and, in appropriate circumstances, the actuality of social and political revolution.

The exodus events are set forth in the Bible in a mixture of literary genres that include sagalike narratives, theophanic descriptions, instructions, lists, and laws. The extent to which we can locate "historical facts" within this mélange of mythico-symbolic origin stories is a matter of great dispute. It can be safely said that at no stage in the development of the single units and complexes of traditions was there any intent of rendering a coherent account according to historiographic conventions. Our hope of recovering the reality of the exodus must be a modest one that respects the nonhistoriographic nature of the traditions, their ultimate unity as a compiled text in late exilic or postexilic times, the prior anchorage of the compiled traditions in a number of different preexilic social horizons, and the indirectly social referential character of literature of this folkloric and instructional type. In short, we must be wise practitioners of "hermeneutical circulation" if we are to discern the sociohistorical contours of the exodus in order to give warrant to our reflections on a theology of exodus.

Nevertheless, there is definite truth to the claim that the exodus is "a fact of history," and this truth has several facets. Most obviously it is a "fact" in literary and theological terms. The reports of these events of exit from Egypt and entrance into Canaan are a given of world literature and, moreover, a given of sacred literature for Jews and Christians. The entire edifice of the Jewish and Christian religions may be said to rest upon the foundation stone of these reports. But can we say more? Is there any way of knowing what relation these reports have to events that actually occurred in Egypt, Sinai, and Canaan sometime between the fifteenth and twelfth centuries B.C.E.? I believe that the answer to this question is a cautious but deliberate yes, but this yes, far from being a simple assertion of facticity, must be a complexly nuanced historical judgment that takes into account the whole field of Israelite origins and not merely some presumed happenings alluded to in the Book of Exodus. It must be emphasized that the entire exodus process encompasses much more than a possible escape of slaves from Egypt insofar as it alludes to the incontestable reality of the birth of Israel out of "bondage in Canaan." Whatever happened in Egypt, Israel sprang to birth in Canaan in the approximate sociohistoric manner attested in the exodus traditions: by resistance to state oppression and by a bold bid for self-determination.

Four Biblical Horizons for Viewing the Exodus

An analysis of the Book of Exodus strongly suggests that the exodus is recounted from the perspective of at least four successive social "horizons" or "moments" that clearly correspond in part to a division by sources and also, more subtly, to "levels" of the text, inasmuch as we can often detect traces of earlier horizons that have been retained in later horizons. To my knowledge, the only interpreter of the exodus who makes an attempt to hold the literary sources, textual levels, and social horizons in systematic correlation is Pixley (1987:xiii–xx). Because it is a commentary, however, his study does not provide a format for bringing the widely scattered observations on the text into a final synthesis.

The literary source, textual level, and social horizon discriminations operative in the Book of Exodus are as follows:

Horizon no. 1 is that of the hypothetical participants in the events reported. No continuous source exists that speaks consistently and coherently from this horizon, precisely because of the liturgical and instructional mythico-symbolic shaping of the traditions. If such a source once existed, it has been so totally excerpted, reworded, and subsumed by traditionists of later horizons that it is irrecoverable. For this reason I refer to "the hypothetical participants in the events reported."

Nevertheless, continuous sources from later horizons now and then display features that do not jibe with the overarching conceptions of those later horizons and thus have the marks of being "literary survivals." For example, when the J source says that "the people of Israel set forth...a mixed multitude went up with them" (Exod 12:37b, 39), this innocent-looking aside explodes the source's presupposition that the Israel that departed Egypt was an already ethnically cohesive and self-contained entity of twelve well-defined tribes. And when all the later sources refer to the exodus Israelites as a people under arms, this surprising concurrence shatters the apparent presumption of the final postexilic horizon (one not necessarily shared by earlier horizons) that Israel did not have to engage Egyptian forces inasmuch as Yahweh saved the people miraculously (Hay).

In addition to the glimmers of horizons no. 1 in later sources, the so-called Song at the Sea in Exod 15:1–18 (short variant in 15:21) contains a poetic celebration of the exodus that could have been composed by the first, or at most, second generation of exodus Israelites (Gottwald, 1979:507–15; Cross, 1973:112–44). Because it tells not only of crossing the sea but of a leading of the people into Canaan, the date of the finished whole implies horizon no. 2 (see below), but vv 1–12 may well have been composed earlier and, in any case, the events underlying the poetry do not seem to correspond to those delineated in later sources. Thus, Exod 15:1–12 enjoys a certain independence uncontaminated by influence from the narratives in the major pentateuchal sources. Although we tend to read the poem's recounted "churning" of the sea through the lens of the miraculous walls of water in the postexilic account, the text of Exod 15:1–12 actually implies no more than a severe windstorm that whipped up gigantic waves in which the Egyptians drowned. Very possibly the poem may also imply that the Egyptian charioteers and archers were crossing a body of water in boats when they were overwhelmed by a sudden storm, so that they "went down like a stone...sank like lead" in the deep waters (Exod 15:5, 10) (Freedman, 1975).

On the basis of the foregoing data from horizon no. 1, I do not think that we have enough bona fide firsthand information to posit categorically a historically verified exodus, if only because the data are so meager. Moreover, the role of "the sea" as a symbol of primordial chaos is so patent that we cannot even be certain that a body of water was involved in the historical events at all. In fact, the sea itself may possess no proper name, for it is now plausibly argued that the so-called Sea of Reeds (sûp) is preferably rendered as Ultimate Sea or Distant Sea (sôp), and is thus more symbolically than geographically identified (Batto). What we conclude, I believe, is that, when joined to our broader knowledge of the conditions of captive peoples in pharaonic service, these data do accord with the genuine possibility that the "historical kernel" of the exodus traditions was a motley group of state slaves who employed stealth and cunning, along with stolen and captured weapons, and even an assist from elements of nature, to make good their escape from Egypt. This possibility is so tenuous, however, that it is unwise to try to build any large-scale sociohistorical or theological conclusions based on it.

Horizon no. 2 is that of the Israelite social revolutionaries and religious confederates in the highlands of Canaan in the twelfth and eleventh centuries. As with horizon no. 1, this perspective on the exodus is not preserved in continuous narrative sources but in certain accents and details in the later narrative strands, some of which are of significance in helping us to correct "quietist" and "pacifist" interpretations of the exodus.

Of particular interest in this regard is the picturing of the Israelite rescue at the sea in terms of holy war ideology, which stressed "having no fear," "standing fast," and "being still" before battle (Exod 14:13–14), with the result that Yahweh energizes and empowers the meager Israelite forces and at the same time augments and multiplies them with elements of nature opportunely wielded against the foe (cf. hail in Josh 10:11, a wadi swelled by rain in Judg 5:21, and snow in Ps 68:14). It is probably in this sense that the J source tells of the sea being driven back by "a strong east wind all that night" (Exod 14:21b) and even of "the column of cloud" (Exod 14:19–20) that intervened between the Egyptian and Israelite forces. A "naturalistic" reconstruction of the battle is not possible on the basis of the terse, disjointed, even nonsequential, way the story is told, but the immobilizing of the chariots (with "locked" or "clogged" wheels; Exod 14:25) may allude to their entrapment in treacherous sand along the seashore. Interestingly, this J version has nothing to say about the Israelites crossing the sea or about the Egyptians trying to cross it, for the Egyptians perish, not because they are pursuing the Israelites into the sea, but because they flee into the waters out of sheer panic (Exod 14:27b).

It is solely the fourth and last horizon on the exodus that speaks of a crossing of the sea. Although the absence of the crossing motif in J and E might be explained by editorial excision in favor of P's dramatic description, the lack of the crossing motif in the early poem of Exodus 15 should give us pause. It is, I think, a more reasonable interpretation that JE simply does not conceive of the sea as a barrier that has to be crossed in order to continue the route of march, but strictly as a point of entrapment from which the Israelites, at first tactically "hemmed in" by the surprise Egyptian attack, extract themselves by "turning the table" on the enemy.

Although we cannot make a secure separation between horizons no. 2 and no. 3 on this issue, it is likely that the practices and ideology of holy war among the citizen militia of the premonarchic tribes have shaped this J version of events at the sea rather than the more professionalized military practices of the monarchy. The import of the holy war influence on the exodus accounts in J is to heighten the agency of God in directly aiding the Israelites, such that a literal reading makes it look as though Israel was utterly passive in the conflict. Yet it is precisely this one-sided impression that is corrected by a look at the holy war traditions of Joshua and Judges, for in those traditions, although their forces are invariably smaller and more poorly armed, the Israelites are definitely active on the field of battle. This means that horizons no. 1, no. 2, and no. 3 remember an exodus deliverance in which Israel used such military weapons and stratagems as it could muster and in which God fought on the people's behalf, but not in their stead (Pixley, 1987:76–80).

The horizon of the early Israelite social revolution is not confined, however, to narrative details in later sources. It shows up in other ways. For instance, the final version of the Song at the Sea closely links exit from Egypt and victory over pharaoh (Exod 15:1–12) with entrance into Canaan and victory over the Canaanites, Philistines, Moabites, and Edomites (15:13–18), and it is characteristic of early Israelite poems celebrating victory over enemies in the land to describe events in the revelatory and theophanic language of Exodus (see Deuteronomy 33 and Judges 5). Moreover, although compiled during the early monarchy, there is a core of social legislation in the Covenant Code (Exod 20:22–23:19) that presupposes the communitarian agrarian practices and judicial system of the confederated tribes prior to the monarchy, and thus attests to the growing formation of an alternative society in Canaan. This developing Israelite society "sees itself" in the exodus, magnifies, and creatively "distorts" the exodus memories, in order to give scope and dimension to its own comparable project of liberation.

Horizon no. 3 is that of Israelite traditionists in monarchic times who conceive Israel of the exodus experience as an essentially national entity in transit toward its secure establishment as a state in Canaan. The J and E traditionists have retained, as we saw above, features of the earlier horizons, but the overarching conceptual frame they employ is that of the relatively secure identity and institutional forms that Israel attained under its own kings. Because the destination that J and E have in mind is the establishment of the nation-state of Israel, they visualize the Israelites of the exodus as embracing all the people of Israel whose descendants went on eventually to occupy Canaan. At the same time, they stress the exodus deliverance as the wonderful action of Israel's God. It is not, as I argue above, that they rule out Israelite military action in the exodus experience, for in fact they seem to presuppose an armed exit from Egypt, but rather that they put their predominant stress upon the divine source and enablement of whatever actions Israel took.

In any case, the telling of the exodus experience by J and E is pervaded by two major emphases: the marvelous work of God in delivering

Egypt and the presentation of Israel as a sharply defined national entity set off from other peoples. This means that our attention is taken away from *the instrumental actions of the people on their way to liberation,* although of course many of these actions are mentioned, and no consideration is given to *the process by which Israel was formed and came to a distinct identity* in the time before it had monarchic definition, even though there are fragments from earlier horizons that hint at the process of Israel's self-composition.

Why was it that, although possessing some earlier traditions about the self-determining actions and mixed origins of the early Israelites, J and E so strongly stressed the transcendent source of the events and the unified, fully-formed status of the people? No doubt two major influences converged to produce this result. One was the liturgical setting in which the exodus traditions had taken shape before J and E put them into connected written form. After all, we can see the impress of liturgy on the poem of Exodus 15, which was composed prior to the monarchy. Liturgy, beginning in the tribal period and continuing on into the monarchy, celebrated the founding of the people under its sovereign God. It did not seek to trace the immanent and instrumental developments of the people's formative history. The other factor at work was that Israel, at the time of J and E, was still a relatively young national state whose leadership and institutions called for explanation and legitimation. The liturgical mode, emphasizing stability and order under a protective God, was well suited to the ideological needs of the new state(s). Even though there are indications that J and E were not simply exponents of monarchic rule, but have shaped the traditions so as to present monarchy with certain cautions, perhaps even warnings, they nonetheless functioned in the first instance to show how the prestate beginnings of Israel prepared the way for the appearance of the monarchy, which aspired to be the conservator of the older traditions.

Horizon no. 4 is that of the late exilic and postexilic restorers of Judah as a religious and cultural community that had lost its political independence. The priestly traditionist has the challenging task of recording the exodus experience as a charter for the rebuilding of Jewish community in the wake of the loss of political independence due to the destruction of both Israelite kingdoms by foreign conquerors. The JE emphases upon the transcendent source and empowerment of Israel and upon the distinctive unity of Israel are taken up and carried to still greater lengths by P. Whereas in the earlier sources, Pharaoh "stiffened his heart" by his own choice, P reports that Yahweh "hardened his heart," virtually against Pharaoh's own better judgment. The terse and obscure allusions in J and E to "a strong east wind" and shifting waters give way in P to a cleft sea with a canyon of dry land between towering walls of water through which the Israelites safely march but into which the Egyptians plunge compulsively to meet their watery death. In JE the Egyptians rush into the sea because they flee from Israel in panic, but in P they pursue Israel into the sea with reckless abandon, goaded on by an obsessive single-mindedness.

The measured narratives of P, together with its great corpus of ritual law, give the picture of a worshiping community going forth in religious procession, a kind of "Salvation Army" on the march. The exodus Israel of P is not so much the national state, which had perished at the hands of Assyria and Neo-Babylonia, as it is the law-observant community of Jewish believers who are defined not by territory or political structure but by a set of religious and ethical norms and practices, which are set forth in the Torah revealed during the exodus march from Egypt to Canaan.

In this horizon on the exodus we observe a decided separation between "religion" and "politics." Whereas in all the preceding horizons, the political dimension of the exodus is very clearly present or presupposed, for P it recedes into the background in favor of the delineation of a religiocultural perspective. Deprived of political autonomy, and dependent on Persian overlords for the success of Jewish restoration in Palestine, the restoration traditionists make the most of their restricted situation and highlight the conditions of communal "law and order" among the exodus Israelites on the basis of which they hope to shape a contemporary Jewish identity that can outlive the loss of statehood. This completely understandable tendency in P's version of exodus joins with the heightened stress on the initiative of God to further separate religious ends and means from the contingencies of political and social history. It is a major interpretive misjudgment when canonical critics take this sort of "apolitical" posture at face value (Gottwald, 1985d).

The Provocative Multivalency of the Exodus

With this postexilic outlook on exodus, we have reached the dominating hermeneutical tradition through which the exodus has been viewed by Jews and Christians: the marvelous and exceptional deliverance of a people from slavery to a new religious identity in which the palpable political purport of the founding events of Israel is "played down," dismissed in some cases, muted in others, and at times delayed or postponed into a messianic future.

Yet, just as the changing sociopolitical Israelite/Jewish horizons for viewing the exodus significantly shaped what the various biblical traditionists saw it to be, so in subsequent Jewish and Christian history the sociopolitical, ethnic, or class positions of interpreters have had a decisive bearing on what was "picked up" as the informing meaning of those delivering events. The protean exodus symbol refuses to be "laid to rest" in the nationalist and ecclesial securities of the horizons of monarchy and religious restoration. Insistently, hermeneutical suspicion reaches back to the originative revolutionary event/process of the first exodus, but only in circles where new exoduses are striven for. Reformist and revolutionary religious and political groups and movements throughout postbiblical history have "latched on" to the exodus as a paradigm for religiously inspired and religiously based reorderings of church and society (Walzer; Bloch:84–105).

Liberation theology is one such "recuperation" of that political dimension of exodus that is normally silenced by religious and political establishments content with Pharaoh's rule. The contemporary recovery of the exodus as a divine-human collaboration in social revolution, already well begun in liberation theology, will be actualized in all its illuminative and energizing power only as the biblical root-metaphor is grasped within the entire spectrum of the biblical social horizons and with discriminating reference to the social horizons where we live and work today:

> It should by now be evident that efforts to draw "religious inspiration" or "biblical values" from the early Israelite heritage will be romantic and utopian unless resolutely correlated to both the ancient and the contemporary cultural-material and social-organizational foundations (Gottwald, 1979:706).

God, Community, Household, Table—A Review of M. Douglas Meeks, God the Economist: The Doctrine of God and Political Economy

ABSTRACT

The book under review breaks many taboos, astutely reading theology economically and economics theologically, as it boldly claims that the biblical/Trinitarian God is a community of persons whose love overflows to the common entitlement of all persons to the basic necessities of life. Insofar as capitalism, with its enthronement of possessive individualism, prevents this fulfillment of human community in the divine image it must be judged as illegitimate. Churches and theologies must stop evading this terrible truth if they wish to be faithful to their mandate. I concur with the author's basic premise but pose the urgency of a more careful reading of economy and society in the Bible so that we do not oversimplify and moralize the struggles it attests. At the same time, I express disappointment that the author does not more fully explore democratic socialism as an alternative to capitalism.

The very title of this book (Minneapolis: Fortress Press, 1989) serves early notice that we are entering unfamiliar theological territory. Douglas Meeks, who teaches systematic theology and philosophy at Eden Theological Seminary in St. Louis, systematically reads theology *economically* and economics *theologically*. North American Christians therefore need to be prepared for a rough ride—one that will challenge and recast most of our basic assumptions about religion and economy.

The foundation of Meeks' analysis is so self-evident that it is constantly overlooked: in order for people to live, they must have the means of subsistence. In reality, the basic necessities of life are simply *not* obtainable for a majority of the world's population, which includes millions of people in the United States. But why?

Here is where Meeks takes the analysis, arguing against much conventional wisdom: People lack these necessities not because they are truly scarce, but because they are unevenly allocated. The "scarcity" of resources for the many is the direct consequence of "hoarding" or "hogging" by the few. Society creates and sustains a situation where some get far more than they need and others get little or nothing. This selective awarding of life necessities is enforced by government and law and is justified by culture and ideology, including religion.

The market society, most highly developed under capitalism, is a clear instance of the use of social power to maintain and increase the gap between those who get more than they need and those who don't get enough. Thus, the economic problematic for Meeks is bluntly statable, "Will everyone in the household [world] get what it takes to live?" (34).

Meeks concludes that the life needs of all people will *never* be met until the present exercise of social power and the theories that support it—including religious theory—are altered. The market society with its privilege of virtually unrestricted personal property rights over public social and economic goods, far from being the answer, is a structural obstacle to providing human livelihood.

So far this doesn't sound like theology, and the reason is that capitalist economics (with socialist economics following suit) formally excludes theology from public life and economic considerations, while it informally assumes that the churches will give their tacit blessing to the way livelihoods are distributed within the economy. By and large the churches have agreed to this arrangement by excluding economics from their theology, but in doing so they have truncated the theology and crippled their mission. Spelling out this claim constitutes the heart of Meeks' reconstruction of a theology of political economy.

To be sure, the premise that all people are entitled to livelihood is often accepted in a vaguely idealistic or sentimental way. But where are its historical and theoretical roots? Who or what says that you and I are entitled to livelihood? The groundings of universal economic entitlement in Western culture are two-fold: humanistic philosophy and ethics, and Jewish-Christian theology and ethics. Simply put, we are all entitled to livelihood either because we are human beings or because we are children of God. These arguments are straightforward enough, but Meeks shows us how both of them have been circumvented and rendered nearly ineffectual in public discourse and action.

The *humanist* basis of the right to economic livelihood has been gutted by the liberal tradition embraced by both "liberals" and "conservatives" in today's political spectrum. From the 18th century on, this liberal theory, on which capitalism is intellectually based, has claimed that everyone has equal political rights, but not equal economic rights. Instead of economic rights, we have economic "opportunity."

Everyone can try to get into the market, even though there will never be places for all. We all have a right to vote and express our opinions, but we don't get to vote for a change in the property rights system that guarantees the continuation of economic inequality.

In the pursuit of livelihood, everyone is on one's own, but the contenders are grossly mismatched from the start because private property rights over the means of livelihood "stack the deck" decisively against those who possess no such rights. Furthermore, this liberal theory assumes that people are isolated individuals whose economic and political needs are in separate spheres, and that somehow "the hand of God" or "ambition to succeed in life" will permit them all to get what they need without society taking the economy in hand as an essential part of the public domain. The liberal outlook does not really have a place in its theory for the social suffering and damage that result from a scramble for economic goods in which many are doomed to die or to live inhuman lives. In short, formal political democracy is far less substantive in meeting real life needs than it appears to be because it excludes economic democracy in favor of economic plutocracy.

The *theological* basis of the right to economic livelihood has been eroded step by step in accommodation to the liberal vision of a capitalist society in which God has nothing to do with the marketplace officially but blesses it "under the table," so to speak. Whether liberal or evangelical, North American theology has accepted—often as God-given—the scenario of individuals who compete for a place in economy and society in a "free" market system.

Moved by religious idealism and sentiment, the churches try to soften the blows for the economic losers with spiritual consolation and charitable services. This "after the fact" aid, however, is never enough to meet all the needs, to say nothing of the damage to human dignity when people are condescendingly, and selectively, "given" the necessities that ought to be their entitlement. In theory and in practice, the best that the church's theology usually offers to economically deprived people is the hope that they will have "riches in heaven." But a modest livelihood on earth for all is not envisioned as a theological or human necessity, much less a conceivable actuality.

The Work of God

Meeks develops his doctrine of the economist God in order to show that provision for all the needs of all people is not a tack-on application of the Christian faith to optional social issues but its very heart and soul,

as well as a key test of Christian discernment and fidelity. He emphasizes this with an arresting and vivid series of images of God as a
community of persons and the world as a household and a table. He
argues that these images render clear the central features of biblical and
classical theological traditions before they were abandoned in the face of
the triumph of economic and religious individualism, which has left us
convinced that we have to "save our necks" and "save our souls" as lone
individuals, in completely separate transactions.

All of these images come together in the portrait of God as
Economist who creates and empowers life against death at all levels of
human existence, including the production, distribution, and consumption of the necessities of life. Far from being a splendidly isolated self-
admiring monarch who blesses similarly powerful humans who lord it
over others, the triune God is a community of divine persons that finds
unity in self-giving love. It is the very nature of this God not to self-
aggrandize and hoard resources, but to give in plenitude to all. The
economy as "household" thus applies not only to the church but to the
world of divine creation. The "table" that Christians gather around for
holy communion is a small-scale model of the whole human community's provisioning in shared fellowship.

When the household and table of the world are violated through
monopolization by some people at the expense of others, the divine
nature is spurned and the divine purpose is frustrated. It is the work of
God to bring about universal access to all that is needed to be human,
beginning with bread, and reaching on to all the other benefits of salvation which are difficult to experience when bread and dignity are denied
God's creatures. Included under dignity is not only the right to work but
the right to have a say in how one works, in what is produced for what
purposes, and in the disposal of the work product in society at large.
Precisely all the fundamental aspects of the nature of God and the divine
work with humanity are mocked and thwarted under the conditions of
capitalism grounded in liberal theory.

Meeks succinctly expresses the vital link between our vision of God
and our vision of humanity:

> God is not a radical individual but rather a community...[and] there is in
> reality no such thing as a radically individual and isolated human
> being...all social goods are given to us communally.... There can't be a just
> society until there is a society (11–12).

The theological betrayal that Meeks uncovers is our Christian collu-
sion in the abandonment of any sense of human society other than as an
arena set up for people to compete ferociously to meet their needs in a
life-and-death game with vastly unequal players.

Because economy is a human creation, the result of power relation-ships, it is inherently political. Christians *must* enter the battle to put universal human entitlement to life necessities on the social and political agenda. On precisely theological grounds, we are obliged to work for limitations in private property rights over the means of livelihood that everyone depends on, and from which so many are presently excluded. To make this economic agenda as much a concern of the churches as it is the divine concern will require a massive reorientation, and reeducation in Bible, theology, and economics. Without that reorientation our pro-grams of social action will continue to be spiritually half-hearted, analyt-ically thin, and strategically weak.

As I see it, Meeks's argument is of timely significance for two reasons. First, he shows that economics is integral to Christian theology and ethics. Bad economic theory is bad theology, and economic depri-vation of people is a violation of divine creation and a frustration of divine redemption. Second, he takes it for granted that Christians in North America are just as involved in economic entitlement and depri-vation as those in situations of deeper want and poverty. Our relative economic privilege does not spare many United States citizens from economic suffering, and it does not give us theological or political exemption from responsibility for economic injustices everywhere. This is so because we are answerable to the claims and concerns of the economist God whose agenda for economic entitlement is inescapably our own, wherever we live and whatever our economic fortune.

Likewise, we North Americans are deeply involved in the economic deprivation of our brothers and sisters everywhere in the world because the economic advantages we have are at the expense of others who are denied them. This system of too much for some and too little for others will not change until sizable numbers of people—including many of the advantaged—see that it has to change and can be changed. God the Economist mandates and enables these changes by awakening in us a nearly lost sense of our social need for one another in a community of cooperation and just allocation of social and economic goods.

Sharing the argument and agenda of Meeks, I have three fundamen-tal questions and some firm impressions about how best to proceed. How are we to assess our biblical and theological heritage concerning economic entitlement? How are we to assess contemporary economic systems in the quest for full economic entitlement? How are we to arouse and involve the Christian churches in the struggle for economic entitlement?

As for our biblical and theological heritage, I concur with Meeks that its main thrust is toward economic entitlement for all. Our heritage, however, is not unitary and unequivocal in this regard; it does not record an unmixed victory but an open-ended struggle. The central moments of the biblical story are economically democratizing: Exodus, Israel's tribal order, the prophets, and the Jesus movement. But the monarchic establishment in Israel and the accommodations to economic inequality made by post-exilic Jewish communities and by early Christian communities once they spread into the Roman world cannot be ignored. Meeks reveals this problem when he notes that Joseph, a model of brotherly love in Genesis, is shown as a clever economist who brings all Egypt into Pharaoh's debt in a master stroke of economic domination, creating the very sort of situation from which Israel had to be delivered by the Exodus and against which the prophets railed.

The theological lesson in all this is that God the Economist has had to struggle with the people of God in carrying out the agenda of economic entitlement because even they tend to forget their mandate and calling. This means that theologically motivated liberation movements today have to read even the Bible and theology critically, in order to discern the issues of struggle in the text and their connection to present struggles. The insistence on reading the tradition critically has been a key contribution of feminist theology, and it applies just as much to the struggle for a humane political economy (as Mosala, 1989, argues brilliantly).

As for economic systems and mechanisms, we are at a particularly chaotic and confused moment in world history. The simplistic ideological reading of the changes in Eastern Europe now encouraged by our leadership and reiterated ad nauseam in the media is that socialism has failed and capitalism triumphed. Unfortunately, Meeks appears to shy away from a comparative critique of socialist theory and liberal theory. Even if the specific shape of his argument did not immediately demand it, the present turn of world events and the possible paths open to us require that this critique be made. Meeks believes that liberal theory is incompatible with God the Economist, and I believe he is absolutely right about that. So we must go on to ask: Is socialist theory also incompatible with God the Economist?

Democratic Socialism

Socialist theory understands people to be interdependent in all facets of life and the means of livelihood for all to be a responsibility of the whole community. In my view, this theory is highly compatible with God the Economist. It is not a necessary part of socialist theory that only one political party, itself controlled by a bureaucratic elite, can justly and wisely act in the interests of the whole community. In fact, this elitist pretension is a breach of socialist theory. If I am correct about this, the faults in Eastern European countries were not that they were socialist but that either they never were actually socialist or they turned away early from a socialist path. Equally then, the solution to their difficulties is not to shift to capitalism and become a part of the dysfunctional system that Meeks clearly sees to be "inhuman" and "ungodly," epithets that we are accustomed to apply only to socialist countries.

Meeks argues tellingly for a limitation on private property rights, subordinating them to the exigencies of livelihood for all people, a condition in which market forces might be given some place as long as they operated within socially limited boundaries that did not legitimate the amassing of private wealth and its attendant political power. What Meeks describes is best characterized as democratic socialism.

Democratic socialists can draw on a significant history of theory and practice. A movement was vibrant in U.S. politics from 1880 to the 1930s, including articulate strands of Christian Socialism, but it went into eclipse over the last half century. Instead, we now have splintered radical movements pushing single issues, all of which are important but which cannot be justly remedied without a larger democratic socialist transformation. Frankly, we need some new critical thinking about what socialism and capitalism have produced for good and ill, and we need to reconnect with the strands of socialism in our own history in order to forge new political movements that will make public the grounds and means of economic entitlement.

As for how to involve the churches in the struggle for economic entitlement, the foregoing sets of questions should make clear how difficult the task will be. If I discern the implications of Meeks's challenge correctly, we are calling the churches to do what our political leadership and our economic masters do not want done. It is also a kind of thinking and acting that a majority of our church leaders do not encourage. We are asking Christians to look at their Bible and theology in an utterly new way, just as we are asking them to think an astonishing "new" image of God as Economist. And we are asking Christian citizens of a complacent capitalist society to challenge the fundamental premises of a system of political economy in which we are made to feel at home and more or less satisfied with our share of the pie.

Awakening to Faithfulness

If this is so, something like a Great Awakening will be needed to involve significant sectors of the churches in such a fundamental questioning and new line of action. Unless some political stirrings in the country complement the church's quest, whatever we do will be fruitless. But probably Meeks would say that the "awakening" has to begin somewhere, and that it would be appropriate for it to begin in the churches. It is also realistic to say that the church is the only institutional setting in the U.S. today that offers a long and broad enough view of history and society to provide space for such inquiry and fresh thinking.

Then, too, there is the theological matter of faithfulness. If you sense, as Meeks does, how urgently God the Economist seeks to overthrow our smug satisfaction with capitalist America, then you really must speak this truth and try to figure out what it means for you as a Christian in community, even if the effort looks meager for the time being.

Every one of us who shares this calling can do certain things. If we are assigned to preach or teach, we can make the economic burden of our faith a part of our conduct of daily duties. If we are assigned to design or administer programs in the church, we can do likewise. If we are in any position as laity to shape the agenda and temper of our churches, we can do the same.

The contradiction is staggering. The task is vast and unpopular at the moment, all too easy to put off. Yet the personal pain and public turmoil of economic deprivation and indignity threaten the social fabric and our own existence. Between the rock and the hard place, we can writhe and fume, or we can take up the piece of the task that is within our grasp. Reading Meeks attentively is a good start.

B

Social and Political Ethics

Prophetic Faith and Contemporary International Relations

ABSTRACT

This article appropriates my work on the international political perspective of Israel's prophets, subsequently published as *All the Kingdoms of
the Earth* (1964), for an ethical grounding of contemporary international
relations. It is characterized on the biblical side by my belief that the
prophetic outlook on politics was not vapidly "utopian" but was perme-
ated by a marked "realism" about the relation between human welfare and
political power. On the contemporary side, it reflects the height of the Cold
War, with its polarization of world powers and threat of nuclear war.

After stating my presuppositions about the relation of church/ synagogue to nation and the prophetic role of the church/synagogue, I articulate prophetic principles of divine transcendence and immanence, the
ethical accountability of nations, the personalization (one might today say,
humanization) of political responsibility, and the necessity of disciplined
political hope. These principles are illustrated by the reported words and
deeds of biblical prophets, notably Isaiah and Jeremiah, and their validity
for our time is developed by analogy. It is evident that this essay does not
yet reflect my later interest in economic and social analysis as the necessary
complement of political analysis, as it also lacks the stimulation of
liberation theologies still to come.

The Hebrew prophets have long been recognized as sharp critics of
the social order and their teaching has had a profound effect upon
Christian Socialism in England and the Social Gospel in the United
States. The related prophetic concern for international order has not
received equal attention. It is the intent of this study to examine the
prophetic attitude toward international relations and to assess its
relevance for today.

Presuppositions

At the outset it is necessary to formulate certain presuppositions concerning the relation of church and nation, the prophetic character of the church, and the propriety of speaking of ethical principles. These presuppositions cannot be argued at length but they must be stated as clearly as possible.

Church and Nation

1. It is recognized that church and nation are two separate "orders" or "realms" whose roles and mandates cannot be interchanged or confused and yet which are intimately related in that both are under the will of God and all members of the church are also members of a national body. This statement does not intend to endorse any particular historic Christian view of the relation of church and world or of church and state, but it is obvious that, on reflection, it would be close to some historic views and perhaps incompatible with others.

2. While church and nation are separate loci for God's work, the Christian church observes the widespread activity of God in the whole of human life and, therefore, in faithfulness to its understanding of God, the church cannot attempt to limit the sphere or the scope of the divine activity.

3. Although the Christian sees God's work everywhere, he does not expect non-Christians to see the same reality except as they become a part of the redemptive center, the church, and thus the church does not attempt to impose its own insights, ethics, or political dicta upon non-Christians.

4. God often deals with men and with nations other than directly through the redemptive community of Israel or the church. This is explicit in the Noachian covenant with pre-Hebrew man (Gen 9:8–10) and in the Pauline assertion that when non-Jews do what is right "they are a law to themselves, even though they do not have the law (of Moses)" (Rom.2:14). It is also apparent in many biblical passages which implicitly claim that a wide knowledge of God is available to man without special revelation (Amos 2:1; 9:7; Isa 1:3; Jer 8:7; Matt 5:44–48; 7:11; 19:3–9; Luke 12:57; 14:8–10; Acts 15:28–29; Rom 12:17; 1 Cor 11:13–15; 1 Pet 2:12; 3:16 [see Dodd; Wilder, 1946]).

5. The church, in fidelity to God the Creator, has the basis and the mandate to speak to men and nations without reference to the special redemptive criteria which she herself knows but solely with respect to what God requires of his creation. This mandate rests upon an impressive body of biblical witness to God's work with men and nations in

creation and providence and not only in the special and familiar biblical sense of God's use of outsiders for the chastisement and restoration of Israel or the church. Without endorsing any particular historic view of "natural law," it is evident that something of the sort must be presupposed to explain this solid testimony.

Prophetic Role of the Church

1. In assessing the relevance of Old Testament prophecy for our situation, one must simply accept the fact that the New Testament stands between us and the prophets of ancient Israel in such a way that we can never directly appropriate Old Testament prophecies. The reconstitution of the church and world in Christ is the touchstone for all Christian use of the Old Testament. Attempts to equate alliance politics in the ancient Near East with alliance politics today, to identify Babylon with Nazi Germany or Soviet Russia, or Israel with the United States or the West, generally ignore the shattering impact of the New Testament which creates the church as a new reality in the world and thus as the basis for another type of politics.

2. Prophecy is a biblically-rooted reality broader than the use of the Hebrew and Greek words for "prophecy" and "prophet."[1] Prophecy is one way of expressing the biblical testimony about God's constant use of humanity to reveal himself and his purposes.

It has often been claimed that prophecy is negligible in the New Testament, yet even a study of the linguistic evidence shows that prophecy was in fact a pervasive and potent factor in the early church. Jesus called himself unequivocally a prophet (Mark 6:4; Matt 13:57–58; Lk 14:33–34) and the first believers so thought of him (Acts 3:22; 7:37). Prophecy is widely attested to as an activity in the early church, but no single office can be confidently delineated. Prophecy is sometimes described as foretelling (Acts 11:27–28; 21:7–14), but more often it is speech addressed "to men for their upbuilding and encouragement and consolation" (1 Cor 14:3; also Acts 15:30; Rom 12:6–8; 1 Cor 12:6–8, 10, 27–31; 14:3; 1 Thess 5:19–20). Prophecy is, in truth, more a power than it is an office and, while some men are noted as prophets, the humblest members of the community may prophesy so long as order is observed (1 Cor 13:2; 14:29–32).

Prophecy in both covenants is primarily the embodiment of God's will in human life, by word and deed, from which it follows that faithful

---

[1] For a thorough analysis of the linguistic data, see the article on *prophētēs* and cognate words in *Theological Dictionary of the New Testament*, 6:781-861. Grand Rapids: Eerdmans, 1968.

prophetic activity today does not imply the duplication of a biblical office but rather the faithful execution of a perpetual function of the church whenever it really listens to its Lord (Younger).

3. Prophecy is an activity of persons *within* the people of God and it is an activity *of* the community itself, both in ancient Israel and in the church. The single prophetic figure speaks to and acts within the empirical community on the basis of its highest traditions and his own experience of God. The community itself, by its existence and by its message, speaks to the nations. While the understanding of Israel as a prophetic word or sign is recessive or nonexistent in much of the Old Testament, it is crystal-clear that the New Testament picks up and transforms the one strong motif in ancient Israel of the obligation of the people of God to the nations. Thus to be the people of God is to nourish prophets within the fellowship and to listen to them in order that the people as a whole may be a prophetic sign on earth.

4. The prophetic function of ancient Israel as the people of God is taken up by synagogue and church and not by any particular theocratic or pseudo-theocratic state, such as modern Israel or the United States of America. When the single prophet or the church as prophet speaks to the nation or the state it speaks not to the covenant people but to man under the aspect of creation. Whatever the church then says to man in society and to man within the state cannot be based on the assumption that the society and the state are answerable to Christian faith or to a Christian ethic. What the church declares is addressed to the knowledge of the right which is written into man's nature. It speaks to and seeks to awaken that latent sense of the right which it believes God the Creator has put in every man. It is a sense of right before which society and state are judged. But to short-circuit this process by speaking to the nation with explicit Christian norms is to betray the biblical foundation of the church's prophetic function, for it pays too little tribute either to Christ and his church or to the wider world which God made and in which He is continually active.

5. The prophetic church has the double task of *internal prophecy* and of *external prophecy*, and the one is impossible without the other. Internally, the church must encourage and heed her own prophets who by word and deed recall her continually to God's purpose for her. Externally, the church, aware of God's wide concern for his world, must summon the state (and all of the natural orders and structures) by her word and deed—and not least in the daily vocation of her members—to listen to that voice which God puts in all men to speak his truth to them. It is apparent that the most obvious elements of the church's prophecy, her ecclesiastical pronouncements and political lobbying, are of small

effect unless they are deeply rooted in a prophetic preaching and teaching ministry and supported round about by the steady vocation of many Christians well-versed in and deeply committed to the several orders and structures to which the church addresses herself.

Ethical Principles

The prophetic clues to international relations may appropriately be called principles. They might also be designated axioms, guidelines, directives, insights, motifs, perspectives; but principle remains the clearest English term for this purpose. By the manner in which the principles are expounded it should be evident that I am not treating abstract rules which took precedence over persons and events or were consciously formulated and codified by the prophets. I am treating rather certain fundamental tendencies and directions in their thought about the political responsibility of man before God.

Divine Transcendence and Immanence

The root belief of the prophets we may describe as the principle of divine transcendence as the point of origin and divine immanence as the means of sustenance for the communion between God and man. God is "above" church and world but "in" them both. This is the radical monotheism of biblical faith, the intensely practical belief that "God is active in all events."[2]

The nearest that prophecy came to stating this as a principle is perhaps the assertion of Isaiah of Jerusalem in connection with Yahweh's plan to break Assyria because it had plundered the nations with arrogance and rapacity:

This is the design designed for all the earth;
   And this is the hand stretched over all the nations.
For Yahweh of Hosts has designed and who shall frustrate it?
   And his hand is stretched forth and who shall deflect it? (14:26–7)

The prophets did not say that God was Lord *only* of those persons and nations who acknowledged him according to Hebrew religious tradition. The reality of Yahweh's rule was a fact observed in the life of every nation. Nations were "condemned" or "vindicated" in his sight not chiefly with reference to their treatment of the Hebrews but primar-

---

[2] C. Gardner (1960, esp. chap. 5); see also Th. C. Vriezen (1958, chap. 6), who contends that "the basis of Israel's conception of God is the reality of an immediate spiritual communion between God, the Holy One, and man and the world."

ily with reference to a sense of right relations planted indigenously within all peoples.

Thus the prophetic assessments of national conduct cut across all the existing religious, political, and ethnic lines. A pagan people could be judged for wronging another pagan people, as when Moab desecrated the royal dead of Edom (Amos 2:1). A pagan people could be judged for wronging the Hebrew people, as when Assyria plundered Judah (Isa 10:5–11). The Hebrews could be judged for wronging a pagan people, as when Judah rebelled against Nebuchadnezzar (Ezek 17:1–21). One Hebrew state could be judged for wronging its sister Hebrew state, as when Israel and Judah launched wars of aggression against one another (Hos 5:8–12). All partisan judgments were immaterial to the one question: How is Yahweh at work in these events and how have people violated or obeyed his will?

There can be no Christian attitude toward international relations that fails to be oriented by this fundamental truth, a truth which at one stroke eliminates such trite but shockingly perennial conceptions as "My country right or wrong" and "God is on our side," including the current version that he must be for us against "those godless communists." All of our self-righteousness and ideological pretensions are called into question. Because we are able to demonstrate that other nations practice different forms of Christianity from ours, or other world religions altogether, or are even officially atheistic, does not mean that we automatically fall heirs to the championship of God's cause. In the mélange of shifting guilt and opportunity among the nations today the moralist is aghast. From the playbill the onlooker is hard put to it to determine who are the good characters and who are the bad ones, for the roles often change and none seems wholly good and none wholly bad. If we are looking for precise means of ranking the nations, often we cannot be more certain than that God is at work in and through each nation. Yet that in itself is a great deal for from such a belief flow important implications.

Concentration of Political Responsibility

The second clue is an inference from the first and I shall call it the principle of the concentration of political responsibility. God speaks to nations primarily with respect to themselves and their own responsibilities. Again and again in prophecy the awful severity of the attack upon Israel and Judah shocks us into dumb amazement. Yet we miss the whole force of the attack if we think that objectively speaking the Hebrews were the world's worst sinners. Rather the nub of the prophetic attack is the decisiveness of those matters over which the listeners have control. No single uniform international obligation lies upon all nations with equal weight. Each nation stands in a unique situation and is responsible in differing degrees and at varying points in the affairs of nations. For some, the obligations take one form and for yet others, the obligations assume quite different shapes and substances.

A nation repents only of its own wrongs and corrects only its own misdeeds. This doubtless strikes us initially as so much sentimental nonsense, but it is at this point that nations must begin their maturation. It was true not only of the Hebrew people for whom the special belief in the covenant with Yahweh made continual self-correction imperative. It was equally assumed that the immediate neighbors, Damascus and Tyre, and the more distant imperial powers, Assyria, Egypt, and Babylon, could understand their crimes of barbarism in war, slave-trading and deportation of captives, and the breaking of treaties. All these crimes were seen to root in a false sense of self-mastery and an egocentric mania to control history which stood condemned before the bar of public conscience even among pagan peoples who are instructed in the rudiments of international conduct by a kind of veiled presence of God.

Similarly today prophetic faith calls each nation to a fundamental self-examination. This may be justified in Western democracies on the theory that a majority of citizens still accept the Jewish-Christian tradition. But it is fully justified in all nations—Christian, non-Christian, or atheistic—on the theory that each people has an inescapable responsibility for its own life and conduct. Therefore, even in a land with complete separation of church and state or in a land without historic Christian traditions, the prophetic challenge to self-examination is not only relevant but imperative.

Is one nation more guilty than another? In given situations it is possible to discern greater or lesser guilt. Yet precisely as in broken or threatened marriages, the legalistic apportionment of guilt in international affairs is generally incapable of touching the deeper problems. The chief prophetic question is not: Am I more or less guilty than another? but rather, How can I respond to God's will in this situation, bearing in mind the guilt in which I am involved and the opportunities which lie at my disposal? Far from implying a double standard of judgment for nations, such a view accepts and acts upon the single standard in the only way possible—by putting it into effect in one's own nation. It is in fact evading it altogether and resorting to a double standard when the West puts off national acceptance of responsibility in certain areas until the communists or the neutrals accept the same responsibility. This is to disregard God by assuming that he can be obeyed or disobeyed at will and that his counsels can prevail only if a quorum of the nations can be found to heed him. But can God's will be so disposed?

In practice, this prophetic conviction summons nations to correct injustices and to develop resources over which they have control. In particular, nations must strive to avoid the rationalizations which regard similar behavior as innocent in themselves and their friends but as hypocritical and even malicious in their enemies. Numerous examples from the Cold War come readily to mind, for instance, political propaganda and nuclear testing, both of which we consider hostile acts in the communist case but simply neutral defensive actions in our own case; and of course the communists see us in reverse image. This rigid self-protecting symmetry of fear and guilt devours and assimilates to itself all facts and feelings which would deny or qualify it. And so only with great effort can a nation keep itself sensitive to the unexpected good in its enemies as well as to the undesired evil in itself and its friends. Any serious attempt to implement this principle would mean the death of propaganda as it is now generally understood, the wilful and systematic misrepresentation of one nation in a good light at the expense of another in a bad light, even when such misrepresentation is rationalized as self-defense.

Personalization of Political Responsibility

Yet another implication of the principle of divine transcendence and immanence is the principle of the personalization of political responsibility. God's expectations of men as individuals and as nations, while not co-extensive and identical, are continuous and of the same order insofar as they involve the same persons subject to the same Lord. This does not compromise the distinction between Christian ethics and "natural" ethics. It simply asserts that the similarities in the ethical obligations of the *individual* in personal relations and the same person in social and political groups are primary and the dissimilarities secondary. It also asserts that the similarities in the ethical obligation of a *Christian* in personal relations and the same person in social and political groups are primary and the dissimilarities secondary. In either instance, whether one works from Christian ethics or from natural ethics, any variation—especially any lessening of ethical behavior in large groups—must prove itself by some more intrinsic criterion than the "difficulty" of doing what is right.

The prophetic claim on life was a total claim. The prophet insisted on a continuum of responsibility extending from the individual through the corporate realms. As the individual Israelite had no warrant for restricting Yahweh's will to his inner feelings or to his conduct toward his friends alone, so the Israelite people had no basis for limiting Yahweh's will to domestic matters such as the cult or the social order, to the exclusion of foreign policy. Nor, if foreign policy were opened to religious considerations, could the loyal Yahweh believer apply those considerations only to friendly nations and not to hostile nations.

Having said this, however, we must carefully note that the prophets did not emasculate political responsibility by dissipating it into a collection of merely individual responsibilities. They understood something of the multiplicity of human roles in social and political affairs. They were not anarchists or egalitarians. They accepted the necessity of political power and political office. The prophets were themselves political non-professionals or, as we might say, "intelligent laymen." Some were close advisors of statesmen, for example, Isaiah and Jeremiah, but they were not approached by kings for the kind of technical information or balanced prudential judgment which many other counselors could supply. None was an official in the sense that he supplied material for national policies or had a voice in formulating or implementing policies. The prophets served government in the manner of a continuing task force which provided, in our terms, a combination of the steady, sharp sniping of a loyal opposition and the soaring, sweeping vision of a properly constituted "committee on national goals."

Crucially illustrative of their respect for the political order was the decision of the prophets not to attempt to replace political leadership with general religious dicta or with other leadership. They criticized policies and practices, but they did not propose anarchy or impeachment as solutions to the misuse of power. In fact, after Elisha's instigation of Jehu's revolt against the house of Ahab, the prophets did not even take a hand in replacing a king faithless from their point of view with a faithful king, although they must have had many opportunities to participate in court plots and intrigues. The prophets recognized that politicians must be trusted to perform their roles and that it was their special task to offer the political leaders the resources of the Yahwistic tradition both in criticism and in encouragement of their office.

It may indeed seem that the kings never had a chance under the terms of the prophetic attack, that they were in fact "damned if they did" and "damned if they didn't." This impression is admittedly heightened by the extreme form of prophetic speech which made it a matter of long-standing convention that judgment be expressed in an absolute and total manner. It is striking, however, that most of the kings showed an extraordinary respect for the prophets, far more than can be explained merely by superstitious awe. The politicians saw in them something more than fumbling crackpots or moralists who could not accept facts. They regarded them as men with a very special task of facing Israel with its total obligation, of laying bare the vast spectrum of its responsibility, of continually organizing the nation's scattered experiences under the unifying word that called them to singular obedience. The kings could not always see their way to incorporate prophetic advice into actual policies, but it is noticeable that they were generally willing and even eager to hear the prophet out.

The prophetic word of the church to national leaders today must also be a word about the totality of the national obligation. It must be a word which distinguishes between the roles of citizens and leaders, but includes them both within the one task of national obedience and which distinguishes between specifically Christian and universally human obligations, but refers them both to the unifying will of God. It must be the word that no one else will speak unless the church speaks it. It is the word about the interests of God and of his creatures in the affairs of nations. It is the word that cuts through form and expedience and strikes unerringly at the heart of deception and indifference. It is the word that must be spoken even when he who speaks it is not at all certain as to which policies should replace the current idolatries of war and propaganda. It is the word that will remind leaders and citizens of what Herbert Butterfield has so well expressed:

> When we speak as though there were a separate ethic for the statesman, a peculiar substance called political morality, we are already moving into a world of trick mirrors and optical illusions. The statesman, like the scientist or the poet, will constantly be confronted by the alternative between an act that is more moral and an act that is less moral. But we must not allow that there can be a difference in the quality of the decision in these cases, or a difference in the ethical principles involved (16).

Today we see a reversal of the general policies favored by the prophets. They were advocates of quietism in foreign policy and activism in domestic policy. When the Assyrian scourge will pass through the land, Isaiah declared, the faithful will have a foundation on which is inscribed the legend: "He who trusts will not be in a hurry" (Isa 28:16). But the same Isaiah urged upon his people that their calling was to social reform and national renewal, for "'This is rest; give rest to the weary; and this is repose,' yet they would not listen" (Isa 28:12 [Blank:24]). Like the ancient Hebrews with whom the prophets reasoned, we, too, prefer activism in foreign policy and quietism in domestic policy. About 60% of our budget goes toward military rivalry with other nations and this very rivalry lures us into cutting back on the development of our own resources. Our energies are concentrated on security at the one obvious danger point of volcanic eruption while all around us the ground of our national life is cracked and fissured by subterranean domestic tremors. By standing too exclusively *against* something, we have forgotten to stand with sufficient clarity *for* anything.

The parallel between the ancient Israelite and the modern American scenes must not be drawn uncritically, but must be approached through the questions: Are our present domestic and foreign policies taking into account the universal human obligations and needs which political structures must serve? If not, can we learn from the evasions of ancient Israel and the critique of those evasions offered by the prophets?

Programmatic Openness

A further implication of the principle of divine transcendence is the principle of programmatic openness. God speaks to man in his political role with such immediacy that all courses of action must be continually subject to revision in the light of the ever new word of God.

There is in fact a rather distressing lack of unity in the prophetic prescriptions for international affairs. They can be quoted to favor isolationism or internationalism, pacifism or militarism, free enterprise or socialism. A policy of internal revolution urged by Elisha was condemned by Hosea (2 Kgs 9:1–10; Hos 1:4–5). A policy of resistance to a foreign power, counseled by Isaiah (37:6–7, 21–32), was replaced by a policy of submission to the foreign power, urged by Jeremiah (27:12–15; 37:6–10; 38:17–18).

Were the prophets actually as unprincipled as they appear? Yes, if we insist on an answer to the question, "What should our nation do now?", for they did not think or write in such a way as to give us any intelligible answer to a policy-oriented question. If, however, we want to ask, "What moment is this in the affairs of nations?", then they offer us amazing resources for preparing our minds and senses to discern the movement of God among the nations and to find our place in relation to it. The prophetic vacillation is not the necessarily worthy openness and flexibility of a statesman. It is rather the openness and flexibility of one who listens for words and signs and who knows that they take different forms in different ages. All principles recede before the one principle that man is engaged as a total being—and therefore also politically engaged—by the God who is his true sovereign.

In place of technical political directives, which we must find for ourselves, we are called to engagement with God and participation in the times. Searching the prophets we must ask: Is ours the time of free sovereign action or of subservience and waiting? Is it the time of resistance or of surrender? Or is it perhaps not any single time but a moment in which the various times of human history are superimposed and interlocked in infinite complexity? If so, what does the personal word of the personal God say to political persons? Are they to put their trust in programs well-suited to habit and tradition or are they to become new persons and to fashion new programs for new times?

We are denied, therefore, the comfort and the fanaticism of slogans. It is true that the prophets indulged in something very like slogans. Isaiah could say of patient waiting that "he who does not believe shall not endure" (7:9) and that "in returning and rest you shall be saved; in quietness and confidence shall be your strength" (30:15), and Ezekiel could see in the pride and punishment of nations the vindication of God "so that they [the nations] will know that I am Yahweh" (25:11; 29:6; 35:15 [Zimmerli]). The slogans in these instances, however, are not visceral responses to complex problems; they are rather insights, prophetic words about a state of mind which men must adopt if they are to see meaning in events and to help shape those events. All prophetic catchwords bring the individual element of politics and international relations to the fore. They do not fog the mind in making political decisions, but rather provide that perspective which remains valid in all political decisions, namely, that even though in aggregations, *man* is after all the stuff of politics.

Yet programmatic openness does not mean vagueness and perpetual indecision. Politics consists in the definite organization of what is organizable in communal life. This excludes sweeping moralism in place of policy and crude expediency instead of that human risk which is the essence of all human relations. We have no choice between absolute love or absolute self-interest in international relations, any more than in interpersonal relations. There is a mania for purity in international relations which must be corrected by the truth of human sinfulness. There is also a mania for security—especially military security—which must be corrected by the truth of our impermanence. We cannot be as pure or as secure as we should like to be, either as men or as nations. If absolute pacifism reaches for too much purity, then our policy of nuclear deterrence reaches for too much security. The first political commandment is not purity nor security but responsibility to the Lord of nations and to men in community, not to theories held in the abstract or by long habit, whether the theory that force must never be used or the theory that freedom and justice can really be defended by threatening nuclear injustice and nihilism.

Possessed of the basic belief in God's transcendence and of the implications of self-responsibility and of the continuity of human obligations from the least unto the largest of political roles, assured of the need for continuous revision of policies, with what spirit do we bear our leadership and citizenship obligations?

Disciplined Political Hope

We are to be moved in all that we do by the spirit of disciplined political hope. I speak now more of a spirit than of a principle, more of the tone of our thought and action than of the actual content. We must fight with steady resolve against the two extreme moods that by turn accost us: the uncritical *acceptance* of all political leadership in the name of a false security and the uncritical *rejection* of all political leadership in the name of a false purity—the attitudes which lead us to say either, "Let the politicians take care of that; it's their business, not mine" or "A plague on the whole lot of them; they're a bunch of crooks, the blind leading the blind." We shall, with the prophets, affirm a hope that springs from our knowledge of God and his purposes, and which, at the same time, is content to work for the attainable. "Attainable" is here understood as that which can grow genuinely out of the present situation instead of as a limit imposed in advance by philosophic or strategic pre-judgments, whether utopian or realist. Allowance must always be made for the open-ended nature of history, for the surprise of unpredicted new elements, especially the surprise of "moral man" ceasing to hide behind the immunity of an "immoral society."

Thus we are entitled to hope in international relations, and not merely that natural sentiment toward the future which makes us feel that things must somehow be better this season or this year—if only because they could hardly be worse. Rather, hope springs up because of the actual measure of hopefulness that we see in the coming of God into human affairs and in the demonstrated fruits of peace and order in human life. Such signs appear more often in this world than our taste for the sensational and the perverse will allow us to realize. It is not the hope that we can somehow save the hopeless situation. It is God's world and he has been here first. Neither purity nor security are our chief burdens but the integrity of human life in the light of the transcendent, which calls forth our constant endeavors lest it be split so deeply that the variety of human life runs to chaos.

Can we really believe that issues of such vast portent and ramification are affected by you and me? If we cannot, then we have not heard the prophetic word although we may have read the prophetic words; our eyes are shut, our ears stopped, and our hearts made fat. Every German had a calling when Hitler gassed the Jews, but the calling concerned not only resistance to the overt crimes but to the situations that brought Hitler to power and made his reasoning seem eminently patriotic. Every American has a calling with respect to nuclear weapons, but the calling concerns not only the crime of their use but also the ways of thought and conduct which persuade us that preparation for indiscriminate murder upholds freedom and justice. Our calling reaches through the whole of life. It may not occur to individual Germans that the way they lived thirty or forty years ago made it either a little harder or a little easier for the Jews to be gassed. But that was exactly the case. It may not occur to individual Americans that the way we live today makes it either a little harder or a little easier for someone to start a nuclear war. But that too is exactly the case.

He who would allow the prophetic faith to shed light upon international relations faces formidable obstacles. The complexity of issues, in which all certainties of guilt and punishment cease to convince, upsets our security so that, paradoxically, we react by thrusting upon the virtually unknown opponent the burden of evil incarnate. It is an act of primitive propitiation by which we unload our dark uneasy guilt upon the distant and unknown ones who may bear it far from us. But whatever is the case, whether we see no national evils at all or see all evil in the enemy, we miss the summons to self-revision as the precondition of politics. To be sure, men have mixed religion and politics in reprehensible ways. More often than not, however, when we reject individual responsibility for international relations as "moralistic" or "utopian" we are really saying that we do not want the arduous task of thinking about problems and helping to solve them. Most of all we do not want to admit that we, the individual citizens, constitute the major problem of world order. We do not want or cannot see how to effect the change in ourselves demanded by serious outward reform. Because we are not prepared to disarm our fears and violent urges we are not prepared to work for disarmament. Because we will not stifle our own inordinate greed we are not eager to share a better life with other peoples of the world. Because we will not surrender the illusion that security lies in our control of the future we will not labor for a community of nations in which national sovereignties are held in check for the common good.

Everything hangs upon the turning, the repentance, which is the key to all prophetic ethics. The same prophet of the Exile who hailed the penitent Jew, "let him return to Yahweh, in order that he may be merciful to him" (Isa 55:7), appealed to the nations of the then-known world: "Turn to me and be saved, all the ends of the earth!" (Isa 45:22). The repentance of men and the repentance of nations are not identical, but they are related and, while the former is the logical precondition of the latter, the two types of repentance must proceed simultaneously. The prophets do not permit us the lame excuse that only when all men are individually converted can anything be done about national repentance. When any individual repents, he repents as a political being, and to that degree the nation repents. In other words, as Christians and humane individuals recognize their own responsibilities as persons, they simultaneously recognize their responsibilities as citizens and their subservience to the moral obligation which stands over all nations. They must not surrender their consciences to the a-moral, all-knowing state but must rather bring the state into subjection to the moral nature of man. Here the insight of Martin Buber into the prophetic faith will serve us well:

> Prophecy has in its way declared that the unique being, man, is created to be a centre of surprise in creation. Because and so long as man exists, factual change of direction can take place towards salvation as well as towards disaster, starting from the world in each hour, no matter how late....As in the life of a single person, so also in the life of the human race; what is possible in a certain hour and what is impossible cannot be adequately ascertained by foreknowledge....But one does not learn the measure and limit of what is attainable in a desired direction otherwise than through going in this direction. The forces of the soul allow themselves to be measured only through one's using them. In the most important moments of our existence neither planning nor surprise rules alone: in the midst of the faithful execution of a plan we are surprised by secret openings and insertions. Room must be left for such surprises, however; planning as though they were impossible renders them impossible....Inner transformation simply means...that the customary soul enlarges and transfigures itself into the surprise soul. This is what the prophets of Israel understood by the turning in their language of faith: not a return to an earlier, guiltless stage of life, but a swinging round to where the wasted hither-and-thither becomes a walking on a way, and guilt is atoned for in the newly-arisen genuineness of existence...the depths of history, which are continually at work to rejuvenate creation, are in league with the prophets (1957:198, 206–7).

In sum, the prophetic interpretation of the relations between states rose on religious grounds but was informed by a high degree of political knowledge and a sound respect for political order. The prophets laid the foundations of internationalism in their view of a single God related to all states and not only to the peoples in a special covenant with him. Many urgent contemporary problems cannot be solved directly from the prophetic traditions, for example, the structure of an international organization to bring about effective disarmament and to settle disputes among nations by arbitration. Yet the genuine will to find solutions and to see that there is a higher arbiter than the sovereign state is the root insight necessary to any and all technical accomplishments in the pursuit of peace. The prophet sharply reminds us that the community of man will find its fruition only as I find mine, and that my own fulfillment will be parasitic unless I seek in it the fulfillment of others. This is the "humanism," the "realism," the "totalism," the "socialism" of prophetic faith.

Before our dimly discerning eyes prophetic faith holds the familiar vision of the community of man which shall rise when "all the nations shall ascend to the mountain of the Lord and learn his ways and walk in his paths," when "instruction shall go forth from Zion and the word of Yahweh from Jerusalem and he shall judge between nations and admonish many peoples," when "nation shall not lift up sword against nation nor shall they continue to learn war" (Isa 2:1–4). In its expectation that all the nations will submit to arbitration from Jerusalem, the prophecy hopes for more than we shall probably ever see. Yet another prophecy, perhaps from Isaiah of Jerusalem or one of his disciples within a century of his death, has given us the lines along which we are more likely to see the unity of the human race manifested: "In that day there shall be a highway from Egypt to Assyria, and Assyria shall come to Egypt and Egypt to Assyria, and Egypt shall worship with Assyria. In that day Israel shall be a blessing, one-third in the midst of the earth, along with Egypt and Assyria, whom Yahweh of Hosts has blessed saying: 'Blessed are my people Egypt, and the work of my hands Assyria, and my inheritance Israel'" (Isa 19:23–25). To catch the true proportions of this, the most universal word in prophecy, let us cast it into equivalent terms drawn from the current international scene: "Blessed by my people the neutrals, and the work of my hands the communists, and my inheritance the free world." Room must indeed be made for such surprises!

Are Biblical and U.S. Societies Comparable? Theopolitical Analogies Toward the Next American Revolution

ABSTRACT

Developed as a reflection on the U.S. Bicentennial, I review the Protestant habit of conceiving this nation as re-living biblical history in its progress out of Europe into a new land of freedom and justice for all. The appropriateness of envisioning the U.S. as the contemporary biblical people of God is assessed in three steps: (1) by typifying biblical society and U.S. society comparatively in concrete economic, social, and political terms; (2) by focusing on the claimed God-people connection in the two societies; and (3) by reviewing the social and political practice deduced from religious understandings in the two societies. Aside from the obvious difference in "church-state" relations in the two societies, the claim that the U.S. is a "New Israel" is grossly mistaken in that the fundamental biblical affirmation of economic entitlement to all Israelites has never been paralleled by a similar fundamental affirmation of economic entitlement for all U.S. citizens. The most that can be said is that many Jews and Christians have struggled to make economic entitlement a structural reality in this country and, in doing so, have been heavily influenced by their biblical heritage. On the whole, the claim that the U.S. is the people of God has served chauvinism, self-righteousness, and the social status quo.

A Christian theological reflection on 200 years of U.S. nationhood requires historical and sociological analyses quite as much as biblical, ethical and theological critiques. The major focus of this article is to analyze the political, economic, and cultural-intellectual structures of tribal-monarchic-dispersed-regathered Israel, on the one hand, and of the United States of America, on the other hand, in order to evaluate the ethico-religious comparisons and equivalencies frequently drawn between biblical Israel and U.S. society.

Theopolitical Analogies

Every society or nation-state understands itself by more or less clearly articulated ruling ideas, sets of notions and symbols that serve to explain, legitimate, and motivate the ongoing social system. Often the ruling ideas are an explicitly religious "reading" or "calculus" of social and political structures and forces, and a religious validation of social and political tendencies and struggles. Ancient Israel had such a religious self-understanding, which was passed on to the British colonies in North America via Christian appropriation in Reformation Europe. I shall call this ethicoreligious mode of national self-identification "theopolitics," after a term coined by Martin Buber.

In *The Prophetic Faith,* in connection with Isaiah's condemnation of alliance with Egypt, Buber remarks:

> Here prevails a special kind of politics, theopolitics, which is concerned to establish a certain people in a certain historical situation under the divine sovereignty, so that this people is brought nearer the fulfillment of its task, to become the beginning of the kingdom of God (1949:135).

The heart of biblical theopolitics is purposeful divine sovereignty to be realized or actualized in a people's collective life. And as such a people stand in a peculiar relation to God, so also do they stand in a peculiar relation to other nations. In the U.S. experience, biblical theopolitical formulations have been used to set forth an analogy by similarity of relation which developed one or more aspects of the assertion that the U.S. people/society/nation now stands in relation to God and the nations as Israel and/or the early church once stood in relation to God and the nations. On the basis of the analogy, one or another public tendency or course of action was urged.

The terms in which U.S. citizens have fought out their social struggles have been much imbued with this biblical theopolitical language of chosenness, covenant, kingdom, and mission in a spirited reliving of biblical scenarios of new exoduses, new wanderings, new conquests, new prophetic declamations, and a new kingdom of God on earth. Theopolitical analogies were not only accessible to church members but also to those in public life who sought a medium of expression that would suit the U.S. dialectic of closeness to and distance from the European forms of politics and culture. The explicit biblical theopolitical rhetoric was further translated into secular counterparts such as "the American dream," "manifest destiny," "melting pot," "guardian of the free world," "last best hope of earth," etc.

Theopolitical validations have been advanced throughout all the major U.S. social and political struggles. The reading of these theopolitical analogies in context makes a rich and exciting resource for under-standing how weighty those struggles were for their participants. Our fascination with the hermeneutics of this theopolitical jousting must not obscure the reality that these battles of words and ideas were social struggle and political warfare by other means. When Nicholas Street preached his 1777 New Haven sermon on "The American States Acting Over the Part of the Children of Israel in the Wilderness and Thereby Impeding Their Entrance into Canaan's Rest," he was striving to encourage and enlarge the ranks of the patriots by isolating tories and winning over the vacillating to the revolutionary cause. When Samuel Langdon delivered his sermon to the General Court of New Hampshire at the Annual Election of 1788, entitled "The Republic of the Israelites an Example to the American States," he was pitching for the adoption of the proposed new federal Constitution of the United States by the State of New Hampshire, which—being the ninth state to approve—would put the plan into effect (Cherry:67–81, 93–105).

The volume and furor of this theopolitical rhetoric raise many questions. In what sense is the U.S.A. a New Israel and a Christian nation? On what grounds can we compare ourselves to early Israel and to the early church? Is it because we have actualized certain norms of Israelite and early Christian social organization and public behavior? Have we realized them more demonstrably than other nations? What norms do we intend, and how would they be embodied in a bourgeois or capitalist society and state?

The theopolitical analogies between Israel and the U.S.A. require attention at three points:

1. What was the nature of the Israelite society, and what has been the nature of U.S. society? Are comparable social entities and situations being compared?

2. In what relation was Israelite society thought to stand to God, and in what relation is U.S. society thought to stand to God? Are compa-rable people-God connections being compared in the two instances?

3. What social and political practice did Israel deduce from its theopolitics, and what social and political practice has the U.S. deduced from its theopolitics? Are dominant and consistent lines and tendencies of action compared in the analogies?

Precisely because the actual social histories of ancient Israel and of the U.S.A. are most often overlooked by those who engage in theopoli-tics and those who assess it more dispassionately, I choose here to focus on the social entities compared in the theological analogies that seek to equate in certain ways two societies separated by a great gulf of time and space. The other issues raised above will be treated less fully but with a view to drawing out materials for the development of more refined theopolitical analogies that orient, legitimate, and motivate with clearer criteria than now obtain.

The Social Entities Compared in the Theopolitical Analogies

Biblical Society

A compressed account of biblical society might proceed as follows. The basic societal component of ancient Israel was a populace, concentrated at first in the Palestinian highlands east and west of the Jordan River, speaking a dialect of the Canaanite language, engaged primarily in intensive rain and spring-irrigated agriculture, practicing supplemental forms of stock-breeding and handcrafts, and eventually selectively engaged in state-sponsored light industry and commerce. The populace was village-based and organized tribally on pseudo-kinship lines, an infrastructure progressively overlaid and fractured by political hierarchy and social stratification. Increasing urbanization, confined to a few centers, dominated and exploited the countryside but failed to draw a majority of the populace into the cities.

In its initial tribal form, Israel's socioeconomic relations were egalitarian in the sense that the entire populace was assured of approximately equal access to basic resources by means of its organization into extended families, protective associations, and tribes federated as an intertribal community. Political hierarchy, introduced by the monarchy to cope with external threats, gave impetus and protection to "creeping" social stratification. Increasingly, the former communally-owned means of production, vested in extended families, fell into the hands of a minority of state officials, merchants, and large landholders, who never constituted more than five to ten percent of the total populace. Between the tenth and the early sixth centuries, the conjunction of domestic social conflict and imperial aggression by Assyria and Neo-Babylonia incrementally destroyed this mixed tribal-statist social system both in the northern and southern kingdoms. Israelite/Jewish survivors of the downfall of the two states, including those who returned to Palestine as an elite under Persian sponsorship, retained features of tribal existence vis-à-vis the great empires to which they were subordinated, while simultaneously incorporating internal social stratification with disproportionate wealth and power vested in native elites.

Certain points in this profile of Israelite social structure through time deserve to be emphasized since they have been often unrecognized among biblical interpreters, not to mention the wider religious and academic communities:

1. Israel took its rise as a social revolutionary tribal movement. Prevailing models of Israel as an invading or immigrating semi-nomadic people of a distinct ethnic type have singularly failed to provide a plausible account of Israelite beginnings. More convincing is the hypothesis that Israel burst into Near Eastern history as an ethnically and socio-economically heterogeneous coalition of insurgent mercenaries and freebooters (*'apiru*), tribally organized farmers and pastoral nomads (*Šosu?*), depressed "feudalized" peasants (*ḫupšu*), assorted crafts-persons (including Kenite-Rechabite metallurgists), and renegade priests, all of whom joined in rebellion against the imperial and entrepreneurial "Asiatic" socio-political structures of Egyptian-dominated Canaan (Gottwald, 1976b). Early Israel was thus an organized and religiously powered resurgence of suppressed rural and village independence against the drafting and taxing powers of the hierarchic state, including Midianites who attempted to build a commercial empire in eleventh century Transjordan, the nascent national states of Ammon, Moab, and Edom, and the Philistine military oligarchy that imposed itself on major Canaanite city-states.

2. The monarchy, intended as a limited instrument for external defense, gradually carried out a counter-revolution that crushed the tribal egalitarian organization under the weight of political centralization and social stratification. Tribally-organized access to basic resources for all Israelites retreated step by step before the concentration of wealth in the state treasury and in the hands of merchants and landlords who were largely urban-based and backed by explicit or implicit state power, including a judicial system compliant to the newly enriched speculators. From time to time, as under Josiah, the state apparatus, while protecting the vital interests of the new propertied classes, strove to stand somewhat above the sectoral conflict and redress the most vocal grievances of the disadvantaged. These measures of "reform" failed, not so much for lack of good intentions, but for structural reasons. To maintain a socially-stratified state Israel had to contend with more powerful states. The Israelite states centralized and deployed their limited wealth—necessarily extracted from the peasants' surpluses—for armaments and a favorable balance of trade, as well as for tribute when they fell into dependency on another state. Monarchic war against foreign states was simultaneously and ineluctably war against the mass of Israelite peasants. Caught up in rounds of state manpower drafts and taxation, crushed beneath the load of accumulated debts, subject to onerous tribute, and physically devastated by wars, the sole authentic sources of

Israel's wealth, its agricultural and pastoral economy, and its courageous laboring people, were decimated to the point that they could no longer sustain the superstructure of the state.

3. The old tribal infrastructure held some of the Israelites together in dispersed existence and gave them the foundation to form semiautonomous communities, including a major restoration to Palestine under Persian auspices. These Israelite/Jewish communities continued to suffer the contradictions of inner elites and of external dominators. The restored Palestinian community was torn by a class struggle in triangular form among the peasant populace and two rival elites: a Samaritan Jewish elite, surviving from the downfall of the northern kingdom, that had penetrated into Judah during the Exile, and a Judahite elite composed of former state functionaries carried into Babylon and now returned to Palestine as protégés of the Persians to establish a buffer state against Egypt. The Judahite elite won out and the Jewish lower classes once again faced economic oppression at the hands of a native elite.

4. The dominant social contradictions in "dispersed-regathered" Israel revolved around two poles: (a) group and class struggles for resources and authority within the community; (b) the ethnic-status struggles between the community as a whole and its various political overlords. The two struggles often opposed and frustrated one another, as most Jews overlooked their differences in order to present a united front to the enemy, only to discover themselves oppressed by their own people. On the other hand, efforts to abolish native elites and restore more equality to the community ran the danger of exposing the entire people to new depredations and repressions by the overlords. Apparently the early Maccabees and the Zealots had in mind not only throwing off the hated foreign bondage but also purging the community of its parasitic elites. The situation of Jesus and of the early Jewish Christian church must be located within the horizons of this phase of Israel's socio-political fortunes.

U.S. Society

A compressed account of American society is more difficult because we are so near to it and think we know so much more about it than about ancient Israelite society. All the more reason that we should attempt a comparable profile of the political economy and the social structure of the U.S.

The American colonies of Great Britain were an outrunner of a type of political economy based on rising trade and manufacture promoted by strong political and military support from the crown (mercantilism).

The emergent capitalist or bourgeois class (burghers or townspeople) at first relied on monarchy for cover and support against the feudal nobility. Once grown strong, however, the bourgeoisie challenged monarchy in three major breakthroughs:

1. the Glorious Revolution of 1688–1689 in Britain wherein parliament as the instrument of the new class gained ascendancy over the crown;

2. the American Revolution of 1776–1783 in which a colonial region directly colonized under the aegis of the bourgeoisie broke away from the crown to form a separate national state and economy;

3. the French Revolution of 1789–1799 in which monarchy and the decadent remnants of feudalism were overthrown from within the country and bourgeois revolutions began to extend over other parts of Europe through the Napoleonic wars.

The function of the North American colonies was primarily threefold:

1. to enlarge the total wealth of the national British bourgeoisie in its competition with other European mercantile powers;

2. to relieve social and economic pressures inside England through population emigration;

3. to serve strategic military needs in the contests with France, Spain, and the Netherlands.

The proper division of wealth produced in the new world became a matter of dispute as the motherland sought to take out more wealth than the colonists wished to give up. The British measures to enforce compliance on the colonists, as though the colonists were not part of the heritage of civil rights that the British bourgeoisie had wrung from the crown, precipitated the final break.

The result of the American revolution was to separate the American bourgeoisie from the British bourgeoisie and to establish political power in a new constitution that assured the ascendancy of property rights over general human rights while also granting civil liberties as a concession to the general populace. The results of the American revolution were thus essentially a transfer of political power from one rising capitalist class to another rising capitalist class, and a firmer consolidation of that class's economic power.

Crucial to our understanding of the American revolution and the founding of a new government is a grasp of the 18th century social struggles within the colonies (Chotiner and the literature he cites). By 1750, the colonies were prospering as the West Indies declined in economic importance. Social strata of wealthy farmers, merchants, and lawyers were gaining control, while close to 70% of the populace—small farmers, wage laborers, and artisans—experienced economic and political disability and deprivation.

Gradually many members of the ruling elite came to see the advantages for themselves in independent control of the colonial political economy. The greatest obstacle to the hopes of the colonial elite for independent control of the colonies was popular hostility. Popular grievances and aspirations burst forth in public disturbances such as the urban Boston antiimpressment riots of 1747 and the rural Paxton riots of 1762–1764, and were continued in Shays' Rebellion of 1786–1787 and the Whisky Insurrection of 1794. Popular movements and uprisings were promised redress and reform, some of which were worked into state constitutions after the Declaration of Independence.

Ultimately, the ruling class succeeded because it preempted the public arena and directed popular unrest either against the British crown or turned it back upon the heads of the people by equating designs for economic and social justice with "lawlessness" and "anarchy." In the tenth Federalist paper Madison expressed confidence that a federal constitution would put a stop to "a rage for paper money, for an abolition of debts, for an equal division of property, or for any other improper or wicked project...."

The revolution thus brought together an alliance of socioeconomic interests under the aegis of major sectors of the colonial ruling elite. The patriots were far from united in what they proposed as an alternative to the crown. A protracted military contest and severe fiscal crises became urgent priorities that deflected attention from full debate on a new form of government. Small farmers, wage laborers and artisans, ridden by debt and devastated by spiraling inflation, had in mind a revolution that would do more than deliver them from the hands of a foreign bourgeoisie into the hands of a colonial bourgeoisie. Only slowly is U.S. historiography beginning to search out the voices of these common people in the 18th century.

The official voices of the revolution equated independence with political separation from England so that existing property holders would be free to reap the maximum benefits from their ascendent positions. The push toward a comprehensive social and economic revolution was aborted. Localism diffused the widespread protests, keeping them from combination into a unified movement. Few from the lower classes benefited from the confiscation of tory property. Most tory property was sold at auction and went to those already monied. In some cases large estates were broken up among small freeholders, as in parts of New York State, but this was not common elsewhere. Economic democracy was not in the cards during the revolution even though the poor and the small farmers and artisans did far more than their share of the fighting for independence.

Supremely masterful was the ruling elite's strategy in devising a federal constitution that channeled popular demands for greater equality into a national political framework that they were able to dominate. The ruling class solution for governing the independent nation was "a republic (that) would guarantee the *liberties* of all adult white males while placing full citizenship *power* only in the hands of property holders" (Chotiner:16). The federal constitution was something of a coup, though not a military one in the sense of Bonaparte's rise to power in revolutionary France. The new constitution was rammed through by political muscle and ideological cunning on the part of thirty-nine men (though clearly they spoke for many others) and approved by a slight majority of 1600 delegates selected by about 5% of the populace who were themselves all propertied males.

Unquestionably the resulting constitution was a novel and impressive achievement, for never had a written constitutional republican form of government been attempted over so large an area. It was, moreover, a signal victory for the American bourgeoisie, for this constitution had as its aim a sufficient centralization of power to enforce sound money and credit, security of trade, and defense of property interests. It was structured to secure merchant, landowning, and financial interests, to firmly rule out all dangers of economic equality. So satisfied were the bourgeoisie with their measure of triumph that they saw no need for anything like the Magna Carta or the Bill of Rights that the British bourgeoisie had demanded and gotten from the British king and parliament. They wanted no bill of rights for the new U.S. government and would have provided none had there been any other way by which they could have garnered the votes needed to eke out their narrow victory (for an interesting fictional treatment of this whole period see Gore Vidal's novel, *Burr*).

The state order established in the new nation supported existing property relations with their built-in inequities. It secured capital wealth over landed wealth, while conceding much to southern landowners to achieve a united front of the bourgeoisie; creditors over debtors; property requirements for the vote, including slaves as a basis for calculating representation; westward expansion that benefited the expansion of capital while providing an outlet for hardpressed small farmers, businessmen, and debtors; and industrial expansion which throughout the 19th century was to mount in productive output and draw droves of workers from the land and from Europe into the great cities. This bourgeois triumph, in many ways analogous to the bourgeois triumphs in Britain and France, kept leading power in existing hands while it could proclaim with some plausibility that it served the general interests of all people through an ever-extending continent of land for farmers and small businessmen and, by its industrial productivity, supplied more and more jobs for factory laborers.

National independence and a strong central government were thus consolidated, but not without intense conflict between business capital and agriculture and between free agriculture and cheap-labor slave agriculture. These conflicts mounted until they precipitated a civil war around the issues of slavery and secession in which the unity of a dominant industrial political economy was at stake. Reconstruction in the south brought a brief experiment in greater social and political equality for blacks and whites, but redistribution of the plantations did not take place and the central government eventually withdrew its support, leaving the former slaves technically free but at the legal and economic mercy of the old society.

Thus, the second American revolution strengthened capital and central government and unexpectedly, almost inadvertently, freed millions of black slaves for whom there was no point of entrance into the going socioeconomic system either of the south or of the north. "Americans have made two revolutions: the first preserved inherited property as it destroyed inherited government, the second enhanced property in factories and railroads as it abolished property in man" (Lynd:3).

In post-civil war U.S., farm productivity and industrial production boomed, haunted by periodic depressions that fell heavily on restive farmers and workers, who fought back through independent associations and unions and electorally through the Populist and Socialist parties. The response of the ruling class to the closing frontier and to overproduction leading to depression, poverty, and labor-farmer insurgency was two-fold, a response that continues to mark the course of U.S. political economy down to the present:

1. to open a new frontier in foreign markets and raw material sources, thereby catapulting the U.S. into an imperial career;

2. to integrate capital and the state in a working alliance known as "the corporate state," on the one side instituting reforms to placate farmer and worker and on the other side offering periodic government intervention as a buffer against the breakdowns of capital.

Instituted under the Progressives, Teddy Roosevelt and Woodrow Wilson, and boldly extended under the New Deal, these external and internal integrations and expansions of capital have been consolidated and refined in order to maintain the rule of capital over the resources and the people. Now, however, there is a perceived limit to the expansion of U.S. capital and political power. Around the world, independent bourgeois states and socialist states are challenging U.S. hegemony. Internally the degradation and regimentation of work and the shifting of capitalist failures onto the working class, including the so-called middle class, creates unrest, further fueled by the unremedied racism and sexism that serve to strengthen capital's total control over a divided people.

The God-People Connection in The Theopolitical Analogies

The God-People Connection in Israelite Society

In Israelite thought, the relation between Israel and God was structured broadly in the following ways:

1. God created Israel midstream in history by delivering the people from subjection to other peoples and setting them free for a life of their own (election; deliverance; national independence).

2. God and Israel entered into a structured reciprocal relationship in which both participants made commitments, but not symmetrical commitments, since God as superior party—while dependable—was not subject to criticism or sanction by Israel (covenant).

3. Israel committed itself to rightly ordered inner-societal relationships and religious obligations which were immediately sanctioned by law and ultimately sanctioned by God; these obligatory relationships coincided with egalitarian tribal social organization (tribal social structure and law).

4. The structured reciprocal relationship between God and Israel held the people under the fundamental obligations of tribal equality even after tribal social organization was undermined and destroyed by a limited monarchy and only very partially retained among small conventicles of Jews in exile and in a semi-autonomous community restored to the land (monarchy; exile; restoration; prophetic judgment).

5. God assured that the just relations begun falteringly in Israel according to tribal norms would one day be realized in Israel and among the nations, either through Israel's agency or in other ways (national eschatology; world judgment and salvation).

The above scheme is a simplification of a wide variety of biblical paradigms of election and covenant, of mission and destiny. Such a catalog must be viewed historically so as not to overlook the mounting tensions in self-understanding as the original tribal homogeneity gave way to layers of monarchy and social stratification and to eddies and riptides of political collapse, dispersion, and partial restoration. The connection of God with Israel was historical, social, dialectical in support and judgment, revolutionary and evolutionary, unmitigated in its insistence that just and equal human relations are the sine qua non of the humanly fulfilling presence of God.

God-People Connection in U.S. Society

The relation between the United States of America and its God has been structured in ways broadly analogous to biblical theopolitics, although postbiblical elements of thought and postbiblical historical developments have strained and altered the analogy in noticeable ways:

1. God created the United States by separating it midstream in history from oppressive and corrupt European nations in order to free it for a life of its own (national independence).

2. God sanctions the U.S. on the principle of republican or democratic government (considerable differences of interpretation here), as embodied in the Constitution, likewise thought to epitomize the justice and freedom of biblical society and of the best Graeco-Roman and/or British traditions and forms of government (constitutionalism rooted in tradition and ethico-religious consensus).

3. God guarantees the national independence and integrity insofar as the nation empowers free and just relations among all its people by providing equal opportunity and legal enforcement of the norms and procedures of republican/democratic government = biblical societal norms (equal opportunity; equality under the law).

4. God upholds the U.S. through an unbroken continuity of adherence to the constitution amid all the changes from limited republican to more mass democratic government, from agrarian to industrial economics, and from continental isolation to worldwide expansion (national continuity and optimism).

5. God assures that the high material and political standards of the U.S., although periodically threatened, will be repeatedly renewed in the nation and will be spread to other nations through U.S. agency—directly or indirectly—by teaching or conquest, or by the contagion of moral example (national triumphalism).

This attempt at a rationalization of American theopolitics may seem even more problematic than the Israelite theopolitical reduction. In any case it serves as an exercise in clearer thinking than when we leave it all unsystematized and unreflected upon. We need to take note of the following problematic features in this theopolitical mythos:

1. Clearly there have been strong differences over whether the God here adduced is the biblical deity of Jewish-Christian delineation or

simply the God of nature and reason. Insofar as a biblical theopolitics predominated in the U.S., the diversification of Christian denominations and the separation of church and state produced a far less homogeneous socio-religious base for theopolitics than was the case in ancient Israel.

2. Striking is the fact that there is nothing in the U.S. theopolitics to allow for the shattering of the first frame of national life for the obvious reason that no great catastrophe has struck the U.S. comparable to the downfall of the Israelite tribal states.

3. Even more significantly, there is nothing built into U.S. theopolitics which could allow for the supersession of the constitution just as the constitution itself, as a document, naturally does not provide for its supersession but only for its amendment. Israel at significant points in its theopolitics allowed for the supersession of its sociopolitical forms by other forms. Almost nothing of that sort appears in the main body of U.S. theopolitics although individual citizens have expressed it.

4. Finally the norms of U.S. theopolitics rest in a constitution and a tradition of government which only formally and indirectly touches on social organization. Israelite theopolitical norms touched the very substance of social structure, whereas U.S. theopolitics does not touch on property relations and thus capitalism can be legitimately understood as that form of political economy which the U.S.'s God mandates. The formal silence or ambiguity on the point, however, leaves the matter in suspension.

The Social and Political Practice Deduced from the Theopolitical Analogies

Social and Political Practice in Biblical Society

The social and political practice deduced from the theopolitical calculus in Israel proceeded unabashedly from a tribal organizational base and thereby constituted a steady measure of and pressure on all subsequent forms of social organization under the monarchy and in marginated existence among the nations. The command against taking interest on loans shows how concretely the tribal mode of equality and mutual aid was taken. Though repeatedly violated, it was as repeatedly invoked and insisted upon as a norm of the only proper life for Israel. Under the impact of capitalism, this bulwark against individual speculation has crumbled both in Judaism and Christianity, for capitalism could no more survive without interest on investments and loans than it could survive without workers who have nothing to sell but their labor power.

Israel was mandated to embody the egalitarian norms of tribalism and at the same time to maintain its identity and independence. Therein lay the rub. Israel's venture in tribalism did not successfully spread to other parts of the ancient Near East. It was surrounded by hostile foes toward whose forms of social organization it progressively shifted in order to survive. Tribalism in the midst of centralized states is a sort of vestigial pocket sooner or later to be wiped out. But this tribalism created a culture and a powerful theopolitics that bore the tribal survivors along in mutual support and in a community of hope. Jesus came along in this Israelite continuum and in his life and death profoundly confronted every feature of oppressive establishments and declared values transvalued. A new religion bearing its own culture and theopolitics cut horizontally across the dispossessed and rootless Roman masses who sought identity and meaning amid their subjection.

In one sense Israel can be seen as a last gasp of tribalism in a world of states and then of slave empires, feudal domains, and bourgeois capitalism. Christianity then universalizes the nostalgia for a lost past and gives us a spiritual and cultural surrogate for a public life we can no longer live. In another sense, however, Israel may be the harbinger of the future, because it did not simply emulate old tribalisms but broke them open with a sense of historical action and destiny. Perhaps Engels was right in a comment that early Christianity was as near to being socialism as could have existed at that point in world historical development (Marx and Engels:316–47). Both the typologies of Israel/early church as vestigial survival and as prophetic harbinger are of course gross models, but it makes some difference which general conception underlies our theopolitics and our critique of theopolitics. If the former, the best we can expect is for our biblical faith to give us some private nerve as capitalism drives on to its grim conclusion. If the latter, we have some basis to move out of biblical faith toward the shaping of the socialist future. Our natural home need no longer be in a lost past but in a long promised future now more nearly within reach than at any time in human history. Which of course is very different from claiming an inevitable triumph of any system by blueprint or prescription.

Social and Political Practice in U.S. Society

U.S. social and political practice began and has continued on a much more divided and circumscribed basis of peoplehood and of equality and justice than in the case of ancient Israel. The national identity from the start incorporated the functional individualism of nascent bourgeois society and thus of civil society as a collectivity of individuals in compact. The notion of communal property held in subservience to the general good was no part of the founding compact although there have always been Americans who have held such a notion. The Bicentennial celebrates above all a political separation from monarchy to republican government evolving into mass democratic forms.

It is one of the pathetic marks of a confused and uncritical theological calculus that it should think that the early biblical tribal egalitarianism offers any deep-going analogy for the founding framework of our nation. Such a misunderstanding is possible, I think, because the enduring problem with theopolitical thought is that it is so highly symbolic, indirect, and ambiguous that it is capable of extrapolation to support almost any position on the socioeconomic spectrum in relation to any given sector of struggle.

We must, in short, be exceedingly careful with our theopolitics, avoiding lazy comparison and false comforts. We must be prepared at every juncture to decode our theopolitical symbols and to say precisely what we mean by them in this or that context, particularly what analysis and what strategy they point toward, lest we be using symbols to mask our lack of analysis or strategy. If we assign to the U.S. the symbols "New Israel" or "Covenant People," or any other theopolitical titles or surrogates, we must be firm in recognizing that the U.S. is no more privileged or virtuous than any bourgeois state, except in very precise ways that require empirical specification: great resources, continental expanse, technological progress, voluntary associationalism, or whatever. The rhetoric and sentiment of theopolitics can easily carry us away. Let's face it. This American "New Israel" was never a tribal people, but rather expelled and exterminated the tribal societies it encountered.

This "New Israel" arose as a very favorably situated extension of statist England, its advantages counterbalanced by the disadvantages of many who remained in the home country. This "New Israel" proceeded under its own national bourgeoisie to do all the things that capitalist states do to subordinate human life and welfare to the primacy of profit for the benefit of a ruling minority. These realities should be recognized at one level with no surprise and no moral opprobrium. That's how it has been and could not easily have been otherwise. Naturally this "New Israel" professed otherwise, and there have always been those who struggled against the dominant trends, but of what bourgeois state is this not also true? There lies many a trap in our claims to "specialness," not least of which is the futile diversionary longing for a "golden age of liberty" that never never was!

Toward a Liberating Theology for U.S. Christians

As far as I can judge, most current theology in North America is not dealing with the kind of critique of theopolitical discourse which I have attempted to offer here. It is too thematically classical or it is too episodically modern. It makes light of liberation theology from Latin America as no more than a "corrective" which in practice is used to correct nothing, or else it treats liberation theology as the latest "fad" or "rage," the current theological commodity, uncritically collected with all the other recent "in" theologies, without reference to the social and cultural practice in which liberation theology is deeply rooted.

For a liberating theology to spring from North American Christians they will have to be engaging in social struggle for liberation. This will have to be more than acts of resistance and symbolic protests. This practice will have to engage with the structures in which we work and live day by day. Groups of Christians will have to practice together and analyze their practice, reflecting upon it with all the available social scientific tools and all the resources of their faith, both as these resources well up from their own experience and as they are communicated through the tradition newly illuminated in the company of socially active fellow Christians. A process of moving outward from immediately lived social practice to the practice of others, and to the way scattered social events are systematically related, will begin to build a world of social analysts and actors rather than the isolated victims or stoics we now are, or else the comfortable operators in a social world that someone else made. Through our growing understanding of the socio-political periodization of human history and through our community with other Christians in social practice, we will find a new route of access to Jesus and the prophets. From them we will draw affirmation, vision, passion, and courage, whereas it will be for us to find the analytic tools for our situation and the organizational forms and strategies for action—all within the historical experience and scientific resources of our age. A recent proposal on doing liberation theology in North America puts it in this way:

> As a conclusion, may we suggest simple criteria for evaluating this process of theological reflection. Each group that goes through these moments...can then ask itself three types of questions.
>
> 1. Is there a systemic understanding of the participant's experience and of the lives of the oppressed?
> 2. Does reflection link immediate actions with a vision of a global alternative and strategies for change as a journey toward God?

3. What is the new experience of God's revelation in the midst of the struggle which challenges our limited perspectives?

With these and other questions that may seem adequate, each group that does liberation theology can attempt to remain faithful to the history of the people and its God (Cormie, Irarrazaval, and Stark: 31).

The most pertinent way I know to celebrate the Bicentennial is to practice and to reflect that kind of theology in continuity with the just ones of all ages and in solidarity with the oppressed of this society and of all the world.

Sociological Method in Biblical Research and Contemporary Peace Studies

ABSTRACT

After a review of the major results of social critical study of the Bible and of peace studies and peace research, the results of these two recently burgeoning areas of inquiry are examined for what they jointly and reciprocally contribute to one another. My reflections are organized around three rubrics: (1) the social structural embeddedness of possibilities for peace and war; (2) a challenge to rethink the classic religiously grounded arguments about war in the three forms of holy war, just war, and pacifism; and (3) the social structural constraints that operate on our individual ethical and political stances toward war and peace.

When the biblical and contemporary war/peace contexts are compared, it is evident that common threads of structured and communally rewarded greed and violence run through both—side by side with restraining and ameliorating structures of justice and compassion—but the situations are sufficiently different that biblical society can only give us broad criteria and sensibilities for assessing human community and not formulas or blueprints for achieving peace with justice.

Either of the two fields of study linked by the deliberately loose copulative in my title could easily occupy the limited time scheduled for this lecture discussion. Since social scientific study of the Bible and peace studies or peace research are both eclectic and protean areas of study, I want to distinguish them as recognizable entities and to note some of the major strands making up their pluriformity. Following mappings of the two areas, I will offer reflections on how a social scientific reading of the Bible bears upon peace studies as a resource for dealing with human conflict and especially with the runaway nuclear threat which has of late elicited deep concern— and often practical strategizing—among religious groups as diverse as the liberal Protestant Riverside Church Disarmament Program, the neo-evangelical *Sojourners* magazine, the U.S. Roman Catholic bishops, and even among professional groups as normally "non-political" as the American Academy of Religion and the Society of Biblical Literature.

My reflections will be from the viewpoint of a biblical scholar long involved in war and peace issues and moderately well informed on peace research. It is my hope that those in the audience more involved in peace research and practiced in various branches of social scientific study of Scripture will contribute other perspectives to the discussion that will follow. Because so little has been done methodically to link a social view of Scripture with peace studies, our undertaking is essentially exploratory and heuristic.

Social Scientific Study of the Bible

Social scientific study of the Bible shares with all other critical methods of biblical study the assumption that biblical documents can be illuminated by applying to them *any* relevant or appropriate method for gaining knowledge. "Any relevant or appropriate method" means primarily that there must be enough of the right kinds of data within the Bible or in the biblical surround for the method to be workable.

Specifically, social scientific method presupposes that biblical documents are social products, i.e., communications of people in networks of social relations, and that the writings when seen in their social contexts through the use of self-conscious methods of study will be much more intelligible than if the social settings are ignored or referred to randomly in undisciplined ways. Dealing with social systems, or social worlds, or social contexts of the past (the language used to characterize the social units under study varies widely) is a matter of social history, and it is a disputed aspect of social sciences. Some social scientists see little possibility of serious study of a society that cannot be observed at first hand or concerning which we lack certain statistical data or documentary evidence. Others contend that for certain aspects of social reality we are likely to have reasonably good data from the past and that, even where we do not, cautious analogies can be made between better known and lesser known social entities when the two are demonstrably comparable in specifiable ways. Everyone who uses social scientific method and theory in biblical studies is convinced of the viability of social history.

For about a century now, various applications of the social sciences to biblical studies have been undertaken, usually from a base in anthropology or macrosociology, i.e., sociology analyzing large-scale social units and systems. The earlier studies were normally peripheral to the main body of biblical scholarship, seldom constructively critiqued or built into a structure of ongoing research and theory. Only in the last decade or so has a sustained application of the social sciences to biblical studies been attempted by scholars already well trained in other methods of biblical study. Furthermore, the present groundswell in social scientific study of Scripture is employing a widening array of methods, often in frankly experimental ways with the conscious intent of developing a body of knowledge within a community of scholarly dialogue where the criteria employed are commonly recognized and where the adequacy of the particular conclusions proposed from case to case can be a matter of ongoing critical assessment.

I want to indicate six kinds of social scientific study of Scripture that are currently in progress and by now sufficiently published to be accessible to the general reader.

1. *Reports and evaluations of particular applications of social scientific methods and theories to biblical subject matter.* The July 1982 issue of *Interpretation: A Journal of Bible and Theology*, with articles by Bruce Malina, Burke Long, John Gager, and Wayne Meeks, is a recent instance of this genre. A further collection of such reports and surveys will appear in a volume I have edited for Orbis Books, to be published late spring 1983: *The Bible and Liberation: Political and Social Hermeneutics.*

Of particular value is an essay on method by Gerd Theissen, translated in his volume of essays, *The Social Setting of Pauline Christianity: Essays on Corinth* (1982:175–200 = Gottwald, 1983a:38–58). Theissen introduces three categories of methods and illustrates them from New Testament texts. First he notes "constructive" methods that mine and process the social data explicitly present in biblical texts. Secondly, there are "analytic" methods that infer social situations and meanings indirectly on the basis of references within the text to events, norms, and symbols. Thirdly, there are "comparative" methods that work with similar and dissimilar social situations or constructs in the immediate world of the biblical text or in analogous situations from elsewhere in time and space. It is a fairly easy matter to supply comparable illustrations from the Hebrew Bible to stand alongside Theissen's New Testament examples.

2. *Social histories or descriptions of ancient Israel or the early church, or of some limited period or region within either.* One thinks of Roland de Vaux's work on ancient Israel and the accounts of early Christianity by Robert Grant and Abraham Malherbe. The work of Theissen mentioned above and Wayne Meeks, *The First Urban Christians,* are social descriptions of Pauline Christianity. In the works to date, the criteria of what is social are not always clear and the extent of the synthesis and depth of treat-

ment vary greatly. For the most part, the theoretical stance in social histories has not been very adequately articulated.

3. *Sociological criticism proper taking for its subject a whole biblical social system, or a subsystem or role cluster, within a specific spatiotemporal span.* Sociological criticism offers either an explanation of the genesis and development of the system or component, or an explanation of the structure and function of the system or component, or it does both, and it does so according to some social scientific theory or combination of theories. Sociological criticism deals with biblical texts but it marshals them according to categories of the social subject matter. The theories employed are drawn from a spectrum of approaches, especially from macrosociology, political economy, anthropology, and social psychology.

With respect to sociological macrotheory and political economy, Max Weber and Karl Marx are the chief contributing theorists, and to a lesser extent Émile Durkheim. S. T. Kimbrough, Jr., has evaluated the use of Durkheimian concepts by the early twentieth-century French Old Testament scholar Antonin Causse, and I have made modest use of Durkheimian theory in my study of premonarchic Israel, *The Tribes of Yahweh*. Weberian macrotheory, apart from its scattered citation in discussions of charismatic authority and leadership, has been applied to premonarchic Israelite society in a limited way in *Tribes*, to Israelite prophecy by Peter Berger, and to Paul's leadership in the early church by John Schütz and Bengt Holmberg. Marxist macrotheory has been tersely applied to all biblical periods by George Pixley (1981), to premonarchic Israelite society in *Tribes*, to Israelite prophets by Henri Mottu, and to the symbolic orders of ancient Israel and first century Palestine by Fernando Belo.

Cultural anthropology, essentially structural-functional in character, has been focused on premonarchic Israelite society, again in *Tribes*, and on the New Testament world by Bruce Malina. Robert R. Wilson (1980) has illuminated the biblical prophets by means of cultural anthropological theory on shamanism and spirit possession. Anthropologically generated theory on conflicting prophetic authorities has been used to clarify biblical prophetic conflicts by Burke Long, and theory on millenarian sects has been applied to Israelite prophets and apocalyptists by Thomas Overholt. Cultural anthropological state-formation theory, especially rich in African data, has supplied a fresh perspective on the rise of Israelite monarchy in the work of Frank Frick (1985) and James Flanagan (1981).

From social psychology, role theory has been taken up to analyze the prophets by David Petersen and to understand wandering radicals and missionary organizers in the early church by Gerd Theissen (1977). Social psychological cognitive dissonance theory has been mustered by Robert Carroll to interpret prophets, especially those deutero-prophets who "piggy back" on earlier prophets, and the same cognitive dissonance theory has been directed to the early church expectation of the end of history by John Gager (chap. 2).

4. *We are also seeing thematic studies of Old Testament and New Testament key words and concepts such as justice and oppression.* These are frequently spinoffs from liberation theology and seem to be open to some of the criticisms levelled against the type of word studies classically represented in Gerhard Kittel's *Theological Dictionary of the New Testament.* Nevertheless, they possess considerable value in alerting scholars to translation and exegetical biases that have obscured the pronounced sociopolitical forcefulness of biblical vocabulary by means of denatured and over-spiritualized renderings of the biblical text into modern languages. I mention here the studies of José Miranda (1974), Severino Croatto, Elsa Tamez, and Thomas Hanks.

5. *Sociological exegesis of biblical texts or books that insert a constitutive sociological dimension into the customary task of exegesis.* John H. Elliott in particular has helped to clarify the specific focus of sociological exegesis on the text as it stands, conceived as a task and process relatively separable from sociological criticism that selects, groups, and subsumes biblical texts according to the social rubrics (1981:chap. 1). Thus far sociological exegesis has been applied to Joshua-Judges in *Tribes*, to Judges 5 by Marvin Chaney (1976), to Amos by Robert Coote (1981), to the Gospel of John by José Miranda (1973), and to 1 Peter by John H. Elliott.

6. *Lastly, I refer to a type of study that might be called sociology of literature, which tends to link with and move into new literary studies and hermeneutics.* Here the attempt is made to join social scientific theory with the symbolic character of language by inquiring into the social status and effects of the text. An instance is Robert Carroll's use of cognitive dissonance theory to explore the prophetic language of "prediction" (1979:parts I–II). Another instance is Fernando Belo's use of Marxist macrotheory and French structuralism to illuminate the emphatic body language of the gospel of Mark with reference to the two competing biblical thought-practice complexes which he calls "the pollution system" and "the debt system," respectively expressed in the Priestly writing and in Deuteronomy (1981:esp. part II, chap. 1 and part IV). From the side of structuralism, the work of David Jobling and Robert Polzin has been reaching out in search of methodological and theoretical bridges that will span literary and social structures. The area

of sociology of literature is likely to be of growing interest, primarily I think because the newer literary and newer sociological approaches sense that they have important affinities and potentially fruitful ways of cooperating that have yet to be realized.

Now it is evident that these varied types and instances of social scientific biblical study focus on different aspects of the subject matter, operate on different levels of abstraction and concretion, and present methodological and theoretical pluriformity. These studies also diverge markedly in whether they show an interest in general hermeneutical theory and in what the social understanding of the Bible means for theology and social ethics today. A number of the studies start from and return to one or another form of political theology, while others show no explicit theological orientation whatsoever. Doubtless this is related to the fact that a large number of scholars using social scientific method and theory in biblical studies—I would judge even a majority—are based in secular institutions of higher education. The church and its theological establishment have not rushed to embrace social scientific study of Scripture, and scholars engaged in it are mostly scattered widely among seminary faculties. Indeed, to date there does not exist anywhere a full-fledged program of graduate study in the sociological criticism or exegesis of Scripture. Nor has there been a periodical or scholarly monograph series devoted to sociological study of the Bible in the way, for instance, that *Semeia* and *Journal for the Study of the Old Testament*, together with their supplement series, have functioned for several years to circulate new literary studies. [Note: in subsequent years, the above publications have increasingly opened their pages to social critical biblical studies, and there now exists a monograph series entitled *The Social World of Biblical Antiquity Series*—NKG.]

In admittedly audacious vein, let me now try to sum up the tendencies and directions of sociological study of Scripture in terms of its key substantive contributions, the ways that it bids to alter the map of biblical studies. Above all, I would say that a social scientific focus on the Bible makes it clear that the origins of ancient Israel and of the early church were far more sociopolitically abrasive and explosive than the redacted biblical tradition, as read in the mainstream of Jewish and Christian exegesis, has previously revealed. Sociological criticism has definitely converged with an unmasking and demystifying project that casts what Paul Ricoeur has called "an ideological suspicion" over biblical texts. This revisioning of the sociopolitical plane or axis on which biblical texts "fall" or "turn" may be seen to operate in four major moments within the Bible.

1. It is now seriously arguable, although not everyone using social scientific methods is so convinced, that intertribal Israel arose from an agrarian social revolution mounted by indigenous Canaanites rather than from an invasion or infiltration of the land by pastoral nomads. A host of issues connected with Israelite origins assume an entirely different cast within this revolutionary sociohistoric matrix: holy war, myth and saga, cult, ethnicity, dependence on Canaanite culture, covenant, religious exclusivity, etc.

2. Seen against a revolutionary origin for Israel, the later stages of state formation, of prophetism, and of the state's collapse invite reexamination in a framework of social revolution and counter-revolution— itself set within an international imperial-colonial context. Exile and restoration are now posed as integral sociocultural and political-economic processes and not merely the means by which the religion of Judaism was distilled from the history of Israel.

3. It is also now apparent that Jesus' politics were critical, confrontational, and disruptive of the Roman-native Jewish elite two-tier alliance of domination in Palestine. The political overtness of the Jesus movement is becoming discernible apart from any effort to make him out as a Zealot. The political intentions, choices, and effects of Jesus and his movement must be looked at much more carefully, including his nonviolence, for all these necessitate reassessment in terms of Jesus' analysis of oppression within the class dynamics of the time, his grass-roots strategies of organizing, the relation between his political reading and the apocalyptic horizon of human agency, and the skewing of Jesus' political meanings by gospel redactions from a very different political world outside Palestine two or three generations later.

4. The work of the Graeco-Roman Christian mission, Paul included among its several streams and tendencies, calls for revaluation in terms of the mechanisms of Roman domination, the social structure of missionized communities, and the place of associations in the Mediterranean world that provided sociocultural activities and meanings in the great void between the Roman apparatus of power and the mass of individuals with their class-specific and culturally varied forms of alienation.

I believe it is true to say that these integrally related sociological perspectives, with their many expressed and implied agenda items for research and theorizing, have considerable bearing on religiously informed attitudes toward peace issues in our time, including the customary ways that pacifism, holy war, and just war have been argued from Scripture.

The Field of Peace Studies/Peace Research

Peace Research has this much in common with social scientific study of the Bible, namely, that they are both mushrooming interdisciplinary areas of study in which social sciences have a large place and in which holistic social relations and the critical role of social actors are front and center in disciplinary attention. As the focus of the one is the elucidation of texts and the religious movements that produced them, the focus of the other is the discovery of factors that make for social and political conflict, war in particular, and the factors that make for social and political conflict closure, harmony, or peace.

Disciplined peace studies have increased almost geometrically since World War II. They were propelled by haunting urgent questions. How could world war have occurred twice within half a century? What are we to do about the cold war and nuclear weaponry? Among the key contributing figures to the peace research boom were the political scientist Quincy Wright through his two-volume *A Study of War* (1942) and Lewis F. Richardson (1960) who developed mathematical and statistical models for predicting when arms races will end in war (see also Wilkinson). The first explicit mapping of peace research in terms of its pluriformity was Theodore Lenz in *Toward a Science of Peace* (1971).

Political scientists took up the challenge first by developing interdisciplinary work in international relations that used simulations, statistical studies, and cognitive maps. Programs at universities and private and governmental peace research centers proliferated, involving more and more of the sciences and an enlarging agenda of issues. UNESCO publications record the existence of 19 institutions for peace and conflict research in 1945, 81 by 1965, and by 1981, 312 institutes in 43 countries. More than 2000 fulltime peace researchers were at work in 1981, not to mention many thousands more engaged in peace education and action projects. A handy resource book on war-peace issues entitled *To End War* by Robert Woito, lists 49 colleges and universities offering peace studies programs, and also cites twelve major periodicals specifically dealing with peace research and education, among them *The Journal of Conflict Resolution* (SAGE Publications, Beverly Hills, CA), *The Journal of Peace Research* (International Peace Research Institute, Oslo, in Irvington-on-Hudson, NY), *Peace Research Reviews* (Dundas, Ontario, Canada), *Journal of Peace Science* (Department of Peace Science, University of Pennsylvania), and *Peace and Change* (Center for Peaceful Change, Kent State University, Ohio). When newsletters and related periodicals in international relations, world affairs, arms control, etc., are included, the periodical literature swells to scores, even hundreds of titles.

As for the many branches of inquiry that constitute the pluriformity of peace studies, we may mention the following: historical studies of past conflicts, often cast as mathematical and statistical studies; arms control and disarmament; conflict resolution or regulation; nonviolence as an action strategy; international law and world government; and, most recently, the emergence to greater prominence of human rights and economic development. Often these same subdivisions are pursued by specialists within geographical area studies programs.

Surveying 682 of these peace studies up to 1969, R. J. Rummel, beginning in 1975, published a field theory of international relations in which war was treated as a result of diverse forces operating in a field of states. For all the erudition, the results often seem vague or truistic, such as Rummel's observation that "conflict or war between states results when those forces causing war outweigh those forces causing peace" (cited in Woito:446). Redundant as the remark appears, it probably intends to stress the multiplicity of peace-war factors in varying combinations such that a seemingly small added factor may tip the fragile balance in a field of states toward war or peace. It would also have to be admitted that similar instances of vapid-sounding conclusions have appeared amid the mountains of biblical scholarship from time to time. Sobering, however, was Rummel's conclusion in 1978, after reviewing the field of states at that time: "This assessment suggests...a new generation is entering a renewed period of dangerous Soviet-American conflict in which war is not only possible, but towards which many forces are pushing" (cited in Woito:439).

Overviews of peace research stress two major phases in the conception of the task. Down to the mid-1960s, peace research focused on what has been called negative peace: preventing or stopping the direct violence of war. Beginning with a critique by Johan Galtung, a second wave of peace research emphasized positive peace, in which not only the elimination of overt violence but the removal of covert structural violence was put on the peace agenda. Most of us, I suspect, may have thought that it was liberation theology that invented the concept of structural violence as the original or precipitating violence, whereas it appears more accurate to say that liberation theology participated in a far wider recognition of and concern for systematic violence.

A UNESCO report speaks of this second phase of peace research as follows:

> The concept of "positive peace" was used as a description of a situation marked by equity, integration, solidarity—perhaps even harmony. Later, the concept of structural violence was introduced for the kind of violence which does not have a direct "sender"—as when starvation results not from

ill-will of any person or group but from distributional inequalities (cited in Woito: 439).

Enlarging on this broader and grimmer view of violence, Galtung says:

> Violence is deprival of life, as in a battle; it is intended and is a quick process. But what if it is not intended, and/or takes place slowly, as in a slum? Is that not violence? It might even be argued that it is usually more violent, for if the victim dies at 32 years of age in a battle, he is usually in good health the moment before, whereas a slow death is usually preceded by a process of increasing near-death (cited in Woito: 440).

In explaining why they include non-physical forms of conflict in their discussion of peacemaking, Adam Curle and Maire A. Dugan give dramatic illustration to the terrible costs of this structural violence which rolls on ineluctably once in place, usually without the sensational attention-grabbing convulsions of war:

> At their extremity, they [non-physical forms of conflict] may result in death just as regularly as, if less obviously than, physical violence. An example of an extreme form of nonphysical conflict may be seen in the apartheid policies in the Republic of South Africa. In this case, it is not only that the freedom of the black population is curtailed in a myriad of ways ranging from limited access to education and income to the forced separation of families, but that their actual physical lives are limited in just as real a way as planned execution. The average life expectancy of a black is over 15 years shorter than that of a white (54 vs. 71 yrs. for females, 50 vs. 65 yrs. for males). The infant mortality rate among black children is 115 per 1,000 whereas that of whites is 18 per 1,000. These early deaths are the result of a systematic discriminatory distribution of social goods (medical care, sanitary conditions, subsistence incomes, etc.) that contribute to longevity. One researcher on South Africa has estimated (using the comparative life expectancy and infant mortality rate figures quoted above) that the equivalent of approximately 100,000 black South African lives are lost each year as a result of unequal distribution (20).

It appears that in significant ways large sectors of peace research have been pushed into recognition of the complicated and intimate connection between peace on the one hand and justice and integral socioeconomic development on the other. Even to secure the absence of open conflict, a deeper penetration of the structural biases toward conflict must be achieved so as to identify what must be changed even to stem open violence. Thus, peace is expected not simply as the result of getting people to stop fighting but as a result of structural change that will make physically destructive fighting less attractive and less necessary. The ethical considerations in all forms of conflict and human deprivation are reflected on, for instance, in conflict resolution theory that asks what the effects of a negotiator's intervention may be on the parties in conflict given the power balance between them. Will open fighting stop at the expense of change adequate to correcting the power imbalance? Conflict resolution conceived in this way not only intends to move a fight into a form of debate but also to move it into a forum for adjudicating substantive issues.

With some frequency one meets in the peace research literature a radical questioning of the practical necessity and the moral legitimacy of enormous inequalities in social goods. John Rawls' way of putting the concept of justice seems to catch up the spirit of this radical analytic exercise and the rigor of fresh thinking needed to get at the preconditions of positive peace in social relations. Rawls puts it this way:

> All social values—liberty and opportunity, income and wealth, and the bases of self-respect—are to be distributed equally unless an unequal distribution of any, or all, of these values is to everyone's advantage (1971:62).

And one may further note Rawls' provocative recasting of social contract theory into a thought exercise proposing that a just social system would be one that all members could agree to if in negotiating its arrangements the contracting parties did not know in advance what positions they would eventually occupy in the newly constructed social order (1975).

The Interface Between Sociological Method in Biblical Research and Peace Studies

What are the implications and potential contributions of social scientific study of the Bible for peace studies, and vice versa? Can we speak of any convergence of understandings in these two fields which has pertinence for our roles as ethically reflective social actors, particularly those of us who stand in a tradition of appeal to the Bible as a fundamental "peace document"? In attempting to treat the interface between these two disciplines I am not able to draw upon any extensive or developed communication between the two bodies of study, and, therefore, I will be giving largely personal assessments that seek to lure and provoke you into thought, discussion, and action.

My reflections are organized around three rubrics: (1) the social structural embeddedness of possibilities for peace and war; (2) the challenge to rethink the standard religiously-grounded arguments about war; (3) the social structural constraints that operate on our individual ethical and political stances toward war and peace.

1. The dominant social structure, with its cultural and ideological assumptions about what is "certainly true," always shapes conflict and

its resolution around particular heated hard-to-avoid issues that seldom can be categorized under a single unambiguous ethical principle. Justice and peace are integral aspects one of the other, as they are aspects of particular structurally defined and constrained conflicts over distribution of social goods, including symbolic goods, i.e., under what descriptive and evaluative categories the situation will be understood. In the Bible, where "peace sentiments and ideals" loom large (as do also "war sentiments and ideals"), the ethicoreligious perspectives are all vested and embodied in particular social settings of a conflictual nature that do not reduce to generalities about war and peace that can be abstracted and applied to current situations. Reflection about war and peace issues in biblical settings and in our own settings must be carefully worked through in terms of the social structural, cultural, and ideological contexts both at the biblical pole and at the contemporary pole of the hermeneutical process.

2. The standard modes of religious argument for pacifism, holy war, and just war need rethinking in the light of Israelite and Christian origins that were far more sociopolitically conflictual, more class-divided, than formerly realized. We must tap into the various biblical voices about justice and peace not as free-floating ideas and principles but as whole responses to conflictual situations in ancient times. Corresponding to a category-collapse in thought about war that nuclear weaponry has precipitated, we may also rightly speak of the collapse of a biblical exegesis that pirates texts for ethical principles pulled out of the structural contexts of the varied conflicts to which the principles remain stubbornly attached. We are, in short, required to undertake a long march through all the justice-peace moments of Scripture, in what Juan Luis Segundo (118–22) has called a first-level process of learning—not to discover the biblical ideas that work formulaically—but to internalize material for our own distinctive task of second-level learning, i.e., learning how to learn for ourselves in a complexly fused situation that does not and cannot reproduce any biblical situation (492–95).

Alfredo Fierro illustrates how a sociopolitical grasp of the Bible gives us exemplary freedom to deal with our own situations rather than prescriptions of exactly what to do:

> To put it concretely, the Exodus is a liberative memory with regard to the possibility of insurrection. The biblical narrative of the escape from Egypt liberates people from fear of revolution. It takes away the fear that rises in us when we advert to the illicit nature of disobedience or insurrection against political authority. Should we be afraid that affiliation with a revolution is incompatible with our faith, the example of the Exodus is there to dispel that particular fear. The Exodus certifies that insurrection is a stance or line of action that is possible for one who has faith (149).

In Fierro's formulation, the words "possibility" and "possible" are pivotal. Whether a "possible" revolution, or any other "possible" political move, is mandated in a given situation can only be judged by our own learning to learn about the conjunction of social forces that has produced our situation and where that complex of forces is tending.

3. Our social structure, together with its culture and ideology, strongly conditions and constrains our private dispositions to act ethically and politically in certain ways, and may even cancel them out or paralyze them altogether. Conformity to prevailing ideology or accepted opinion, combined with tangible economic rewards and penalties, works powerfully upon us and must be deliberately held in our awareness and corrected for if we have any hope at all of acting consistently and decisively for a just peace.

It is particularly important to recognize that the major institutions that shape our thought and life options (and one would have to include the church here) are structured to expedite the orderly execution of ends that are assumed to be benign. No one working in bureaucracy or subject to bureaucracy is asked to do more than carry out their tasks and duties as means toward fulfillment of the organizational ends. If we are to think ethically with cogency and act politically with effect we must be able to evaluate the *actual* ends and means of institutions, above and beyond their *alleged* ends and means. The key problem at this point is that most of our socialization and education does not equip or encourage us to think independently. Biblical-style obedience and courage presuppose a capacity and readiness to think critically in this manner, and sociological criticism of the Bible makes clear how costly it was for people in biblical times to do so, just as it is hard work and sometimes dangerous work in our time and place.

Studies in social psychology, which have had measurable influence on peace studies, help to illuminate how extremely difficult it is for rational or ethicoreligious analyses and motivations to break through the web of convention and self-justification that surrounds the way daily life is lived within our society. The experiments of S. Milgram with subjects who were instructed to give presumably painful, even lethal, electric shocks to slow learners and of P. Zimbardo (summary in Sabini and Silver, chap. 4) who constructed prisoner and guard simulations make it clear that, once a social situation is defined in a certain way by some accepted authority, it becomes very difficult for people playing roles in that situation either to dissent from taking part in actions they disapprove or to dissuade others from taking part.

In a fascinating study of the moral difficulties of everyday emotions and behavior patterns, running a gamut from envy, gossip, flirtation, procrastination, and anger to moral reproach in public contexts, John Sabini and Maury Silver lay bare why widely shared moralities often have little effect in the actual dynamics of everyday life situations constrained by social structure. Those lived situations simply do not give us the ways and means to reflect and dissent ethically, since they assure us that we are, as it were, "acting under orders," if not of a specific authority at least of a general consensus as to what can be expected or excused. It is this "social domestication" of human abuse and murder, at the extreme, that is far more threatening than emotionally-triggered violence. National Socialism could only manage to kill millions of Jews by regularizing the process so that it seemed like something naturally decreed from above and beyond any of its executors. Hannah Arendt speaks tellingly of how this process worked in the case of a notorious Nazi functionary:

> As Eichmann told it, the most potent factor in the soothing of his own conscience was the simple fact that he could see no one, no one at all, who actually was against the Final Solution (cited in Sabini and Silver:52).

While there may be individual cases in which all conscience has been lost, Eichmann typifies the more human reality that even among the most notorious and efficient abusers of human beings, conscience is at work and must be somehow appeased and laid to rest with convincing self-justifications. As Sabini and Silver go on to remark, the self-justification does not finally suffice:

> In *these* cases [acting under orders or habits that your conscience objects to] the question of intent is irrelevant to the question of responsibility. No matter how much the evil that was a part, say, of dispatching the trains, when those trains went from Warsaw to Auschwitz, *felt* accidental, it was not. Eichmann knew what his actions caused. Eichmann may well have been personally indifferent to whether the Jews were annihilated, or sent to Madagascar, or, for that matter, allowed to fulfill the Zionist dream, and in that sense he didn't intend the Holocaust. But he was still responsible because people *are* responsible for all that they *cause* so long as they can see that they cause it and can do otherwise. We may *feel* responsible only for what we intend; we *are* responsible for all that we do. And we know it (66).

Thus, the high importance of seeing what we cause at the time we cause it and of exploring what we could do differently.

There is a further strong impression from these social psychological experiments and reflections that ethical capacities which people privately hold will dwindle and waste away if they find no forum for public and joint expression. Thus in acting on threats to peace and justice, the sole consideration is not political effectiveness; also involved is the very survival and nurture of our moral identity, even of our humanity per se. Otherwise there comes a time, not only when it is politically too late to act ethically but when, even in and of ourselves, it is morally too late because we have lost the context and means to express what our private moral language may still feebly assert.

These psychosocial dimensions of public morality suggest further that the forms and levels of our action against the constraints of social structure, culture, and ideology may have to be boldly commensurate with the human abuse we are addressing. From one million people protesting nuclear arms in Central Park, for instance, we may appropriately have to move to one million people committing civil disobedience to gain the attention of the organs of government and to mobilize public support. However, with every such "upping of the ante" of ethically motivated action, there is also a concomitant "upping of the ante" of political analysis and strategy. The bold action that gets attention both mobilizes support and opposition.

What is the political end toward which this ethically induced public action tends? The current romanticizing of Gandhi and fetishizing of nonviolence exhibit a want of political thinking. It is essential to analyze and strategize about the political and socioeconomic factors and consequences in bold actions of conscience. Gandhi's politics had the result of transferring India from the control of British capitalists to the control of Indian capitalists. Do we simply want nuclear weapons abolished, leaving the cold war establishments in Russia and the U.S. firmly in place? As long as we are not engulfed in major war, is it tolerable that human needs and interests are sacrificed to corporate wealth controlled and inherited by a small fraction of the human race?

One consequence of sociological criticism and exegesis of the Bible is to bring the biblical world and its people closer to hand as we see our common immersion in social realities. The other consequence is to underscore how distinctive and unformulaic our situation is and how inescapable it is that we build our own political analysis and program of action toward which the biblical scenarios are exemplary backdrops and not blueprints.

C H A P T E R   26

How Does Social Scientific Criticism Shape Our Understanding of the Bible as a Resource for Economic Ethics?

ABSTRACT

Ethical judgments and injunctions in the Bible are part of the warp and woof of its history, literature, and theology. While "unsystematic," they are repeatedly generated and expressed as an integral aspect of collective Israelite and early Christian experience. To grasp this diffuse social and cultural embeddedness of biblical ethics, we need to be analytically aware of the social and cultural embeddedness of our own ethics, ceasing to think of them as some "universal truth" by which we peremptorily dismiss biblical ethics or naively conflate them with our own ethics.

Biblical ethics conceive the world and life in it as an ongoing site of struggle for the realization of community in which all members will have a secure and fulfilling place. Because the world is not yet complete, futurity becomes a central biblical ethical category. Thus, biblical eschatology signals that the normal discourse of ethics is conflictual discourse. In this regard biblical ethics are neither simply deontological or teleological, but a dialectical interweaving of both what is required and what is possible. Taking economic ethics as an example, the Bible as a whole favors communitarian over tributary economics but it does not address all kinds of practical issues that have arisen in the contest between capitalism and socialism in our world. The overriding perspective of the Bible on economic ethics is that people—literally all people—matter more than property and that the building of a materially just society is an indispensable counterpart and precondition for the spiritual welfare of humanity.

Although it is correct to recognize that the Bible does not display an elaborated ethic—any more than it displays an elaborated theology— almost every page of scripture expresses ethical values and judgments. How are we to access the ground and substance of biblical ethical discourse so that it can take its place as one voice among many in our own ethical life and reflection?

Any approach to biblical ethics is shaped by one's understanding of the ethical mode of discourse and action. In my view, ethics are deeply embedded in everything else people think, feel, and do. Therefore, I do not find it surprising, and certainly not disappointing, that biblical ethics are embedded in biblical literature and history in a confusingly "unsystematic" way. In this respect biblical ethics are frankly reflective of the way that the great majority of humanity—outside the community of academic ethicists—evaluate what they do and what is done to them as being "good" or "bad," "better" or "worse," "right" or "wrong," "deserved" or "undeserved," "just" or "unjust"—or any similar terms in which ethical assessments are typically expressed.

Accordingly, we best grasp and appropriate biblical ethics by seeing the whole history, literature, and society of which they were a part. By the same token, we can only carry out that sort of biblical inquiry profitably if we have located ourselves in our own situation, discovering what kind of socially and culturally embedded people we are. The objectivity that matters in our quest consists not of finding the most neutral generalizations about biblical ethics and about our own, but of identifying those life issues we and the biblical actors care about in the sense that we see ourselves as moral agents with the responsibility and capacity to do something about them. By starting off with a critical understanding of our own ethical biases, we stand the best chance of accessing biblical ethics over their entire range, as we uncover the points of coherence and dissonance among various biblical ethical views and the points where we find biblical ethics clashing with our own. In all this we are trying to counter a superficial harmonization of diverse ethical outlooks within the Bible and an illusory conflation of biblical ethical views with our own.

Biblical ethics are embedded in literary genres and streams of tradition of lush variety: law, prophecy, songs, wisdom, and apocalyptic. Each of these genres and traditions affirms, or at least presupposes, some sort of trustworthy ethical structure to life and each at the same time struggles with threats to and denials of such structure. Biblical ethics are diverse not only because of the manifold history and literature of Israel and the early Christian church, but because the rightness and wrongness of living is not "sewed up" in the Bible. Daily life is seen as ethically problematic because the world is experienced not simply as given without question or issue. It is known rather as a place of struggle. The world is still in formation and will always be so until "the end," conceived imaginatively as the ultimate horizon of the redemption of humanity or the establishment of the Reign of God. The various biblical ethical strands are, therefore, partial and in process as life itself is partial and in process.

Because life is in process and the world is being shaped in the midst of power struggles and moral ambiguities, futurity becomes a central biblical ethical category. Eschatology, our clumsy word for this mythic "end" of worlds—and even of the entire world—in God's purposes, is the ethos and symbolic ground where theology and ethics converge. How is God to impact and overcome the contradiction-riddled situations of biblical communities so that a worthy "end" will be reached? How are believers in communion with God to live at risk and with uncertainty on the frontiers of the world's contradictions so that they help rather than hinder movement toward the desired completion/fulfillment of human life?

The eschatological offense of biblical ethics is not primarily an offense against logical thinking. Rather it is a discomfiting exposure of our determined resistance to the scandalous truth that human life itself—and our ethical wisdom in particular—is socially and culturally limited and conflict-ridden. The eschatological mode works against the illusion of controlled stability and customary routine as the sole and decisive factors in shaping reality. It stresses that each situation passes over into another, and yet another, always with costs and benefits in the process. Biblical eschatology signals that the normal discourse of ethics is precisely conflictual discourse.

Moreover, the interpenetration of ethics and eschatology in biblical traditions resists either/or categories common to formal ethical discourse. For example, biblical ethics refuse to stay within the boundaries of deontological ethics or of teleological ethics. It is, I believe, a serious misreading to think that the biblical language of revelation is merely another form of deontological ethics, solely grounded in a transcendent deity, and that the ends-means concerns of teleological ethics are therefore immaterial to the Bible.

In his enduringly significant work on the connection between ethics and eschatology in the teaching of Jesus, Amos Wilder correctly grasped the dialectical mixture of deontological "demand" and teleological "situation" in the ethic of Jesus:

> Not the nearness of the end but the supreme significance of his errand and the resistance from the old order governs the world-renouncing claims. And this was not something which denied human relationship or led to asceticism or anarchy necessarily, but enriched relationships, save that in an emergency it could require renunciation, and save that its newness had in it the possibility of cleavages (1950:188).

Amid all their diversity on issues treated and warrants advanced, the varied strands of biblical ethics are keenly aware of the "renunciations" and "cleavages" of life in the tumultuous conditions of the ancient Mediterranean world.

In this sense, apocalyptic discourse is simply a mythic, pictorial way of stating what is elsewhere well recognized in the Bible: there is no way of realizing the Reign of God except through painful costly struggle in which our dreams for a better life are not simply progressively realized but frequently punctured and recast contrary to our wishes. In a perceptive study that traces significant formal and thematic affinities between biblical apocalyptic and science fiction, Frederick Kreuziger bluntly states this crisis aspect of eschatological ethics: "Fulfillment is never the simple matter of granting human desires, but a terrible tearing apart and transcending of those desires, so that a radically new life can flourish in their stead" (114).

This, then, is a key point where our ethics are challenged by biblical ethical discourse. The world as we know it—and our lives as we live them—do not go as any of us would design them to go. Yet how things do go depends in a measure on us and is not simply done to us. We are both "out of control" and "in control."

With this perspective on biblical ethics and their challenging juncture with our ethical struggles, what are the implications for the theme of this Conference: economic ethics? How are economic ethics embedded in the Bible and in our world?

Economics has to do with the way we produce and reproduce our lives within certain structures and systems that have changed over time and will continue to change. The particular way that our lives are produced and reproduced is called a mode of production and this reality shapes class consciousness according to differing notions of what life in community is about: its entitlements and obligations, its scope and limits, its empowerments and disabilities.

In spite of repeated claims over recent decades about an end to economic ideologies, we do live within capitalist and socialist modes of production which bit by bit have driven out or subordinated earlier modes of production. They are presently locked in a dance of competition and accommodation, neither able to achieve a clear victory in the meeting of basic needs for the majority of humanity. What light, if indeed any, do biblical economic ethics cast on our tangled situation?

Biblical economic ethics come to us from pre-capitalist and pre-socialist modes of production. The dominant mode was tributary, in which a strong state and the upperclasses dominated the majority of people through taxes, rents, and debts. Early Israel was a socioreligious movement confronting and challenging this tributary system with a communitarian mode of production that renounced statehood and retained economic power in the hands of free agrarians. A fierce political and ideological struggle over which of these modes of production should prevail runs throughout the entire course of biblical history. Once Israel became a monarchy, the tributary system had the upper hand, but economic and political battles were waged again and again to reclaim or hold communitarian ground lost to kings, merchants, and landlords.

The dominant voices in biblical economic ethics are emphatically communitarian, resolutely critiquing tributary power by seeking state reforms, urging resistance to oppressive power, upbraiding ruthless exploiters and speaking to the collective religious conscience of a nation with a communitarian premise at its base. Above all, it is this protracted conflict between tributary and communitarian understandings of economics that gives biblical economic ethics such a strident voice. It is the stridency of people who know of a "beginning" in community and seek for an "end" in community that has been thrown into jeopardy by the sacrifice of communal welfare to private indulgence and profit.

No ethical prescription or model from the Bible can be lifted out and employed today without considering its context and ours. Broadly speaking, there is no good reason to believe that we can ever return to earlier modes of production such as prevailed in biblical times. Of course small-scale communities may institute modified forms of communitarian sharing with biblical models as an example, and there is room for individuals to maneuver inside capitalist and socialist systems, provided they can maintain livelihood in doing so. But a sectarian "exceptionalist" approach will not build comprehensive economic structures and secure justice and equity over entire societies.

Given the reality that economic systems cannot be "imported" from the Bible to meet our needs, the ethical force of the Bible on issues of economics will have to be perspectival and motivational rather than prescriptive and technical. Once we recognize that the most basic questions about economic systems were entwined with biblical religion and fought over as an intrinsic aspect of living religiously, we gain leverage to criticize and evaluate economic systems today. We are freer to break the taboos against thinking big and thinking critically about capitalism and socialism. From our capitalist captivity in western society, in which we are indoctrinated with the wonders of capitalism and the woes of socialism, we will be empowered to explore the larger economic reality that includes the miseries of capitalism and the strengths of socialism. We will be less satisfied to echo the dominant economic voices of our society in their self-satisfaction and disregard for human suffering caused by economic structures that systematically favor some and disadvantage others. Economic domination of the many by the few will no longer seem so obviously natural and necessary.

When we interface communitarian biblical economics with our own economic systems, the results are instructive. The biblical premise of the primacy of communal welfare over individual achievement is much closer to the premises of socialism than to those of capitalism. The bias of communitarian biblical economics for control of production, distribution, and consumption by the producers themselves rather than an authoritarian hierarchy is likewise at odds with capitalist fundamentals, but it also is out of joint with state socialism that imposes economics by an ingrown bureaucracy.

There is one fundamental economic challenge in our day that the Bible throws no light upon, and that is the challenge of rapidly increasing technological development coupled with a growing complexity in economic organization. Capitalism largely dodges the question of the human effects of this set of issues, and socialism, which in principle espouses economic democracy, has had great difficulty in developing forms of economic organization that are both effective and democratic. Bible economics, because of the low level of technology and the small scale of the societies involved, are therefore virtually voiceless on the details of what is certain to become an ever more serious problem and stumbling block to humane economics. Communitarian biblical economics can only provide a general principle that technology and economic organization should be developed in such a way as to benefit all members of the society and that this goal is attainable only by involving large numbers of people, representing all sectors of society, in economic decision-making.

Thus the realities of biblical economic ethics all hang together in the knotted structures of a distant past, while our own economic ethics are bound up in a present intricate structural fabric. What links the two worlds of economic ethics, in spite of all the important differences, is a common thread of economic inequity and oppression and a common thread of struggle against needless economic suffering, a struggle fueled by religious convictions and aspirations. So we must exegete the biblical world and our world separately while we also lay claim to their continuities.

In conclusion, is it possible to identify a perspective emerging from biblical economics that will orient our analysis and reflection on capitalist/socialist economic systems in our time? I think we can.

Biblical economic ethics, in their several strands, show an abiding concern for the welfare of persons in damaged but perfectible communities. People matter. People are social and communal creatures. In important ways community structures, especially economic production, distort, and destroy people. As creatures of God, it is both possible and obligatory to build better forms of economic community in which more people benefit more equitably in deciding economic priorities and in the production and consumption of goods, services, and ideas. What the God of the Bible "reveals," behind and within all the many voices of the biblical traditions, is that this building of a materially just society is an indispensable precondition for the spiritual welfare of humanity.

CHAPTER 27

The Biblical Prophetic Critique of Political Economy: Its Ground and Import

ABSTRACT

The economic justice mandated in the Bible necessitates an examination of actual biblical economic systems. Israel developed out of an Egyptian-Canaanite "tributary" economy and in time developed its own form of "tributary" economy, in which a minority of people at the top lived off the labor of the majority. In its beginnings, Israel practiced a "communitarian" economy of approximate equality among family producers, reinforced by its religion. The charter communitarian economics of Israel can be amply illustrated from biblical stories, songs, and laws. When Israel became a state with a growing class structure, a deep conflict developed between tributary and communitarian beliefs and practices. This conflict runs all through biblical history, right into New Testament times. The Israelite prophets brought a powerful critique of the tributary political economy of their day by drawing on communitarian criteria and practices. Biblical law and prophecy leave us a tantalizing legacy: on the one hand, no specific model of economics that we can directly apply but, on the other hand, searching criteria for any economics: Do those economics serve the welfare of all members of the community as co-equals before God? In addition, biblical economic ethics give us a framework and ground for accepting personal responsibility for our economic views and actions as a specifically religious mandate.

Is there a biblical perspective on economics? This is both an ethical and a historical question, and neither question can be answered properly without also addressing the other. Ethically, it is recognized that the Bible calls for economic "justice." But biblical economic justice remains a vague generalization unless biblical economic systems can be recognized—and that is where the historical analysis becomes relevant.

Normally, not much thought is given to the historical nature of economic systems. Still, it is worth noting that the economic system of the United States is at most two hundred years old, and it undergoes considerable changes every fifty years or so. It is certainly not an eternal system, although it has been portrayed that way by its most ardent defenders. Thus, a historical view of how economies have come to be the way they are provides a much needed perspective in contemplating economic change.

In addition, Jews and Christians should have an interest in the views of economics expressed in the Bible. Some Jews and Christians argue that religion has little or nothing to do with economics and that if there were a dominant economic system favored in the Bible it would be irrelevant today because so much has changed since then. A review of biblical history sharply qualifies both of these arguments, particularly if the focus is placed on the prophetic movement and the socioeconomic structural context in which prophecy arose. The central question to be explored can be put in this way: Is there a biblical economics that is prescriptive, obligatory, or in any way exemplary for Jews and Christians today? The answer developed here is basically that the Bible will not solve our economic problems, but that knowledge of its economics is necessary if religious resources are to be called upon to deal with economics intelligently. The prophets will be used to suggest a concrete, working solution to this thorny question.

Some of the categories to be applied in this analysis are not often used in biblical interpretation. One such concept is "political economy," which can be described as the means by which people produce and reproduce their lives. Political economy has to do with how we keep ourselves going from day to day, develop our social relations, assert and accept authority, and generate ways of thinking about what we are doing. These thought patterns concern the way the system works, from provision for the most elementary needs, such as getting food and shelter, to the notions entertained about the ultimate meaning of life. This essay will inquire into the forms of political economy in ancient Israel as reflected in the Bible.

Another key concept is that of labor, the outlay of human energy that is required for the maintenance of life. The simplest requirements for life must be satisfied before higher cultural products can be created. Labor and the labor product encompass all human productions from foodstuffs and clothing to works of art and religious faith. Among the products of such labor are written texts, including the biblical books. The political economy of biblical times is therefore expressed in various kinds of labor products generated by people living in those times, including their religious ideas, practices, and texts.

Within this process of production, another concept of importance is that of "power relations." These relations among people determine the volume and flow of labor products: who decides what gets produced and who benefits from the use of what is produced. Only by learning something about the power struggles that went on in biblical communities is it possible to discern their economic system and to estimate its connection with the so-called market economics of modernity. A key aspect of power in all situations is who has the means to "explain" or "interpret" what is happening in the society, so that their view of political economy (including how labor is applied according to prevailing power relations) is accepted as correct. Power conflict is often a struggle over correct ideas, as is amply demonstrated in the Bible.

The major form of production in the ancient world in which Israel arose has been called "tributary" (Amin: 46–70; Gottwald, 1992; and cf. Bailey and Llobera). The tributary form of production was pre-capitalist: it did not involve capital formation in anything like the modern sense. But it did include relationships of domination, and the structure of that power system was bipolar: a powerful central state (such as Egypt, Assyria, or Babylon) or a smaller city-state (such as characterized Canaan or Syria) dominated a considerable stretch of land made up largely of villages engaged in agriculture and animal breeding. These villages contained up to 98 percent of the state's population. Peasants had "use ownership" of the land, but the state claimed entitlement to tax the villages first in the form of payment in kind and second in the form of conscription of labor for public works or army service. So the state regularly intruded into the village communities and took a good part of their labor products. Many peasants, already living on the margin, were further impoverished and driven into debt by these measures. Many were compelled to take loans at staggering interest rates offered by a money-lending merchant and absentee-landlord class that grew up with state blessing and support. While not precisely comparable in all respects, the political economies of many Third World countries today exhibit features very much like this tributary pattern in the ancient Near East. This helps to explain why Bible readers in Third World countries are often quicker to grasp the stark realities of biblical economics than those of us in more protected economic environments where inequities and hardships are less blatant. This also helps to explain why Third World peasants and workers can grasp the fundamentals of a liberation theology that baffles First World intellectuals.

Israel arose within the tributary political economy just described, and it did so in a very unusual way (Gottwald, 1979). There is something notably different about the religion of the Bible, and it is definitely connected with the peculiarity of its earliest political economy. What is unusual about the first communities of Israelites is that they did not give or take tribute. They refused allegiance to the states that taxed and conscripted their subjects, and they themselves strove not to extract tribute from one another. These first Israelites were residents of the small villages in the highlands of Canaan, and they banded together in large families and tribes to protect themselves from the Canaanite city-states and ultimately from the Egyptian empire.

Simply expressed, earliest Israel was in rebellion against the tributary system and the political and religious arrangements that legitimated and enforced it. These people of the new deity Yahweh were not willing to pay taxes, to be conscripted into the city-state armies, or to be debt-obligated. They asserted the full and free use of their own labor products, and they did so within the context of a society and culture where cooperation took precedence over competition.

How was their emphatic break with the all-powerful tributary system achieved? Israel attributed this "new beginning" to her delivering God. Historically, however, the factors that contributed to this deliverance must be sought. One way of understanding what happened is that the Canaanite city-states were weakening and in virtual collapse. No doubt this was true. Yet the books of Joshua and Judges (which, though written much later, preserve earlier traditions) contain significant indications that these assertive peasants were taking advantage of weaknesses in the political system and joining together in the common cause of becoming free agrarians. In particular, they developed their own distinctive measures of self-help, cooperative labor, and mutual aid, extending assistance from one family or clan to another, making grants-in-aid that passed among the people without interest charges. They also created their own culture, and it is especially through their religious culture—which they passed on to Western society— that we know these Israelites best. It is the specific contention of this analysis that Israel's religion can be understood adequately only when it is seen as an important dimension of Israel's political economy.

The Hebrew language appears to have been a dialect of the Canaanite language. It was apparently the dialect of the underclass Canaanites who became Israelites, mostly cultivators of the soil, but including pastoral nomads, artisans, and priests. They emerged bit by bit as a new people whose ethnic identity was formed in the midst of their struggle to establish themselves firmly in the hill country of western Palestine. The difficulty in saying exactly what it meant to be "Israelite" at the time stems from the fact that Israel was just then coming into being. Later on, what it meant to be "Jewish," especially in the midst of geographical dispersion and political domination, was shaped in good measure by Israel's original background of political and economic resistance to the overwhelming power of the state and its wealthy and privileged clients (Gottwald, 1988b).

The exodus from Egypt served as a metaphor to describe all kinds of experiences of oppression and resistance shared by the Israelites in Canaan, who had to contend not only with the Canaanite city-states, but also with the Philistines, Midianites, Ammonites, and Moabites, as well as the Egyptians, who exerted an imperial claim over Canaan. One could fairly say, therefore, that every Israelite group had its own experience of a pharaoh and an exodus. When early Israel speaks in legend or saga about those delivering experiences under Moses or Joshua, the historicity of the events lies not so much in details of time and place as in testimony to the process of social and political struggle by which Israel emerged from disparate groups of politically and economically subject peoples. There is a pattern of community formation that runs through these diverse, sometimes fanciful, traditions: Israel, under tributary oppression, resists and is delivered into a new communitarian society that it strives to sustain through covenant and law (Gottwald, 1989a).

How did the religion of Israel fit within the situation just described? A striking feature of the traditions from the very start is that the God of this people, known as Yahweh, is distinctively a delivering God who takes a strong stand on behalf of the oppressed underclasses that compose Israel. God creates a people out of those who were counted as no people according to the estimate of the political and economic leaders of the time. Yahweh not only sets these former "nobodies" on a new foundation that gives them identity and self-worth, but grants them alternative social and economic forms of life so that they need not lapse back into tributary domination or be torn apart by unbridled selfseeking. Very roughly, this may be called a "communitarian" mode of production in contrast to the tributary mode of production from which Israel dissented and withdrew and against which it had to defend itself.

To be sure, this communitarian mode of production did not prevail once Israel itself became a monarchic state with its own kings. And it was this turn to monarchy that set the stage for Israel's prophets to appear. The rise of Israelite monarchy is usually explained by Israel's military need to unify its forces in order to defeat the Philistines, who were a more formidable enemy than the divided Canaanite city-states had been. But the return of Israel to a tributary system was probably more complicated than that. Power struggles within the tribes probably weakened the communitarian manner of life, especially the judicial system designed to secure evenhanded preservation of rights. Families that had prospered on particularly good land seem to have used their influence to press for strengthened state power under David and

Solomon. The communitarian spirit and practice of the people did not disappear overnight, but now it was dominated and threatened by Israelite state power.

What this means is that within about two centuries the Israelite tribes had gone full circle. Arising in opposition to a foreign tributary mode of production—or one that became "foreign" to them as they withdrew from it—they now returned to a native tributary mode of production. One could say that they were now able to be ruled and oppressed by Israelite kings, merchants, and landlords instead of by non-Israelites. But many Israelites found no consolation in the fact that they were now oppressed by fellow Israelites instead of outsiders. Indeed, it struck many as an affront to and violation of their history and constitution as a communitarian people. Precisely this ironic situation is played upon by many of the prophets, some of whom came to prefer the prospect of foreign oppression to continued exploitation by Israelite kings and upper classes.

At any rate, the practical result for political economy was that a three-cornered conflict developed. The villages did not simply disappear. The Israelite state did not suddenly urbanize in the way that modern industrializing states have been able to do. The economy continued to consist of fundamentally small-scale agriculture organized by village networks. But the key political decision making was vested in the Israelite monarchy, and this meant taxing and conscripting policies, without which the state could not have thrived and taken its place among the other ancient Near East states. It also meant coercing peasants into growing lucrative export crops, a policy that often exacted a heavy sacrifice in the peasants' own standard of living and capacity to survive (Gottwald, 1985b).

Alongside the state and the agrarian populace, coexisting in uneasy tension that sometimes broke into open conflict, was a third power: the foreign tributary mode of production that became an increasing threat both to the Israelite state and to its peasant subjects. Foreign conquerors began to exact tribute and indemnities from Israel, and these payments had to come out of the same Israelite villages that paid taxes to Jerusalem or Samaria (double taxation without representation!). Eventually Assyria wiped out the northern kingdom of Israel, and Babylonia overthrew the southern kingdom of Judah. Israel's experiment in monarchic statehood had died. Henceforth, except for less than a century under the Hasmonean dynasty, the descendants of the Israelite tribes and states were a people subject to other powers. After Babylonia came Persia, the Hellenistic empires, and Rome. But by this time the Israelite people (now identified as Jewish) had developed such a distinctive culture and religion that they survived with remarkable tenacity, integrity, and flexibility, even when restricted by colonial servitude. This culture, known now as Judaism, has continued in its main contours to the present day (Gottwald, 1985a:419–56).

Although not strictly called for in the scope of this essay, a word should be said about Jesus and political economy. This is necessary because Christians are inclined to think that Jesus led a solely ethical and spiritual movement that had little or nothing to do with social and economic conditions. This is an entirely mistaken notion. The location of the work of Jesus and of the Jesus movement in Palestine—before Christianity became a primarily Gentile faith—was in alignment with the communitarian values and practices of the countryside of Galilee. This placed Jesus in opposition to the native tributary power represented by the Sadducees and the Jewish elite in Jerusalem and ultimately to the foreign tributary power of Rome. The strategy of Jesus and his movement seems to have been to aim at the Jewish elite and the temple economy rather than to target Rome directly. It was this Jewish elite and temple economy that imposed native tributary servitude on the people, while it simultaneously served Roman interests. The clearest single piece of historical information about Jesus is that he died as a political provocateur or disturber of that "alliance of convenience" between the Roman and the Jewish tributary modes of production.

This sketch of the place of Jesus in the political economy of his time is crucial for Christian reasoning about biblical economics and contemporary economics alike. It means, for instance, that discussion about whether or not Jesus was violent, politically speaking, is a red herring, since to answer positively or negatively ignores substantive questions about the politics of Jesus. He was implicated in politics of a communitarian stripe, whatever his precise methods were or whatever he thought he was accomplishing. He was killed for primarily political reasons. His followers went on to live in various relations and accommodations to political economies in Palestine and throughout the Roman Empire. The interconnection of religion and political economy was from the beginning as intimate and inescapable for Christians as for Jews, and the same is true today. Religion and political economy cannot simply be pulled apart and regarded in isolation. That is not only a general principle that can be illustrated from many known religions; it is concretely demonstrated in the provocative, controversial stance of Jesus toward his own society (Gottwald, 1989b).

Attention should be turned now to the ancient Israelite prophets who were active during the time of the independent Israelite kingdoms and into the period of Babylonian and Persian domination of the Jews. It clearly does not do the prophets justice to see them as foretellers of predetermined events or as teachers of ethics or theology in a formal or scholastic sense. They are more nearly commentators, analysts, and critics of the social and religious orders. The prophetic movement is a long-sustained exploration and criticism of how the tributary mode of production permeates and distorts Israelite (and later Jewish) culture and religion. For the most part, the prophets do not evaluate society from an abstract position of religious doctrine, mysticism, or spirituality, but from the perspective of the communitarian mode of production and its values. These had become well defined in the time of the judges and still existed in the village communities throughout Palestine. All the developments in later Israelite history that jeopardize this communitarian mode of life are severely judged by the prophets. To state it religiously, prophetic theology and ethics are unrelentingly communitarian in their conception of what God wants of human beings (Coote, 1981; Doorly).

Not all the prophets came from villages or from the ranks of the poor, to be sure. Some may have been from higher echelons of society, just as throughout history advocates of the unprivileged have come from higher classes. These prophets were troubled by the chauvinist and elitist assumptions about Israelite superiority to other peoples and about the virtues and wisdom of established rulers. They exposed smug self-righteousness and narrow self-interest in the politically and socially powerful who claimed to be serving Israel as a whole. They turned a pitiless eye on the inhuman effects of national leadership on the majority of ordinary Israelites. They foresaw the ruin of the nation through internal spoliation and external conquest.

How truly "practical" or "realistic" the prophetic criticisms actually were is a serious question, and this same uncertainty haunts attempts to apply their analyses (even by loose analogy) to modern societies. The political leaders of Israel and Judah had a number of understandable objections to these prophets; sometimes these objections are voiced in the Bible. Yet it is clear that Israelite leaders were not more evil than other leaders in tributary systems of political economy. To make their systems thrive and to keep control as leaders they felt compelled to maintain tax policies and launch building and military programs that were humanly very costly to their subjects. These same leaders also felt themselves entitled to privilege and luxury. The difference in the prophetic outlook was that the prophets were measuring present performance by communitarian rather than tributary standards, which meant that they felt compelled to represent the welfare of the majority of Israelites, who did not have entrée or voice in the royal court or in the circles of the powerful merchants and landgrabbers. In particular, the prophets were caustic about the way judicial verdicts and religious blessings were obtainable virtually on demand, if one had enough money or favors to dispense to judges, priests, or prophets "for hire."

So, in substance, most of the prophets were quarreling with aspects of a tributary political economy, as practiced by Israelite leaders and foreign powers, that threatened the communitarian integrity of the people. And because they saw the religion of Yahweh rooted in the old covenantal, communitarian style of life, with its mutual commitment among equals and sharp limitation of leadership powers, they regarded the prevailing forms of domination in Israel as irreligious, that is, contrary to the will of Israel's God. The consequences they foresaw were the ruination of the people and the collapse or overthrow of the institutions of national life. A clearer understanding of the prophetic mixture of religion and political economy can be gained if a closer look is given to some of the features of communitarian political economy and religion as they are expressed in older texts from the tribal period.

A very early text is the Song of Deborah in Judges 5, which expresses the exuberance of the Israelite tribes on the occasion of their victory over the chariot forces of Canaanite city-states in the plain of Jezreel, an event that occurred about 1100 B.C.E. The guerrilla fighters of Israel came down out of the hills of Galilee and Samaria and successfully overpowered the massed Canaanite chariotry, probably through a combination of surprise attack and a torrential rainstorm that immobilized the enemy's superior weaponry.

> In the days of Shamgar, son of Anath,
>   in the days of Jael, caravans/campaigns [of the Canaanites] ceased
>   and travelers kept to the byways.
> The peasantry grew fat
>   In Israel, they grew fat on booty.[1]
> When you arose, O Deborah,
>   when you arose, a mother in Israel!...
> Tell of it, you who ride on tawny asses,
>   you who sit on rich carpets
>   and you who walk by the way.
> To the sound of musicians at the watering places,
>   there they repeat the triumphs of Yahweh,
>   the triumphs of his peasantry in Israel.
>   (Judg 5:6–7, 10–11; trans. Gottwald)

---

[1] This translation of Judg 5:7, in which Israel's peasantry is celebrated as "growing fat" on booty, has been proposed by Marvin L. Chaney (1976). Explanations of the grounds for this undoubtedly correct rendering are presented in Gottwald (1979:503–7).

A more stylized liturgical text in Deuteronomy 33 also celebrates some of these early victories of the insurgent Israelites over their more numerous and powerfully armed enemies:

> Yahweh came from Sinai,
>   and dawned from Seir upon them;
>   he shown forth from Mount Paran.
> He came with the consecrated fighting forces,[2]
>   fire flashing from his right hand.
> Yes, he loved his people;
>   all those consecrated to him were in his hand;
> so they followed in your steps,
>   receiving direction from you,
> when Moses commanded us a law,
>   as a possession for the assembly of Jacob.
> Thus Yahweh became king in Jeshurun,[3]
>   when the heads of the people were gathered,
>   all the tribes of Israel together....
>
> There is none like God, O Jeshurun,
>   who rides through the heavens to your help,
>   and in his majesty through the skies.
> The enduring God is your dwelling place,
>   and underneath are the ever secure arms.
> And he thrust out the enemy before you,
>   and said "Destroy!"
> So Israel dwelt in safety,
>   the fountain of Jacob alone,
> in a land of grain and wine;
>   yes, his heavens drop down dew.
> Happy are you, O Israel!
> Who is like you, a people saved by Yahweh,
>   the shield of your help,
>   and the sword of your triumph!
> Your enemies shall come fawning to you,
>   and you shall tread upon their high places.
>   (Deut 33:2–5, 26–29; trans. Gottwald)

These early poems are shot through with martial and chauvinist rhetoric, but if it is seen in the context of political economy—as part of the struggle to build and defend a communitarian society—what comes to view is a bunch of rag-tag farmers who, though of no account in previous history, had achieved something by combining forces under the aegis of their empowering deity. Their exuberance and boasting makes sense in the circumstances. There is no God like Yahweh and no

---

[2] My translation of "consecrated fighting forces" as a double entendre on Israel's army and on supportive heavenly elements as an army is explained in Gottwald (1979:278–82).

[3] "Upright one," poetic term of endearment for Israel.

people like Israel! The nobodies of the earth "speak up" about how one of the high gods has lifted up this "scum of the earth" and made an autonomous people out of them.

We have to grasp the social placement of this kind of language to hear what it means for a country like the United States of America when its Jewish and Christian citizens imagine this nation to be the equivalent of biblical Israel and begin drawing conclusions about God's blessings that follow from such an equation (Gottwald, 1976a)! Language from the lips of underdog, insurgent peasants, when put in the mouths of citizens of the dominant oppressive power in the world today, simply will not work in the way it did originally. This is what Israel's prophets already recognized when they told Israel's later ruling classes that they could not speak and act as if they had warrants from God when they were at the same time oppressing their own people and violating the norms of the communitarian law. Religious claims should be valued differently depending upon the particular political economy in which they are made and the power position of those making them.

In this connection, a brief look should be given at the content and setting of communitarian laws and practices traditionally attached to Moses and thus placed in the foundation period of ancient Israel (von Waldow). A body of laws in Exodus 21–23, called the Covenant Code, probably dates from the northern kingdom of Israel about a century after David. Indications are, however, that these laws originated in the tribal period when Israel was trying to exclude relations of social and economic domination from its common life. One of these ancient instructions reads in this way: "If you lend money to any of my people who is poor, you shall not be to him as a creditor; you shall not exact interest from him" (Exod 22:25). What sort of a "loan" is in view? Normally a financial grant would not be called a loan unless there were some interest attached to it to compensate the creditor. Likewise, it was customary in ancient tributary societies to charge interest on loans to tax-encumbered and famine-devastated peasants. The Bible does not tell us the actual size of the tax and interest burdens, but informed estimates suggest that anywhere from 75 to 90 percent of a cultivator's annual yield might be consumed in taxes and interest on loans (Oakman: 57–80). In the face of this onerous economic practice, the Israelite law speaks emphatically: You Israelites may not exact tribute in that way. If you extend help to a brother in need, you may not charge anything for it because you are not permitted to make profit on the unavoidable suffering of others.

Furthermore, the same corpus of laws requires that Israel must practice equitable justice in deciding disputes among fellow Israelites.

"'You shall not pervert the justice due to your poor in his suit. Keep far from a false charge and do not slay the innocent and righteous, for I will not acquit the wicked. And you shall take no bribe, for a bribe blinds the officials and subverts the cause of those who are in the right'" (Exod 23:6–8).

It is precisely laws of this sort that the prophets saw violated all around them. Bribes were being lavishly extended and greedily received, and crushing interest rates were applied to loans that culminated in forfeiture of land and debt servitude. It is clear that the prophets did not regard these infractions as the isolated acts of a few anti-social persons. They found, rather, that the law was being systematically and deliberately ignored by rulers, officials, and the newly affluent who had prospered under the conditions of monarchic "economic growth." In one way or another the political and social leaders justified this unbridled use of power to enrich and enhance themselves. Military adventurism and conspicuous consumption among the well-to-do had laid heavier conscription and tax burdens on the people. Debt foreclosures had concentrated land in the hands of profiteers. Once-productive land lay in neglect or had been devastated by war. Isaiah is typical of his radical prophetic colleagues when he blasts the leaders of Israel for plundering and destroying the people of Israel put in their charge:

> Yahweh has taken his place to contend,
>   he stands to judge his people.
> Yahweh enters into judgment
>   with the elders and the princes of his people.
> "It is you who have devoured the vineyard,
>   the spoil of the poor is in your houses.
> What do you mean by crushing my people,
>   by grinding the faces of the poor?" says the Lord God of Hosts.
>   (Isa 3:13–15; trans. Gottwald)

From Isaiah's perspective, Yahweh's people are not just the elders and the princes who have been able to do whatever they can get away with in wronging others for their own advantage. Yahweh's people include the poor, and the deity wants to know what the leaders think they are doing in crushing and grinding their own citizenry so mercilessly. For it is these very leaders who have "devoured the vineyard" of Israel that Yahweh planted in the expectation of producing good grapes, but to no avail (Sheppard, 1985a:204–11). Numerous other examples could be given of prophetic indictments against the moral dereliction of Israel's leaders, together with their warnings of severe judgment to come. The examples given here should serve, however, to establish the communitarian measuring rod by which these prophets evaluated public life.

A question naturally arises about this heavily moralized social preaching, just as it is asked about the moral critics of our own capitalist economy. Were the prophets exaggerating, laying it on a little thick for effect? Were they perhaps "grinding axes," being envious or resentful of leaders with whom they had personal quarrels? Such doubts and reservations are raised today about those who question the supposed achievements of the capitalist success story. Such critics are often dismissed as disgruntled "prophets of doom." It is objected that nobody need be poor in our society. If people really want to advance economically, they can do so. If there are a few "glitches" in the economy here and there, they will be cleared up soon enough to reward everybody who honestly tries to get ahead. So, in biblical times as now, it was always possible to dismiss the prophets as troublesome cranks or dangerous charlatans.

In the last analysis, the only way to respond to what critics of society are saying is to make an independent judgment. There is no other court of appeals to adjudicate individual judgment. The "vindication of history" and the "judgment of God" may represent higher tribunals, but they take inordinate time to emerge, and even then they remain subject to dispute. For example, the prophetic announcements of public ruin and collapse did receive verification of a sort when the Israelite kingdoms fell. Even then, however, there were those who did not agree with the prophets' alleged reasons for catastrophe. Some thought that God had simply abandoned them without cause, or that the prophetic agitation had created social unrest and division that caused the public ruin.[4] The same range of contradictory explanations for historical reversals continues to show up: Is the United States weak abroad because it is a big bully among the nations or because it is not tough enough? Does our economy suffer because it is built on contradictory premises or because we have not given it free reign? It matters greatly with what eyes we see events and with what ears we hear contending voices. What do we read? To whom do we listen? What do we choose to see and what to ignore? When are the dark truths about our society and our culture too painful to look upon?

---

[4] That the radical prophets and other reformist elements in ancient Israel, including the Deuteronomists, were actually the cause of the downfall of the Israelite kingdoms has been argued by M. Silver (1983). In my judgment, Silver is able to reach this conclusion only by ignoring taxation and debt burdens within Israel and the balance of power among ancient Near East states.

The political context of the prophets can be summed up as follows: The original impulse of Israel was to create a communitarian society that empowered the poor and denied to anyone the right to lord it over others. This impulse was sharply challenged and frustrated by Israel's own resort to kingship and also by her experience of exile and dispersion among the tributary world empires. During this long retreat from communitarian social practice, the prophets of Israel and Jesus himself upheld the neglected and violated communitarian norms and practices. The later history of Judaism and Christianity suggests that the synagogue and church have usually adapted to whatever political economy in which they were found, whether it was tributary, slave, feudal, capitalist, or socialist. On the other hand, courageous dissent and resistance to oppression and exploitation have been carried on by a significant minority of Jews and Christians, inspired and directed by the communitarian voices of the Bible and the liberative traditions of both religions.

How, then, might a biblical economic scheme be applied today? Does the Bible give a clear plan or model for economic life? Given the methodological difficulties already mentioned, any answer must remain personal.

The Bible does not give a plan or model of economics proper, but it does give something more valuable: a perspective and criteria for evaluating political economies and a framework and ground for accepting personal responsibility for one's economic views and actions.[5] The "communitarian" yardstick is a significant one for assessing any political economy: Does that mode of production, and the power relations governing it, build up the whole community, providing it basic services and creating opportunities to realize the life possibilities of the greatest number of people? If that is roughly the biblical measure of political economy, then I would conclude that the failures of socialist economies, while extensive and severe in many respects, are matched and even exceeded by the failures of capitalist societies. This "greater failure" of capitalism can be stated in various ways, but one of the plainest ways to say it is this: The most powerful capitalist nation in the world gains the advantage of wealth that it has by "bleeding" and dominating smaller

---

5 J. L. Segundo (1976:97–124) articulates this point by means of a distinction between "faith" as the commitment to liberation and "ideologies" as political analyses and actions pertinent to particular historical situations. The Bible is rich in ideologies, and familiarity with them inspires us, not to try to copy one or another of them—which we cannot do in any case—but to seek out the necessary ideology for our situation in order to fill "the empty space between the conception of God that we receive from our faith and the problems that come to us from an ever-changing history" (116).

nations, the majority of whose citizens live in deepening poverty, and at the same time it allows a very large part of its own population to suffer in poverty. Public needs go begging, while a small part of the populace lives in opulence and surfeit of goods. The political leadership is almost totally captive to the ruling economic interests.

Does the Bible address the problem of developing a political economy that serves the basic needs of all and does so by involving people in a process of self-government—not only politically, but economically? No economic plan or model in the Bible can be used because they are all pre-capitalist and pre-socialist, predating the state of the economic universe as it now exists. Small groups of Jews or Christians can certainly develop communitarian economic groupings, but political economy on a large scale must be developed afresh.

In this regard, it may be that humane economics will have to develop in the direction of democratic socialism, since capitalism contains the fundamental flaw of selfish egoism at its very foundation. But the details of all this, and the specific mechanisms and processes for working it out, are not to be found in the Bible as prescriptions translatable into the contemporary situation. The current task is to work them out along the lines of the communitarian impulse that runs in tandem with the Jewish and Christian religions. To the degree that the communitarian impulse to equality and justice tempers the harsh features of unrestrained capitalism, it can be said that the resulting political economy is more humanly fulfilling than capitalism (when allowed to run riot). Personally speaking, however, the capitalist structure is the wrong starting point for the economy because it begins from a crude self-seeking individualism that simply fails to serve the full range of human needs in community. [6]

What the Bible can do in a very powerful way is to sensitize persons to look across class lines to the world as people in different circumstances see it. Since most of the kind of analytic thinking represented in this essay is carried out by people in relatively advantaged positions, some help is needed to see the world as the poor and the disadvantaged see it.

Surprisingly, the voice of the poor and needy sounds throughout the Bible more persistently than in any other classical literature. The danger is that its stirring scenes and messages will be turned into an ancient morality play that no longer connects with our world. The truth is that the cruelty and neglect suffered by the poor and deprived of the earth

---

[6] More extensive ethical assessments of the theory and practice of capitalism and socialism are set forth elsewhere by Gottwald (1986a; 1991a; 1991b).

continue in our time without any surcease and threaten the security and integrity of everyone in the process. On this point the Bible is as contemporary a document as can be imagined. Without giving specific instructions, it says again and again in stunning ways that something must be done about mass economic injustice in our world if this is to become God's earth and we are to be God's people.7

So, we are left with the logically perplexing but morally empowering paradox that the Bible is both grossly irrelevant in direct application to current economic problems and incredibly relevant in vision and principle for grasping opportunities and obligations to make the whole earth and its bounty serve the welfare of the whole human family. Such is the tantalizing economic legacy of biblical law and prophecy.

---

7 M. D. Meeks (1989) pursues the provocative and original theological method of examining what economic assumptions and behaviors are most in accord with God conceived under the metaphor of "the economist," i.e., as "householder" or "manager" of creation, society, and church. Among works on the biblical grounding of liberation theologies, the one that makes most sophisticated and trenchant use of political economy, ancient and modern, is I. J. Mosala (1989).

Biblical Views on "Church-State" Relations and Their Influence on Existing Political Ideologies

ABSTRACT

In this document assigned by the World Alliance of Reformed Churches for a Consultation on Christian Community in a Changing Society, I was given two far-reaching questions. One was descriptive: What role has biblical social history and ideology played in shaping current political ideologies? The other was normative: How are current ideologies to be evaluated in the light of principles or norms drawn from biblical social history and ideology? To tackle these questions, I had first to sketch the biblical views in their social historical context, which I identified as (1) a tribal communitarian view of the socioreligious community as a surrogate state; (2) a monarchic view of the socioreligious community as protected by and represented in the state; and (3) a colonial tributary view of the socioreligious community as an enclave within a state beyond its control.

In answer to the descriptive question, I concluded that the three major current political ideologies—bourgeois liberalism/capitalism, Marxist socialism and political romanticism (polities based on blood, soil, or religion)—have *not* been consistently or profoundly influenced by biblical social history and ideology, although the first and third of those ideologies have often had religious spokespersons who defended the ideologies biblically. In answer to the normative question, I concluded paradoxically that the one ideology that has been most anti-biblical, namely Marxist socialism, comes closer to biblical communitarianism than either of the other two ideologies. Socialism's weaknesses have been in its difficulty of integrating economic democracy with social and political democracy because of reliance on a corruptible central command structure which tends to lose sight of the very persons whom it seeks to benefit. In my judgment, economic democracy is central to human welfare. Since by its own premises, capitalism cannot provide economic democracy and, since in its predominant practice, state socialism has not provided economic democracy, an uncertain future opens before us in which the only human path visible seems to be democratic socialism. I would judge that there is substantial biblical "moral" support for that route, but for all the details and strategies we are "on our own."

There is no overarching systematic statement in the Bible of the relations between the religious community and the political community, either in terms of theory or in terms of institutional accords. What we find instead is a changeful account of the actual interplay between various religious communities and polities over the course of biblical history. From this interplay emerge several key issues and strategies for articulating the conjunction and disjunction between religious and political institutions at particular points in Israelite and early Christian history. Possibly the book of Deuteronomy gives us the fullest such account, apparently applicable to the Kingdom of Judah in the time of Josiah, but even Deuteronomy falls short of a fully developed church-state theory and is also incomplete when one attempts to read it as an actual constitution of the kingdom or as a concordat between church and state.

It seems to this writer that the best synoptic view is to be gained by assessing church-state relations within the broad sweep of political economy in the biblical period, distinguishing three phases of political economy: the *tribal* phase (approximately 1250–1000 B.C.E.); the *monarchic* phase (1000–586 B.C.E.); and the *colonial* phase (586 B.C.E.–100 C.E.). This tribal-monarch-colonial periodization emphasizes the sociopolitical dimension of Israelite life. To accentuate the specifically economic component of this history, we may also characterize tribal Israel as exhibiting a *communitarian* mode of production, monarchic Israel as dominated by a *native tributary* mode of production, and colonial Israel as subject to a *foreign tributary* mode of production. Each of these historic phases, seen both politically and economically, displays a distinctive perspective on the way religious and political communities are related.[1]

1. The tribal communitarian view
of the religious community as surrogate state.

It is increasingly recognized that Israel was an indigenous growth within Canaan from a mainly agrarian populace rather than a pastoral nomadic intrusion from without as formerly thought. Through some combination of Canaanite city-state decline and Israelite insurgency, the coalition of tribes secured livelihood and autonomous communal existence in the hill country of western Palestine. This was accomplished materially by intensive rain agriculture based on a grain-wine-oil pattern, supplemented by animal husbandry (Hopkins, 1985). It was

---

[1] For a fuller treatment of the history of Israel in terms of modes of production, see Gottwald (1992).

accomplished socially by a network of grassroots support systems that replaced the organs of centralized government.[2]

At the same time, Israel developed a strong religious ideology and practice that both validated and regulated its anti-statist communitarian life.[3] The religious community was itself coterminous with the social body which governed itself without specialized political institutions in a manner best paralleled in tribal forms of society that have survived into modern times. It is clear that while this loose form of communal governance had its problems in securing cooperation and compliance among all its members, it was by no means "anarchic" in the popular pejorative sense. Tribal Israel recognized the sovereignty of its deity which it sought to embody in social and religious compacts and practices implemented through a variety of limited leadership roles, as it also strove for social control through the proclamation of norms and the adjudication of disputes (von Waldow; Wilson, 1983).

2. The monarchic view of the religious community as protected and represented in the state.

In order to avert the dire threat of subjugation by the Philistines, the Israelite tribes centralized their military command. Over the course of the reigns of Saul, David and Solomon, the trend toward centralization of power led, step by step, to the entrenchment of a native Israelite state

---

[2] In recent years, many Old Testament scholars have come to doubt that we have any reliable biblical data for discerning the premonarchic history of Israel. While I concur that a detailed sequential history of tribal Israel is unattainable, it is my firm judgment that, in spite of their late redaction, numerous specimens of the various genres that speak about early Israel do in fact give us a reliable profile and much of the substance of the social formation of communitarian Israel. A review of this evidence concerning the genres of narratives, annals, lists, blessings and victory songs, legal directives and covenant texts will be found in Gottwald (1979; 1985a) and in Chaney (1983). The archaeological evidence is broadly supportive of this indigenous communitarian reconstruction of Israel's origin, but to date falls short of clarifying many of the social and political aspects of its tribal life (Dever, 1990: chap. 2). There is reason to expect that further excavations and more refined methods will in time enhance the contribution of archaeology to reconstructing Israel's early social history.

[3] By "communitarian" mode of production, I refer to a way of producing, distributing, and consuming goods, services, and ideas in which all the people, gathered in extended family structure, have entitlement to economic support and empowerment to develop cultural values and symbols through a form of self-rule that excludes domination and exploitation by foreign or native elites. The sense in which this society was "egalitarian" is more fully elaborated by the author elsewhere (Gottwald, 1979: see especially 798–99 n. 635).

apparatus roughly comparable to the type of Egyptian and Canaanite centralized power from which earliest Israel had broken away (Frick, 1985; Gottwald, 1986b). Domestic resistance, stemming from the tribal mode of self-rule, ruptured this kingdom into two parts. This division lasted until both kingdoms, north and south, were successively overthrown by foreign powers. During this period, the religious community of Israel existed within two sovereign states that at times were at war with one another in spite of their shared religious loyalties.

The religious ideology for legitimating centralized state power in Israel was the notion of the king and his agents as conduits of the will of God for the defense and welfare of the people. This ideology is most succinctly set forth in the conception of a covenant with David in contrast to the tribal ideology of a covenant with the people through Moses. The Israelite royal ideology was markedly similar to the notions of kingship throughout the ancient Near East, although Israelite kings seem never to have been deified in the manner customary in Egypt and occasionally practiced in Mesopotamia (Mettinger, 1976). In actuality, Israelite monarchy had to contend with an active communitarian constituency in continuity with its tribal past, and this social reality created resistance to royal policies that probably made the Israelite state somewhat less "absolute" or "arbitrary" than was the case with other ancient Near Eastern states (Halpern, 1981).

The economic consequences of the adoption of monarchy were far-reaching insofar as centralized government opened the door to social class stratification and to big power politics which put enormous strains on the majority of the Israelite populace (Chaney, 1986). The tribal communitarian ways of life stood in tension with and were progressively undermined by the state and its clients through an accumulating burden of taxation and debt, which constituted a tributary mode of production.[4] Prophets repeatedly underscored the contradiction between the lavish claims of royal ideology and the spoliation of the people (Coote, 1981; Mosala:chaps. 4–5). Nonetheless, the conception of the king and his courtiers as exemplary defenders of the people at the pleasure of God was strongly articulated and held sway against all criticisms, until the state apparatuses eventually were crushed by foreign conquerors. The reformation of Josiah toward the end of the seventh century, as reflected in Deuteronomy, seems to have attempted to tighten the control of the state over its populace while simultaneously

---

4 The term "tributary" for this mode of production (following Amin) is preferable to Marx's less precise term "Asiatic" mode of production (Bailey and Llobera; Krader).

checking the abusive socioeconomic practices of big merchants and landowners. This attempted "reform from above" pictures the Davidic king as one who serves the stipulations of the Mosaic covenant. Except for its centralization of worship at Jerusalem, the reform was short-lived.

3. The colonial tributary view of the religious community as an enclave within a state beyond its control.

With the cessation of political independence, Israel regrouped itself as communities of Jews, some of whom were restored to Judah while others were dispersed throughout the world empires that followed in succession down to the hegemony of Rome over Palestine. These communities, granted a measure of internal autonomy by their non-Jewish overlords, sought to achieve an integral civil and religious existence amid dominant political institutions that were by turns friendly, hostile or indifferent to them. The political institutions of Babylon, Persia, the Hellenistic empires, and Rome were all constituted on non-Jewish grounds. While Jews held that their one true God gave to these empires whatever legitimacy they had, they did not look to these powers for more than the protection of their communities and for whatever converts they could make among their peoples. Jewish recognition of the disjunction between the political institutions they could not control and the religious institutions they could build created an ongoing tension and conflict that set off Jewish interests as a distinct province from the interests of the empires they sought to exploit to their advantage (Gottwald, 1985a:chap. 10).

This was a decisively "colonial" situation, in which the aspiration for national independence smoldered and at times flamed up, as in the Maccabean-Hasmonean period from 175 to 63 B.C.E. and again in the open revolts against Rome in 66–74 and 132–135 C.E. Jewish leadership, caught between foreign and native constituencies, sought to extract maximal benefits for their communities from the world empires and also to keep their own nationalist elements from rash actions that would bring reprisal or devastation upon the Jewish enclaves.

The economic reality in this colonial situation was a two-tier form of the tributary mode of production, which was eventually overarched by the slave mode of production.[5] Overall it was a foreign tributary mode

---

[5] With the penetration of Hellenistic and Roman empires into the biblical world, the legal notion of private property, including property in slaves, became a critical factor in imperial political economy (Ste. Croix). In Palestine, however, slavery did not occur on a large scale, as in other parts of the empire, although Roman worldwide hegemony was made possible by slave labor and the concept of

because the world empires "called the shots" through their taxation policies and their decisions as to how the Jewish sectors of their empires would be favored or disfavored in the flow of trade and the dispensing of imperial funds. By way of example, the restored community of Jews in Judah seems to have been singled out for considerable support from the Persians who wished to strengthen their frontier against Egypt. By contrast, Hellenistic and Roman policies toward the Jews in Palestine were less generous and the tax burden in particular increased oppressively.

Of course the colonial policies of the great powers could not succeed without native officials and entrepreneurs who carried out the details of imperial administration and commerce, and kept civil order according to prevailing local practices. In the process, these native elites were in a privileged position to enhance their own power and wealth, thus exposing themselves to disdain when their actions were perceived as more self-serving than protective of the community as a whole. In Judah, this privileged elite was centered on the temple cult around which the civil and religious life of the community revolved, and through which the wealth of the society flowed. In Hellenistic and Roman times, lay elites developed alongside priestly elites as opportunities in trade, estate building, and tax-farming broadened the ranks of the comprador class that prospered under foreign rule (Belo, 1981:part II, chap. 2).

The relatively brief success of Jews in reestablishing a state of their own, under the Hasmonean dynasty, highlighted the issue of which political institutions their aspirations for national independence should strive to establish. Which political institutions would serve the communitarian interests of the whole people as articulated in the tribal origins of Israel and variously expressed in the people's canonical Torah? (Gottwald, 1985a:458–69; 1985d). Although battered and beleaguered throughout centuries of native and foreign tributary rule, these communitarian sensibilities and strategies of life survived tenaciously. At this juncture, the two preceding conceptions of the relation between religious and political communities came into play as alternative visions and programs for Jewish national independence. The monarchic or temple tributary format in which a Jewish state would protect and represent Jewish religion stood in tension with the tribal communitarian mode of life in which a Jewish state was seen to be a contradiction in terms since it automatically granted hierarchic powers to some Jews over others, thereby undercutting the religion and society it was intended to serve.

---

private property no doubt influenced the Jewish elite in their tributary exploitation of the populace.

We can see these contending visions and programs at odds in the Maccabean-Hasmonean era and during the uprisings against Rome. The Maccabees and Hasideans, from whom the Pharisees sprang and from whom the Essenes may have split off, were ardent for religious and communal autonomy but extremely suspicious, and eventually hostile, toward a church-state alliance such as the Hasmoneans developed once they were able to break free of Hellenistic rule. From their perspective, the Jewish Hasmonean state became an illegitimate Hellenistic princedom which mocked Jewish religion and exploited the majority of Jews as mercilessly as any foreign conqueror. Although Rome no doubt would have eventually swallowed up the Hasmoneans, the end of that dynasty came abruptly when a majority of Jews grew weary of the murderous infighting of their leaders and disaffected by the utter cruelty and avarice of their rule.

The wars against Rome were crushed so quickly that no particular program of national independence had opportunity to be fully enacted. Clearly there were those who wanted to establish a Jewish state shorn of its Roman collaborators and, in the second revolt against Rome, Bar-Cochba was endorsed by the rebels as the messianic head of the independent Judah they briefly established. In Josephus's accounts of the rebels in the first revolt against Rome, he drops enough information to show that some factions among the rebels had in mind a limited communitarian order. Josephus tells us that among the first acts of the rebels on seizing Jerusalem was to burn the tax records and to institute a method of electing the high priest by casting lots so that personal power and wealth could not influence the choice. It is also evident that the Pharisees, who had had their fill of Hasmonean and Sadducean connivance with state power, were intent on building parallel communal structures that imbued daily life with religious significance and did not hang on state or temple authority. It was of course these very Pharisees who eventually reconstructed Judaism in the wake of the unsuccessful uprisings against Rome.

In this connection, the position of Jesus and his followers in Palestine becomes of special interest for our topic. Any reconstruction of the political economy envisioned by Jesus labors under severe limitations. His style of teaching was anecdotal and aphoristic. His life was reported in retrospect and is overshadowed in the Gospels by his resurrected presence in the church. Also, as with the abortive uprisings against Rome, Jesus's specific communal intentions for his people never had a chance to show themselves on a large scale because his life was cut short. We simply do not know what he would have done had he gained a large enough following to successfully challenge and replace the existing order. Most limiting for our purposes was the rapid transfer of the church out of Palestine and into the wider Roman world, for this meant that the New Testament writers had mostly lost touch with the problem of Jewish-Roman relations as they existed in Palestine before 70 C.E.

Nevertheless, I believe we can make some approximations of Jesus's vision and program for political economy by ruling out those church-state options patently foreign to his outlook. We can rule out that Jesus was in favor of collaboration with Rome. We can also rule out that he favored a direct insurrection against Rome. Equally, we can rule out that Jesus was merely a moral and spiritual teacher who had no interest in communal life and wanted merely to change people's hearts. Furthermore, we can exclude that he wanted a return to monarchic tributary rule with a Jewish state where some "lorded it" over others (Oakman; Horsley).

In my judgment, the exclusions cited help us to locate Jesus in the position of a radical reformer with a communitarian vision of Jews as equals under God who express their "Kingdom commitment" in all aspects of personal and communal life. His "program" toward this end seems to have been threefold: (1) to activate personal commitment to this vision among followers whom he gathered around him; (2) to begin to exhibit this vision communally by the cultivation of mutual trust and sharing of goods within the movement he was leading; (3) to challenge the native tributary rule of his people at its center in Jerusalem by exposing the bankruptcy of the prevalent Jewish leadership. It seems to me that the nearest analogy to the interplay between vision and program in the stance of Jesus will be found among nonviolent confrontational agitators for social change, as, for example, Martin Luther King and Mohandas Gandhi: there is an overarching conception of the proper social order, a personal involvement in social change that begins small and aims for big changes, and an assertive confrontational style that coerces the opposition through social shaming and moral coercion.

I doubt that we can specify much more about Jesus's conception of public power except to say that it ought to be seen as highly communitarian, subordinating all its instruments and actions to the precious life of people as immediate children of God and as immediate brothers and sisters in community (Fiorenza: chap. 4; C. Myers: chaps. 1–2). I have so far said nothing about the "eschatological proviso," because I don't think we can know what Jesus expected as "the end of history." I suspect that his eschatological rhetoric was far more moral-decisional than it was cosmological-descriptive (Wilder, 1950). What Jesus expected is less important in this context than his bold speaking and acting in the direction of re-forming communal life radically in communitarian terms. He taught and acted as though there was a vital and necessary connection between what he was attempting and a fuller realization of God's beneficent love and justice among humankind.

In spite of the radicality of their Lord, the early Christians had to go on living in a world where the resurrected presence of Jesus did not break up the old state structures. They were left with a mix of communitarian, monarchic, and imperial-colonial institutions to which they accommodated in part and from which they sought to wrest some social and cultural space to build communities that would approximate what Jesus had talked about and enacted and was summoning them now to try to do in their own circumstances and in their own way. Still, they had no blueprint from Jesus on church-state relations. These Christians, while escaping the specific form of church-state confrontation that the Jews of Palestine faced, were themselves thrown into collaborative and adversarial relations with the Roman society and state. They adopted strategies and tactics not greatly different from those taken up by Jews over the centuries (Coote and Coote, 1990).

Only with the Constantinian era did Christians have to face what it meant to be part of a state that claimed to be Christian. When they did have to face it, they too, like the Jews before them, struggled between the contradictory poles of communitarian and hierarchic conceptions of religious and political community. There were differences, of course. The scale of conversion to Christianity over the Roman world and beyond it dwarfed anything that Jewish proselytism had achieved. Greek body-soul dualism, combined with the long Christian "sectarian" status within the Empire, freely encouraged a spiritualization of life in this world that discounted political structures and activities as of secondary importance. And, as Christians came to a majority in the Empire, the absoluteness of their religious claims translated readily into an intolerant repression of all opposing religious expressions.

Biblical Influence on Existing Political Ideologies

This topic has two dimensions. One is descriptive: What role has biblical social history and ideology played in shaping current ideologies? The other is normative: How are current ideologies to be evaluated in the light of principles or norms drawn from biblical social history and ideology? I shall give attention to both facets of our topic.

What are the relevant existing political ideologies that shape church-state relations today? There should be little disagreement that *bourgeois liberalism* and *Marxist socialism* are primary candidates. Beyond these, there is a family of related ideologies which, following Tillich's characterization, I shall call *political romanticism*. These are the "nationalisms" that take various shapes according to their respective emphases on the constitutive elements of soil, blood, culture, or religion. These political ideologies, with their appeal to "the mythical powers of origin," do not constitute a clear set of political and economic institutions. They may take aristocratic, feudal, populist, fascist, and even bourgeois liberal or socialist forms. I shall attempt to characterize and assess the core of each of these ideologies vis-à-vis biblical theories and practices at the interface of religious communities and political economies.[6]

1. *Bourgeois Liberalism.* Propelled by the British, American and French Revolutions of the 17th and 18th centuries, which overthrew aristocratic and feudal orders, this has been the dominant pace-setting political ideology of the last two centuries. It has been intimately connected throughout with the rise and triumph of the capitalist mode of production and western imperialist expansion into the rest of the world (Wolf, 1982). The heart of its ideology is the integrity of individuals as citizens of a polity with powers to choose their form of government, with civil liberties honored by the state, and with the right to personal ownership of the means of production (Macpherson). Freedom is understood as the protection of the rights of individual citizens. Government is that minimal exercise of administrative force necessary to protect these citizen rights from domestic or foreign infringements.

Culture, religion, economy, and social welfare are not of primary concern to the state, since these spheres are proper to the individual citizenry according to their respective powers, assets, and preferences. Government should enter these spheres only when there is a direct threat to the security of the polity. The organs of the state are shaped by parliamentary democratic forms subject to direct or indirect vote of the citizenry. The day-to-day administration of government is in the hands of a bureaucracy which is indirectly accountable through the parliamentary system. Over time, the role of government in liberal democratic states has tended to expand in the perceived interests of one or another sector of the populace, but always against the grain of the formal political philosophy.

---

[6] Paul Tillich (1933) brilliantly analyzed the roots and contours of what he called "political romanticism," "the bourgeois principle," and "the socialist principle." His grasp of the interaction of these political ideologies, and their relation to biblical "prophetism," is in my judgment still by far the most succinct and trenchant assessment of these political ideologies from the perspective of Jewish and Christian views of religious and political community.

Biblical views have been ingredient to the shaping of bourgeois liberalism, but only as one source among others, such as Greek and Roman political theory, Enlightenment, laissez faire economics, and accelerated technological developments. Through the Protestant Reformation, emerging liberalism imbibed a sense of the competency and right of the individual to reshape or overthrow traditional institutions. The anti-monarchic and Mosaic covenant strains in the Bible were seen to validate the removal or limitation of monarchs in favor of a political community of consensual processes and accords (Walzer). At first a very Protestant phenomenon, a progressively liberalized Catholicism has in this century accommodated itself to the regnant liberal political ideology (Fierro).

With the mediation of Protestant hermeneutics, the Bible was felt to endorse a vigorous entrepreneurial ethic which assumed that the development of a privately controlled economy would prosper the whole body politic. The triumphant universalism which had been a part of Christianity from the Constantinian era was put at the service of imperialism and colonialism. National independence movements in the 20th century have wrested much of the world from the direct political domination of western states. In that process, the liberal model of the state has been widely adopted in former imperialized regions. On the other hand, the enormous economic base of western liberal states, acquired through the economic and military plunder of their own lower classes and of the world at large, has left much of the now formally independent world so deliberately underdeveloped that, even where liberal democratic institutions have been adopted, there is little hope for securing a decent human life for a majority of citizens. Feeding on structural injustice and popular frustration, political romanticism has spread widely in these once imperialized regions.

In the appropriation of anti-monarchic and covenantal biblical motifs, bourgeois liberalism has failed to grasp the decisive communitarian thrust of those biblical rejections of absolutist rule. By focusing freedom on individual rights that did not, by their very design, secure the economic and social welfare of all citizens, the overthrow of aristocracy and monarchy was far more advantageous to those who had the private means to begin with than it was for those who lacked such means and could never count on the body politic to provide them. Freedom from arbitrary interference with individuals was not matched by freedom as commitment to uplifting the life conditions of the whole people. In biblical communitarian practice, freedom from hierarchic rule was not *freedom from* but a *mandate for* mutual economic and social sharing (Gnuse; Soares-Prabhu; C. J. H. Wright).

This hiatus in liberalism's view of public life has never been satisfactorily addressed or corrected (Hinkelammert). Emergency measures to care for the casualties of liberalism's economic and social blindspots have always been slow in coming and insufficient to meet the basic needs of all citizens. Predictions that the capitalist free market mechanisms protected by liberal democracy will in time benefit everyone have consistently proven to be "false promises." The significant contribution of liberalism to the protection of civil rights and liberties, a heritage deserving to be kept alive and expanded, is constantly undermined by the begrudging and half-hearted application of these rights and liberties to the socially deprived and marginal who suffer from liberalism's principled denial of economic entitlement for all citizens. Bourgeois liberalism's starting point is economic plutocracy which stands in fundamental contradiction to its platform of political democracy (M. D. Meeks). It is difficult to see how liberal political theory can ever overcome this double standard. The criterion of biblical communitarianism seems to suggest that it matters little what form of government is adopted if large numbers of people are denied resources to live a fully human life. Political equality is unable to compensate for economic inequality, for without the latter we have the former in name but not in substance.

2. *Marxist Socialism.* Fusing Enlightenment reason with utopian passion, and sharpened by an analysis of how wealth is generated and withheld from the producers under capitalism, Marxism offers a political philosophy that starts from the socialized individual in association with others. It views the liberal state as a mask that only thinly disguises the processes by which a few live off the labor of many. The socioeconomic divisions and inequities ramify until all aspects of personal and communal life are thrown out of balance. The key to a human politics is to honor and serve the basic needs of people, which include not only physical goods but dignity and self-fulfillment through participation in work and self-governance. The state, having historically served to meet principally the needs of a privileged minority, must be seized by the working majority and eventually rendered unnecessary as economic and social parity is attained for all citizens (Avineri; Gilbert).

This political ideology has been implemented in the attempted reconstruction of a fair number of states and societies in the twentieth century. It is probably accurate to say that socialism has had more success in improving the living conditions of people in the economically depressed lands where it has come to power than it has had in involving its citizens in participatory politics. In the socialist process, religion has usually been actively discouraged, and sometimes repressed, because it is seen as a bulwark of the liberal state or of political romanticism. Where Christians, however, have played a role in the revolutionary process, as in Nicaragua from the beginning and in Cuba in recent years, the church has been treated more sympathetically (McLellan).

By and large, Marxists have categorically denied any influence by religious ideas or motivations. But as a good number of Marxists, Jews and Christians have recognized, the Marxist passion for social justice and its impulse "to remake the world" have definite affinities with major strands of biblical thought. It can even be said that Marxism is a form of religious naturalism in which humans acting in history are accorded the creative novelty that the Bible attributes to God, and in many respects the human community envisioned by Marx is similar to notions of the people of God in biblical communitarian thought (Jacobson). There are of course major differences. A scientific analysis of how surplus wealth is produced was unknown to biblical writers. Reasonably firm moral notions that anchor much of biblical thought are not explicit in Marxism beyond the expectation that a new socialist morality will emerge as people begin to work and live together cooperatively rather than competitively (Nielsen).

If this prospect seems naive, it may be no more so than the biblical confidence that God is going to set things right in the world. In this respect, Marxism and much biblical thought share an optimism that major changes for the better are possible if people will throw themselves into the effort because there is an objective reality to the world, whether God-given or not, that will reward human effort. This passionate way of believing may lead to insufficient attention to means employed in pursuing ends, and it can issue in manipulation and coercion, whether Christian or Marxist, that tend to defeat the realization of laudable goals, or at least long delay them.

How much of this affinity between biblical views and Marxist views was present in the mind of Marx is unimportant compared to the reality of the appeal that Marxism has held for many Jews and Christians, even in the face of its atheistic stance. This has been possible, it seems to me, because biblical views allow for God to work through secular forces which sometimes are turned against the religious community for punishment or enlightenment.

It has been common for modern believers to view Marxism as a chastisement or "corrective" to the laxness of religion in addressing social injustice. This notion flows understandably from the history of the interplay and conflict among communitarian, monarchic, and imperial/colonial biblical views of church-state relations as outlined above.

When Marxists have occasionally identified their affinity with biblical views, it has usually been the prophets and Jesus in their advocacy of the poor that has drawn favorable comment. Following up on Engels' identification of pre-socialist tendencies in the Reformation sects, some Marxists have traced a "messianic" strain within the Bible and episodically throughout Jewish and Christian history, which they view as "unscientific" forerunners and seedbeds of contemporary socialism (Bloch). Some have even seen this religiously based commitment to social change as exemplary of a humanistic depth dimension that secular socialism has lacked to its own detriment (Gardavsky). An evaluation of Marxism in terms of biblical views, however, must proceed in recognition of the fact that as a whole Marxists have not made any explicit appropriation of biblical views.

It is evident to this writer that Marxism posits an understanding of humans as socialized actors in community which accords closely with the communitarian dimension of biblical thought and practice. The Marxist aim of spreading wealth and power among equals in community is markedly congruent with the vision and program of the early Israelite tribes and the prophetic-apocalyptic depictions of the proper human community. But it is unwise to make sweeping superficial comparisons and correspondences. Israel's communitarian mode of production was pre-capitalist and at a simple level of technology, loosely organized in its social formation, and without the stimulation of utopian secular goals and aspirations of the sort to which modern socialism has fallen heir in company with bourgeois liberalism. The obstacles and difficulties confronting the Israelite communitarian revolution, while formidable enough, did not begin to compare with the complexity and scale of the task of socialist transformation in a modern state.

In assessing Marxism as a political ideology from a biblical perspective, I doubt that there is anything specific to be said about the inefficiencies of Marxist socialism in practice or about its record of violence. With respect to the former, the Bible offers little beyond saying that a particular political form does or does not serve people in some specific regards, and the weight is usually on openly moral and theological criteria rather than on an assessment of the effectiveness of means taken to meet expressed goals. With respect to the latter, the Bible is itself so riddled with religiously endorsed violence that, unless we derive a principled pacifist stance from a certain interpretation of the practice of Jesus, there is little biblical basis to rule out political violence categorically on moral or theological grounds (Schwager).

Anti-Marxist Christians and Jews have regularly assessed socialist outcomes on these matters with a corresponding blindness about the massive ineffectiveness of liberal polity to produce a decent life for all and obliviousness to the millions of deaths that have been directly or indirectly inflicted by liberal states both on their own citizens and others throughout the world. In sheer magnitude of suffering and death, I would estimate that more of it has been produced in the name of bourgeois liberalism than in the name of Marxist socialism. It is of course possible to attribute bourgeois liberalism's death-dealing to "accident" or "miscalculation," while attributing Marxism's death-dealing to "deliberation" and "malevolence," or vice versa, but this maneuver is so patently untrue to all the facts and so evasive of the fundamental systemic issues that it serves no honest purpose.

More to the point is to ask whether Marxism has been true to its own philosophic foundations in the attempt to build socialist societies. From a biblical communitarian perspective, it is here that socialist practice may be judged to have made its most serious errors. The reluctance to honor civil rights and liberties and the direct equation of the will of communist parties with the welfare of the people go hand in hand with the naive assumption that one faction among the populace is able to determine the true needs of all and to provide the motive and means for a state apparatus to meet them. In short, instrumentalist and techno-cratic impulses that permeate bourgeois liberal practice have lived on in Marxist socialist practice.

To be sure, these tendencies have been exacerbated by the unrelent-ing siege that liberal states have mounted against socialist regimes the world over, doing everything in their power to make them closed and administratively rigid authoritarian societies, in order to strangle them to death. Yet this is not a sufficient justification for the drift of socialist societies into thought conformity and uninventive practice. It means regrettably that old hierarchic habits and attitudes were brought into the presumed service of the socialist revolution without adequate scrutiny. Worse yet, the privilege of socialist leadership too often turned into corruption of office for personal gain in a manner abundantly modeled in liberal democratic states. But precisely because the liberal state does not undertake a project of the social ethical magnitude and import of the socialist state, the moral failures of socialist leadership are more politi-cally damaging, both objectively and subjectively, than the like failures of liberal leaders. With respect to this point, biblical church-state notions have much to say about the urgent requirement for leadership that is integral to the people and subservient to their needs. The biblical voices have more to say to us about the moral culture in which any polity is founded than about the specific form of polity appropriate to a given situation. It is essential that the political economy be structurally congruent with social ethical goals and policies, but it must also be worked by agents whose personal integrity is evident in their social behavior at every administrative juncture.

3. *Political Romanticism.* I will comment more briefly on a category of political ideologies which is far less clearly defined than the preceding ideologies. The chief feature of these political ideologies is that they elevate one group of people, distinguished along territorial, ethnic, racial, cultural, or religious lines, above all others. Opposing the progressivism and universalism implicit in liberalism and socialism, they build polity on the rhetoric, tradition, and mythology of "purity of origins." Political romanticism often emerges in newly independent states whose people have long been under the heel of other groups, and it also comes to the fore in liberal and socialist polities when a once-strong state begins to weaken. It appears that no group of people is assuredly immune to the inroads of these romantic ideologies. In fact, the most virulent outburst of political romanticism occurred in fascist Germany in the heartland of "liberal" Europe.

In its benign forms, ethnocentric nationalism may function constructively in a transitional separatist mode, providing experience in self-governance and the development of culture that produces self-confidence and pride, meeting the long-neglected needs of a downtrodden people who can eventually take their place in the family of nations. Sadly, however, states formed by the cultivation of such inherently chauvinist and xenophobic ideologies are highly vulnerable to demagogic leadership which justifies all manner of corruption and personal luxury in the name of national pride. In the end, they may poorly serve the real needs of their people while offering them illusory "bread and circuses." Curiously, these politically romantic polities may be either "leftist" or "rightist" in their announced policies, but their overall drift is in a reactionary direction even when they appear to be "populist" or "socialist." When ethnocentric ideologies appear in countries that are already ethnically mixed, the result may be the monopolization of state power by one of the groups, or they may relativize parochial rivalries by espousing transnational religious identities, typically of a Christian, Muslim, or Hindu stripe. In these cases, the bond between church and state is apt to be intimate. Some of these ethnocentric polities may be integrated into international capitalism and others into socialist alliances.

It appears to me that within the biblical political economies there were strands of ethnocentrism, some fairly benign and others highly destructive. This is evident both in the Israelite-Jewish communities and in the early Christian communities. But, as noted above, the repeated tendency to equate particular ethnic groups or polities with the reified will of God on earth was again and again challenged and deflated by communitarian ideology and practice throughout the course of biblical history, even though the communitarian outlook usually worked under severe political restrictions. It is evident, however, that "unenlightened" and "absolutized" readings of biblical religion continue to fuel destructive political romanticism in the forms of nationalism, patriarchalism, racialism, and religious arrogance. In these respects, Jewish and Christian faith stand under the instruction and judgment of the universalizing outlooks of liberalism and socialism.

Christian Faith and the Future of Political Economy

In my own hermeneutical judgment, it is the communitarian ethos within the Bible, seeking to shape corporate life for the benefit of all its members, that constitutes the cutting edge of our heritage concerning the relations of church and state. This is our specific Jewish-Christian contribution to understanding and overcoming the present world political impasse in which non-communitarian political (and ecclesial) power dominates and frustrates human development. Privileged minorities everywhere benefit disproportionately from these power arrangements in the political economy that spill over into all aspects of life, including church structures and theologies. We face a daunting contradiction in theory and praxis: in order for political economy to serve the human race in its vast majority, abusive power must be broken "at the top" and alternative consensual practices and structures must be built "at the bottom." It is also apparent that these two tasks must go forward simultaneously. Moreover, it is clear that the rational and humane impulses in community must do constant battle with the irrationalities and parochial visions of political romanticism, which means that social psychology, culture, and religion are integral dimensions of the political project.

In giving precedence to communitarianism as our principal biblical political heritage, it is of utmost importance that we distinguish carefully between the priority of communitarianism in biblical political economy, on the one hand, and the desirability and feasibility of communitarianism in contemporary political economy. They are not identical, nor do they stand in simple continuity with one another. Each stands on its own. Historically, I believe Israel's communitarianism shaped its initial and enduring identity and that it was this current in Israel that contributed substantially to its survival in the religion and culture of Judaism, thereby creating the matrix for Christian faith. The seminal moments in the biblical history—the Mosaic tradition, prophecy, and the Jesus movement—were powerful outcroppings of communitarian ethos and practice.

As for today, however, the decision which I favor, namely, to give precedence to democratic socialism over capitalism in any of its forms is not a conclusion that follows automatically from the priority of communitarianism in biblical times. Rather, it is a choice based on philosophical, ethical, and practical grounds in which the Bible plays only a partial role. Jews and Christians will take biblical history into account insofar as the biblical traditions possess some form of authority for them, and those traditions will be exemplary of ever-renewed possibilities for a just human community under God. But it seems to me that our option today must be freshly formulated "from the ground up" and not preferred because it is allegedly "biblical." We must fully "own" our option, in the first place because there is no monolithic view of political order in the Bible, communitarian or otherwise, but rather conflicting tendencies. Moreover, in our world, shaped by novel forms of political economy—all of which are marked by practical and moral difficulties—we need to clearly articulate and concretely demonstrate exactly what form of communitarianism can truly address our present situation.

An adequate political ideology to realize this communitarian heritage of the Bible and to meet crying human need everywhere must be reconstructed in the face of the manifest inability of bourgeois liberalism, Marxist socialism, or political romanticism as they have been practiced to produce what they aspire to. This does not mean that we are at "the end of ideology," as some fancy. The ideologies are alive, and in spite of malaise, stagnation, and stalemate, they will struggle on in their efforts to offer workable political paradigms for our times. Of the three, probably political romanticism retains the strongest air of confidence, just because it is the most naively unreflective and feeds on political disillusion and despair. Nor does any "fourth way out" conveniently present itself to break the deadlock of the ideologies. The rearranged map of political ideologies necessary for our world will have to be a better way of putting together "the pieces of the puzzle" we have presently in hand. The key pieces I believe to be as follows:

1. Genuine economic democracy (the strong card of Marxist ideology).

2. Genuine respect for the personhood of all citizens (the strong card of bourgeois liberal ideology).

3. Genuine respect for the particularities of ethnicity, culture, and religion (the strong card of benign political romanticism).

But the "pieces" resist being randomly or arbitrarily joined as so many "good ideas." They require a design that prioritizes and connects them. The structural reality is that some ways of prioritizing and connecting these goals and criteria will encourage them to work together symbiotically, while other ways of bringing them together will block or violate one or more of the goals in such a way that none of them can be adequately realized. But which design and by what criteria?

In my judgment, political order adequate for human development and congruent with biblical communitarianism must be economically democratic as its foundational precondition. But that very prime condition can only be sustained in a polis that respects personhood and the particularities of subgroups within it. If this be so, socialism alone among existing ideologies provides a sufficient overarching framework for securing the maximal recognition and expression both of individual personhood and of group particularity, so that no person or group is over or underadvantaged (Cort; Dorrien). Neither bourgeois liberalism, which is premised on favoring persons who are private owners, nor political romanticism, which is premised on favoring one group with superior pedigree over others, can possibly provide this kind of framework. But, at the same time, socialism will be a lifeless shell, indeed can never truly thrive in cooperative human community, unless it encourages the enhancement of personhood and cultural particularities as its very reason for being.

Looked at in this manner, the political order toward which we press—or more often grope?— is not likely to emerge in a straight line of development from existing political ideologies and institutions, any more than from the biblical models themselves, either singly or patched together eclectically. The way forward is through transformations of all that has gone before in our political and ecclesial histories, and it will be "pre-lived" more than it will be "pre-planned" (Altizer). It will be a new birth, a birth at first undetected, barely to be trusted, amid all that will be dying around it. While we in the churches necessarily relate to the political ideologies and institutions as they are, our crucial role is to keep pointing and living toward the new polis that is biblical promise and present necessity. In doing so, we also commit ourselves to a reborn church whose shape is not one bit clearer—nor less clear—than the shape of that reborn polis that is on the way.

Works Consulted

Abernethy, T. P.

1932   *Frontier to Plantation.* Chapel Hill: University of North Carolina.

1937   *Western Land and the American Revolution.* New York: Macmillan.

1938   "Democracy and the Southern Frontier." *Journal of Southern History* 4: 3–13.

1940   *Three Virginia Frontiers.* Baton Rouge: University of Louisiana Press.

Adams, R. N.

1966   "Power and Power Domains." *América Latina* 9: 3–21.

Albrektson, Bertil

1963   *Studies in the Text and Theology of the Book of Lamentations.* Lund: Gleerup.

1967   *History and the Gods: An Essay on the Idea of Historical Events as Divine Manifestations in the Ancient Near East and in Israel.* Lund: Gleerup.

Almack, J. C.

1925   "The Shibboleth of the Frontier." *Historical Outlook* 16: 197–201.

Alt, Albrecht

1966a   "The Formation of the Israelite State in Palestine." Pp. 171–237 in *Essays on Old Testament History and Religion.* Oxford: Basil Blackwell. [German original, 1930].

1966b   "The God of the Fathers." Pp. 1–77 in *Essays on Old Testament History and Religion.* Oxford: Basil Blackwell. [German original, 1929].

1966c   "The Monarchy in the Kingdoms of Israel and Judah." Pp. 239–59 in *Essays on Old Testament History and Religion.* Oxford: Basil Blackwell. [German original, 1951].

1966d   "The Settlement of the Israelites in Palestine." Pp. 133–69 in *Essays on Old Testament History and Religion.* Oxford: Basil Blackwell. [German original, 1925].

Alter, Robert

1981   *The Art of Biblical Narrative.* New York: Basic Books.

Altizer, Thomas J. J.
1985   *History as Apocalypse.* Albany: State University of New York.

Amin, Samir
1980   *Class and Nation, Historically and in the Current Crisis.* New York/London: Monthly Review.

Anderson, Bernard W.
1981   Review of *The Tribes of Yahweh. Theology Today* 38:107–8.

Aronowitz, Stanley
1981   *The Crisis in Historical Materialism: Class, Politics and Culture in Marxist Theory.* New York: Praeger.

Auerbach, Erich
1957   *Mimesis: The Representation of Reality in Western Literature.* Garden City: Doubleday.

Auld, A. Graeme
1980   *Joshua, Moses and the Land. Tetrateuch-Pentateuch-Hexateuch in a Generation Since 1938.* Edinburgh: T. and T. Clark.

Avineri, Shlomo
1968   *The Social and Political Thought of Karl Marx.* Cambridge: Cambridge University.

Bailey, Anne M., and Joseph R. Llobera, eds.
1981   *The Asiatic Mode of Production: Science and Politics.* London/Boston: Routledge & Kegan Paul.

Barber, Bernard
1968   "Stratification, Social (Introduction)." Pp. 288–97 in *International Encyclopedia of the Social Sciences,* Vol. 15. New York: Free Press.

Batto, Bernard F.
1983   "The Reed Sea: *Requiescat in Pace.*" *JBL* 102: 27–35.

Belo, Fernando
1981   *A Materialist Reading of the Gospel of Mark.* Maryknoll: Orbis Books.

Berger, Peter L.
1963   "Charisma and Religious Innovation: The Social Location of Israelite Prophecy." *American Sociological Review* 28: 940–50.

Best, Michael H., and William E. Connolly
1976   *The Politicized Economy.* Lexington, MA: D.C.Heath.

Blank, Sheldon H.
1958   *Prophetic Faith in Isaiah.* New York: Harper & Brothers.

Blenkinsopp, Joseph
1977   *Prophecy and Canon: A Contribution to the Study of Jewish Origins.*. Notre Dame/London: University of Notre Dame.

Bloch, Ernst
1972   *Atheism in Christianity: The Religion of the Exodus and the Kingdom.* New York: Herder and Herder.

Boling, Robert G.
1988   *The Early Israelite Community in Transjordan* [The Social World of Biblical Antiquity Series, 6]. Sheffield: Almond.

Borowski, Oded
1987   *Agriculture in Iron Age Israel.* Winona Lake: Eisenbrauns.

Brandfon, Frederic R.
1987a   "Kinship, Culture and 'Longue Durée'." *JSOT* 39: 30–38
1987b   "The Limits of Evidence: Archaeology and Objectivity." *Maarav* 4: 5–43.

Bright, John
1981   *A History of Israel.* 3rd ed. Philadelphia: Westminster.

Brown, Bruce
1973   *Marx, Freud, and the Critique of Everyday Life: Toward a Permanent Cultural Revolution.* New York: Monthly Review.

Brueggemann, Walter
1968   "David and His Theologian." *CBQ* 30: 156–81.
1977   "Israel's Social Criticism and Yahweh's Sexuality." *JAARSup* 45/3, B: 739–72*.
1980   "The Tribes of Yahweh: An Essay Review." *JAAR* 48: 441–51.
1985a   *David's Truth in Israel's Imagination and Memory.* Philadelphia: Fortress.
1985b   "Shape for Old Testament Theology, I: Structure Legitimation." *CBQ* 47: 28–46.

Buber, Martin
1949   *The Prophetic Faith.* New York: Macmillan.
1957   "Prophecy, Apocalyptic and the Historical Hour." Pp. 192–207 in *Pointing the Way.* Collected Essays. London: Routledge & Kegan Paul.

Buccellati, Giorgio
1967   *Cities and Nations of Ancient Syria: An Essay on Political Institutions with Special Reference to the Israelite Kingdoms* [Studi Semitici, 26]. Rome: Instituto di Studi del Vicino Oriente.

Buss, Martin J.
1980   Review of *The Tribes of Yahweh. RelSRev* 6:271–74.

Butterfield, Herbert
1960   *International Conflict in The Twentieth Century*. London: Epworth.

Campbell, Edward E., Jr.
1975   *Ruth*. Garden City: Doubleday.

Cancian, Frank
1976   "Social Stratification." *Annual Review of Anthropology* 5: 227–48.

Carroll, Robert
1979   *When Prophecy Failed: Cognitive Dissonance and the Prophetic Traditions of the Old Testament*. New York: Seabury.

Chaney, Marvin L.
1976   "ḤDL-II and the 'Song of Deborah': Textual, Philological and Sociological Studies in Judges 5, with special Reference to the Verbal Occurrences of ḤDL in Biblical Hebrew." Ph.D. Diss., Harvard University.

1981   Review of *The Tribes of Yahweh. Pacific Theological Review* 14:28–33.

1982   "You Shall Not Covet Your Neighbor's House." *Pacific Theological Review* 15/2: 3–13.

1983   "Ancient Palestinian Peasant Movements and the Formation of Premonarchic Israel." Pp. 39–90 in *Palestine in Transition: The Emergence of Ancient Israel* [The Social World of Biblical Antiquity Series, 2]. Ed. D. N. Freedman and D. F. Graf. Sheffield: Almond.

1986   "Systemic Study of the Israelite Monarchy." *Semeia* 37: 53–76.

Cherry, Conrad, ed.
1971   *God's New Israel: Religious Interpretations of American Destiny*. Englewood Cliffs: Prentice-Hall.

Childs, Brevard S.
1972   "The Old Testament as Scripture of the Church." *CTM* 43: 709–722.

1977   "The Exegetical Significance of Canon for the Study of the Old Testament." VTSup 28: 66–80.

1979   *Introduction to the Old Testament as Scripture*. Philadelphia: Fortress.

1985   *The New Testament as Canon: An Introduction*. Philadelphia: Fortress.

Chotiner, Harry
1976   "The American Revolution and the American Left." *Socialist Revolution* No. 28 (April-June 1976): 6–28.

Christensen, Duane L.
1980   Review of *The Tribes of Yahweh. JSOT* 18:113–20.

Claburn, W. Eugene
1973   "The Fiscal Basis of Josiah's Reforms." *JBL* 92: 11–22.

Clapham, Lynn
1976 "Mythopoeic Antecedents of the Biblical World-view and Their Transformation in Early Israelite Thought." Pp. 108–19 in *Magnalia Dei: The Mighty Acts of God*. Ed. F. F. Cross et al. Garden City: Doubleday.

Clévenot, Michel
1985 *Materialist Approaches to the Bible*. Maryknoll: Orbis Books.

Coote, Robert B.
1981 *Amos Among the Prophets. Composition and Theology*. Philadelphia: Fortress.

1990 *Early Israel: A New Horizon*. Minneapolis: Fortress.

Coote, Robert B., and Mary P. Coote
1990 *Power, Politics, and the Making of the Bible: An Introduction*. Minneapolis: Fortress.

Coote, Robert B., and Keith W. Whitelam
1987 *The Emergence of Early Israel in Historical Perspective* [The Social World of Biblical Antiquity Series, 5]. Sheffield: Almond.

Cormie, Lee; Irarrazaval, Diego; and Robert Stark
1976 "How Do We Do Liberation Theology?" *Radical Religion* 2/4: 23–31.

Cort, John C.
1988 *Christian Socialism: An Informal History*. Maryknoll: Orbis Books.

Croatto, J. Severino
1981 *Exodus: Hermeneutics of Freedom*. Maryknoll: Orbis Books.

Cross, Frank M.
1973 *Canaanite Myth and Hebrew Epic*. Cambridge: Harvard University.

1983 "The Epic Traditions of Early Israel: Epic Narrative and the Reconstruction of Early Israelite Institutions." Pp. 13–39 in *The Poet and the Historian: Essays in Literary and Historical Biblical Criticism* [Harvard Semitic Studies, 26]. Ed. R. E. Friedman. Chico, CA: Scholars Press.

Crüsemann, Frank
1984 "State Tax and Temple Tithe in Israel's Monarchical Period." Unpublished paper for the ASOR/SBL Seminar on Sociology of the Monarchy, Annual Meeting.

Culley, Robert C., and Thomas W. Overholt, eds.
1982 *Anthropological Perspectives on Old Testament Prophecy*. Semeia 21.

Curle, Adam and Maire A. Dugan
1982 "Peacemaking: Stages and Sequence." *Peace and Change* 8 2/3: 15–30.

Des Pres, Terrence
1988   *Praises and Dispraises: Poetry and Politics in the Twentieth Century.* New York: Viking.

Dever, William G.
1983   "Material Remains and the Cult in Ancient Israel: An Essay in Archaeological Systematics." Pp. 571–87 in *The Word of the Lord Shall Go Forth: Essays in Honor of David Noel Freedman.* Ed. C. Meyers and M. O'Connor. Winona Lake: Eisenbrauns.

1987   "The Contribution of Archaeology to the Study of Canaanite and Early Israelite Religion." Pp. 209–47 in *Ancient Israelite Religion: Essays in Honor of Frank Moore Cross.* Ed. P. D. Miller, Jr., et al. Philadelphia: Fortress.

1990   *Recent Archaeological Discoveries and Biblical Research.* Seattle/London: University of Washington.

1992   "Archaeology and the Israelite 'Conquest.'" Pp. 545–58 in *The Anchor Bible Dictionary*, Vol. 3. Garden City: Doubleday.

Diakanoff, I. M., ed.
1969   *Ancient Mesopotamia: Socio-economic History. A Collection of Studies by Soviet Scholars.* Moscow: Nauka.

Dodd, C. H.
1953   "Natural Law in the New Testament." Pp. 129–42 in *New Testament Studies.* Manchester: Manchester University.

Doorly, W. J.
1989   *Prophet of Justice: Understanding the Book of Amos.* New York: Paulist.

Dorrien, G. J.
1990   *Reconstructing the Common Good: Theology and Social Order.* Maryknoll: Orbis Books.

Dybdahl, Jon L.
1981   "Israelite Village Land Tenure: Settlement to Exile." Ph.D. Diss., Fuller Theological Seminary. Ann Arbor: UMI.

Eagleton, Terry
1976   *Criticism and Ideology: A Study in Marxist Literary Theory.* London: Verso.

Edelstein, G. and M. Kislev
1981   "Mevasseret Yerushalayim: The Ancient Settlement and its Agricultural Terraces." *BA* 44: 53–56.

Elliott, John H.
1981   *A Home for the Homeless: A Sociological Exegesis of 1 Peter.* Philadelphia: Fortress Press.

Farley, Edward
1981 "The Reform of Theological Education as a Theological Task." *Theological Education* 18 (Spring issue): 93–117.

Fierro, Alfredo
1975 *The Militant Gospel: A Critical Introduction to Political Theologies.* Maryknoll: Orbis Books.

Finkelstein, Israel
1988 *The Archaeology of the Israelite Settlement.* Jerusalem: Israel Exploration Society.

Finley, Moses
1983 "Ancient Society." Pp. 19–22 in *A Dictionary of Marxist Thought.* Ed. T. Bottomore. Cambridge: Harvard University.

Fiorenza, Elisabeth S.
1983 *In Memory of Her: A Feminist Theological Reconstruction of Christian Origins.* New York: Crossroad.

Flanagan, James W.
1981 "Chiefs in Israel." *JSOT* 20: 47–73.

1988 *David's Social Drama: A Hologram of Israel's Early Iron Age* [The Social World of Biblical Antiquity Series, 7]. Sheffield: Almond.

Fohrer, Georg
1972 *History of Israelite Religion.* Nashville: Abingdon.

Freedman, David N.
1975 "Early Israelite History in the Light of Early Israelite Poetry." Pp. 3–35 in *Unity and Diversity: Essays in the History, Literature, and Religion of the Ancient Near East.* Eds. H. Goedicke and J. J. M. Roberts. Baltimore: The Johns Hopkins University.

1979 "Early Israelite Poetry and Historical Reconstructions." Pp. 85–96 in *Symposia Celebrating the 75th Anniversary of the ASOR (1900–1975).* Ed. F. M. Cross. Cambridge: ASOR.

Freud, Sigmund
1939 *Moses and Monotheism.* New York: Vintage Books.

Frick, Frank S.
1971 "The Rechabites Reconsidered," *JBL* 90: 279–87.

1979 "Religion and Sociopolitical Structures in Early Israel: An Ethnoarchaeological Approach." *SBLSP* 18: 233–53.

1985 *The Formation of the State in Ancient Israel. A Survey of Models and Theories* [The Social World of Biblical Antiquity Series, 4]. Decatur, GA: Almond.

Fried, Morton H.
1967   *The Evolution of Political Society: An Essay in Political Anthropology.* New York: Random House.

Fromm, Erich
1966   *You Shall Be As Gods: A Radical Interpretation of the Old Testament and its Traditions.* New York: Holt, Rinehart and Winston.

Gager, John G.
1975   *Kingdom and Community: The Social World of Early Christianity.* Englewood Cliffs: Prentice-Hall.

Gardavsky, V.
1973   *God is Not Yet Dead.* Baltimore: Penguin Books.

Gardner, E. Clinton
1960   *Biblical Faith and Social Ethics.* New York: Harper & Brothers.

de Geus, C. H. J.
1975   "The Importance of Archaeological Research into the Palestinian Agricultural Terraces...." *Palestine Exploration Quarterly* 107: 65–74.

1976   *The Tribes of Israel: An Investigation into Some of the Presuppositions of Martin Noth's Amphictyony Hypothesis.* Amsterdam/Assen: van Gorcum.

Giddens, Anthony, and David Held, eds.
1982   *Classes, Power, and Conflict: Classical and Contemporary Debates.* Berkeley: University of California.

Gilbert, Alan
1981   *Marx's Politics: Communists and Citizens.* New Brunswick, NJ: Rutgers University.

Girard, René
1977   *Violence and the Sacred.* Baltimore: The Johns Hopkins University.

Gitay, Yehoshua
1980   "Deutero-Isaiah: Oral or Written?" *JBL* 99: 185–97.

Glock, Albert E.
1970   "Early Israel as the Kingdom of Yahweh. The Influence of Archaeological Evidence on the Reconstruction of Religion in Early Israel." *CTM* 41: 558–605.

Gnuse, Robert
1985   *You Shall Not Steal: Community and Property in the Biblical Tradition.* Maryknoll: Orbis Books.

Golomb, B., and Y. Kedar
1971   "Ancient Agriculture in the Galilee Mountains." *IEJ* 21: 136:40.

Goodrich, C., and Sol Davison

1935-36 "The Wage-earner in the Westward Movement." *Political Science Quarterly* 50: 161–85; 51: 61–116.

1938 "The Frontier as a Safety-Valve: A Rejoinder." *Political Science Quarterly* 53: 268–71.

Gottwald, Norman K.

[titles marked * are included in this volume]

1962 *Studies in the Book of Lamentations*. Rev. ed. London: SCM Press.

1964 *All the Kingdoms of the Earth: Israelite Prophecy and International Relations in the Ancient Near East.* New York: Harper and Row.

1974 "Were the Early Israelites Pastoral Nomads?" Pp. 223–55 in *Rhetorical Criticism: Essays in Honor of James Muilenburg.* Ed. by J. Jackson and M. Kessler. Pittsburgh: Pickwick Press = pp. 165–89 in *The Proceedings of the Sixth World Congress of Jewish Studies* I. Jerusalem, 1977.

*1976a "Are Biblical and U. S. Societies Comparable? Theopolitical Analogies Toward the Next American Revolution." *Radical Religion* 3/1: 17–24.

1976b "Early Israel and 'The Asiatic Mode of Production' in Canaan." *SBLSP* 15: 145–54.

1976c "Israel, Social and Economic Development of." *IDB Sup:* 465–68.

1978 "The Hypothesis of the Revolutionary Origins of Ancient Israel: A Response to A. J. Hauser & T. L. Thompson." *JSOT* 7: 37–52.

1979 *The Tribes of Yahweh: A Sociology of the Religion of Liberated Israel, 1250–1050 B.C.E.* Maryknoll: Orbis Books. [2nd corrected printing: 1981].

1981 "'Church and State' in Ancient Israel: Example or Caution to our Age?" Pamphlet, Department of Religion Lecture Series. Gainesville: University of Florida.

1983a *The Bible and Liberation: Political and Social Hermeneutics.* Ed. by N. K. Gottwald. Maryknoll: Orbis Books.

1983b "Early Israel and the Canaanite Socioeconomic System" Pp. 25–37 in *Palestine in Transition: The Emergence of Ancient Israel.* Ed. by D. N. Freedman and D. F. Graf. Sheffield: Almond [revision of Gottwald, 1976b].

*1983c "Sociological Method in Biblical Research and Contemporary Peace Studies." *American Baptist Quarterly* 2/2: 142–56.

*1983d "The Theological Task After *The Tribes of Yahweh.*" Pp. 190–200 in *The Bible and Liberation: Social and Political Hermeneutics.* Ed. by N. K. Gottwald. Maryknoll: Orbis Books.

*1983e "Two Models for the Origins of Ancient Israel: Social Revolution or Frontier Development." Pp. 5–24 in *The Quest for the Kingdom of God. Studies in Honor of George E. Mendenhall.* Ed. H. B. Huffmon et al. Winona Lake: Eisenbrauns.

1983f "Bibliography on the Sociological Study of the Old Testament." *American Baptist Quarterly* 2/2:168–84.

1985a *The Hebrew Bible—A Socio-Literary Introduction.* Philadelphia: Fortress. [3rd corrected printing: 1990].

*1985b "A Hypothesis About Social Class in Monarchic Israel in the Light of Contemporary Studies of Social Class and Social Stratification." Paper presented to the Sociology of the Monarchy Group, ASOR-SBL, annual meeting.

1985c "The Israelite Settlement as a Social Revolutionary Movement." Pp. 34–46 in *Biblical Archaeology Today: Proceedings of the International Congress on Biblical Archaeology, Jerusalem, April 1984.* Jerusalem: Israel Exploration Society.

1985d "Social Matrix and Canonical Shape." *Theology Today* 42: 307–21.

1986a "From Biblical Economies to Modern Economies: A Bridge Over Troubled Waters." Pp. 138–48 in *Churches in Struggle. Liberation Theologies and Social Change in North America.* Ed. W. K. Tabb. New York: Monthly Review.

1986b "The Participation of Free Agrarians in the Introduction of Monarchy to Ancient Israel: An application of H. A. Landsberger's Framework for the Analysis of Peasant Movements." *Semeia* 37: 77–106.

*1986c "Review of I. M. Zeitlin, *Ancient Judaism: Biblical Criticism from Max Weber to the Present.*" *Religion* 16: 383–400.

1986d "Sozialgeschichtliche Praezision in der biblischen Verankerung der Befreiungstheologie." Pp. 88–107 in *Wer ist unser Gott? Beitraege zu einer Befreiungstheologie im Kontext der 'ersten' Welt.* Ed. L. Schottroff and W. Schottroff. Muenchen: Kaiser Verlag [trans. of address to the Catholic Biblical Association of America, San Francisco, August 1985].

1988a "Lamentations." Pp. 646–51 in *Harper's Bible Commentary*. Ed. by J. L. Mays. San Francisco: Harper & Row.

*1988b "Religious Conversion and the Societal Origins of Ancient Israel." *Perspectives in Religious Studies* 15: 49–65.

*1989a "The Exodus as Event and Process: A Test Case in The Biblical Grounding of Liberation Theology." Pp. 250–60 in *The Future of Liberation Theology: Essays in Honor of Gustavo Gutiérrez.* Ed. by M. H. Ellis and O. Maduro. Maryknoll: Orbis Books.

1989b *Proclamation 4: Aids for Interpreting the Lessons of the Church Year, Series A: Pentecost 3.* Minneapolis: Fortress.

*1991a "Biblical Views on 'Church-State' Relations and Their Influence on Existing Political Ideologies." Pp. 1–18 in *Christian Community in a Changing Society: Studies from the World Alliance of Reformed Churches.* Ed. by H. S. Wilson. Geneva: World Alliance of Reformed Churches.

1991b "Values and Economic Structures." Pp. 53–77 in *Religion and Economic Justice.* Ed. M. Zweig. Philadelphia: Temple University.

1992   "Sociology of Ancient Israel." Pp. 79–89 in *The Anchor Bible Dictionary*, Vol. 6. Garden City: Doubleday.

Gouldner, Alvin W.
1970   *The Coming Crisis of Western Sociology*. New York: Avon Books.

Graham, Billy
1985   *Approaching Hoofbeats: The Four Horsemen of the Apocalypse*. Waco: Word Books.

Grant, Robert M.
1977   *Early Christianity and Society: Seven Studies*. San Francisco: Harper & Row.

Gressley, G. M.
1968   "The Turner Thesis—A Problem in Historiography." Pp. 261–90 in *American Themes: Essays in Historiography*. New York: Oxford University.

Gunkel, Hermann
1910   *Genesis*. 3rd ed. Göttingen: Vandenhoeck & Ruprecht.

Gunn, David M.
1978   *The Story of King David: Genre and Interpretation* [JSOT Supplement Series, 6]. Sheffield: JSOT.

Gutiérrez, Gustavo
1988   *A Theology of Liberation: History, Politics and Salvation*. Rev. ed. Maryknoll: Orbis Books.

Gwaltney, W. C., Jr.
1983   "The Biblical Book of Lamentations in the Context of Near Eastern Lament Literature." Pp. 191–211 in *Scripture in Context II: More Essays in Comparative Method*. Ed. W. W. Hallo et al. Winona Lake: Eisenbrauns.

Hacker, L. M.
1933   "Sections or Classes?" *The Nation* 137: 108–10.

Halpern, Baruch
1975   "Gibeon: Israelite Diplomacy in the Conquest Era." *CBQ* 37: 303–16.
1981   *The Constitution of the Monarchy in Israel* [Harvard Semitic Monographs, 25]. Chico, CA: Scholars.
1983   *The Emergence of Israel in Canaan* [SBL Monograph Series, 29]. Chico, CA: Scholars.

Hanks, Thomas D.
1983   *God So Loved the Third World. The Biblical Vocabulary of Oppression*. Maryknoll: Orbis Books.

Hanson, Paul D.
1975   *The Dawn of Apocalyptic: The Historical and Sociological Roots of Jewish Apocalyptic Eschatology.* Philadelphia: Fortress.

Harris, Marvin
1968   *The Rise of Anthropological Theory: A History of Theories of Culture.* New York: Thomas Y. Crowell Co.

Hauser, Alan J.
1980   "Judges 5: Parataxis in Hebrew Poetry." *JBL* 99: 23–41.

Hay, Lewis S.
1964   "What Really Happened at the Sea of Reeds?" *JBL* 83: 397–403.

Hayes, C. J. H.
1946   "The American Frontier—Frontier of What?" *American Historical Review* 51: 199–210.

Hayes, John H., and J. Maxwell Miller, eds.
1977   *Israelite and Judaean History.* Philadelphia: Westminster .

Helm, J. ed.
1968   *Essays on the Problem of Tribe.* Seattle: University of Washington.

Hendel, Ronald S.
1988   "The Social Origins of the Aniconic Tradition in Early Israel." *CBQ* 50: 365–82.

Herbrechtsmeier, William
1987   "False Prophecy and Canonical Thinking." Ph. D. dissertation, Columbia University.

Herzog, Frederick
1980   *Justice Church: The New Function of the Church in North American Christianity.* Maryknoll: Orbis Books.

Hillers, Delbert R.
1972   *Lamentations.* Garden City: Doubleday.
1985   "Analyzing the Abominable: Our Understanding of Canaanite Religion." *JQR* 75: 253–69.

Hindess, B., and P. Q. Hirst
1975   *Pre-capitalist Modes of Production.* London: Routledge & Kegan Paul.
1977   *An Autocritique of "Pre-capitalist Modes of Production."* London: Macmillan.

Hindley, D.
1965   "Political Conflict Potential, Politicization, and the Peasants in Underdeveloped Countries." *Asian Studies* 3: 470–89.

Hinkelammert, F. J.

1986   *The Ideological Weapons of Death: A Theological Critique of Capitalism.* Maryknoll: Orbis Books.

Hofstadter, Richard

1949   "Turner and the Frontier Myth." *American Scholar* 18:433–43.

1955   *The Age of Reform.* New York: Alfred Knopf.

Holmberg, Bengt

1978   *Paul and Power.* Philadelphia: Fortress.

Hopkins, David C.

1983   "The Dynamics of Agriculture in Monarchical Israel." *SBLSP* 22:177–202.

1985   *The Highlands of Canaan: Agricultural Life in the Early Iron Age* [The Social World of Biblical Antiquity Series, 3]. Decatur, GA: Almond.

Horsley, Richard A.

1987   *Jesus and the Spiral of Violence: Popular Jewish Resistance in Roman Palestine.* San Francisco: Harper & Row.

Horton, Robin

1971   "African Conversion." *Journal of the International African Institute* 41: 85–108.

1975   "On the Rationality of Conversion." *Journal of the International African Institute* 45: 373–98.

Innis, Harold A.

1951   *The Bias of Communication.* Toronto: University of Toronto.

Ishida, Tomoo

1977   *The Royal Dynasties in Ancient Israel: A Study on the Formation and Development of Royal-Dynastic Ideology.* Berlin/New York: Walter de Gruyter.

Jacobson, Norman P.

1949   "Marxism and Religious Naturalism." *JR* 29 : 95–113.

Jameson, Fredric

1981   *The Political Unconscious: Narrative as a Socially Symbolic Act.* Ithica: Cornell University.

Jellinek, F.

1937   *The Paris Commune.* London: Gollancz.

Jepsen, Alfred

1934   *NABI: Soziologische Studien zur alttestamentlichen Literatur und Religionsgeschichte.* Muenchen: C. H. Beck.

Jobling, David

1978   *The Sense of Biblical Narrative: Three Structural Analyses in The Old Testament—1 Samuel 13–31, Numbers 11–12, 1 Kings 17–18* [JSOT Supplement Series, 7]. Sheffield: JSOT.

1980a   "'The Jordan A Boundary': A Reading of Numbers 32 and Joshua 22." *SBLSP* 19: 183–207.

1980b   "The Myth Semantics of Genesis 2:4b–3:24." *Semeia* 18: 41–49.

1992   "Deconstruction and the Political Analysis of Biblical Texts: A Jamesonian Reading of Psalm 72." *Semeia* 59:95–127.

Jones, Larry, and Gerald T. Sheppard

1984   "The Politics of Biblical Eschatology: Ronald Reagan and the Impending Nuclear Armageddon." *Theological Students Fellowship Bulletin* 8/1: 16–19.

Kamp, Kathryn A., and Norman Yoffee

1980   "Ethnicity in Ancient Western Asia During the Early Second Millennium B.C.: Archaeological Assessments and Ethno-archaeological Perspectives." *BASOR* 234: 85–104.

Kane, M.

1936   "Some Considerations on the Safety-valve Doctrine." *Mississippi Valley Historical Review* 23: 169–88.

Kaufmann, Yehezkel

1961   *The Religion of Israel from its Beginnings to the Babylonian Exile.* Chicago: University of Chicago.

1970   *The Babylonian Captivity and Deutero-Isaiah.* New York: Union of American Hebrew Congregations.

Kennedy, James M.

1987   "The Social Background of Early Israel's Rejection of Cultic Images: A Proposal." *BTB* 17: 138–44.

Kimbrough, S. T., Jr.

1978   *Israelite Religion in Sociological Perspective: The Work of Antonin Causse.* Wiesbaden: Harrassowitz.

Klein, Ralph W.

1981   Review of *The Tribes of Yahweh. Currents in Theology and Mission* 8 (February):53–54.

Krader, Lawrence

1985   *The Asiatic Mode of Production: Sources, Development and Critique in the Writings of Karl Marx.* Assen: Van Gorcum.

Kraemer, Helmut et al.
1968 "Prophētēs." Pp. 781–861 in *Theological Dictionary of the New Testament*, Vol. 6. Ed. G. Kittel and G. Friedrich. Trans. G. Bromiley. Grand Rapids: Eerdmans.

Kreuziger, Frederick A.
1982 *Apocalypse and Science Fiction: A Dialectic of Religious and Secular Soteriologies*. Chico, CA: Scholars.

Kristjánsson, Jónas
1980 *Icelandic Sagas and Manuscripts*. Reykjavik: Iceland Review.

Ladd, George E.
1956 *The Blessed Hope*. Grand Rapids: Eerdmans.

Lanahan, W. F.
1974 "The Speaking Voice in The Book of Lamentations." *JBL* 93: 41–49.

LeGuin, Ursula
1976 *The Left Hand of Darkness*. New York: Ace Books.

Lemche, Niels P.
1985 *Early Israel: Anthropological and Historical Studies on Israelite Society Before the Monarchy* [VTSup, 37]. Leiden: E. J. Brill.

1988 *Ancient Israel: A New History of Israelite Society* [The Biblical Seminar, 5]. Sheffield: JSOT.

Lenski, Gerhard
1966 *Power and Privilege: A Theory of Social Stratification*. New York: McGraw-Hill.

1976 "History and Social Change." *American Journal of Sociology* 82:548–64.

1980 "Review of N. K. Gottwald, *The Tribes of Yahweh*" *RelSRev* 6:275–78.

Lenski, Gerhard, and Jean Lenski
1978 *Human Societies: An Introduction to Macrosociology*. 3rd ed. New York: McGraw-Hill.

Lenz, Theodore
1971 *Toward a Science of Peace*. 5th ed. Portland, OR: Halcyon.

L'Heureux, Conrad E.
1981 "Searching for the Origins of God." Pp. 33–57 in *Traditions in Transformation: Turning Points in Biblical Faith*. Ed. B. Halpern and J. Levenson. Winona Lake: Eisenbrauns.

Lindsey, Hal, and C. C. Carlson
1976 *The Late Great Planet Earth*. Grand Rapids: Zondervan.

Lipset, Seymour M.
1968   "Stratification, Social (Social Class)." Pp. 296–316 in *International Encyclopedia of the Social Sciences.* Vol. 15. New York: Free Press.

Long, Burke O.
1982   "Social Dimensions of Prophetic Conflict," *Semeia* 21: 31–53.

Lynd, Staughton
1968   *Intellectual Origins of American Radicalism.* New York: Vintage Books.

Maccoby, Hyam
1982   *The Sacred Executioner: Human Sacrifice and the Legacy of Guilt.* New York: W. W. Norton.

Macpherson, C. B.
1975   *The Political Theory of Possessive Individualism: Hobbes to Locke.* Oxford: Oxford University.

Maduro, Otto
1982   *Religion and Social Conflicts.* Maryknoll: Orbis Books.

Malamat, Abraham
1983   "The Proto-History of Israel: A Study in Method." Pp. 303–13 in *The Word of the Lord Shall Go Forth. Essays in Honor of David Noel Freedman*. Ed. C. L. Meyers and M. O'Connor. Philadelphia: American Schools of Oriental Research.

1989   *Mari and the Early Israelite Experience* [The Schweich Lectures 1984]. Oxford: Oxford University.

Malherbe, Abraham J.
1977   *Social Aspects of Early Christianity.* Baton Rouge: University of Louisiana.

Malina, Bruce J.
1981a   *The New Testament World: Insights from Cultural Anthropology.* Atlanta: John Knox.

1981b   Review of *The Tribes of Yahweh. BTB* 12:61.

Mansueto, Anthony
1983   "From Historical Criticism to Historical Materialism." Unpublished paper submitted to a graduate seminar on Social Scientific Method in Biblical Studies at the Graduate Theological Union, Berkeley, California, spring term.

Marfoe, Leon
1979   "The Integrative Transformation: Patterns of Sociopolitical Organization in Southern Syria." *BASOR* 234: 1–42.

Marx, Karl

1857/8 *Grundrisse: Foundations of the Critique of Political Economy (Rough Draft).* Pelican Marx Library. Harmondsworth/Baltimore: Penguin Books.

1867 *Capital.* Vol. I. Pelican Marx Library. Harmondsworth/Baltimore: Penguin Books.

1972 "The Civil War in France." Pp. 526–76 in *The Marx-Engels Reader.* Ed. R. C.
[1871] Tucker. New York: W. W. Norton.

Marx, Karl, and Friedrich Engels,

1964 *Karl Marx and Friedrich Engels on Religion.* Ed. R. Niebuhr. New York: Schocken Books.

McCarthy, Brian R.

1980 Review of *The Tribes of Yahweh. The Economist* 18:17–22.

McKnight, Edgar V.

1985 *The Bible and the Reader: An Introduction to Literary Criticism.* Philadelphia: Fortress.

McLellan, David

1987 *Marxism and Religion: A Description and Assessment of the Marxist Critique of Chrisitanity.* New York: Harper & Row.

McNutt, Paula

1987 "Interpreting Israel's 'Folk Traditions'." *JSOT* 39: 44–52.

Meeks, M. Douglas

1989 *God the Economist: The Doctrine of God and Political Economy.* Minneapolis: Fortress.

Meeks, Wayne A.

1983 *The First Urban Christians: The Social World of the Apostle Paul.* New Haven: Yale University.

Melotti, Umberto

1977 *Marx and the Third World.* London: Macmillan.

Mendenhall, George E.

1962 "The Hebrew Conquest of Palestine." *BA* 25: 66–87 = *BAR* 3 (1970): 100–20.

1973 *The Tenth Generation: The Origins of the Biblical Tradition.* Baltimore: Johns Hopkins University.

1976a "'Change and Decay in All Around I See': Conquest, Covenant, and *The Tenth Generation.*" *BA* 39: 152–57.

1976b "Social Organization in Early Israel." Pp. 132–51 in *Magnalia Dei, The Mighty Acts of God: Essays on the Bible and Archaeology in Memory of G. Ernest Wright.* Ed. F. M. Cross et al. Garden City: Doubleday.

Mettinger, T. N. D.

1971   *Solomonic State Officials: A Study of the Civil Government Officials of the Israelite Monarchy* [Coniectanea Biblica Old Testament Monograph Series, 5]. Lund: Gleerup.

1976   *King and Messiah: The Civil and Sacral Legitimation of the Israelite Kings* [Coniectanea Biblica Old Testament Monograph Series, 8]. Lund: Gleerup.

Meyers, Carol L.

1981   Review of *The Tribes of Yahweh*. CBQ 43:104–9.

1988   *Discovering Eve: Ancient Israelite Women in Context*. New York/Oxford: Oxford University.

Milgram, Stanley

1974   *Obedience to Authority*. New York: Harper & Row.

Milgrom, Jacob

1978   "Priestly Terminology and the Political and Social Structure of Pre-Monarchic Israel." *JQR* 69: 65–81.

1982   "Religious Conversion and the Revolt Model for the Formation of Israel." *JBL* 101: 169–76.

Miller, J. Maxwell

1977   "The Israelite Occupation of Canaan." Pp. 213–84 in *Israelite and Judaean History*. Ed. J. H. Hayes and J. M. Miller. Philadelphia: Westminster.

Mintz, Alan

1982   "The Rhetoric of Lamentations and the Representation of Catastrophe." *Prooftexts* 2: 1–17.

Miranda, José P.

1973   *Being and Messiah: The Message of St. John*. Maryknoll: Orbis Books.

1974   *Marx and the Bible: A Critique of the Philosophy of Oppression*. Maryknoll: Orbis Books.

Miyakawa, T. S.

1964   *Protestants and Pioneers: Individualism and Conformity on the American Frontier*. Chicago/London: University of Chicago.

Mosala, Itumeleng J.

1989   *Biblical Hermeneutics and Black Theology in South Africa*. Grand Rapids: Eerdmans.

Mottu, Henri

1983   "Jeremiah vs. Hananiah: Ideology and Truth in Old Testament Prophecy." Pp. 235–51 in *The Bible and Liberation*. Ed. N. K. Gottwald. Maryknoll: Orbis Books.

Mowinckel, Sigmund
1964   *Tetrateuch-Pentateuch-Hexateuch. Die Berichte über die Landnahme in den drei altisraelitischen Geschichtswerken.* Berlin: Walter de Gruyter.

Murray, D. F.
1979   "Narrative Structure and Technique in the Deborah and Barak Story." VTSup 30: 155–89.

Myers, Allen C.
1981   Review of *The Tribes of Yahweh. The Reformed Journal* 31 (March):20–23.

Myers, Ched
1988   *Binding the Strong Man. A Political Reading of Mark's Story of Jesus.* Maryknoll: Orbis Books.

Nelson, Richard D.
1981   "Josiah in the Book of Joshua." *JBL* 100: 531–40.

Newman, Katherine S.
1983   *Law and Economic Organization: A Comparative Study of Preindustrial Societies.* Cambridge/New York: Cambridge University.

Niebuhr, Reinhold, ed. and intro.
1964   *Karl Marx and Friedrich Engels on Religion.* New York: Schocken Books.

Nielsen, Kai
1989   *Marxism and the Moral Point of View: Morality, Ideology and Historical Materialism.* Boulder/London: Westview.

Njardvik, Njödur P.
1978   *Birth of a Nation: The Story of the Icelandic Commonwealth.* Reykjavik: Iceland Review.

North, Robert
1985   "Violence and the Bible: The Girard Connection," *CBQ* 47: 1–27.

Noth, Martin
1930   *Das System der zwoelf Staemme Israels.* Stuttgart: Kohlhammer.
1960   *The History of Israel.* 2nd ed. New York: Harper.
1972   *A History of the Pentateuchal Traditions.* Englewood Cliffs: Prentice-Hall.

Oakman, Douglas E.
1986   *Jesus and the Economic Questions of His Day.* Lewiston, NY: Edwin Mellen.

Ollman, Bertell
1978   *Alienation: Marx's Conception of Man in Capitalist Society.* 2nd ed. Cambridge, MA: Harvard University.

Overholt, Thomas W.

1974   "The Ghost Dance of 1890 and the Nature of the Prophetic Process."
        Ethnohistory 21: 37–63.

1982   "Prophecy: The Problem of Cross-Cultural Comparison." *Semeia* 21: 55–78.

Petersen, David L.

1981   *The Roles of Israel's Prophets* [JSOT Supplement Series, 17]. Sheffield: JSOT.

Pixley, George V.

1981   *God's Kingdom: A Guide to Biblical Study.* Maryknoll: Orbis Books.

1987   *On Exodus: A Liberation Perspective.* Maryknoll: Orbis Books.

Polzin, Robert

1980   *Moses and the Deuteronomist: A Literary Study of the Deuteronomic History.*
        New York: Seabury.

Propp, Vladímir

1968   *Morphology of the Folktale.* 2nd ed. Austin/London: University of Texas.

von Rad, Gerhard

1965   *Old Testament Theology.* 2 vols. New York: Harper & Row.

Rambo, Lewis R.

1982   "Current Research on Religious Conversion." *RelSRev* 8: 146–59.

Rawls, John

1971   *A Theory of Justice.* Cambridge: Harvard University.

1975   "The Justification of Civil Disobedience." Pp. 346–58 in *Today's Moral
        Problems.* Ed. R. Wasserstrom. New York: Macmillan.

Reik, Theodor

1959   *Mystery on the Mountain: The Drama of the Sinai Revelation.* New York:
        Harper & Brothers.

Richardson, Lewis F., ed.

1960   *Arms and Insecurity: A Mathematical Study of the Causes and Origins of War.*
        Ed. with N. Rashevski and E. Trucco. Pacific Grove, CA: Boxwood.

Richter, Wolfgang

1963   *Traditionsgeschichtliche Untersuchungen zum Richterbuch.* Bonn: Hanstein.

Ringgren, Helmer

1966   *Israelite Religion.* Philadelphia: Fortress.

Robertson, Pat, and Bob Slosser

1984   *The Secret Kingdom.* New York: Bantam Books.

Rofé, Alexander

1970   "The Classification of the Prophetical Stories." *JBL* 89: 427–40.

Rogerson, John W.
1978   *Anthropology and the Old Testament.* Atlanta: John Knox.
1985   "The Use of Sociology in Old Testament Studies." VTSup 36: 245–56.

Ron, Z.
1966   "Agricultural Terraces in the Judean Mountains." *IEJ* 16: 33–49.

Rummel, Rudolph J.
1975–77, 1979 *Understanding Conflict and War.* 4 Vols. Beverly Hills: Sage
         Publications.

Runciman, W. G.
1983   *A Treatise on Social Theory, Vol. I: The Methodology of Social Theory.*
         Cambridge: University of Cambridge.

Sabini, John, and Maury Silver
1982   *Moralities of Everyday Life.* Oxford/New York: Oxford University.

Sahlins, Marshall
1968   *Tribesmen.* Englewood Cliffs: Prentice-Hall.

Ste. Croix, G. E. M. de
1981   *Class Struggle in the Ancient Greek World from the Archaic Age to the Arab
         Conquests.* London: Duckworth.

Sanders, James A.
1972   *Torah and Canon.* Philadelphia: Fortress.
1976   "Adaptable for Life: The Nature and Function of the Canon." Pp. 531–60 in
         Magnalia Dei—The Mighty Acts of God. Ed F. M. Cross et al. Garden City:
         Doubleday.
1980   "Canonical Context and Canonical Criticism." *Horizons in Biblical Theology*
         2: 173–97.
1984   *Canon and Community: A Guide to Canonical Criticism.* Philadelphia: Fortress.

Sauer, James A.
1986   "Transjordan in the Bronze and Iron Ages: A Critique of Glueck's
         Synthesis." *BASOR* 263: 1–26.

Schlesinger, Arthur M., Jr.
1946   *The Age of Jackson.* Boston: Little, Brown.

Schneider, Michael
1975   *Neurosis and Civilization: A Marxist/Freudian Synthesis.* New York: Seabury.

Schütz, John H.
1975   *Paul and the Anatomy of Apostolic Authority.* Cambridge: Cambridge
         University.

Schwager, Raymond
1987   *Must There be Scapegoats? Violence and Redemption in the Bible.* San Francisco: Harper & Row.

Segundo, Juan Luis
1976   *The Liberation of Theology.* Maryknoll: Orbis Books.

Shannon, F. A.
1936   "The Homestead Act and the Labor Surplus." *American Historical Review* 41: 637–51.

Sheppard, Gerald T.
1974   "Canon Criticism: The Proposal of Brevard Childs and an Assessment of Evangelical Hermeneutics." *Studia Biblica et Theologica* 4: 3–17.

1980   *Wisdom as a Hermeneutical Construct: A Study in the Sapientializing of the Old Testament.* New York/Berlin: Walter de Gruyter.

1982   "Canonization: Hearing the Voice of the Same God Through Historically Dissimilar Traditions." *Interpretation* 37: 21–33.

1985a   "The Anti-Assyrian Redaction and the Canonical Context of Isaiah 1–39." *JBL* 104: 193–216.

1985b   "The Use of Scripture within the Christian Ethical Debate Concerning Same-Sex Oriented Persons." *Union Seminary Quarterly Review* 40/1–2: 13–35.

Silver, Morris
1983   *Prophets and Markets: The Political Economy of Ancient Israel.* Boston/The Hague/London: Kluwer-Nijhoff.

Smith, Mark S.
1990   *The Early History of God: Yahweh and the Other Deities of Ancient Israel.* San Francisco: Harper & Row.

Smith, Morton
1952   "The Common Theology of The Ancient Near East." *JBL* 71: 135–47.

Soares-Prabhu, G. M.
1985   "Class in the Bible: The Biblical Poor a Social Class?" *Vidyajyoti* 49: 322–46.

Soelle, Dorothee
1974   *Political Theology.* Philadelphia: Fortress.

Spencer, J. E., and G. A. Hale
1961   "The Origin, Nature and Distribution of Agricultural Terracing." *Pacific Viewpoint* 2: 1–40.

Sperling, S. David
1986   "Israel's Religion in the Ancient Near East." Pp. 5–31 in *Jewish Spirituality.* Ed. A. Green. New York: Crossroad.

1987   "Joshua 24 Re-examined." *Hebrew Union College Annual* 58: 119–36.

Spina, Frank
1983   "Israelites as gērîm, 'Sojourners,' in Social and Historical Context." Pp. 321–35 in *The Word of the Lord Shall Go Forth. Essays in Honor of David Noel Freedman*. Ed. by C. Meyers and M. O'Connor. Winona Lake: Eisenbrauns.

Stager, Lawrence E.
1976   "Agriculture." *IDBSup*: 11–13.

1985   "The Archaeology of the Family in Ancient Israel." *BASOR* 260: 1–35.

1988   "Archaeology, Ecology and Social History: Background Themes to the Song of Deborah." VTSup 40: 221–34.

Steck, Odil H.
1968   *Ueberlieferung und Zeitgeschichte in den Elia-Erzaehlungen*. Neukirchen-Vluyn: Neukirchener.

Sternberg, Meir
1985   *The Poetics of Biblical Narrative: Ideological Literature and the Drama of Reading*. Bloomington: Indiana University.

Tamez, Elsa
1982   *The Bible of the Oppressed*. Maryknoll: Orbis Books.

Taylor, G. R., ed.
1972   *The Turner Thesis Concerning the Role of the Frontier in American History*. 3rd ed. Lexington, MA: D. C. Heath.

Theissen, Gerd
1977   *Sociology of Early Palestinian Christianity*. Philadelphia: Fortress.

1982   "The Sociological Interpretation of Religious Traditions: Its Methodological Problems as Exemplified in Early Christianity." Pp. 175–200 in *The Social Setting of Pauline Christianity. Essays on Corinth*. Philadelphia: Fortress = Gottwald, 1983a: 38–58.

Thompson, Leonard L.
1978   *Introducing Biblical Literature: A More Fantastic Country*. Englewood Cliffs: Prentice-Hall.

Thompson, Thomas L.
1987   *The Origin Tradition of Ancient Israel. I. The Literary Formation of Genesis and Exodus 1–23* [JSOT Supplement Series, 55]. Sheffield: JSOT.

Tillich, Paul
1977   *The Socialist Decision*. Lanham, MD/London: University Press of America [German original, 1933].

Tippett, A. R.
1977   "Conversion as a Dynamic Process in Christian Mission." *Missiology* 5: 203–21.

Turner, B. S.
1978   *Marx and the End of Orientalism.* London: Allen & Unwin.

Turner, Frederick J.
1921   *The Frontier in American History.* New York: Henry Holt.

UNESCO
1979   *Peace Research, Trend Report and World Directory.* UNESCO: International Peace Research Institute, Oslo.

1981   *World Directory of Peace Institutes.* 4th ed. UNESCO: Unipub.

Vansina, Jan
1985   *Oral Tradition as History.* Madison: University of Wisconsin.

de Vaux, Roland
1961   *Ancient Israel: Its Life and Institutions.* New York: McGraw-Hill.

Vriezen, Th. C.
1958   *An Outline of Old Testament Theology.* Oxford: Basil Blackwell [rev. ed., 1970].

1963   *The Religion of Ancient Israel.* Philadelphia: Westminster.

von Waldow, Hans E.
1970   "Social Responsibility and Social Structure in Early Israel." *CBQ* 32: 182–204.

Wallace, A. F. C.
1956   "Revitalization Movements." *American Anthropologist* 58: 264–81.

Walzer, Michael
1985   *Exodus and Revolution.* New York: Basic Books.

Webb, W. P.
1952   *The Great Frontier.* Cambridge: Harvard University.

Weber, Max
1952   *Ancient Judaism.* Glencoe, IL: Free Press [German original, 1921].

Weber, Timothy P.
1987   *Living in the Shadow of the Second Coming: American Premillennialism 1875–1925.* Rev. ed. Chicago: University of Chicago.

Whybray, R. Norman
1968   *The Succession Narrative.* London: SMC.

1978   *Thanksgiving for a Liberated Prophet: An Interpretation of Isaiah 53* [JSOT Supplement Series, 4]. Sheffield: JSOT.

Wifall, Walter, Jr.
1982   "Israel's Origins: Beyond Noth and Gottwald." *BTB* 12: 8–11.

Wilcoxen, Jay A.
1974   "Narrative." Pp. 57–98 in *Old Testament Form Criticism*. San Antonio: Trinity University.

Wildavsky, Aaron
1984   *The Nursing Father: Moses as a Political Leader*. Birmingham: University of Alabama.

Wilder, Amos
1946   "Equivalents of Natural Law in the Teaching of Jesus." *JR* 26: 125–35.

1950   *Eschatology and Ethics in the Teaching of Jesus*. New York: Harper & Row.

Wilkinson, David
1980   *Deadly Quarrels, Lewis F. Richardson and the Statistical Study of War*. Berkeley: University of California.

Williams, James G.
1969   "The Social Location of Israelite Prophecy." *JAAR* 37: 153–65.

Williams, William A.
1969   *The Roots of American Empire: A Study of the Growth and Shaping of Social Consciousness in a Marketplace Society*. New York: Random House.

Wilson, Robert R.
1980   *Prophecy and Society in Ancient Israel*. Philadelphia: Fortress.

1983   "Enforcing the Covenant: the Mechanisms of Judicial Authority in Early Israel." Pp. 59–75 in *The Quest for the Kingdom of God: Essays in Honor of George E. Mendenhall*. Ed. H. G. Huffmon et al. Winona Lake, IN: Eisenbrauns.

1984   *Sociological Approaches to the Old Testament*. Philadelphia: Fortress.

Woito, Robert
1982   *To End War: A New Approach to International Conflict*. Rev. ed. New York: Pilgrim.

Wolf, Eric R.
1966   *Peasants*. Englewood Cliffs: Prentice-Hall.

1969   *Peasant Wars of the Twentieth Century*. New York: Harper & Row.

1982   *Europe and the People Without History*. Berkeley: University of California.

Woo, Franklin J.
1980   Review of *The Tribes of Yahweh*. *China Notes* 18:142–43.

Wright, Christopher J. H.
1990   *God's People in God's Land: Family, Land and Property in the Old Testament.*
         Grand Rapids: Eerdmans.

Wright, Quincy
1942   *A Study of War.* 2 Vols. Chicago: University of Chicago.

Wyman, W. D., and C. Kroeber, eds.
1957   *The Frontier in Perspective.* Madison: University of Wisconsin.

Younger, George D.
1960   "The Prophetic Function of the Church in Society." *Foundations* 3: 306–25.

Zeitlin, Irving M.
1981   *Ideology and the Development of Social Theory.* 2nd ed. Englewood Cliffs:
         Prentice-Hall.

1984   *Ancient Judaism. Biblical Criticism from Max Weber to the Present.* Oxford:
         Polity.

Zimmerli, Walther
1954   *Erkenntnis Gottes nach dem Buche Ezechiel.* Zürich: Zwingli.

Abbreviations

BA	*Biblical Archaeologist*
BAR	*Biblical Archaeologist Reader*
BASOR	*Bulletin of the American Schools of Oriental Research*
BTB	*Biblical Theology Bulletin*
CBQ	*Catholic Biblical Quarterly*
CTM	*Concordia Theological Monthly*
IDBSup	*The Interpreter's Dictionary of the Bible Supplementary Volume*
IEJ	*Israel Exploration Journal*
JAAR	*Journal of the American Academy of Religion*
JBL	*Journal of Biblical Literature*
JAARSup	*Journal of the American Academy of Religion Supplement*
JQR	*Jewish Quarterly Review*
JR	*Journal of Religion*
JSOT	*Journal for the Study of the Old Testament*
RelSRev	*Religious Studies Review*
SBLSP	*Society of Biblical Literature Seminar Papers*
VTSup	Supplements to Vetus Testamentum

Author Index

Abercrombie, N., 142
Albrektson, B., 171
Albright, W. F., 22, 64, 198
Alt, A., xxv, 19, 45, 66, 134, 194, 198
Alter, R., 213, 217
Althusser, L., 140–42, 221–22
Amin, S., xxvi, 152, 351
Arendt, H., 338
Auerbach, E., 217
Batto, B., 274
Belo, F., 204, 246, 328–29
Berger, P., 111, 328
Blauner, R., 143
Blenkinsopp, J., 182, 185–86, 189
Braverman, H., 141
Bright, J., 17–26, 34, 39, 239
Brueggemann, W., 25, 84, 184, 188, 201–205
Buber, M., 305, 308
Buccellatti, G., 134
Bultmann, R., xvii
Butterfield, H., 300
Carroll, R., 198, 329
Causse, A., 328
Chaney, M. L., 45, 63, 75, 329, 357
Chesneaux, J., 153
Childs, B. S., 180–82, 185, 187–91
Clevenot, M., 24
Connell, R. W., 141
Coote, R. B., 66–69, 329
Croatto, S., 268, 329
Cross, F. M., 8, 84, 240
Curle, A., 334
de Geus, C. H. J., 25, 38, 68–69, 198
de Vaux, R., 327
Dhoquois, G., 158

Diakonoff, I. M., 153
Doeringer, P., 142
Dugan, M. A., 334
Durkheim, E., xvi, xxii, 34, 140, 146–47, 178, 328
Eagleton, T., xxix, 204, 220–21
Elliott, J. H., 329
Engels, F., 143, 150, 320, 378
Evans-Pritchard, E., 81
Farley, E., 246–47
Fierro, A., 243, 269–70, 336
Finkelstein, I., 64
Flanagan, J. W., 58, 328
Fohrer, G., 34, 39, 199, 239
Frankel, B., 141
Freud, S., xvii, 105, 193, 243
Frick, F. S., 70, 328
Fried, M., 11–14, 48
Fromm, E., 193
Fuentes, C., 231
Gager, J., 327, 329
Galtung, J., 333–34
Gandhi, M., 339 , 372
Gardner, C., 295
Garnsey, E., 143
Giddens, A., 141
Girard, R., 252
Godelier, M., 152, 158
Gouldner, A., 5
Grant, R., 327
Greimas, A. J., 221
Gunkel, H., 127
Gutiérrez, G., 268
Hanks, T., 329
Hanson, P. D., 189, 198
Hartmann, H., 143

Hegel, G. W. F., 243
Hendel, R., 193
Herbrechtsmeier, W., 215–216
Hillers, D. R., 84
Hobsbawm, E., 152
Holmberg, B., 328
Horton, R., 81–83
Humphries, J., 143
Ishida, T., 134
Jameson, F., xxix, 204, 220–23
Jepsen, A., 130
Jobling, D., 215, 218–19, 223, 329
Kant, I., 243
Kaufmann, Y., 193–99
Kennedy, J,. 193
Kimbrought, Jr., S. T., 328
King, Jr., M. L., 372
Kittel, G., 329
Kreuziger, F., 344
LeGuin, U., 26
Lemche, N. P., 68
Lenski, G., 40–55
Lenz, T., 332
Lockwood, D., 143
Long, B. O., 189, 198, 327–28
Maccoby, H., 249–53
Madison, J., 314
Maduro, O., 29–32
Malherbe, A., 327
Malina, B., 327–28
Mann, M., 142
Mansueto, A., 152, 159–60
Marfoe, L., 137
Marglin, S. A., 141
Marx, K., xvi–xvii, xxiii, xxv, 50–51,
    105–106, 140, 146, 148, 150–51, 153,
    157–58, 162, 199, 243, 328
McBride, Jr., S. D., 191
McGrath, T., xv
McKnight, E., 209
Meeks, M. D., 281–88, 364
Meeks, W., 327
Melotti, U., 144, 151–53, 157
Mendenhall, G. E., xxvii, 6, 8–9,13–14,
    22, 25, 34, 37–39, 50, 55, 66–67, 69, 72,
    74, 90, 93, 97, 102–103, 198, 239
Mettinger, T. N. D., 136–37
Milgram, S., 337

Milgrom, J., 71–87
Miranda, J., 329
Mosala, I. J., 364
Mottu, H., 328
Newman, K. S., 146–47, 216
Nietzche, F., 196
Noth, M., 6, 66, 77, 194, 196, 198
Offe, C., 141
Otis, G., 258
Overholt, T., 328
Parkin, F., 141
Petersen, D., 328
Pixley, G. V., 246, 268, 273, 276, 328
Plekhanov, G. V., 152
Polzin, R., 87, 214–15, 329
Poulantzas, N., 140
Priore, M., 142
Propp, V., 119–20
Rawls, J., 335
Reagan, R., 258–59
Reik, T., 193
Richardson, L. F., 332
Ringgren, H., 199
Rodinson, M., 152
Rogerson, J. W., 27–35, 198
Ronge, V., 141
Rubery, J., 142
Rummel, R. J., 333
Runciman, W. G., 30–35
Sabini, J., 338
Sanders, J. A., 181–82, 185, 189
Sandmel, S., 251
Schleiermacher, F., xvii
Schütz, J., 328
Schwager, R., 184
Segundo, J. L., 336, 362
Service, E., 12
Shanks, H., 89–107
Sheppard, G. T., 181–82, 185, 189, 192
Silver, Maury, 338
Silver, Morris, 193, 361
Smith, M, 198
Soelle, D., xvii
Sperling, S. D., 84
Stager, L. E., 70, 99
Stark, D., 142
Steck, O. H., 128
Sternberg, M., 213, 217

Swanson, G., 146
Tamez, E., 329
Theissen, G., 327, 329
Therborn, G., 141
Thompson, E. P., 142
Thompson, L., 209
Tillich, P., 374
Tökei, F., 152
Turner, B. S., 142
Turner, F. J., 43
Turner, V., 81
von Rad, G., 128, 130, 188
Vriezen, T. C., 199
Walzer, M., 193, 197
Weber, M., xvi, xxii, 32, 135, 140–42,
    146–48, 156, 178, 193–99, 328
Wellhausen, J., 198

Whitelam, K., 66–69
Wifall, Jr., W. R., 25
Wildavsky, A., 193, 197
Wilder, A., 343
Williams, J. G., 111
Williams, W. A., 44
Wilson, R. R., 198, 328
Wittfogel, K. A., 152, 158
Woito, R., 332
Wolf, E., xxvii, 45, 47, 58, 65, 78
Wright, E. O., 141, 143
Wright, G. E., 8, 22, 188
Wright, Q, 332
Zeitlin, I., 193–99
Zeitlin, M., 141
Zimbardo, P., 337

Subject Index

Aaron, 215
Abimelech, 11, 100, 132
Abraham, 19, 250
Acrostics, 166–67
African societies, 11–13, 81–82, 137, 328
Agriculture, 10, 34, 40, 59, 65–66, 83–84, 95, 99, 136, 158–61, 238
Ahab, 299
Amarna Age/Letters, xxv, 45, 101–102
American Revolution, 374
Amerindians, 11–13, 78, 137
Ammon(ites), 15, 311
Amorites, 19
Amphictyony, xxi, xxiii, 6, 14, 23, 38
Animal husbandry. *See* Pastoralism
Anthropology, xxii, 6–7, 10–13, 28, 81–83, 137, 144–45, 327–28
ʿapiru, 14, 23, 68, 101–102
Apocalyptic, 198, 255–65, 328, 342, 378.
    See also Dispensationalism;
    Eschatology
Arad, 22
Aram(eans), 19
Archaeology, xxiii, 15, 18, 20, 22, 59–70, 78, 91, 94–95, 98–99, 178, 194, 367
Armageddon, battle of, 257–59
Art, theology compared to, 243–45, 262–65
Artisans, 161, 251
Asiatic mode of production, 51, 136, 151–64, 368. *See also* Tributary mode of production
Assyria, 53, 217, 278, 295–97, 300, 306, 310, 351, 354
Baal, 42, 46, 84, 97, 124, 127

Babylon(ians), 167, 169–70, 172–73, 217, 264, 278, 293, 296–97, 310, 351, 354
Banditry, social, 40
Bar Cochba, 371
Barak, 213
Bill of Rights, U.S., 315
Bourgeois liberalism, 373–383.
    See also Capitalism; Liberal theory
British (Glorious) Revolution, 374
Bureaucracy, 134, 141, 155, 160, 163, 337, 346, 368, 374, 379
Caiaphas, 252
Cain, 250
Canaan(ites), xxiii, xxviii, 11–15, 19, 22–24, 39, 42, 45–54, 63–70, 71–87, 93–103, 196, 217, 230, 271–76, 310–11, 331, 351–53, 357, 366, 368.
    See also City-states, of Canaan
Canon, 177–192, 261, 272
Canonical criticism, 177–92, 211, 228–29, 278
Capitalism, 43–45, 50–51, 140–43, 149, 245, 282–88, 309, 312–17, 319–321, 339, 344–46, 351, 361–64, 373–83
Carmel, 127
Charismatic rule, 134, 329.
    See also Dynastic rule
Chiefdom, 11
China, 12, 157
Christian Socialism, 287, 291.
    See also Democratic socialism;
    Socialism
Christianity, 7, 54, 81, 104, 173, 226, 244–53, 272, 278–79. 320–23, 350, 355, 359, 362–63, 373, 376, 381–83.
    See also Church/churches

Chronicles, biblical books of, 135
Church/churches, 287–88, 292–95, 300–
    306, 319, 362–64, 381–83.
    See also Christianity
City-states, of Canaan, xxviii, 13–14, 39,
    44, 66–68, 75, 80, 82–84, 96–97, 99–
    100, 161, 179, 366. See also
    Canaan(ites); State, as a social
    organizational form
Civil liberties, xxvi, 383
Civil society, 149, 320–21
Civil War, U.S., 316
Class. See Social Class
Class conflict, 147–48.
    See also Social conflict/struggle
Classical (slave-based) mode of
    production, 150–55, 369–70
Cognitive dissonance theory, 329
Colonialism, 11–13, 87, 204, 369–73, 375.
    See also Imperialism
Commerce. See Trade
Commercialization of property, 136–37.
    See also Land tenure; Private
    property
Communal lament, 166–67, 170
Communism/communist parties, 144,
    150–52, 296, 306, 379
Communitarian mode of production,
    xxv–xxviii, 60, 84–87, 344–46, 352–
    62, 366–73. See also Egalitarian
    society
Comparative literary studies, 214
Comparative social scientific studies,
    91, 137, 144–47, 178–79, 214, 216–17,
    327
Conflict. See Class conflict; Social
    conflict/struggle
Conflict resolution theory, 215, 233–35
Conflict theory, of social inequality, 151,
    245
Conquest/invasion model, for early
    Israel, 6–7, 22–23, 38, 72, 85–86, 91–
    92, 96, 196, 271
Constitution, U.S., 315, 318–19
Conversion, religious, 71–87, 373
Coordinates (literary, social,
    theological), 208–11. See also
    Cross-methodological readings

Corvée/conscripted labor, 134–35, 351,
    354
Counter-culture, xxviii–xxix, 47, 67, 117,
    216, 276–77
Counterrevolution, 52, 311, 331
Covenant, 24, 117, 172, 184, 202, 216,
    297, 239, 241, 292–94, 297, 308, 317,
    321, 368–69, 375
Cross-cultural studies, 144–45, 178.
    See also Comparative social scientific
    studies
Cross-methodological readings, 203–
    204, 208–23, 225–31.
    See also Coordinates
Cult/ritual/worship, 69–70, 111–15,
    159, 167–69, 172–73, 198–99, 238–40,
    276–77
Cult community, Israel as a, 75–76, 203–
    204, 277–78, 369–70
Cultic prophecy, 111–17.
    See also Prophets/prophecy
Cultural anthropology, 7.
    See also Anthropology
Cultural continuity, 64–65
Culture, 7–9, 69–70, 80, 161–62, 238–39,
    320, 337, 381–82
Damascus, 126, 297
Daniel, book of, 255–65
David, 47–48, 85, 91, 132–35, 201–205,
    213, 367
Davidic-Zion theology, 171–73.
    See also Zion
Death, as viewed in Israel, 240–42
Deborah. See Song of Deborah
Debt, 122, 125, 130, 132, 136–37, 155–57,
    163–64, 311, 319, 329, 351, 359–61.
    See also Interest/usury; Tributary
    mode of production
Democracy. See Economic democracy;
    Political democracy
Democratic socialism, 286–87, 316, 363.
    See also Economic democracy;
    Socialism
Demotic Chronicle, 190
Demythologization, socioeconomic,
    241–42. See also Symbolism, religious
Deontological ethics, 343

Determination/fatalism, in history, 151, 221–22, 258–65, 303–306.
See also Freedom, in history
Deuteronomistic history/theology, xxviii, 60–61, 75–76, 86–87, 128–29, 133–36, 171–73, 214–15, 229–30
Deuteronomy, book of, 73–76, 85, 171, 182, 191, 215–16, 329, 358, 361, 366, 368
Diachronic social analysis, 10, 178, 212
Dispensationalism, 256–61.
See also Apocalyptic
Divine warrior, Yahweh as, 25, 46, 240.
See also Holy war, texts and ideology
Division of labor, 140–41, 144
Dynastic rule, 134, 171–72, 202–203.
See also Charismatic rule
Ebla texts, 20
Economic democracy, 283–87, 314–15, 375–76, 382–83. See also Democratic socialism; Socialism
Economic development theory, 333–34
Economic ethics, 281–88, 344–47, 349–64
Economy, 11, 34, 105.
See also Historical materialism; Mode of production; Political economy
Edom(ites), 15, 127, 169, 276, 296, 311
Egalitarian society, xxv–xxvi, 14, 48–50, 80, 87, 132, 184, 241–42, 310–18, 321, 367, 375–76. See also Communitarian mode of production
Egypt(ians), 11, 14, 17–20, 47, 65, 68, 77–78, 94–102, 132, 155, 190, 196–97, 217, 267–78, 286, 297, 306, 308, 311–12, 351–53, 368
El, 19, 23–24, 46, 84, 97, 240
Eli, 133
Elijah, 119–30
Elisha, 119–30, 299, 301
Elohist (E) source, 275–77
Emic social science theories, 32–33
Enlightenment, xviii, 375–76
Eschatology, 241, 255–65, 317, 343–44, 372–73. See also Apocalyptic
Essenes, 371
Ethical judgment, on the past, 50–54, 84, 204, 361–64

Ethics/morality, xxii, 103–104, 142, 147–48, 173, 261–65, 282–88, 295–306, 330–39, 341–47, 377.
See also Economic ethics; Political ethics; Values
Ethnicity/Ethnic groups, 7, 25, 68–69, 74–80, 143, 145, 312, 352, 380, 382
Ethnocentrism. See Political romanticism
Etic social science theories, 32–33
Evolutionary social theory, 40–41, 179
Exile, 87, 168, 172, 217, 312, 317, 331, 362
Exodus, 17, 19, 21, 62–63, 77–78, 96, 98–101, 196, 267–79, 286, 336, 353
Exploitation. See Surplus labor, expropriation of
Ezekiel, 302
Family, 11, 49, 136, 150
Famine, 122, 125–27
Fascism/National Socialism, 293, 303–304, 338, 380
Feminist theology, 286
Feminist theory, 142–43, 270
Feudal mode of production, xxv, 51, 150–53, 158
Folklore, 20, 62, 76–78, 119–20
Forces of production, 147.
See also Mode of production
Foreign tribute, 160, 163, 311, 354
Form/genre criticism, 229
Free agrarians, 161.
See also Communitarian mode of production; Peasant revolt model
Freedom, in history, 53–54, 58–59, 204, 221–22, 262–65, 303–306.
See also Determinism/fatalism, in history
French Revolution, 374
Freudian theory, xvii, 245–46
Frontier model, for early Israel, 41–48
Functional theory, of social inequality, 246
Funeral song, 166
Galilee, 133, 357
Gedaliah, 172
Gehazi, 126, 129
Gender, 142–43, 145
Genealogies, 77–78

Germanic mode of production, 152–53, 155, 162
Germany, under Nazism.
    See Fascism/National Socialism
Gibeon(ites), 22, 215
Gideon, 11, 132
Gog of Magog, 257, 260
Greece, 14, 38, 104, 137, 162, 218
Guilt, national/corporate, 249–53, 297–98, 303–306
Hasmoneans, 354, 369–71
Hebrews, 23, 68, 101
Hebron, 22
Hellenism/hellenization, 87, 354, 369–71
Hermeneutical circle/circulation, 203, 230–31, 269–70, 272
Hermeneutics, xvii–xviii, 180, 192, 201, 204–205, 208–209, 211–12, 227–31, 262–65, 268–71, 309, 329–30, 336
Herod, 251–52
Hierarchic society, 13–14, 500–53, 87, 179, 198, 202, 346, 370–72, 379.
    See also Tributary mode of production
High god, 239–42.
    See also Monotheism
Historical criticism, 180, 195–96, 208, 213–14, 228–30
Historical materialism, 53, 57–60, 140–53, 211–12, 219–223, 244–46.
    See also Marxist social theory; Political economy
Historiography, 17–26.
    See also Models, historiographic
History, as Yahweh's sphere, 25, 46, 84
Hittites, 14
Holocaust, 250, 303–305, 338
Holy war, texts and ideology, 127, 230, 275–76, 330. *See also* Divine warrior, Yahweh as
Hormah, 22
Hosea, 301
Hurrians, 14
Ibzan, 11
Icelandic sagas/society, 20, 78, 162, 214
Ideal types, 146, 194, 197.
    See also Weber, M. in Author Index

Idealist religious/social theory, 33–35, 50, 55, 59, 67 , 81–82, 103, 106, 196, 283, 304–305
Ideology, 9–10, 31–35, 58, 69–70, 83–84, 103, 115–17, 130, 142, 148–49, 161–63, 179, 184, 190–92, 217–222, 243–45, 264–65, 277–79, 330, 336–37, 345–47, 350–51, 362, 367–68.
    See also Political ideologies
Idolatry, rejection of, 70, 193–99
Immanence, divine, 295–96
Immigration model, for early Israel, 6–7, 64–65, 85–86, 91–92, 96, 215
Imperialism, 316–17, 374–75.
    See also Colonialism
Individual lament, 166–67, 169
Innovative marvels, 125, 128
Interest/usury, 319, 351, 359.
    See also Debt; Tributary mode of production
Intermarriage, 25, 72–73
Internal relations, in social theory, 54–55, 106
International relations, xxi, 291–306, 311–12
Isaac, 19, 250
Isaiah, of Jerusalem, 295, 299–302, 306, 308, 361
Isaiah, of the Exile, 304
Islam, 81, 137
Israel, modern state, 256–59, 293–94
Israel, northern kingdom, 296–301
Israel, people of Yahweh, 297, 306–12, 317–20
Jacob, 19, 77
Jehu, 130
Jeremiah, 156, 171, 299, 301
Jerusalem, 166–68, 171–73, 256, 355, 369
Jesus, xvii, xxv, 249–52, 270, 286, 293, 312, 320, 331, 343, 355, 362, 371–73, 378, 382
Jezreel, plain of, 357
Joash, 123, 126
Joseph, 286
Joseph tribes, 13, 135
Josephus, 371
Joshua, 18, 85, 196

Joshua, book of, xxviii, 22, 67, 74–75, 86–87, 92, 100, 179, 214–15, 230, 276, 352, 366

Josiah, 67, 86, 156, 229, 311, 368

Judah, 91, 133, 135, 167–68, 170–73, 296–301, 312, 370

Judaism, 7, 54, 87, 104, 173, 194–95, 226, 244–53, 278–79, 350, 355, 359, 362–63, 373, 377, 381–83

Judges, 18, 67.
  See also Law; Laws

Judges, book of, xxviii, 74–75, 87, 92, 100, 179, 230, 276, 352, 357

Judicial administration.
  See Law/legal institutions

Just war theory, 336

Khirbet Rabud, 22

King Arthur legends, 214

Kingdom/reign of God, 308, 342–44, 372

Kings, books of, 119–30

Labor, 141–43, 149–50, 154, 350.
  See also Surplus labor

Lamech, 250

Lamentations, book of, xx, 165–73

Land tenure, 128–30, 135–37, 153–56, 154–63, 360.
  See also Commercialization of property; Debt

Language, 8, 94, 186–88, 329–30, 352

Late Bronze Age, 18–19, 66

Latifundaries, 161, 163–64.
  See also Land tenure; Tributary mode of production

Law/legal institutions, 117, 124–25, 129–30, 135, 161, 215–16, 311, 317–18, 357, 359–60, 367

Laws, 60, 62, 86, 146–47, 179, 183, 187, 272, 276, 278, 342, 359–60

Levites, 11, 47 , 65, 83–85, 191, 215.
  See also Priests

Liberal theory, political and economic, 282–87. See also Bourgeois liberalism; Capitalism

Liberation theologies, generic, xvii–xviii

Liberation theology, Latin American, 267–79, 329, 333

Literary criticism, 180, 27–23, 227–30, 329–30

Liturgy, 86, 203, 277.
  See also Cult/ritual/worship

Livelihood, entitlement to, 282–87, 346–47

Luwians, 14

Maccabees, 312, 369, 371

Macrosociology, 326.

Malachi, 182

Manasseh, 63, 132

Marginality, social. See Social class

Mari, 20

Marvel story, 119–130

Marxist literary theory, xxix, 219–23

Marxist social theory, xvi–xxvi, 29–32, 105–107, 140–44, 146–58, 178, 198–99, 243–46, 269, 329.
  See also Historical materialism

Marxist socialism, 376–83.
  See also Communism/communist parties; Socialism

Materialist exegesis, 270

Mediations, in cross-methodological readings (literary, religious, social), 198–99, 219–223. See also Coordinates; Cross-methodological readings

Mercantilism, 312

Merchants. See trade

Merneptah stele, 68

Messiah, 251.
  See also Apocalyptic; Eschatology

Methodological fundamentalism, 186.
  See also Reductionism, in methodology

Middle Bronze Age, 18, 64

Midianites, 20–21, 311

Midrash, 182

Military organization, 86, 97, 135, 273–78, 357. See also Holy war, texts and ideology

Millennial kingdom, 258.
  See also Dispensationalism

Miracle story. See Marvel story

Miriam, 215

Mizpah, 172

Moab(ites), 15, 276, 311

Mode of production, xxv, 58–60, 140–41, 145, 147–63, 204, 221, 296, 344–47. *See also* Political economy

Models, historiographic, 5–15, 91. *See also* Historiography

Models, social scientific, 5–15, 27–35, 91, 144–46

Monarchy, of Israel/Judah, 85–87, 91, 128–37, 158–64, 196, 217–18, 276–77, 286, 299–300, 311–12, 317, 328, 353–55, 367–68. *See also* State, as a social organizational form

Money-lending. *See* Debt; Interest/usury

Mono-Yahwism, 198. *See also* High god; Monotheism

Monotheism, 193–99, 217, 195–96. *See also* High god

Moses, xxi, 18–21, 23–24, 78, 85, 96, 102, 104, 162, 196–97, 215, 250, 359, 382

Myth. *See* Symbolism, religious

Myths, as blaming devices, 249–53. *See also* Guilt, national/corporate

Naaman, 126

Nabal, 132

Narrative plot structure, in marvel stories, 119–28

Nation state, contemporary, 291–306

Nation state, Israel as a, 68, 75–76, 78, 276–77

Nationalism. *See* Nation state, contemporary; Political romanticism

Natural law, in ethics, 292–94, 298

Nature, as Yahweh's sphere, 25, 46, 84

Nebuchadnezzar, 296

New Testament, 250–52, 292–93, 371–72

Noah, 250, 292

Nomadic model, for early Israel, 271

Nomads. *See* Pastoral nomads

Omri, 134

Oppression. *See* Surplus labor; Tributary mode of production

Oral tradition, 127–28, 218

Origin stories, of Israel, 77–78, 272–78

Pacifism, 336, 378

Pastoral nomads, xxviii, 6–8, 13, 19, 23, 25, 38, 65–66, 78, 94, 98, 199

Pastoralism, 10, 65–66, 95, 98

Patriarchs, 18–20, 77, 85, 97, 101, 196

Paul, 250–51, 292, 327–28, 331

Peace studies/research, 332–39

Peasant revolt model, for early Israel, xxv, xxvii, 22–23, 66, 90, 102. *See also* Social revolution model

Peasants, xxvi–xxviii, 26, 39, 46, 78, 102, 106, 136, 144–45, 154–63, 179, 196–98, 351–52, 354, 357, 359

Pedagogy, in biblical instruction, 225–31, 246–48. *See also* Theological education

Pentateuch. *See* Torah

Persia(ns), 190–91, 278, 310, 312, 354

Pharisees, 251, 371

Philistines, 52, 96, 100–101, 132–33, 276, 311, 353, 367

Philosophy, 243–45

Poems, biblical, 60–61, 183, 342, 357–58

Political anthropology, 145. *See also* Anthropology

Political democracy, 283–87, 314–15, 375–76

Political economy, 58–60, 136–37, 204, 271, 281–88, 349–64, 373–83. *See also* Historical materialism; Marxist social theory; Mode of production

Political ethics, 295–306, 332–39, 373–83

Political hope, 303–306, 381–83. *See also* Freedom, in history

Political ideologies, 365–83. *See also* Ideology

Political romanticism, 380–83

Political strategy, 262–63

Polytheism, 195–96, 240. *See also* Idolatry, rejection of

Positivism, 196, 204, 260

Power relations, 9–10, 350–51. *See also* Social class; Social conflict/struggle

Praxis, 244–48, 271, 309, 322–23. *See also* Marxist social theory

Pre-capitalist modes of production, 149–58, 344–45, 378

Priestly (P) source, 73–76, 189, 191, 275, 277–78, 329

Priests, 160, 170–73, 190, 241–42, 251–52, 357, 371. *See also* Levites

Primitive communist mode of production, 150, 162

Principles, in ethical reasoning, 291–306

Private property, 153–57, 160–61, 221, 282–83, 287, 313–316, 319, 370, 374–76, 383. *See also* Commercialization of property

Problem resolution story, 123

Progressives, U.S., 316–17

Prophets/prophecy, 53, 111–17, 119–30, 135–36, 170–73, 179, 182, 191, 197–98, 256–59, 261, 265, 270, 286, 291–306, 317, 328–29, 331, 342, 349–64, 368, 374, 378, 382

Prophets, as consultative specialists, 114–15

Prophets, as liturgists, 114–15

Psalms, book of, 166–67

Puritans, 93–94

Qumran, 20

Race, 142–43.
    See also Ethnicity/ethnic groups

Radical prophecy, 111–17.
    See also Prophets/prophecy

Rahab, 215

Rapture, 257–59.
    See also Dispensationalism

Rechabites, 11, 102

Recruitment, in early Israel, 79–83.
    See also Conversion, religious

Redaction criticism, 167–68, 180–82, 331, 372

Reductionism, in methodology, 210.
    See also Methodological fundamentalism

Reformation, Deuteronomic, 136, 172.
    See also Josiah

Reformation, Protestant, 93, 247, 308, 375, 378

Relations of production, 147.
    See also Mode of production

Religion, Canaanite, xxiii, 42, 46–47, 70, 82–84, 93, 97

Religion, Israelite (Yahwism), xxviii, 7–9, 19, 21–26, 33–35, 39, 42, 46–47, 69–70, 79–84, 87, 93, 95, 102–103, 106, 163, 167, 172–73, 179, 193–99, 238–42, 352–55. *See also* Theology, Israelite

Religious Right, 255–65

Restoration marvels, 124–25, 128

Retribalization, in early Israel, 6, 9, 12–13, 40, 44, 52, 216.
    See also Tribalism; Tribes, of Israel

Revelation, book of, 255–65

Revelation, divine, 67, 81–82, 192, 247, 259. *See also* Theology, contemporary; Theology, Israelite

Rome/Roman empire, 12, 87, 137, 153–55, 162, 251–52, 264, 320, 331, 354–55, 369–73

Root metaphors, 77, 100, 279, 353.
    See also Symbolism, religious

Sacrifice, human, 249–53

Sacrifices, religious, 84, 94, 172, 249–53.
    See also Cult/ritual/worship

Sadducees, 355, 371

Saga, 20, 60–61, 179, 214, 272

Samaria, 357

Samaritans, 312

Samuel, 133

Saul, 133–34, 367

Sea of Reeds, 274. *See also* Exodus

Sea Peoples, 15. *See also* Philistines

Segmentary social organization, 10, 12–13. *See also* Social organization/structure

Servants/slaves, xxvi, 132–33, 360, 369

Sexuality, in Israel, 240–42

Shechem, 63

Shunem, woman of, 123–27, 129

Sinai, 2–21, 97, 272

Slavery. *See* Servants/slaves

Social analysis, 262–65, 269–71, 322–23.
    See also Marxist social theory

Social change, 7–9, 48–49, 85, 105, 131–37, 140, 145–46, 214.
    See also Social conflict/struggle

Social class/stratification, 47, 76, 93, 139–64, 241–42, 310–16, 319–21, 363, 368

Social conflict/struggle, 66–70, 80, 131–37, 179, 238–42, 263–65, 307–23, 331–39, 341–47, 352 –53.
    See also Social change

Social contradictions, 189, 312, 343, 381
Social ethics.
    See Ethics/morality; Social justice
Social Gospel, 291
Social history, 61–64, 137, 214, 227, 230,
    269–79, 309–10, 326–28, 365–81
Social justice, 333–39, 346–47, 378–79.
    See also Ethics/morality
Social location/matrix, 177–92, 244–48,
    251, 260–61, 263–64
Social organization/structure, 7–15, 34,
    39, 49, 52, 68–70, 75–76, 92–93, 95,
    133–37, 179, 198–99, 238–42, 269–79,
    309–17, 333–39
Social psychology, 328–29, 337–39, 381
Social revolutions, post-biblical, 13, 52,
    197, 279, 312–21, 336–37
Social revolution model, for early Israel,
    XXV, XXVII–XXIX, 13, 22–26, 37–40, 45–
    50, 54–55, 59, 66–69, 74–76, 79–80,
    85–86, 161, 163, 179, 197–99, 215,
    241–42, 275–79, 311–12, 317, 319–20,
    331. See also Peasant revolt model
Social role(s), 112–17, 328–29
Social science methodology. See Social
    scientific criticism
Social sciences, XXI, 326–27.
    See also Anthropology; Political
    economy; Sociology
Social scientific criticism, of the Bible,
    XVI, XXI–XXII, 179–92, 208–10, 214–17,
    228–29, 237–48, 269–71, 325–31, 335–
    37, 341–47
Social theory, 27–35. See also Marxist
    social theory; Social analysis
Socialism/socialist mode of production,
    143–44, 282, 286–87, 320, 344–46,
    362–64
Sociology, 6, 27–35, 193–99
Sociology of literature, 183–84, 186–88,
    203–204, 329–30
Solomon, 47, 135, 161, 367
Song of Deborah, 91, 213, 230, 357
Songs. See Poems, biblical
Soviet Union, 256–57, 260, 293, 339.
    See also Communism/communist
    parties

State, as a social organizational form,
    11–14, 42, 132–37, 141, 144, 149–56,
    158–63, 202–204, 276–77, 365–83.
    See also City-states, of Canaan;
    Monarchy, of Judah/Israel
Status group, 140.
    See also Social class/stratification
Stratum, 140.
    See also Social class/stratification
Structuralism, literary, 214–15, 218–219,
    329. See also Literary criticism
Surplus labor, expropriation of, XXII, 60,
    70, 75, 144–45, 147–50, 155–56, 158–
    59, 163, 377. See also Labor; Marxist
    social theory; Political economy
Suzerainty treaty, 24, 216.
    See also Covenant
Symbolism, religious, 34, 69–70, 83, 96,
    100, 154, 237–48, 259–65, 269, 272–79,
    283–84, 307–23, 344, 353.
    See also Myths, as blaming devices;
    Theology
Synchronic social analysis, 10, 178, 212
Syria, 95, 137, 351
Taxes/taxation, 134, 136, 153–55, 158–
    63, 311, 351, 354, 356, 359, 361, 370–
    71. See also Tributary mode of
    production
Technology, 34, 42, 45–46, 51, 54–55, 59,
    141–42, 346, 375, 378
Teleological ethics, 343
Temple, at Jerusalem, 168, 171–72, 203,
    370–71
Theodicy, 168–73
Theological education, 246–48, 270–71.
    See also Pedagogy, in biblical
    instruction
Theological representations, 243–46.
    See also Symbolism, religious;
    Theology
Theology, ancient Near Eastern, 239–42
Theology, contemporary, XXII, 25–26,
    104, 180, 192, 218–19, 237–48, 281–88,
    292–306, 330, 381–83.
    See also Ideology
Theology, in Israel, 33–35, 49, 69–70, 98,
    170–73, 184, 189, 208, 210–11, 217–19,
    238–42.

See also Ideology; Religion, Israelite (Yahwism); Symbolism, religious

Theopolitics, 307–23.
See also Ideology

Timna, 20

Torah/Pentateuch, 182–83, 188–91, 213, 274, 370

Trade, 134, 155–57, 160, 251, 351, 370

Transcendence, divine, 197, 276–78, 295–96, 301–302

Transjordan, 15, 20, 24, 65, 133, 215

Tribe, as a social organizational form, 10–14, 31, 144–45, 317.
See also Retribalization; Tribes, of Israel

Tribes, of Israel, xxix, 10–14, 23–25, 49, 93, 132, 135–37, 198, 202–204, 217–18, 229, 271, 273–76, 286, 310–11, 328, 352–54, 366–67.
See also Retribalization

Tribulation, 257–59.
See also Dispensationalism

Tributary mode of production, xxv–xxviii, 51, 60, 82, 84, 161, 344–46, 351–54, 356, 366–73.
See also Asiatic mode of production; Debt; Surplus labor; Taxes/taxation

Trinity, 284

Tyre, 297

Ugarit, 20

Uniqueness, of Israel, 38, 193–99, 240–42

United States of America, 245, 256–60, 264–65, 281–88, 292–95, 304–309, 312–23, 339, 349, 359, 361, 374

Use-ownership, of land, 351.
See also Commercialization of property; Land tenure

Values, 50–54, 115–17, 142, 243–45, 260–65, 319–21, 341–47.
See also Ethics/morality

Village social organization, 8, 98–99, 154, 158–59, 199, 351, 354.
See also Peasants; Retribalization

Violence, contemporary, 332–39, 378

Violence, in the Bible, 184–85, 355

Wisdom, 171–73, 179, 182, 342

Women. *See* Feminist theology; Feminist theory; Gender

Women, in ancient Israel, 241

Working class, 141–43, 314–16, 319–20, 375–76. *See also* Social class/stratification; Labor; Surplus labor

Yahweh, xxi, 19–20, 23–25, 97–98, 126, 128, 130, 169–71, 184, 218–19, 240–42, 306. *See also* Religion, Israelite (Yahwism)

Yahwist (J) source, 60, 273–78

Zealots, 312, 331

Zion, 166–73, 306.
See also Jerusalem

Zionism, 106, 194–95, 252, 338